HISTORICAL DICTIONARIES OF LITERATURE AND THE ARTS

Jon Woronoff, Series Editor

Historical Dictionary of English Music: ca. 1400–1958

Charles Edward McGuire
Steven E. Plank

The Scarecrow Press, Inc.
Lanham • Toronto • Plymouth, UK
2011

Published by Scarecrow Press, Inc.
A wholly owned subsidiary of The Rowman & Littlefield Publishing Group, Inc.
4501 Forbes Boulevard, Suite 200, Lanham, Maryland 20706
http://www.scarecrowpress.com

Estover Road, Plymouth PL6 7PY, United Kingdom

British Library Cataloguing in Publication Information Available

Library of Congress Cataloging-in-Publication Data

McGuire, Charles Edward.
  Historical dictionary of English music: ca. 1400–1958 / Charles Edward McGuire, Steven E. Plank.
      p. cm. — (Historical dictionaries of literature and the arts)
  Includes bibliographical references.
  ISBN 978-0-8108-5750-6 (cloth : alk. paper) — ISBN 978-0-8108-7951-5 (ebook)
  1. Music—England—Dictionaries. I. Plank, Steven Eric. II. Title.
  ML101.E5M34 2011
  780.942'03—dc22   2010049351

Printed in the United States of America

A man will turn over half a library to make one book.

—Samuel Johnson, 6 April 1775, recorded in
James Boswell, *Life of Johnson*

Contents

Editor's Foreword

The *Historical Dictionary of English Music: ca. 1400–1958* deals with just that—English music over the ages, here focused on music from the early Renaissance to the mid-20th century, ending with the death of Ralph Vaughan Williams. Moreover, this is indeed English music and does not include Irish, Scottish, or Welsh derivations. It may seem a bit nationalistic to focus on English music, but today the primary concern is what England has contributed to the world of music, which it turns out is quite a bit. Some of the truly great composers of English music figuring in this volume include Johann Christian Bach, Felix Mendelssohn, and George Frideric Handel, along with singers like Jenny Lind and Farinelli. Yet they do not overshadow the remarkable role of locals Thomas Tallis, Henry Purcell, and Sir Edward Elgar among the composers, Sir Adrian Boult and Sir John Barbirolli among the conductors, and John Dowland and Robert Lindley among the instrumentalists.

This historical dictionary begins with a list of acronyms, an ample chronology that covers high points of approximately six centuries, and an introduction that provides a broader view of English music. The dictionary section fills in many of the details in some 600 entries, which not only provide considerable information but, in many cases, provide a point of view by contemporaries or later observers. It covers the most significant and many of the lesser but still remarkable composers, conductors, instrumentalists, and singers as well as some of the impresarios and critics who made the music scene vibrant for so long. Other entries are on the most popular theaters and concert halls, numerous musical instruments, genres, particularly notable musical works, professional and other societies, and crucial technical terms. The bibliography is last but hardly least, since it is the first step toward a much broader literature.

This volume was written by two authors with a long and abiding interest in English music. Both are American, not British, which gives them some physical and intellectual distance and perhaps a clearer perspective. Both have been struck by the richness and beauty of English music, strongly enough indeed for them to study it intensively and teach it at Oberlin College in Ohio, which is known for its Conservatory of Music. The main interest of Charles

Edward McGuire is British music of the 19th and 20th centuries, particularly that of Edward Elgar and Ralph Vaughan Williams. He has written extensively on both of these composers and other topics in leading journals and has published two books. After teaching at various other universities, he is now an associate professor of musicology at the Oberlin Conservatory of Music. Steven E. Plank is professor and chair of the Department of Musicology at Oberlin, where he has been teaching since 1980. His main historical interest is earlier, namely Restoration England, and also the role of liturgy in music and the oratorio. He, too, has written numerous articles and two books. Between them, they have produced a reference work that is not only informative but helps us understand just why English music is so special and delightful.

Jon Woronoff
Series Editor

Preface

This *Historical Dictionary of English Music: ca. 1400–1958* seeks to identify and briefly annotate a wide range of subjects relating to English musical culture, largely from the early 15th century through 1958, dates that reflect the coalescence of an identifiable English style in the early Renaissance and the death of the iconic Ralph Vaughan Williams in the mid-20th century. Although the chronological span is an arbitrary one, its compass embraces the emergence of distinctively English repertories until the successful establishment of English modernism. Entries include people, venues, repertory, genre, and sources: the landmarks in the geography of English musical history. But in appropriating the notion of "landmark," the authors also understand that landmarks themselves range from the monumental to the mundane, and accordingly, the scope of the entries is, of necessity, selective, but of design "democratic." We also acknowledge that dictionaries, unlike encyclopedias, are meant to be concise. Thus even a series of democratic descriptions needs limits, else concision would be lost. Therefore, within this dictionary we have focused on the music and musical infrastructure of England and those at work within England and have not attempted to evaluate the rest of Great Britain, including Northern Ireland, Scotland, and Wales, in any detail, except when individuals and institutions active in England overlapped with these areas.

Entries in the dictionary aim to be "first reference" sources for students and researchers. Our aim is to give readers information in an efficient format that will help clarify and position the landmarks of English music that readers may encounter in the many scholarly and popular discussions now available. The modern reference bibliography offers a number of possibilities for comprehensive articles on many of these subjects, with the *New Grove Dictionary of Music and Musicians* and its many contributors being the most notable example. We are naturally indebted to the authors of this monumental source, as well as to other writers who have pursued these topics at length, and seek to complement them with material that is compellingly content-rich, though less developed in scope.

These debts are acknowledged in the bibliography of this volume, which includes both works consulted and works for further reference. Additionally, in some cases where a specific reference proved necessary, we have supplied an author-date note within the text itself. In all instances, we have been deeply aware of our part in a chain of information and discourse and are grateful for the enabling work of so many colleagues in the field of English musical studies.

The writing of this dictionary is also an occasion for gratitude in the opportunity for collaboration that it has so richly presented. We have been fortunate, indeed, to find our respective passions for English music to be something that we have shared and celebrated for so many years as friends and colleagues at Oberlin College. In general, our division of labor has been a chronological one, with articles on subjects after Handel largely the work of Charles Edward McGuire and those on subjects Handelian and earlier the work of Steven E. Plank. Each of our individual efforts, however, has been much enriched by an ongoing dialogue with each other over several decades, and our efforts are much the richer and warmly congenial for it.

In the preface to his *The Mirror of Music, 1844–1944: A Century of Musical Life in Britain as Reflected in the Pages of the* Musical Times (1947), Percy A. Scholes noted,

> Of all historical study, the most interesting is that which leads us to a conception of the means by which have come about the conditions of the period in which we are ourselves living. That is what this book will, I hope, achieve for others, as it had done for me. It will demonstrate to the British musicians and music people of today the processes that have been at work to create their own artistic and educational *milieu*.

Scholes published his two-volume social history of music through the lens of the *Musical Times* in 1947, when few understood the history of all classical music to have been so affected by the tastes of the English. Fewer still thought of writing a history that encompassed more than just national and nationalist events. As authors of this dictionary, we have been lucky to have Scholes and others break this flawed supposition before us, so that we can present elements of the rich landscape of English music over the course of some six centuries. We can, further, identify with Scholes's notion that the demonstration of the historical process is an edifying one: the more than 600 entries in this dictionary allowed us latitude to explore concepts, genres, people, and places that were new to us, and continually illuminated just how complex the history of music in England has been—and still is. It is our hope that you, gentle reader, will find at least some of our excitement and wonder at the revelations within these pages.

Reader's Notes

1. Cross-references are indicated through the use of **bold** type within the entry or in a *See also* at the end.
2. Acts in plays, operas, and operettas are identified by capital Roman numerals while scenes are identified by lowercase ones; thus *The Tempest* II/ii would mean the second act, second scene of **Shakespeare**'s play, and *The Mikado* I/iii would mean the first act, third scene of **Gilbert** and **Sullivan**'s *The Mikado*.
3. References to manuscripts follow the library sigla standardized in *Répertoire International des Sources Musicales*.

Acronyms and Abbreviations

ADCM	Archbishop of Canterbury's Diploma in Church Music
ARCM	Associate of the Royal College of Music
ARCO	Associate of the Royal College of Organists
Blwl	*Blackwell History of Music in Britain* (Ian Spink, general editor)
CBE	Commander, Order of the British Empire
CBSO	City of Birmingham Symphony Orchestra
CH	Companion of Honour
CHM	Choir Training Diploma of the Royal College of Organists
CVO	Companion of the Victorian Order
DBE	Dame Commander, Order of the British Empire
DipCHD	Choral Directing Diploma of the Royal College of Organists
DNB	Reference to the corresponding article in the *Oxford Dictionary of National Biography*
FRAM	Fellow of the Royal Academy of Music
FRCM	Fellow of the Royal College of Music
FRCO	Fellow of the Royal College of Organists
GCVO	Grand Cross, Victorian Order
GSM	Guildhall School of Music
KB	Knight Bachelor
KCVO	Knight Commander, Victorian Order
LSO	London Symphony Orchestra
MBE	Member, Order of the British Empire
MT	*The Musical Times*
MVO	Member of the Victorian Order
NG	Reference to the corresponding article in the *New Grove Dictionary of Music and Musicians*
OHEM	*Oxford History of English Music* (John Caldwell, editor)
OM	Order of Merit
RAM	Royal Academy of Music, London
RCM	Royal College of Music, London
RMA	Royal Musical Association

RMCM	Royal Manchester College of Music
RNCM	Royal Northern College of Music
RVO	Royal Victorian Order
SPCK	Society for the Propagation (later "Promotion") of Christian Knowledge
SPNM	Society for the Promotion of New Music

Chronology

ca. 1325   Robertsbridge Codex written.

1382   Winchester College founded.

1399   Accession of Henry IV.

1413   Accession of Henry V.

1415   **25 October:** Battle of Agincourt.

ca. 1415–1421   Major compilation of the *Old Hall Manuscript*.

1422   Accession of Henry VI.

1440   Eton College founded.

1441   King's College, Cambridge, founded.

1461   Accession of Edward IV.

1483   Incorporation of Chapel Royal; Accession of Edward V; Accession of Richard III.

1485   **22 August:** The Battle of Bosworth Field; Accession of Henry VII.

ca. 1490   *Eton Choirbook* copied.

ca. 1505   Birth of Thomas Tallis.

1509   Accession of Henry VIII.

1520   Field of Cloth of Gold.

1535   Coverdale English Bible translation published.

ca. 1540   Birth of William Byrd.

1547   Accession of Edward VI.

1549   First *Book of Common Prayer* published.

1550   Marbeck, *The Booke of Common Praier Noted*, published.

1553 Accession of Mary I.

1558 Accession of Elizabeth I.

1564 Birth of William Shakespeare.

1575 Tallis and Byrd, *Cantiones Sacrae*, I, published.

1581 **1 December:** Execution of Edmund Campion.

1583 Birth of Orlando Gibbons.

1587 **8 February:** Execution of Mary, Queen of Scots.

1588 **8 August:** Defeat of the Spanish Armada.

1593 **3 April:** Birth of George Herbert.

1597 Morley, *A Plaine and Easie Introduction to Practicall Musick*, published.

1599 Morley, *The First Booke of Consort Lessons*, published.

1601 *The Triumphs of Oriana* published.

1603 Accession of James I.

1604 Dowland, *Lachrimae or Seven Teares*, published.

1611 *The King James Bible* published.

1613 *Parthenia* published.

1617 Jonson and Lanier, *Lovers Made Men*, first performed.

1621 John Adson, *Courtly Masquing Ayres*, published.

1623 Shakespeare, *The First Folio*, published.

1625 Accession of Charles I.

1646 Westminster Confession of Faith.

1649 Beginning of the Commonwealth. **30 January:** Execution of Charles I.

1656 Davenant, *The Siege of Rhodes*, performed.

1659 Birth of Henry Purcell.

1660 Restoration of the Monarchy; Accession of Charles II.

1663 Drury Lane Theatre built.

1671 Father Smith appointed royal organ maker.

1672 Bannister's public concerts begun.

1676 Performance of *Musick: or a Parley of Instruments.*

1683 **22 November:** First of the annual St. Cecilia's Day Musick Feasts in London.

1685 Accession of James II; Grabu and Dryden, *Albion and Albanius*, first performed; Birth of Handel.

1689 Accession of William and Mary.

1691 Purcell and Dryden, *King Arthur*, first performed.

1700 Blow, *Amphion Anglicus*, published.

1701 *Judgment of Paris* first performed.

1702 **8 March:** Accession of Anne.

1705 Clayton, *Arsinoe*, performed.

1711 Handel, *Rinaldo*, first performed.

1714 **1 August:** Accession of George I.

1719 Durfey, *Pills to Purge Melancholy*, published; First Royal Academy of Music begun.

ca. 1720 Three Choirs Festival Founded.

1727 **11 June:** Accession of George II.

1728 Gay, *The Beggar's Opera*, first performed.

1729 Second Royal Academy of Music begun.

1732 Opening of Covent Garden.

1733 "The Opera of the Nobility" begun.

1738 Fund for Decayed Musicians (later Royal Society of Musicians) founded.

1742 **13 April:** Handel's *Messiah* first performed in Dublin.

1753 British Museum founded.

1760 **25 October:** Accession of George III.

1761 Noblemen and Gentlemen's Catch Club founded.

1772 Opening of the Pantheon.

1776   Hawkins, *A General History of the Science and Practice of Music*, published; Concerts of Ancient Music founded.

1784   Birmingham Musical Festival founded.

1785   Professional Concert founded.

1813   Philharmonic Society (later Royal Philharmonic Society) founded.

1820   **29 January:** Accession of George IV.

1822   Royal Academy of Music (RAM) founded.

1830   **26 June:** Accession of William IV; Opening of Novello & Co.

1831   Opening of Exeter Hall.

1832   Sacred Harmonic Society founded.

1834   Society of British Musicians founded.

1837   **20 June:** Accession of Victoria.

1839   Society of Female Musicians (later Royal Society of Female Musicians) founded.

1844   **1 June:** *Musical Times* began publication as *Mainzer's Musical Times and Singing Class Circular*.

1845   Musical Union founded.

1846   **August 26:** Mendelssohn, *Elijah*, first performed.

1849   Mendelssohn Scholarship founded.

1850   St. Martin's Hall opened for concerts.

1851   Crystal Palace completed; Tonic Sol-fa Association founded. **1 May 1–15 October:** Great Exhibition.

1854   Bach Society founded.

1855   Henry Leslie Choir founded.

1858   St. James's Hall opened; Hallé Orchestra founded.

1864   Royal College of Organists founded.

1866   Royal Society of Female Musicians and Royal Society of Musicians merged.

1869   Tonic Sol-fa College founded.

1871 Royal Albert Hall opened.

1872 Church Choral Society (forerunner of Trinity School of Music) founded.

1875 Musical Association (later Royal Musical Association) founded.

1876 National Training School for Music (forerunner of the RCM) founded.

1878 People's Concert Society founded. **25 May:** Gilbert and Sullivan, *H.M.S. Pinafore*, first performed.

1879 D'Oyly Carte Opera Company founded; *A Dictionary of Music and Musicians* (edited by Grove) began publication; Richter Concerts commenced.

1880 **3 April:** Gilbert and Sullivan, *Pirates of Penzance*, first performed in London (New York premiere: 31 December 1879). **7 September:** Parry, *Prometheus Unbound*, first performed; traditional date for the beginning of the "English Musical Renaissance."

1882 Royal College of Music (RCM) founded.

1885 **14 March:** Gilbert and Sullivan, *The Mikado*, first performed.

1893 Manchester College of Music (later Royal Northern College of Music [RNCM]) founded.

1895 Proms and Queen's Hall Orchestra founded.

1898 Folk-Song Society (forerunner of English Folk Dance and Song Society) founded.

1899 **19 June:** Elgar, *Variations on an Original Theme* ("Enigma"), first performed.

1900 **3 October:** Elgar, *The Dream of Gerontius*, first performed.

1901 **22 January:** Accession of Edward VII.

1904 London Symphony Orchestra founded.

1910 **6 May:** Accession of George V. **6 September:** Vaughan Williams, *Fantasia on a Theme by Thomas Tallis*, first performed.

1911 Society of Women musicians founded.

1920 City of Birmingham Symphony Orchestra founded.

1922 BBC began broadcasting.

1925 Haslemere Festival founded.

1927 School of English Church Music (later Royal School of Church Music) founded.

1931 **8 October:** Walton, *Belshazzar's Feast*, first performed.

1932 MacNaughten-Lemare Concerts founded.

1936 **20 January:** Accession of Edward VIII. **11 December:** Accession of George VI.

1943 Society for the Promotion of New Music founded.

1944 **19 March:** Tippett, *A Child of Our Time*, first performed.

1945 Philharmonia Orchestra founded.

1948 Bryanston Summer School (forerunner of Dartington International Summer School) founded.

1951 **3 May:** Festival of Britain opens; Opening of the Royal Festival Hall.

1952 **6 February:** Accession of Elizabeth II.

1958 **26 August:** Death of Vaughan Williams.

Introduction

The musical history of a nation brings diverse notions into play. "Nationalistic" music, for instance, is a music that in its gestures, idioms, and expression evokes something of the character of the nation itself, and something that the people of the nation might recognize as familiarly their own. Ralph Vaughan Williams in his lectures entitled *National Music* explores this moment of recognition in the music of Edward Elgar. He fondly writes, "When I hear the fifth variation of the 'Engima' series I feel the same sense of familiarity, the same sense of the something peculiarly belonging to me as an Englishman which I also felt when I first heard [the English folk songs] 'Bushes and Briars' or 'Lazarus.'"[1]

"National style," on the other hand, is a concept that identifies the musical procedures of a nation as distinctive, whether the style particularly evokes the nation or not. With respect to English music this idea of distinction is well established in the early 15th century, the start of the European musical Renaissance. English composers such as Leonel Power and John Dunstaple pioneered a musical style rich in consonant thirds and full triadic sonorities that was held to be both identifiably English and a foundation of the emerging Renaissance style. The music theorist Johannes Tinctoris, writing of the modern Franco-Flemish composers, notes that

> At this time [ca. 1476], consequently, the possibilities of our music have been so marvelously increased that there appears to be a new art, if I may so call it, whose fount and origin is held to be among the English, of whom Dunstable stood forth as chief.[2]

And the French poet Martin le Franc in his *Le champion des dames* describes the Franco-Flemish composers of the day, composers like Dufay and Binchois, as following Dunstaple and wearing an "English guise": "Et ont prins de la contenance / Angloise et ensuy Dunstable." Additionally, it seems that national distinctiveness extended to the manner of performance as well. Tinctoris, for example, writes that the English cannot be compared to the French, for they are "popularly said to shout while the French sing."[3] More favorably,

Ornithoparcus, in his *Musice active micrologus* (1517), translated by John Dowland in 1609, notes that

> Every man lives after his owne humour; neither are all men governed by the same lawes, and divers Nations have divers fashions, and differ in habite, diet, studies, speech, and song. Hence is it, that the English doe carroll; the French sing; the Spaniards weepe; the Italians, which dwell about the Coasts of *Ianua* caper about with their Voyces; the others barke: but the Germanes (which I am ashamed to vtter) doe howle like Wolves.[4]

Yet another strand in considering the musical history of a country would be the tension between a country's reliance on native composers on the one hand and a reliance on musical importation on the other. This, too, surfaces relatively early and is certainly prominent in the record of English music, where it often bears the stamp of political and religious circumstance. In 1575 the preface to William Byrd and Thomas Tallis's *Cantiones Sacrae* declared with confidence the strength of "British Music":

> British Music, already contemplating battle, saw that she, who yields to none of the nine Muses in art, could safely proceed by one course: if the Queen would declare herself her [British music's] patron, and if she could include as her own such distinguished authors who if they would compose would astonish the rest of the multitude. Therefore, blessed with the patronage of so learned a Ruler, she fears neither the boundaries nor the reproach of any nation. Proclaiming Tallis and Byrd her parents, she [British music] boldly advances where no voice has sung.[5]

However, the confidence here would bow to foreign incursion, especially in the 17th and 18th centuries. In writing the royal opera *Albion and Albanius* (1685), the poet John Dryden chose not an English composer but rather the Francofied Spaniard Louis Grabu, long resident in England. If the choice of composer for this patriotic opera seemed unpatriotic, Dryden explained, "When any of our Countrymen excel him, I shall be glad, for the sake of old England, to be shown my error."[6] The issue was keen in the 18th century as well. In a 1732 letter to Handel, himself an import, the theater manager Aaron Hill pleaded for an operatic liberation from Italy: "My meaning is, that you would be resolute enough, to deliver us from our *Italian bondage*; and demonstrate, that *English* is soft enough for Opera, when compos'd by poets, who know how to distinguish the *sweetness* of our tongue, from the *strength* of it, where the last is less necessary."[7] Such pleas proved idle. At the end of the 18th century, the redoubtable music historian Charles Burney lamented the short lives of Orlando Gibbons, Pelham Humfrey, and Henry Purcell, concluding that "If these admirable composers had been blest with long life, we [the English] might have had a music of our own. . . . As it is, we have no school for composition, no well digested method of study, nor indeed, models of our own."[8] For Burney the perception of foreign ascendancy was complete, even if the reality differed greatly, as this *Dictionary* shows.

What picture emerges? England's music in the early 15th century establishes aesthetic norms for the new Renaissance style, a style in which the formerly dissonant interval of the third became sweetly consonant, a new fullness of sound was essayed, and a fluidity of rhythm with frequent vertical and horizontal hemiolas graced the whole. This music, in the main Marian motets and mass movements, features in manuscript collections like the lavish "Old Hall Manuscript," wherein the chief composer is Leonel Power. The nature of the transmission of this style to the Continent, where it became "mainstream," remains speculative. However, John Dunstaple, Power's more famous contemporary, perhaps found his way to the Continent in the retinue of the Duke of Bedford, a possibility that would help to explain the transmission of this style to the Franco-Flemish world.[9]

Inherent in this early 15th-century style is a striking sense of sonority, a robust embrace of the sound itself—its amenity—that seems to trump the objective mathematics governing counterpoint. It is easy to hear the continuity of this interest in sonority in the generation of English composers coming into blossom around 1500. Notably, in the music of the Eton Choirbook we see a dramatic expansion of range in both bass and treble registers; the old three-voice core polyphony of the earlier generation has now added soaring treble lines on top and profound bass lines below, as well as oftentimes an enrichment of the middle voices. And while this does indeed extend contrapuntal technique, it more substantially seems to revel in the creating of new sound effects, as heard for instance in works like Robert Wylkynson's stunning nine-voice *Salve Regina* in the Eton collection.

The English exploration of sonority in the 15th and early 16th centuries was distinctive. So too, to a degree, was their exploration of musical form and genre, as seen in the cultivation of the carol. Compilations like the Fayrfax Manuscript and the Ritson Manuscript document the prominence of the carol at the early Tudor court, where one finds it not only celebrative but also affectively contemplative, as in the Passion carols by John Browne, William Cornysh, and others. And while the carol remains much an English form, its reliance on periodic repetition—it is strophically set with a refrain (the burden)—is suggestive of the appetite for repetition that one also encounters in the continental *formes fixes*.

The 16th century in England is marked by both a striking degree of exigent heterogeneity as well as a "Golden Age" at the end of the century. The heterogeneity is sparked chiefly by the religious reforms and reversals that characterized the reigns of Henry VIII and his children. The establishment of the autonomous Church of England gave reform-minded clerics an arena in which to establish a vernacular liturgy—the first *Book of Common Prayer* appeared in 1549—and to explore a concomitant simpler, devotional style. This simpler style, eschewing counterpoint, melisma, and development, is clear in collections like the Lumley Partbooks—Anglican devotional music before the *Book of Common Prayer*—and the Wanley Partbooks from the reign of Edward VI, and it commanded the attention of major composers like Thomas Tallis, whose proficiency in the earlier, elaborate style was both masterful and well established. The austere style was in some contexts explicitly urged. Archbishop Cranmer, architect of the *Book of Common Prayer*, famously wrote to the King about his English Litany (1544), saying:

> I trust it will much excitate and stir the hearts of all men unto devotion and godliness; but in mine opinion, the song that shall be made thereunto would not be full of notes, but, as near as may be, for every syllable a note; so that it may be sung distinctly and devoutly.[10]

The return to the Roman Church under Mary Tudor (1553–58) saw the return to the more florid, contrapuntal style as well, with Tallis and others able to re-animate the earlier tradition with works like his sumptuous *Missa Puer Natus*.

The reign of Elizabeth (1558–1603), while often characterized as a "Golden Age," buoyed by Shakespeare, western exploration, the rousing defeat of the Spanish Armada, and a general flourishing of the arts, proves to be complex. With the Act of Supremacy of 1559, Elizabeth severed England's ecclesiastical ties to Rome. This did not, however, prompt a uniform return to an austere liturgical practice; the Elizabethan church forged its now much heralded via media between Roman and Protestant sensibilities, and in that middle path liturgical music continued to embrace the Latin motet, as seen in Byrd and Tallis's famous *Cantiones Sacrae* of 1575, as well as to nurture vernacular forms of anthem and service music that show little signs of austere constraint, as the complexity and ebullience of works like Byrd's "Great Service" or his anthem "Sing Joyfully" attest. Additionally, developing out of the consort song, the verse anthem moved church music in a new formal direction that would stay active well into the 18th century. Tellingly, too, the coexistence of different scorings for verse anthems—versions for viols and versions for organ—likely point to different venues, a reminder that sacred music was often a domestic concern as well as a public ecclesiastical one.

Elizabethan secular music fostered the ayre, generally a strophic composition of an accompanied melody, often taking the form of a lute song, but equally apt as an ensemble partsong, as one sees in the music of John Dowland, Thomas Campion, and others. The strophic form made declamation and textual emphasis rare, in contrast to the direction in which Italian monodic song was notably developing. (Dowland's through-composed "In Darkness Let Me Dwell" is a significant exception.) However, the influence of the Italians in Elizabethan music is especially evident in the cultivation of the madrigal. The English madrigal drew more directly on lighter Italian forms like the *canzonetta* than it did on the more literary Italian madrigal itself, although several collections of "Englished" Italian madrigals appeared in the 1580s and 1590s, suggesting that the Italian influence was broad. The English form, like its Italian counterparts, reveled in iconic text painting, a technique that sought to render the meaning of the word audible, but at the same time a technique that was prone to exaggerated extreme.

Instrumental music also flourished under Elizabeth, royally blessed by the monarch's own abilities to play both the lute and the virginals. Solo music for lute and for keyboard well documents the virtuosic abilities of their most accomplished practitioners—lutanists like John Dowland, keyboardists like John Bull—and ensemble music for full and mixed consorts shows a high degree of cultivation. The full consort, in England most classically the chest of viols, is often, though not exclusively, associated with the contrapuntal fantasia, learned and sophisticated: the instrumental equivalent of the motet. The mixed consort, here most notably the so-called English Consort, was more associated with dance and popular music, and in its florid divisions gave to the lute one of its most characteristic solo outlets.

The Stuart 17th century is marked by the rise of Puritanism and its clash with the monarchical government, a pronounced and heightened interplay of foreign and native musical elements, the development of the English music drama, and the cultivation of public concert life. Although these may seem discrete elements, in many ways they are closely intertwined. The turbulent mid-century saw the continental exile of Prince Charles and others of the nobility, and this exile nurtured continental tastes in those who upon the restoration of the monarchy would have the power to gratify them. Accordingly, the musical establishment of Prince Charles, now Charles II, was infused with a violin band on the model of the French court; foreign musicians, such as Louis Grabu, placed in leadership positions in the royal musical establishment; and a ceremonial-liturgical style in the modern symphony anthem that imitated the ceremonial musical idioms of J. B. Lully. The foreign queens consort—Henrietta Maria of France, Catherine of Braganza, and Mary of Modena—were also influential in heightening a foreign presence; Catherine of Braganza's Roman Catholic Chapel, for instance, featured musicians such as the organist Giovanni Battista Draghi and the castrato Siface. In part, London's professional public music-making was a lure to foreign virtuosi, who were featured in early public concerts and in the theater. Indeed, the presence of foreign singers in the theater both anticipated the rise of Italian opera in the early 18th century and also undermined the English theater, where the integrity of productions was strained in order to give the singers an outlet. Similarly, the presence of foreign instrumentalists, especially violinists like Nicola Matteis, would undermine the contrapuntal viol consort tradition, as sonatas and concertos for violin began to replace fantasias for viols.

The development of English music drama in the 17th century charts a distinctive path, not oblivious to the development of fully sung opera in Italy, but tellingly different in its course. The Jonsonian masque at the early Stuart court—a dazzlingly multimedia genre of dance, music, and stagecraft—was strongly monarchical in its allegorical content and lavish in its style, both qualities that would render the genre problematic for the ascendant Puritans. Unsurprisingly, the Commonwealth (1649–60) sounded the death knell for the masque in its courtly form. However, following the Restoration of the monarchy, masquelike entertainments resurfaced, not so much in their own right, but inserted into the tradition of the spoken play, where they gave rise to the popular hybrid of "semi-opera" or "dramatick opera," masterfully rendered at the end of the century in collaborations by Henry Purcell and John Dryden, and pioneered in works like *Psyche* (1675) by Thomas Shadwell, Matthew Locke, and G. B. Draghi. To the English audience, this was "opera." The fully sung music drama, on the Italian model, had several notable 17th-century manifestations, but they were not to the native taste; in 1692 Peter Motteux pointedly observed that "experience hath taught us that our English genius will not relish that perpetual singing."[11] Most notable among the fully sung music dramas are Purcell's stunning *Dido and Aeneas* and John Blow's *Venus and Adonis*, but even as early as 1617 Nicholas Lanier had attempted a fully sung work in the masque *Lovers Made Men*.

Establishing the theatrical trajectory of the 17th century is especially important as it sets the stage for the Handelian decades at the beginning of the 18th. The first decade of the 18th century featured Italian operas in translation—newly set, as for example *Arsinoe* (1705), and old scores adapted to English words, as for example *Camilla* (1706), a work that eventually was performed bilingually, as were works like the 1707 *Thomyris* or the 1708 *Love's Triumph*. The most "English" of the operas performed in this decade was Joseph Addison and Thomas Clayton's decidedly unsuccessful *Rosamond* (1707), a work that was conceived from the beginning as an English work, and as such found little sympathy or echo. Against this background, it is easy to envision the operatic triumph of Handel with his London performance of *Rinaldo* in 1711. In its wake, the ascendancy of Italian opera and foreign musicians was well launched. Though for a period the fashionability of Italian opera was generally uncontested, its expense, its status as an import, its close ties to the aristocracy, and a rivalry between theater companies eventually led to the its demise in 1737 with the closing of both the Royal Academy of Music (Handel's opera company) and the "Opera of the Nobility." Early signs of the demise were apparent in the huge success of John Gay's *The Beggar's Opera* (1728), a ballad opera that drew on popular melodies and lowlife Hogarthian situations to satirize the aristocracy and the conventions of *opera seria*.

Handel was naturalized as an English citizen in 1727, a situation that seems in retrospect handily to emblemize foreign culture taking root in England. Certainly Handel, the Anglicized Saxon, historically emerges as a touchstone of musical Englishness. This is vividly seen in ceremonial works like his coronation anthem, "Zadok the Priest," but more extensively in his establishment of English oratorio. Developed in part to try to offer a viable theatrical alternative to opera, English oratorio has endured as one of the more long-lived, distinctively English genres, especially as the backbone of the 19th- and 20th-century choral festivals; Handel's model has both inspired and haunted later oratorio composers.

George Bernard Shaw would eventually claim that Handel's pervasive influence on English music led to "withering religion into dead bones,"[12] yet the oratorio *Messiah* was more than partly responsible for democratizing music throughout the English classes. The 18th-century charity festivals of the Three Choirs (Hereford, Worcester, and Gloucester) and at Birmingham, Cambridge, Oxford, and York—inter alia, founded to present *Messiah* and selections of other works—were increasingly controlled not by the higher echelons of the church and members of the nobility (though such individuals would remain on their lists of patrons for many years to come), but by middle-class volunteers out to "improve" their own localities through the introduction of good music to the public. Such festivals ensured two things: first, that the English public would never forget Handel's music; second, that the provincial audiences (or congregations, as they became styled at cathedral and church festivals at the end of the 19th century) would hear the best choral music from both the Continent and England. In the 18th century this meant glees, opera selections, and newly composed or pastiche oratorios that were derivative of Handel. In the 19th century this meant that composers and performers with the best reputations from England and abroad were invited to present works, sometimes in the "English style" (oratorios and cantatas), and sometimes not. The parade of foreign composers that benefited from the English love of Handel is far too long to list here but includes Ludwig van Beethoven (*Christus am Ölberg* [Norwich, 1836]), Hector Berlioz (*Damnation of Faust*, *L'Enfance du Christ*), Antonin Dvorak (*St. Ludimilla*), Charles Gounod (*Redemption*), Franz Liszt (*Christus*), Felix Mendelssohn (*St. Paul* and *Elijah*), and countless others.

While the oratorio steadily lost its hold on the musical festival in the 19th century, the idea that festivals could cultivate the best music did not, and increasingly symphonies, concert overtures, opera excerpts, cantatas, and even chamber music were mixed into the programs. Such mixing of genres was especially welcome to the domestic composers, who at the end of the 19th century were able to take great advantage of the opportunity to compose oratorios if they wished to do so. Many, including Edward Elgar, Hubert Parry, Alexander Mackenzie, Charles Villiers Stanford, Arthur Sullivan, and William Walton, did, while others, including Benjamin Britten, Samuel Coleridge-Taylor, Gustav Holst, Ethel Smyth, and Ralph Vaughan Williams, did not—at least for the traditional musical festivals. Their works, both choral and instrumental, showed that English composers could not only break away from the genres supported by the middle class but also become successful not just nationally, but internationally.

The love of Handel brought another great democratizing ideal to English music: a long-standing belief in the power of music was turned proactive throughout the 19th century. Part of this can be seen in the purpose of many of the 18th- and 19th-century festivals. These concerts had a purpose, and that was not merely entertainment, but to raise money for a particular charity, be it a fund for widows and orphans of the clergy (the Three Choirs Festival), a local hospital (Birmingham, Leeds, and Norwich), or a cathedral restoration fund (Lincoln and Peterborough). The other part, the more powerful part, which led England to be the most important country for the production of all music—classical, popular, world, or otherwise—through the first half of the 20th century, was the idea that music should be learned by all, because it could be good for all. Such was the constant refrain in magazines and journals throughout the century, as here in an anonymous excerpt from the *Tonic Sol-fa Reporter*:

> Music was not merely amusing, but an important element in education, physical, mental, and moral. Plato had said so, and the moderns concurred. He contended for music linked with poetry as a vehicle of high and holy truth, tending to secure its reception, and to aid its development. It exerted a mighty sympathetic influence, to which none were insensible. Children were led by it to yield themselves to feelings which they heard so pleasantly expressed. While it thus helped to raise the heart to God, statistics proved that the practice of public singing and speaking was conductive to longevity. Those who loved song were less liable to waste their time and associate with vile companions.[13]

This belief in music's power could be as simple as the trope that singing moral words would help instill a moral message into the heart, or as complex as using classical music as a distraction from other potential vices, as Evangelical philanthropists such as John Curwen and John Spencer Curwen believed. Whatever the reason, the educational establishments—the Royal Academy of Music, the National Training School for Music, the Royal College of Music, the Guildhall School for Music, among others—founded to teach professionals their craft for churches, orchestras, opera companies, and the like were increasingly joined by the end of the 19th century by institutions dedicated to teaching the amateur, or teaching others to teach amateurs, such as the Tonic Sol-fa College and competition festivals. The latter combined an English love of competition with the desire to promote good music to the working and middle classes and employment opportunities—either as commissioned composers of test works or as adjudicators—for many English music teachers and composers. The nominal founders of the competition festival movement, Henry Leslie (Oswestry Fetival), John Spencer Curwen (Stratford Festival), and Mary Wakefield (Kendal Festival), borrowed the Welsh *eisteddfod* and turned it from a solo competition into one that included both solo and community elements, almost always with a large, combined performance at the end, as Vaughan Williams would concentrate on within the Leith Hill Festival at Dorking. These festivals are one of the reasons that adult summer music camps for amateurs are still so popular within England today.

Opera, too, benefited from the hybrid ideals of English music-making and spurred on the production of popular music in ways heretofore not seen in the West. The London opera houses of the 18th century sponsored a truly European amalgamation of composers, singers, and instrumentalists: Germans composing Italian opera (Handel), English composers trained in Italy (Stephen Storace) or writing Italian opera (Thomas Arne's *Artaxerxes* [1729]), and Italian singers whipsawing between the English and Italian languages. For most of the 18th century, Italian opera was the most prestigious genre in England, but this is not saying much: operas themselves were not the only thing on the program at the great opera theaters of Drury Lane, Covent Garden, and elsewhere. Pastiches, afterpieces, and oratorio seasons were all part of the mix, and most of the London opera musicians worked as well in the many pleasure gardens such as Marylebone, Ranelagh, and Vauxhall. Here, the high costs that prohibited all but the elite to attend were relaxed, and members of many classes could—and often did—rub shoulders while listening to popular works often in the same style as many of the operatic greats of the time. Some of the pleasure gardens even included dramas and operalike pieces in their repertoires.

The 18th-century pleasure garden begat the 19th-century music hall (one of the potential vices the Curwens were ever so vigilantly on guard against with the promotion of singing), where popular music continued on its own way; the polyglot opera of the 18th century begat in the 19th even more presentations of Italian opera by English companies, but now also French, German, and even Russian opera made inroads, as well as interesting pastiches (Henry Bishop's rendering of Mozart's *Marriage of Figaro*, for instance) and continual attempts at English opera. Some, like Sullivan's *Ivanhoe* (1891), were presented on a grand scale; others, like Frederic Corder's *Nordissa* (1887), were much more modest in their pretensions. Into the 20th century, English composers still sought to present a convincing opera: Elgar attempted one (*The Spanish Lady*, which remained unfinished at his death); and Vaughan Williams and Holst both wrote operas that were somewhat successfully premiered. By the middle of the 20th century, Britten could boast several that traveled well beyond the shores of England. Throughout the period, though, operetta, in the style of Gilbert and Sullivan, remained much more popular both nationally and internationally than other English-language opera and would further lead English music down a successful populist path.

Sullivan, Elgar, Holst, Vaughan Williams, and Britten were all conscious of working and composing in a new musical environment, one in which English music was once again accepted by the populace as something good in and of itself, not necessarily something that had to be hybridized. The self-conscious notion was referred to at the time as the "English Musical Renaissance" (now sometimes called the "Second English Musical Renaissance" and the "British Musical Renaissance"). The pedigree of the title is as venerable as the title itself is misleading. In 1907, for instance, Ernest Walker identified "a Renaissance of English composition" within his *History of Music in England*.[14] The litany of developments causing this purported "renaissance" is well-known: the increase of musical literacy, the foundation of professional musical training institutions, and the gradual acceptance of the musical profession as a proper middle-class career were all important in the increase in literature written in English about music, both popular and scholarly, and led to a wide discussion of indigenous composers involved with these institutions. By 1882 the music critic Joseph Bennett could easily champion British composers and discuss such renewal, as he did in the *Daily Telegraph* (4 September 1882). A few years later, Morton Latham could make a passing reference to the idea of an "English Musical Renaissance" in a lecture at Trinity College, Oxford, and in 1890 publish a book entitled *The Renaissance of Music* in which he linked burgeoning contemporary British musical composition with that of the Tudor and Elizabethan schools.[15] By 1892 critics could discuss the hoped-for end of a long period of musical derision, with British music "on the rise" and matching international standards, as in the November 1892 issue of the *Musical Herald* in an article titled "Dr. Parry and the English School":

> Already there are in our land the first stirrings of a revolution which may raise English music once more to the position which it has abrogated. Our means of musical education are wide-spread and successful, our choral societies are

growing more numerous in aim, the level of performance is steadily rising throughout the country: all that is needed is a proper direction and impetus that these newly awakened forces may be trained to serve the national cause. In one word, we have everything ready for the establishment of a school of composition through which, and through which alone, we can take our place in the musical art of Europe. . . . We have not so far degenerated as to have lost the gift of song which we possessed in "the spacious times of great Elizabeth." The capacity may have been weakened by misuse, but it still exists latent in the hearts of our people. Let English music recover its national language, let it work in its own field, and develop its own resources, and it may look forward to the future not only with hope, but with confidence.[16]

Typical of this passage is both the optimistic enthusiasm with which the writer speaks of an English "Golden Age" of music during the Elizabethan period and addresses the potential of contemporary English music, and the complete dismissal of the music that had come between the two from the time of Purcell to his own. While this was not the case (as has been discussed above), it remained a common trope throughout most of the 20th century.

Indeed, there was a great deal of music to be had in England between Charles Burney and the English Musical Renaissance, some made by foreigners, either resident in the country (Michael Costa, Alberto Randegger, etc.) or visiting, either in person (Hector Berlioz, Johannes Brahms, Fryderyk Chopin, Charles Gounod, Joseph Joachim, Franz Liszt, Clara Schumann, Pyotr Tchaikovsky, Giuseppe Verdi, Richard Wagner, etc.) or through their compositions (Ludwig van Beethoven's Ninth Symphony in D minor, op. 125, was commissioned by the London Philharmonic Society, under the auspices of Sir George Smart). But even more music was composed by indigenous English composers, frequently working within the churches and cathedrals on predominantly sacred music (Samuel Sebastian Wesley), and sometimes presenting secular instrumental music to the London public (William Crotch and Sir Henry Bishop). Such would be the pattern for the rest of the 19th and the 20th centuries: England would welcome some of the best musicians from the Continent (and increasingly, the rest of the world), sometimes temporarily, sometimes permanently, while its own composers and musicians grew steadily more prestigious in the eyes of England's public. By the beginning of the 20th century, more classical music from more parts of Europe and North America was available to the London middle-class music lover than to his counterpart anywhere else in the world, a situation that continued long into the 20th century. Other English cities followed suit, founding orchestras and theaters that supplemented the still-booming provincial musical festivals.

This has led to an interesting tension throughout the entire 20th century: England has great music, celebrates great music, and studies great music from all over the world daily within its borders. But what attention does it pay to its own great music? Even by the 1920s English composers split into multiple aesthetic camps, including those who would follow a "National Style" in their works, in a conscious attempt to keep the attention of the audience for classical music that peaked at the end of the 19th century, and those who would follow a more "International" style. The aesthetic divide is much more complicated than between those composers who used folk music and antique music as their models and those who used serialism, aleatoricism, and other high-modernist methods within their works, as befits a musical culture coming to terms with its own newfound international appeal in an age when the audience for classical music began shrinking. Even after the artificial end date of 1958 used in this *Dictionary*, both coexist. Perhaps the only difference between the two is that "Internationalist" composers could always find acceptance in the work of academic musicologists and music theorists, while those following the "National Style" were frequently celebrated by amateur music lovers, until the renaissance of scholarship on English music, alluded to above, when the importance of all elements of English music, especially that created by the English themselves, became open for inquiry, criticism, and celebration. England *is* a place with so much vibrant classical music today because England *was* a place, from the 15th century until the late 20th, that continued to strive for a balance between the foreign and the domestic, to value the music of yesterday and today, and never feared to juxtapose all of these things.

NOTES

1. Ralph Vaughan Williams, *National Music* (London: Oxford University Press, 1934), 76.
2. *Proportionale musices* in *Strunk's Source Readings in Music History: The Renaissance*, ed. Gary Tomlinson (New York: W. W. Norton, 1998), 14–15.
3. Ibid., 15.
4. John Dowland, *Andreas Ornithoparcus His* Micrologus . . . (London, 1609; rpt. New York: Dover, 1973), 208.
5. William Byrd, *Cantiones Sacrae (1575)*, ed. Craig Monson (London: Stainer and Bell, 1977), xxv.
6. *The Works of John Dryden*, vol. 15, ed. Earl Miner, George Guffey, and Franklin B. Zimmerman (Berkeley: University of California Press, 1976), 8.
7. In Christopher Hogwood, *Handel* (London: Thames and Hudson, 1984), 101.
8. Charles Burney, *A General History of Music*, vol. 2 (1789; rpt. New York: Dover, 1957), 405.
9. See Margaret Bent, *Dunstaple* (Oxford: Oxford University Press, 1981), 1; Andrew Wathey, "Dunstable in France," *Music & Letters* 67 (1986): 5.

10. In Oliver Strunk, *Source Readings in Music History* (New York: W. W. Norton, 1950), 351.

11. *Gentleman's Journal*, January 1692.

12. George Bernard Shaw, *Music in London, 1890–1894*, vol. 3 (New York: Vienna House, 1973), 210.

13. *Tonic Sol-fa Reporter*, May 1856, 133.

14. Ernest Walker, *A History of Music in England* (Oxford: Oxford University Press, 1907), 286.

15. Robert Stradling and Meirion Hughes, *The English Musical Renaissance, 1860–1940: Construction and Deconstruction* (London: Routledge, 1993), 34.

16. *Musical Herald*, November 1892, 323–26.

A

ABEL, CARL FRIEDRICH (1723–87). Composer, impresario, and bass-violist. Abel was born in Cöthen, held an early position in Dresden with the court orchestra there under Johann Adolph Hasse, and arrived in England for the 1758–59 season. After several years of presenting his own concerts, he began a long association with **Johann Christian Bach**; their first concert together occurred in 1764, and the famous Bach-Abel subscription concert series occurred between 1765 and 1781. The **Hanover Square Rooms** were partly built to house this series. After J. C. Bach's death in 1782, Abel attempted his own series and, following a trip to the Continent, produced further concerts at Hanover Square until his death. At these concerts, Abel was a composer, performer (on both harpsichord and bass **viol**), and conductor. His music, as described by Roger Fiske, was Italianate and *galant*, and consisted of symphonies, concerti, and solo sonatas. It was published contemporaneously and available to the London public. Abel was a well-regarded figure within the London musical establishment; according to **Charles Burney**, Abel "became the umpire in all musical controversy, and was consulted in difficult and knotty points as an infallible oracle."

ABELL (ABEL), JOHN (1653–AFTER 1716). Countertenor, lutanist, and composer. Abell enjoyed royal favor at the courts of Charles II and James II as a gentleman of the **Chapel Royal**, the **Private Musick**, and, during the reign of James II, the monarch's Roman Catholic Chapel. With the accession of William and Mary, Abell joined the exiled Stuart court at Saint-Germain, returning to England in 1699, where he sought to recover financial stability through concerts and teaching. As a countertenor, he was known for his high range; as the diarist **John Evelyn** described his voice, "one would have sworne it had been a Womans it was so high, and so well and skillfully manag'd" (27 January 1682).

The *Post Boy*, the *Post Man*, the *London Post*, the *English Post*, the *Daily Courant*, and the *Edinburgh Courant* document his concert activity in the early 18th century, including performances in his native Scotland. Though he seems not to have been involved in stage music to any significant degree, he performed the title role in **Daniel Purcell**'s *The Judgment of Paris*

(1702). The early years of the century also saw the publication of several song anthologies, including *A Collection of Songs, In English* . . . (1701), *A Collection of Songs, In Several Languages* . . . (1701), and *A Choice Collection of Italian Ayres* . . . (1703). Of his two contributions to **Thomas Durfey**'s *Pills to Purge Melancholy*, **Sir John Hawkins** noted that they were "very elegant tunes."

Several aspects of Abell's career seem colorful to the modern reader. Hawkins, for example, describes how the singer had spurned a royal request to sing at the Polish court in Warsaw; upon finally appearing at court Abell was given a choice of singing or being thrown to wild bears that had been assembled in the hall. Wisely, he chose to sing. Contemporary advertisements also underscore his ability to sing in many different languages, including not only the expected English, Italian, and French, but Greek, Latin, Danish, Swedish, Turkish, and two varieties of Dutch, among others.

ABRAMS, HARRIET (ca. 1758–1821). Singer (soprano) and composer. Abrams came from a musical family: her sister Theodosia was a contralto; her sister Eliza, a singer and pianist; her brother Charles, a cellist; and her brother William, a violinist. The family may have been Jewish immigrants from Germany; Abrams and her siblings were baptized at St. George's, Hanover Square, in 1791. Though Roger Fiske and others state that she was a pupil of **Thomas Arne** (citing her performance in his 1775 afterpiece **opera** *May Day* as evidence), she was likely trained by her family, since Arne complained of David Garrick engaging "a jewess" for the performance instead of one of Arne's own pupils. Her career at **Drury Lane** lasted from her 1775 debut until 1780, when she left the dramatic stage to concentrate on **oratorio** singing, especially at the provincial **musical festivals**. She held a yearly benefit concert for herself from 1781 to 1796, at times singing in the **Hanover Square Rooms**. Abrams published four collections of vocal music, including **ballads** such as the popular "Crazy Jane" and "Orphan's Prayer", duets, and trios; the last of these collections was dedicated to Queen Charlotte in 1803.

ACADEMY OF ANCIENT MUSIC (ALSO ACADEMY OF ANCIENT MUSICK AND ACADEMY OF ANTIENT MUSICK). A London musical society founded to promote the "study and practice of vocal and instrumental harmony" with a focus on 16th-century composers as well as those who "in our own Time have become famous" (**Sir John Hawkins**). Founded in 1726 as the Academy of Vocal Music, it changed its name to the Academy of Ancient Music in 1731, and remained active until 1797. Prominent at its founding were Henry Needler, **John Ernest Galliard**, **Bernard Gates**, and

Johann Christoph Pepusch, whose antiquarianism and library were well suited to the aims of the society. Other early members include **Maurice Greene, Giovanni Bononcini**, Agostino Steffani (elected president in 1727), **Francesco Geminiani**, Nicola Haym, Jean Baptiste Loeillet, Giuseppe Riva, and the celebrated castrato **Senesino**. The number of foreign musicians in such a list is a significant indicator of the musical cosmopolitanism of London at the time. *See also* COOKE, BENJAMIN.

Through its many decades of activity, the nature of the society varied. Initially, the private meetings were held at the Crown and Anchor Tavern on alternate Friday evenings. In the 1730s the academy became a "seminary for the instruction of youth in the principles of music and the laws of harmony" (Hawkins), with Pepusch providing the tutelage. The scale of its concerts increased toward the end of the century, prompting a move to the Freemasons' Hall in 1784, where it remained until 1795.

The Academy was much involved in the plagiarism scandal involving Greene, Bononcini, and Antonio Lotti. Greene had performed before the Academy a **madrigal**, "In una siepe ombrosa," ostensibly by Bononcini. When several years later (1731) the same madrigal resurfaced as a work by Lotti in an Academy performance by Gates, scandal ensued. The Academy's investigations were reported in *Letters from the Academy of Ancient Music at London to Signor Antonio Lotti of Venice, with answers and testimonies* (London, 1732) and confirmed Lotti's authorship.

In 1776 Hawkins summarized the Academy's achievement as allowing students and performers "to form an idea of classical purity and elegance; and, in short, to fix the standard of a judicious and rational taste. One of the principal ends of the institution was a retrospect to those excellent compositions of former ages . . . ; and in the prosecution thereof ere brought forth to public view, the works of very many authors, whose names, though celebrated with all the applauses of panegyric, had else been consigned to oblivion."

ACTS OF UNIFORMITY. Various statutes enacted in 1549, 1552, 1559, and 1662 to establish a common liturgical rite in England and other royal dominions. The provisions made the *Book of Common Prayer* the exclusive liturgical text and mandated its use without interference or derogation. In establishing a vernacular rite, the effect on musical practice was strong, as was the reduction of the daily offices to two—Matins and **Evensong**. Significantly, exceptions to the rule were granted in particular circumstances. For instance, private prayer might be in Latin, Greek, or Hebrew if one understood those languages (1549), and the University Chapels at Cambridge and Oxford were similarly allowed to use Latin, Greek, or Hebrew liturgically, except in the service of Holy Communion (1549).

ADAMS, THOMAS (1785–1858). Organist and composer, chiefly in London, considered one of the most important of his time. A pupil of Thomas Busby, Adams served as organist at Carlisle Chapel, Lambeth (1802), St. Paul's, Deptford (1814), St. George's, Camberwell (1824), and St. Dunstan-in-the-West, Fleet Street (1833). Between 1817 and 1821, and again from 1823 to 1825, he directed other organists, including at times C. Guichard, Walter Augustus Lord, George Cooper, Alfred J. S. Moxley, and Joseph Warren, in performances of **oratorios** on Benjamin Flight and Joseph Robinson's **Apollonicon**. Here he introduced the English public to sacred music by Wolfgang Amadeus Mozart and **Franz Joseph Haydn**, and frequently performed the **organ** works of Johann Sebastian Bach. From 1819 these concerts included a quartet of vocalists and began to include popular operatic and oratorio arias. A virtuosic player and skilled improviser (he was called "the Thalberg of the organ" by Edward John Hopkins), English firms frequently used him to advertise the capabilities of their instruments. His compositions—mostly for organ and piano—were highly contrapuntal, differing from his contemporaries by density of texture and his attempts to strive for orchestral-like effects using keyboard instruments.

ADCM. *See* ROYAL COLLEGE OF ORGANISTS; ROYAL SCHOOL OF CHURCH MUSIC.

ADSON, JOHN (1587?–1640). Wind musician and composer. Following a time of employment on the Continent, Adson was appointed a member of the London **Waits** (1614), and documentary references to him as a player of both **cornett** and flute (recorder) are suggestive of the waits' versatility. In 1633 he was appointed a court wind player. Adson supplemented his activities at court and in the city wind band with work in the theater, playing in productions of the King's Men, an association that prompted his being named in William Cavendish's play *The Country Captain*. When asked for music in the play, a musician questions: "Do you meane Master *Adsons* new **ayres** sir?" The Captain replies, "I sir. But they are such phantasticall ayres, as it puts a Poet out of his witts to ryme them."

In 1621 he published his collection of five- and six-voice pieces, *Courtly Masquing Ayres for Violins, Consorts and Cornetts*, dedicated to George, Duke of Buckingham, "remembering how I have hereby in some measure discharged my present obligation of duty and have taken a happy incouragement for a future service."

AKEROYDE, SAMUEL (fl. 1684–1706). Violinist and composer. Akeroyde was sworn a musician-in-ordinary to James II in 1687, taking the place of the deceased John Twist; in 1689 he was sworn a member of the **Private Musick** at the court of William III, in whose entourage he traveled to Holland in 1691. As a composer, he contributed to a number of song collections and plays, and he was described by his contemporary **John Blow** as a "good scholar," knowing French and Italian. Ian Spink (1974) notes that "he composed fluently but innocuously."

ALBERT HALL. *See* ROYAL ALBERT HALL.

ALBRICI, VINCENZO (1631–90 OR 1696), BARTOLOMEO (ca. 1640–AFTER 1687), AND LEONORA (n.d.). Italian musicians in service to Charles II and (Bartolomeo) James II. The brothers Vincenzo and Bartolomeo entered royal service as musicians in 1665, as confirmed in official documents. Their sister likely entered royal service as a musician at the same time as well, though she is not named apart from references to "the Woman." Later, with the establishment of James II's Roman Catholic Chapel, Bartolomeo was appointed as a "Gregorian" and also played the **organ**. As a mark of royal favor, all three siblings received gold medals and chains from Charles II (1668).

The high esteem in which the brothers were held is confirmed by the diarists **Samuel Pepys** and **John Evelyn**. Evelyn employed Bartolomeo as music master to his daughter: "My daughter Mary now first began to learne Musick of Signor Bartholomeo, and Dauncing of Monsieur Isaac, both reputed the best Masters, etc." (7 February 1682). Pepys records that Vincenzo was the "chief composer" among the Italian musicians at court (12 February 1666/67).

The initial connection between the Albrici family and England was likely Bulstrode Whitelocke, Oliver Cromwell's representative to the Swedish court, where both brothers were employed in the 1650s. Westrup (1941) reports that Queen Christina's musicians visited and played for Whitelocke on several occasions.

ALCOCK, JOHN (1715–1806). English organist, composer, and novelist. Trained as a chorister at St. Paul's Cathedral (London) under Charles King, he was later an apprentice to **John Stanley**. He took the BMus and DMus from Oxford (1755 and 1766) and was employed as organist of Lichfield Cathedral and a number of parish churches, including St. Andrew's (Plymouth), St. Laurence's (Reading), Sutton Coldfield (Warwickshire), and Tamworth.

Alcock's interest in earlier English church music forms an important presage of **William Boyce**'s *Cathedral Music*, a connection made all the more compelling in that both he and Boyce were choristers together at St. Paul's. In 1752 Alcock published a proposal to print editions of English church music by such composers as **Thomas Tallis, William Byrd**, and **Orlando Gibbons**, "[h]aving observed how incorrect the **Service**s, &c. are at Cathedrals, and as I have now by me an exceeding valuable Collection of the choicest antient and modern Services[.]" However, **Maurice Greene**'s ongoing activity to the same end caused Alcock to abandon his plan: "As I have the Pleasure of assuring my Friends that the famous Dr. GREENE designs to publish a Collection of the choicest Cathedral SERVICES, I take this Opportunity of thanking those Gentlemen, &c. who have already subscribed to my Scheme of that Kind . . . and likewise of acquainting them, that I think it advisable to decline that Undertaking . . ." (*London Evening-Post*, 29–31 March 1753).

Alcock's experience at Litchfield was an unhappy one, characterized by difficulties with the **vicars-choral**. The trials and tribulations of his cathedral years surface in his novel, *The Life of Miss Fanny Brown* (1761), written under the musically suggestive pseudonym John Piper.

ALDRICH, HENRY (1648–1710). Scholar, cleric, amateur composer, and collector. Aldrich was strongly associated with Christ Church, Oxford, where he both studied as a young man and spent the full length of his career in various capacities, notably as canon (from 1681) and dean (1689–1710); for several years he also served as vice-chancellor of the University. He was a man of diverse abilities and interests. **Charles Burney** describes him as not only a musician but a "polemical writer, a polite scholar, a theologian, a profound critic, an architect, and a man of sound judgement, and exquisite taste in arts, science and literature in general." His architectural skill remains evident in his design of Peckwater Quad at Christ Church and the Chapel of Trinity College. Although he was an amateur musician, he exercised significant authority over musical matters at Christ Church. Burney notes that "he became so profound and skilled in the theory and practice of harmony, that his compositions, particularly for the church, equal in number and excellence those of the greatest masters of his time."

Aldrich's classical education, his strong Tory convictions, and his high-church views would all predispose him to embrace historical music with an appreciative sense. One manifestation of this was his activity as a music collector. **Sir John Hawkins** records that Aldrich "made a noble collection of church-music, consisting of the works of Palestrina, Carissimi, Victoria, and other Italian composers for the church," a sizeable collection given to Christ Church upon his death. Burney, who relied on the collection for source material in the writing of his history of music, said that it was "one of the most complete [collections], in old masters, that I have seen." Aldrich's reputation has been extensively associated with the amassing of this important musical library; however, recent research (Pinto, 1990, and Wainwright, 1997) has clarified that much of the collection was actually obtained and built by the Hatton family, the first Baron Hatton of Kirby (Christopher Hatton III) passing the collection to Aldrich ca. 1670. Significantly, the collection supported Aldrich's extensive practice of "recomposing" works by Giacomo Carissimi, Giovanni Pierluigi da Palestrina, **William Byrd**, **Thomas Tallis**, and others, a practice that may be seen to be resonant with the Renaissance educational ideal of *imitatio* (Shay, 1996). Although newly supplied with English texts, the recomposed pieces were more extensively adapted than the simple making of a *contrafactum*. Aldrich employed variously truncation, the addition of reworked material, and conflation of material from different contexts in the act of adaptation. Hawkins likened the practice to "naturalizing" the pieces, "accommodating them to an English ear, by words perhaps as well suited to the music as those to which they were originally framed."

As a churchman, Aldrich's interest in sacred music is unsurprising. In a lighter vein, he also composed the **catch** "O the Bonny Christ Church Bells." It and similar fare may have found a place in the music meetings held in his rooms, along with, more predictably, choral church music. An extant Latin verse by Aldrich seems to confirm that he possessed a convivial side:

> If on my theme I rightly think
> There are five reasons why men drink,
> Good wine, a friend, or being dry,
> Or lest we should be, by and by,
> Or any other reason why.
> (*Oxford Book of Oxford*, 1978)

ALEXANDRA PALACE. Recreation grounds in North London including a concert hall, built as a companion to the **Crystal Palace**. Initially proposed in 1860, Alexandra Palace was completed in 1873, only to be destroyed by fire shortly thereafter. A new Palace was built and opened in 1875, which included a 3,500-seat concert hall and a concert **organ** designed by Henry Willis & Sons. The BBC leased part of the site from 1935 onward, using it for broadcasting.

ALEYN, JOHN (?–1373). Canon of the **Chapel Royal** and composer. Aleyn was a canon at St. George's Chapel, Windsor, from 1362, where inventories from the late 14th and early 15th centuries note music given by him to the chapel. He composed a three-voice motet, "Sub Arturo plebs vallata" in I Bol Q15 and Fch 1047, the text of which names not only English musicians but English music theorists as well. There is speculation that this Windsor John Aleyn may also be the composer of two works, a Gloria and an Agnus Dei, in the **Old Hall Manuscript**. However, the ascriptions in the manuscript are inconclusive: the Gloria lacks an initial, and the Agnus, as Margaret Bent (NG, 2001) observes, "appears to read 'W. Aleyn,'" thus challenging a linkage to the Windsor canon.

ALLEN, SIR HUGH PERCY (1869–1946). Musical administrator, conductor, and organist. When Allen held joint appointments as professor of music at Oxford (1918–46) and director of the **Royal College of Music** (RCM; 1918–37), there were few elements of music-making in Great Britain not directly or indirectly touched by him. Early training with the organist Frederick John Read culminated with his being named Read's assistant at Chichester Cathedral (1887). Allen took a BMus at Oxford in 1892 and was then an **organ** scholar at Christ's College, Cambridge (1892–95). He passed the examination for DMus at Oxford in 1895 but was not awarded the degree until 1898. Early appointments at St. Asaph Cathedral (1897) and Ely Cathedral (1898) culminated in his being named organist at New College, Oxford (1901); within this position, he conducted the Oxford Bach Choir and an orchestra. Allen also conducted **musical festivals** (including Peterborough and Leeds), was the conductor of the **Bach Choir** (1907–20), and was the director of music at University College, Reading (1908–18), and Cheltenham Ladies' College (1910–18). Following his appointments as professor of music at Oxford and director of the RCM, his conducting slowed for administration, including being head of the Music Advisory Committee for the **British Broadcasting Corporation** (1937). He expanded the faculty and staff of the RCM and helped create the music faculty at Oxford in 1944. Allen was knighted in 1920, made CVO in 1926, KCVO in 1928, and GCVO in 1935.

ALLISON, RICHARD (1560/70?–BEFORE 1610). English composer of consort music and settings of **metrical psalms**. Allison contributed a number of works scored for the so-called **English Consort** to **Thomas Morley**'s *First Booke of Consort Lessons* (1599) and to the Walsingham partbooks. In his consort pieces he shows an affinity for varied textures and instrumental dialogue. In 1599 he published *The Psalmes of David in Meter*, which provided harmonizations of standard psalm tunes in the Sternhold and Hopkins Psalter. His settings were published with an eye toward flexible performance: "the common tunne to be sung and plaide upon the **Lute**, Orpharyon, **Cittern** or Base **Violl**, severally or altogether, the singing part to be either Tenor or Treble to the Instrument, according to the nature of the voice, or for fowre voices. . . ." In other words, one might sing the tune in either octave, with diverse instrumental accompaniment, or as a four-part vocal setting, a flexible approach embodied in the printer's format as well. Moreover, the particular instruments involved strongly suggest the domestic performance of devotional works. Richard Day, holder of a monopoly for printing the Sternhold and Hopkins psalms, claimed that Allison's psalter infringed upon his rights, although the outcome of the dispute is unclear.

Contemporary praise of Allison was strong. **Anthony Wood**, for instance, noted that he "was then most excellent in his facultie, as several of his compositions which we have in our musick school shew." Morley's dedication to the *First Booke of Consort Lessons* includes Allison among "the most perfect men in their quality, that in the censure of many which can well judge in Musicke, have beene, and are at this day held very rare and excellent, both for their skill and practice." **Charles Burney** was less enthusiastic in the 18th century. Of Allison's psalter he wrote: "If the author's friends may be credited, . . . it abounds with uncommon excellence. However, the puff-direct, in the shape of friendly panegyrics prefixed to books, was no more to be depended on by the public in Queen Elizabeth's time, than the puffs oblique of present newspapers. The book has no merit, but that was very common, at the time it was printed."

ALTERNATIM. The liturgical practice of alternating monophonic chant with sung or played polyphony based on that chant or its **faburden**. The practice was established in the Middle Ages, documented, for instance, in the 14th-century Exeter Ordinal of Bishop Grandisson that specifies that the Gloria of the Lady Mass could be performed in this fashion, and in England extends well into the 16th century. The practice was associated with masses, **hymns**, *Te Deums*, and Magnificats.

Early examples include **John Dunstaple**'s hymn "Ave maris stella" and his Magnificat on the second tone, a work existing in two versions, one that alternates three- and two-voiced polyphony and another that alternates the three-voiced sections with monophonic chant. **Thomas Tallis**'s eight chant-based hymns and **Robert Fayrfax**'s Magnificats document the persistence of the practice.

The only surviving English **organ** mass is that of **Philip ap Rhys** (GB lbl add 29996), where troped Kyrie, Gloria, Sanctus, and Agnus alternate organ and vocal sections. **Nicholas Ludford**'s Lady Masses (ca. 1520–30) are preserved in partbooks that include a separate book giving the chant melodies for alternating sections. As the chants are given with only text incipits, it seems likely (Harrison, 1963) that they were used for organ improvisation.

ALWOOD, RICHARD (fl. 16th CENTURY). Composer and priest. Allwood is the composer of five works in the **Mulliner Book**, including a contrapuntal piece entitled "**Voluntary**," one of the earliest examples of this nomenclature. His *In nomine* in the Mulliner Book is distinctive in being based not on the *Gloria tibi trinitas* melody but rather on the cantus firmus of his Mass, "Praise Him Praiseworthy." This cantus firmus—F, G, A, B-flat, A—has been associated with the plainsong "Sponsus amat sponsam" by Roger Bray (*Blwl*, v 2).

AMNER, JOHN (1579–1641). Organist and composer. Amner was *informator choristarum* at Ely Cathedral from 1610 until the year of his death. He took a BMus from Oxford in 1613 and shortly before his death received a MusB from Cambridge (1640). Unsurprisingly, his compositions are chiefly Anglican church music, including several **services** and a large number of **anthems**, a significant number of which were published in his *Sacred Hymnes of 3, 4, 5 and 6 parts for Voyces and Vyols* (1615). Amner's anthems were in use beyond Ely, as **Anthony Wood** confirms: Amner was well known for "certaine Anthemes, wh[ich] were in his time & after sung in Cathedralls." His keyboard variations on "O Lord in Thee is all my trust" (US NYp) are unusual in being based on a psalm tune.

Amner's family was a musical one that included an uncle, Michael, who was a lay clerk at Ely and a brother or cousin, Ralph (d. 1644), who was a bass singer at Ely, Westminster Abbey, St. George's, Windsor (where he was curate of the Castle and Dean's Curate), and the **Chapel Royal**.

ANACREONTIC SOCIETY. Society for amateur and professional musicians founded in 1766. At a series of 12 to 14 weekly or biweekly concerts starting in November of each year, "honorary members" (professional musicians) would entertain the music-loving members (up to 80 gentlemen and members of the professional classes, plus their guests) with **glees** and songs, some written especially for the society, such as **John Stafford Smith**'s "The Anacreontic Song" or "To Anacreon in Heaven"—a tune popularly known today as that for the "Star Spangled Banner." A supper would be served afterward. By the end of the 18th century, the Society's season included mixed concerts of vocal and instrumental music, including symphonies by **Franz Joseph Haydn**.

ANGLICAN CHANT. A 19th-century term for harmonic formulas composed for the sung recitation of prose psalms and **canticles**, chiefly employed in the Prayer Book liturgies of morning and evening prayer. In its classic form, Anglican chant consists of a top-voice melody harmonized in four parts (SATB), arranged in a binary structure of three measures, followed by four measures. The first three measures correspond to the first half of the psalm verse (to the asterisk in the Prayer Book orthography); the last four bring the verse to conclusion. The first measure of each half is a chord of recitation, accommodating a varying number of text syllables. Since the 19th century, this chord of recitation has been of flexible length, lasting as long as is necessary to accommodate the words in a free, declamatory recitation, while the other measures move in a more mensural fashion to the cadence. This combination of flexibly free time and measured time is confirmed in Benjamin Jacob's *National Psalmody* of 1817: "The metronomic figures do not apply to the recitation, which is unmeasured, but to the succeeding bars." Nicholas Temperley (1979) has documented that in the 18th century the chord of recitation had an equal length in each verse: "When [in the 18th century] there are many syllables to be recited, they are not, as in modern chanting, sung in natural rhythm to a note of indefinite length; they are provided with shorter notes, so that the total time taken up is the same in each verse." The classic seven-bar form is often doubled in its length (3+4; 3+4) in what are termed "double chants."

Anglican chant has its roots in earlier practices including both the improvised harmonization of psalm tones (**faburden**) and written harmonizations of psalm tones with the melody in the tenor, harmonizations that were associated with festal as opposed to daily usage. **Thomas Tallis** wrote the earliest examples of these harmonized festal psalms, using a measured declamation throughout. **Thomas Morley** also gives examples in his *Plaine and Easie Introduction to Practicall Musicke* (1597). Restoration sources, specifically Edward Lowes's *A Short Direction for the Performance of Cathedrall Service* (1661), James Clifford's *Brief Directions for the understanding of that part of the Divine Service performed with the Organ in S. Paul's Cathedrall on Sundayes and Holy-dayes* (1664), and **John Playford**'s *The Order of Performing the Divine Service in Cathedrals and Collegiate Chappels* (1674), document the persistence of psalm-tone based chanting; although, in the late 17th and 18th centuries, the repertory embraces newly composed melody, the later norm.

Anglican chanting in the modern day has achieved a highly stylized performance practice in the daily offices of cathedrals and collegiate chapels, where expert choirs lavish attention on nuanced declamation. This emphasis on declamation has generally made Anglican chanting ill suited for congregational use.

The musical content provided by the harmony, in distinction to the textual content of the declamation, seems analogous to the lyricism of the antiphons that accompany plainsong recitation. In both cases, declamation receives an added musical layer, though in the one case it is successive and in the other simultaneous.

ANTHEM. A vernacular composition set to devotional, biblical, or liturgical texts to be sung most particularly at Anglican services of Morning and Evening Prayer, but also finding broader use in various ceremonial contexts and in domestic settings. The musical style of the anthem varies with historical period under the influence of changes in both aesthetics and piety, but significantly the anthem has at times commanded the attention of leading composers and has been an area in which national style has received much development.

Anthems were first rubrically specified in the fifth edition of the *Book of Common Prayer* (1662). In the liturgies of both Morning and Evening Prayer, following the third Collect—thus toward the end of the **service**—a rubric specifies: "In Quires and Places where they sing, here followeth the Anthem." And though here explicitly authorized, a more general authorization is found a hundred years earlier in the Elizabethan Injunctions of 1559: "[I]t may be permitted, that in the beginning, or in the end of Common Prayers, either at morning or evening, there may be sung an **hymn**, or suchlike song, to the praise of Almighty God, in the best sort of melody and music that may be conveniently devised, having respect that the sentence of the hymn may be understanded and perceived."

The positioning of the anthem at the end of the liturgy allows a compelling link to be forged between this modern usage and the earlier tradition of **votive antiphons**, most particularly those to the Blessed Virgin Mary. Pre-Reformation Roman rite usage prescribed one of four seasonal Marian antiphons—*Regina caeli*, *Alma redemptoris mater*, *Ave regina coelorum*, and *Salve regina*—at the conclusion of Compline. Harrison (1963) documents the extensive allegiance to this practice, which reaches its apex around 1500, as seen in the richly sonorous repertory of the **Eton Choirbook**. It is a short leap from a lyrical coda at the end of the Office to the lyrical pause close to the end of the Prayer Service. Additionally, the linkage is strengthened by the close etymological relationship between "antiphon" and "anthem."

Early forms of English anthem coincide with or predate the advent of the first *Book of Common Prayer* (1549), as seen in the works of **Thomas Tallis**, **John Sheppard**, and Robert Okeland in the **Wanley Partbooks**. Tallis's well-known "If Ye Love Me" and "Hear the Voice and Prayer" from this collection exemplify the note-against-note style and simplicity of counterpoint that were typical. Drawing on the model of **consort songs** and modes of performing **metrical psalms**, subsequent development was in the direction of the verse anthem. The verse anthem features extensive passages for solo singer(s) accompanied by **organ** or **viol** consort in alternation with choral tuttis. The existence of the two different instrumentations reflects the diversity of venue—organ in church and viols in domestic contexts. Notable examples include **William Byrd**'s "Christ Rising" and **Orlando Gibbons**'s "This is the Record of John."

With the restoration of the monarchy in the 17th century, the verse anthem received much attention with infusions of continental idioms, including

Italianate declamation, harmonic pathos, and passages of French-style dance music. The substantial instrumental contribution in the Restoration anthem—overtures and ritornelli—make some pieces appropriately styled "symphony anthems," represented at their grandest by the coronation anthems of **John Blow** and **Henry Purcell**—for example, Blow's "God Spake Sometime in Visions" or Purcell's "My Heart is Inditing."

Full anthems, those not written in a verse style, persisted, often with intricate interplay, as in Byrd's "Sing Joyfully," or rich contrapuntal writing, as in Purcell's expressive "Hear my Prayer." **George Frideric Handel** furthered the tradition in a number of anthems for the Duke of Chandos, and his coronation anthem "Zadok the Priest" has become iconic of the English ceremonial style.

The period after Handel's death witnessed two trends in the singing of anthems in cathedrals and churches with sufficient forces: one was the adaptation of music from Handel's **oratorios**, especially *Messiah*, to be sung as anthems; the other was a sense of preservation of older anthems in the repertory; both continued well into the next century. Choirs sang anthems primarily from manuscript partbooks, and therefore many anthems had only local or regional significance. But composers could still be known for their contributions to the genre, including **William Boyce** and **William Crotch**, who alternated simple styles and forms with counterpoint occasionally inspired by the counterpoint and harmonies of Johann Sebastian Bach, as can be heard in Crotch's "How Dear are Thy Counsels" (1796). Crotch also advocated a return to 16th-century counterpoint, believing that modern secular styles were not appropriate for anthems; well into the 19th century, "antique" touches, such as plainsong incipits (**Thomas Attwood**, "Enter Not into Judgment" [1834]) could be found.

Thus, creativity did not decline in the beginning of the 19th century, but standards of singing—in both cathedral and parish church—did. Simpler and shorter anthems consequently appeared, such as Attwood's "Turn Thy Face from My Sins" (1835), a reserved, even touching verse anthem with mostly homophonic choral tutti sections, occasionally poignant in its harmonies. The number of anthems composed in the century would continue to rise, a phenomenon helped in the 1830s when **Novello & Co.** began publishing a cheap anthem service in octavo scores. Parish churches largely discarded the manuscript partbooks (cathedrals would retain them until the 1860s). The Gresham Prize for best service or anthem was also instituted in this decade, made possible by a subvention from Maria Hackett; Crotch was one of the first judges, ensuring that "antique" styles would continue. The anthem continued a journey to the affective and even sentimental throughout the middle of the century, partially because of the harmonic flexibility borrowing from the ancients provided, and partly too because the congregation began to believe that the anthem was to be sung to them—not just the officiants. Churches and cathedrals still adapted music from other sources—particularly oratorios—for their anthems; **Sir William Sterndale Bennett**'s "God is a Spirit" from his *Woman of Samaria* (1867) was particularly popular, and few oratorios were composed without an eye toward such recycling. The music of non-English composers, including Johann Sebastian Bach, **Franz Joseph Haydn**, Wolfgang Amadeus Mozart, Franz Schubert, Ludwig Spohr, and many others, was translated and rearranged a great deal.

From the middle to the end of the 19th century, composers sought increasingly dramatic effects (to cater to the congregation) while still maintaining a good sense of text setting. The *Twelve Anthems* (1853) of **Samuel Sebastian Wesley** are a particularly good example of this. In the last 40 years of the century, the number of anthems exploded, just as did the composition of **oratorios** and **cantatas**, and composers increasingly looked to these other genres as models for drama and effect. Congregations demanded facility and emotion from church and cathedral choirs since they could easily find them in concerts by amateur choral associations. Additional organ registers and colors helped give a sense of drama to late-century works, and the parade of great composers (**Sir George Smart**, **Sir Arthur Sullivan**, **Sir John Stainer**, **Sir Charles Villiers Stanford**, **Sir Hubert Parry**, and **Charles Wood**, among many others) wrote poignant examples of anthems where the organ accompaniment sounds almost like an orchestra.

Of course, some anthems were orchestrated. Parry's "I was glad" (1902), used for the coronation of Edward VII, is a good example. This explosion of anthem development was not to last. After 1914 composers increasingly turned away from church music, as they did from most choral music. Those who did continue to compose frequently used older styles or worked to make modern styles palatable to both choir and congregation. Successful examples of the latter include **Herbert Howells**'s "Take Him Earth for Cherishing" (1964), which is poignant in its expression of grief—made even more so by its a cappella setting.

AP RHYS, PHILIP (fl. 1545–60). Welsh composer and organist. Ap Rhys held appointments at two London churches, St. Mary-at-Hill and St. Paul's Cathedral, the latter position confirmed in a descriptive note in GB Lbl Add. Ms. 29996. This manuscript contains all of Ap Rhys's compositions, which are exclusively liturgical **organ** works, in all likelihood written for use before the advent of the Prayer Book liturgies of 1549. His organ mass is the only such surviving English work, and consists of a troped Kyrie (*Deus Creator*), Gloria, Sanctus, Agnus, and, unusually, an Offertory (*Benedictus sit* for the

Feast of the Holy Trinity). The organ movements are chant based and to be played in *alternatim* with sung sections.

APOLLONICON. Five-console, equally tempered finger and barrel **organ** built and used at the premises of Benjamin Flight and Joseph Robinson between 1817 and 1832. It took five years to construct, had 45 stops, and was one of the largest organs of its time. Its home, the business premises of Flight and Robinson, became one of the first venues in England for secular organ recitals. The high status of these recitals was assured through the direct patronage of the Prince Regent. The instrument was likely designed for a museum (never built) to promote English trade and industry. Originally, Flight and Robinson proposed a subscription for the estimated £10,000 to complete the organ, but eventually paid for the instrument themselves. In their 1814 prospectus for the Apollonicon, Flight and Robinson stated that the instrument was designed to "produce the real effect of a *whole orchestra of performers.*" The four types of performances heard on the Apollonicon included concerts of self-playing music as a barrel organ; solo organ recitals by figures such as **John Purkis** and **Thomas Adams**, five-player ensemble performances, and organ and vocal recitals. Repertoire performed on the instrument included popular **opera** overtures, variations on popular songs, and **oratorio** and opera arias. The Apollonicon remained a fixture of the London concert scene until the bankruptcy of Flight & Robinson in 1832. After this, the Fleet Street premises were purchased by Hill & Co., who used the instrument sporadically until 1840, selling it off as spare parts in 1865.

APPLEBY, THOMAS (?–1563/64). English organist and composer. Appleby's surviving works consist of a Magnificat in GB Cu Peterhouse 471–74 and a Mass in the so-called **Gyffard Partbooks** (GB lbl Add. Ms. 17802–5). He maintained a long association with Lincoln Cathedral as organist and master of the choristers (1537–38; 1541–50; 1559–63) but was also briefly *informator choristarum* at Magdalen College, Oxford. Harrison (1963) notes that in 1539 this was a post he held jointly with a "Master Jaquet."

ARNE, MICHAEL (1740–86). Composer, keyboard player, conductor, and singer. Michael Arne was thought by contemporaries to be the illegitimate son of **Thomas Arne**; during his early childhood he lived with his aunt, the famous stage actress Susannah Maria Cibber. After an early attempt on the stage as an actor and singer, he turned to keyboard playing (particularly the works of Thomas Arne) and composing for London's theaters and **pleasure gardens**. On tour in Germany, he conducted the first public performance of **George Frideric Handel**'s *Messiah* there (Hamburg, 1772). His compositions were mostly songs (such as "Lass with the Delicate Air") and stage works. Aside from music, he also dabbled in alchemy, which led him to debtors' prison twice.

ARNE, THOMAS AUGUSTINE (1710–78). English composer, especially prolific in the realm of theater music. While a student at Eton, Arne developed his interest in music. Like **George Frideric Handel**, with whom he is frequently compared on grounds of both proximity and devotion to the theater, he was for a time trained at law, though musical interests in both cases won out. Arne's setting of Milton's **masque** *Comus* (1738), his settings of **William Shakespeare**'s songs for **Drury Lane** productions (published in a 1741 collection, *The Songs in* As You Like It *and* Twelfth Night), and the **masque** *Alfred* (1740) all served to establish and strengthen Arne's leading position in musical circles. And in *Alfred* he gives us one of England's most enduring icons of musical patriotism, the song **"Rule, Britannia,"** a song that in the early 1740s would have had compelling resonance with the so-called War of Jenkins' Ear.

Arne's long career was prolific—he wrote for over 80 stage productions, for instance—but was not uniformly successful. A telling example is his attempt to write an Italian language *opera seria*, *L'Olimpiade* (1765), which closed after only two performances. His output is largely music for the theater, although he also wrote **oratorios**, a few masses (he was Roman Catholic), keyboard concertos, overtures, and **catches**. His stylistic range is notable, often elegant, lilting, and gallant, sometimes Handelian. Holman and Gilman (*NG*, 2001) have also underscored the imaginative capacity of his orchestration.

A look at Arne's career also interestingly documents the interconnectedness of the London performance world. His sister, Susannah, married to Theophilus Cibber, son of the poet laureate, was one of the leading tragic actresses of the day and a notable singer as well (she was, for instance, one of the soloists at the first performance of Handel's *Messiah*); his wife, Cecilia Young, was an accomplished singer whom he married, as he confessed in a draft of his will, seeking "profit or advantage" from her skill as a "Public Singer"; his mistress, Charlotte Brent, under his tutelage and nurture also became a prominent singer; and his supposed natural son, **Michael Arne**, who later went on to become a keyboard player and composer in London, came into his keyboard skills at an early age and was featured as a child soloist in an **organ** concerto by his father.

ARNOLD, SIR MALCOLM (1921–2006). Composer, conductor, trumpeter. Arnold, initially a self-taught trumpeter (inspired by Louis Armstrong, which led him to include blues idioms in his compositions), attended the **Royal College of Music**, studying composition with Gordon Jacob and trumpet with Ernest Hall. Between 1941 and 1948, he played in the **London**

Philharmonic Orchestra and the **British Broadcasting Corporation** Symphony Orchestra (with a short hiatus in the army). After this, he turned to composition full-time. As a composer he was prolific and popular, working in genres from overtures, dance suites, concertos, and symphonies to film music; his score to *The Bridge on the River Kwai* won the 1957 Academy Award for best score. His melodies and mostly tonal harmony (Jackson [2003] refers to his idiom as "proto-postmodern") have made his music especially popular for student bands and orchestras. He was knighted in 1993.

ARNOLD, SAMUEL (1740–1802). Composer, organist, conductor, impresario, editor. He was thought by some to be the illegitimate child of a commoner and Princess Amelia. His early education was at the **Chapel Royal**, and throughout his life he held posts such as harpsichordist and composer in **Covent Garden** (1764), composer at the Little Theatre, **Haymarket** (1777 until his death), organist of the Chapel Royal (appointed 1783), conductor of the **Academy of Ancient Music** (1789–94), and organist of Westminster Abbey (appointed 1793). He also owned and managed the Marylebone **pleasure garden** between 1769 and 1774. His compositions were mostly vocal, and he frequently created pastiches of **operas** and **oratorios** (the former drawing from sources as diverse as Irish folk melodies, **Franz Joseph Haydn**, and Wolfgang Amadeus Mozart, the latter based mostly on the work of **George Frideric Handel**). He edited or contributed to numerous magazines and music books, and for a time attempted a complete works edition of Handel's music (26 volumes, published between 1787–97).

ASHEWELL, THOMAS (ca. 1478–AFTER 1513). English composer. Ashewell was trained as a chorister at Windsor and held posts at Tattershall College, Lincolnshire (a clerk, 1502–3), Lincoln Cathedral (*informator choristarum*, 1508–13), and Durham Cathedral (cantor, from 1513). Two masses, *Missa Jesu Christe* and *Missa Ave Maria*, survive complete and reveal a notable complexity of structure. Among his other masses is one to Saint Cuthbert, unsurprising from the Durham cantor, and one on "God Save King Harry." Bray (*Blwl*, vol. 2) links the cantus firmus to *Sponsus amat sponsam* and thus postulates it may have been written in celebration of the wedding of Henry VIII and Catherine of Aragon.

ASTON (ASHTON), HUGH (ca. 1485–BURIED 1558). English composer. Aston took the BMus at Oxford in 1510 by supplication and in 1528 is found as *magister choristarum* at St. Mary Newarke Hospital and College in Leicester. His compositional output unsurprisingly focuses on liturgical settings (*Missa Te Deum*, *Missa Videte Manus*, possibly a third mass as well, and several motets and antiphons). However, he is best known as the composer of a keyboard "Hornepype" in GB L Roy App 58, distinctive in its unusually expansive right-hand figuration.

Aston has a nominal appearance in **William Byrd**'s "My Ladye Nevells Booke" with "Hugh Ashton's Grownde"; the same work appears in the **Fitzwilliam Virginal Book** as "Treg[ian's] Ground." Byrd's variations are on an ostinato that corresponds to the missing bass part of "Hugh Ashton's Maske."

ATKINS (ATKINSON), JOHN (?–1671). English violinist and composer. Atkins became a member of Charles II's Twenty-four Violins at the Restoration and is also referred to as a member of the king's "private consort." A number of his songs survive in US Nyp Drexel 4041, suggesting he was active in the pre-Commonwealth theater. Some of the songs are dance airs, while some include declamatory elements. His setting of "This lady ripe and fair and fresh" may have been written for the 1629 production of **Sir William Davenant**'s *The Just Italian*. This significantly not only places him in important theater circles, but also helps document the chronological range of what appears to have been a long career.

ATTEY, JOHN (fl. 1622; d. ca. 1640). Lute song composer. Attey's single publication of lute songs, *The First Booke of Ayres* (London, 1622), marks the end of the lute ayre tradition in print. Little is known of him, although the text of the dedication of his book of airs documents a time of service to the family of John Egerton, Earl of Bridgwater. Poulton and Spencer (*NG*, 2001) point to the singularity of Attey's suggestion that these four-part ayres might be performed not only with one voice, lute, and bass **viol**—a customary alternative—but also on lute alone.

ATTWOOD, THOMAS (1765–1838). Composer and organist. His early education was as a chorister in the **Chapel Royal** (1774–81), a student in Naples with Felipe Cinque and Gaetano Latilla (1783–85), and a student in Vienna with Mozart (1785–87)—the latter two likely under the patronage of the Prince of Wales. Upon his return to London, Atwood served as a hired musician to members of the nobility before being appointed organist at St. Paul's Cathedral and composer to the Chapel Royal (both in 1795). He was a founding member of the **Philharmonic Society** (1813) and one of the original professors at the **Royal Academy of Music** (2; 1823). He was appointed organist at the Chapel Royal in 1836. Wolfgang Amadeus Mozart's influence remained with him throughout his life, whether it was as a point of imitation for his early dramatic vocal music, or in introducing the English public to Mozart's symphonies at the concerts of the **Royal Philharmonic Society**. Most of his operatic and dramatic works were composed before 1800, after which he turned predominantly (but not exclusively) to **organ** and sacred music.

AVISON, CHARLES (1709–70). Composer, organist, and writer on musical topics. The son of a Newcastle **wait**, Avison spent his entire career attached to Newcastle as longtime organist at St. Nicholas and as director of the Newcastle Musical Society. He also was active in producing concerts concurrently in Durham. His musical prominence brought him job offers in London, Edinburgh, and York, but his allegiance to Newcastle was unseverable. As a composer he wrote a large body of concertos that show the influence of **Francesco Geminiani**, with whom tradition holds he studied; his concertos include as well arrangements of harpsichord pieces by Domenico Scarlatti. He also composed "accompanied sonatas," which were keyboard works accompanied by violins and cello.

Modern appraisal of Avison's concertos has been positive; late 18th-century views were less flattering. However, **Sir John Hawkins** held that "the music of Avison is light and elegant, but it wants originality, a necessary consequence of his too close attachment to the style of Geminiani, which in a few particulars only he was able to imitate." **Charles Burney** wrote that Avison's compositions "want force, correctness, and originality, sufficient to be ranked very high among the works of masters of the first class." One suspects that Burney's harsh view in part reflects a degree of resentment at Avison's critique of **George Frideric Handel.**

Avison was much given to writing about music and in 1752 published his significant *Essay on Musical Expression*, "the most notable contribution of the period to musical aesthetics" (Caldwell, *OHEM*, vol. 2). The *Essay* was controversial enough to engender a printed attack and defense between Avison and **William Hayes**. The range of the *Essay* is broad, covering issues of emotional response, the performance of concertos, and critiques of individual composers. Avison praised Benedetto Marcello and Francesco Geminiani as ideals (for vocal and instrumental composition, respectively), and found fault with Handel—a bold move—for privileging counterpoint over melody. Burney saw Avison as a lone and pioneering figure in English music criticism: "Indeed, musical criticism has been so little cultivated in our country, that its first elements are hardly known. In justice to the late Mr. Avison, it must be owned, that he was the first, and almost the only writer, who attempted it." And though he found his judgment biased, he noted that Avison was "an ingenious man, and an elegant writer upon his art."

"THE AWAKENING." Suffrage song by Teresa del Riego (1876–1968) with lyrics by Ella Wheeler Wilcox (1850–1919) first published in 1911 and used especially by the National Union of Women's Suffrage Societies.

AYLIFF, MRS. (fl. 1692–96). Soprano. Mrs. Ayliff was one of the leading sopranos on the Restoration stage, and in contrast to the singing-actor model of performer, she performed exclusively as a musician. **John Dryden** makes this distinction in describing her as one "whose trade it was to sing." She was praised in the press by Peter Motteux for her performance of **Henry Purcell**'s "Ah Me! To Many Deaths Decreed," and as that song features an ornamental cast to the line, one might infer from this and other songs ("When First I Saw the Bright Aurelia's Eyes," for instance) that she was adept at florid rendition.

AYRE (ALSO AIR). The term *ayre* has diverse usage in 16th- and 17th-century England, but is particularly associated with the genre of **lute** song appearing in print from 1597 (**John Dowland**'s *First Booke of Songes or Ayres*) to 1622 (**John Attey**'s *The First Booke of Ayres*). The lute ayre was typically a strophic composition, often setting texts of high quality. The literary quality and its close synergy with the music was brought into focus by the poet-composer **Thomas Campion**, who observed, "In these *English* ayres I have chiefly aymed to couple my words and notes lovingly together, which will be much for him to doe that hath not power over both." And Campion was ardent in defense of the ayre's brevity and sometime lightness. He notes, "Short ayres if they be skillfully framed, and naturally exprest, are like quicke and good epigrammes in poesie, many of them shewing as much artifice, and breeding as great difficultie as a larger poeme." Elsewhere he adds, "The Apothecaries have Bookes of Gold, whose leaves being opened are so light as that they are subject to be shaken with the least breath, yet rightly handled, they serve both for ornament and use; such are light Ayres."

The musical style of the lute ayre is varied. Some are simple accompanied melodies, as for instance Campion's "Never Weather-beaten Sail"; others conform to dance-patterns, such as Dowland's "Can She Excuse," "If my Complaints," or "Now, O Now, I Needs Must Part," this latter known elsewhere as the "Frog Galliard." Less common are those that seem to show the influence of Italian monody, such as Dowland's intensely brooding "In Darkness Let Me Dwell," a work unusual in being through-composed as well.

The publication format of the lute ayres promoted a commercially advantageous flexibility of performance. The page layout included the solo voice part with intabulated lute accompaniment as well as alto, tenor, and bass vocal parts and a part for bass **viol**. Thus the ayre could be performed as an accompanied solo or as a partsong.

"Ayre" was also used in the 17th century for instrumental movements of various sorts, often with the implication of something tuneful. (See for instance the **fantasia-suites** of **John Hingeston**.) **Thomas Mace** compared the ayre to the allmain: "*Ayres*, are, or should be, of the *same Time* [as Allmaines] . . . only they differ from *Allmaines*, by being commonly *Shorter*, and of a more *Quick and Nimble* Performance." Ayre was also treated as an aesthetic quality in the writings of **Roger North**. *See also* ADSON, JOHN; BARTLET, JOHN; CAVENDISH, MICHAEL; COPRARIO, JOHN; FANTASIA-SUITE; FORD, THOMAS; HILTON, JOHN; HUME, TOBIAS; LAWES, HENRY; *MUSICA BRITANNICA*; NORTH, ROGER; PILKINGTON, FRANCIS; PLAYFORD, JOHN; ROSSETER, PHILIP; WILSON, JON.

AYRTON, WILLIAM (1777–1858). Editor, historian, and collector. While not a prolific performing musician himself, Ayrton was known for his organizational skills. Institutions he aided included the **Royal Philharmonic Society** and the King's Theatre, **Haymarket** (1816–17, 1821, and 1825). He is perhaps best known, though, for his editorship of the early musical journal the *Harmonicon* (1823–33) and its successor, the *Musical Library* (1834–37), and for his large collection of materials for a music dictionary he never completed.

B

BABELL, WILLIAM (ca. 1690–1723). Harpsichord virtuoso, organist, violinist, and composer. Babell was a student of his father, a long-serving bassoonist in the orchestra at **Drury Lane**, and later with **Johann Christoph Pepusch** and perhaps with **George Frideric Handel.** He was a member of the **Private Musick** of George I (appointed 1709), active at **Lincoln's Inn Fields**, and the organist at the parish church of All Hallows, Bread Street (London) from 1718. Most distinctive, however, was his presence in London concerts as a harpsichord soloist. **Charles Burney** suggests his virtuosity was empty, gratifying "idleness and vanity," and he likens his performance to the "glare and glitter" of tinsel. However, **Sir John Hawkins** describes his playing as "admirable proficient."

Babell is particularly associated with keyboard arranging of material from Handel **operas**, as seen in his 1717 *Suits of the Most Celebrated Lessons Collected and Fitted to the Harpsicord or Spinnet . . . with Variety of Passages by the Author*, arrangements that can require an unusual degree of virtuosic technique. Additionally, his sonatas, likely for oboe, are supplied "with proper graces adapted to each Adagio by the author."

BACH, JOHANN CHRISTIAN (1735–82). Composer, impresario, and keyboardist of German origin. The 11th son of Johann Sebastian Bach, his early training occurred in Leipzig at the studio of his father and then in Berlin in 1750, where he studied with Carl Philipp Emanuel Bach. From 1755 to 1762 he worked in Milan as a student of Padre Martini and under the patronage of Count Agostino Litta, eventually taking a position as an organist in the cathedral. Bach arrived in England in 1762 to take up an appointment as music master to Queen Charlotte, wife of George III. Other than short trips to the Continent, he made London his home for the rest of his life. For the next two decades he became one of the most visible members of London's musical establishment through working intermittently at the King's Theatre, **Haymarket**, as a performer and composer, publishing, and, with **Carl Friederich Abel**, organizing the Bach-Abel series of subscription concerts at various locations before settling finally at the **Hanover Square Rooms**. In London Bach was most famous for his *opera seria* and his contributions to pasticcios, but he also composed and published numerous symphonies, keyboard sonatas, concerti, and vocal works for such contemporary institutions as the **Vauxhall Gardens**. His style was heavily influenced by *galanterie*, and he was an early adopter of publishing for and performing on the pianoforte.

BACH CHOIR. London amateur choir founded in 1875 to perform the music of Johann Sebastian Bach, particularly the Mass in B minor. The impetus to found the choir was from Arthur Duke Coleridge, barrister and amateur musician. The first conductor was Otto Goldschmidt (1875–85), and the first concerts occurred in 1876. The Choir quickly became one of the most important amateur ensembles in Great Britain, conducted by many significant figures, who broadened the repertoire from Bach to contemporary music. These included **Charles Villiers Stanford** (1885–1902), **Henry Walford Davies** (1902–7), **Sir Hugh Percy Allen** (1907–21), **Ralph Vaughan Williams** (1921–28), **Gustav Holst** (1928), **Sir Adrian Boult** (1928-31), Reginald Jacques (1932–60), and Sir David Wilcocks (1960–98). Under Jacques and Wilcocks, the choir became well-known for its recordings.

BACH SOCIETY. Organization active between 1849 and 1870, founded to promote Johann Sebastian Bach's music in Great Britain. Aside from presenting concerts of Bach's music including four dedicated to the *St. Matthew Passion*, the Society also collected an extensive library of scores and biographies of Bach and his family, housed at the **Hanover Square Rooms**.

BACHELER, DANIEL (1572–1619). Lutanist and composer. Bacheler served an apprenticeship with his uncle, Thomas Cardell, a lutanist and dancing master at the Elizabethan court; subsequently, in 1587 his apprenticeship was transferred to Sir Francis Walsingham. He later entered the service of Robert Devereaux, the Earl of Essex—Lady Essex was Sir Francis's daughter, Frances—and his song "To Plead my Faith" represents a musical approach to the Queen on Essex's behalf. In 1603 Bacheler received appointment as Groom to Queen Anne's Privy Chamber.

In addition to a substantial quantity of **lute** solos there are also a number of pieces for **English consort** (broken consort) in the Walsingham Consort Books under his name. The date of compilation of this source—1588—has given rise to the suggestion (Poulton, 1982; Caldwell, *OHEM*, vol. 1) that these consort pieces may represent the work of an older member of the family. Failing that, they would well document a degree of precocity in so young a composer.

BAIRSTOW, SIR EDWARD CUTHBERT (1874–1946). Organist, conductor, lecturer, and adjudicator. After early training at Westminster Abbey with Walter Alcock, Bairstow held **organ** posts in London and Wigan before being named organist at Leeds Parish Church in 1907. From this point on, he became a fixture in music-making of the north. He was organist of the Leeds Triennial **Musical Festival** from 1910, was appointed organist at York Minster and director of the York Musical Society in 1913, directed the Leeds Philharmonic Society from 1917, and was appointed professor of music in Durham in 1929. His few liturgical compositions were offset by his many appearances as a guest conductor, lecturer, and adjudicator at competition festivals.

BALFE, MICHAEL WILLIAM (1808–70). Composer, conductor, and singer of Irish origin. He was one of the premier composers of 19th-century London (a posthumous article in the *Times* referred to him as "our Rossini"). As a singer, he was a protégé of Gioachino Rossini and performed with Maria Malibran (for whom he composed *The Maid of Artois*) and Gulia Grisi. He worked with or composed works for most of the well-known singers of the day, including the previously mentioned Malibran and Grisi, as well as **Jenny Lind**, Giovanni Battista Rubini, Antonio Tamburini, Luigi Lablache, and others. While Basil Walsh's description of Balfe as the "Dickens of music" (2007) may be an exaggeration, it is only a slight one: Balfe's music was well known and enjoyed in the British Isles and far beyond.

After early training with his father in Dublin and as an articled pupil of C. F. Horn in London, Balfe spent from 1825 to 1835 on the Continent, studying, singing, and composing **operas** primarily in Italy and Paris. Upon his return to London, he quickly established himself as one of the most popular composers in Great Britain with two operatic triumphs: *The Siege of Rochelle* (1835) and the aforementioned *The Maid of Artois* (1836), both performed at **Drury Lane**. Over the next few years, Balfe's operatic successes in London—as both a composer and a singer—were many, which led him to attempt an English opera company at the **Lyceum Theatre**. While initially successful, it quickly ran aground financially, and Balfe returned to the Continent for several years of performances and commissions. In 1843 his best-known opera, *The Bohemian Girl*, premiered at Drury Lane and quickly became both a national and an international success.

Balfe directed the Italian Opera at Her Majesty's Theatre, **Haymarket**, from 1846 to 1852, during which time he published several pedagogical manuals for voice training. He spent the middle of the 1850s traveling on the Continent, visiting Germany, Austria, and Russia. In the last years of his life, he composed *The Rose of Castille* for the newly formed Pyne-Harrison Opera Company at the Lyceum Theatre (1857) and then retired to the country in 1864, though he continued to work on a number of operas until his death in

1870. Besides stage works, Balfe was particularly noted for his songs (which became staple repertoire at chamber concerts at numerous **musical festivals** in the last part of the 19th century).

BALLAD. The ballad is a genre of popular song in England that emerged in the Middle Ages, though it came into particular blossom in the 16th and 17th centuries, especially with the so-called broadside ballad, printed on large single folios and popularly vended. The genesis and transmission of ballads is complex to trace, combining elements of oral tradition as well as professional authorship. The text subjects are diverse, though oftentimes narrative, and in the genre's heyday, the ballad could be dynamically political. Ballad meter, a commonly found pattern for the texts, consists of a quatrain with alternating eight- and six-syllable lines, the second and fourth of which rhyme.

The tunes to which ballads were sung come from diverse sources—folk song, fiddle tune, and theater songs—**Henry Purcell**'s "If Love's a Sweet Passion" from *The Fairy Queen*, for instance—all contribute to the repertory, and sources like **John Playford**'s *The English Dancing Master* or **Thomas Durfey**'s *Pills to Purge Melancholy* are helpful in recovering melodies that were associated with ballad texts. Significantly, melodies were rarely notated with ballad texts, but most typically were indicated with a verbal reference of "to the tune of . . ." Thus, like the popular musician of our own day, the ballad singer would draw on a repertoire of familiar and standard tunes.

The ballad's impact on the English theater is significant. Several theatrical genres, notably the **jig** and the **ballad opera**, drew on ballads for their musical substance. Additionally, Ross Duffin (2004) has shown the striking degree to which **William Shakespeare** alluded to ballads, allusions that show great potential for adding multiple layers of interpretative meaning to the plays. *See* BALLAD OPERA, PERCY SOCIETY.

BALLAD OPERA. Ballad **opera** is a form of musical play combining spoken dialogue and integral songs, often set to popular, familiar melodies. Price and Hume (*NG*, 2001) caution that the term *ballad opera* is something of a misnomer as the majority of the songs are not from the **ballad** repertory. The progenitor of the ballad opera was the hugely successful *The Beggar's Opera* by **John Gay**, performed at **Lincoln's Inn Fields** in 1728 an impressive 62 times. Fiske (1986) called it "the greatest theatrical success of the century." Over 100 ballad operas followed in the wake of *The Beggar's Opera*, although by and large the success of Gay's work proved unrepeatable and the genre had waned by the late 1730s.

Notable features of *The Beggar's Opera* include its lowlife setting and cast and its satire of the Whig administration of Robert Walpole and the reigning conventions of Italian *opera seria*. (Modern comment has cautioned against an exaggerated view of its satirical thrust, however.) The prison setting and thieving cast were distinctive at a time when opera librettos followed an antique, heroic model; later ballad operas took on a variety of subjects, including English rurality, as for example in Charles Johnson's *The Village Opera*.

The music for *The Beggar's Opera* incorporates not only ballad tunes but also works by **Henry Purcell**, **John Eccles**, and **George Frideric Handel**. Tellingly, the original context of the music can inform its use by Gay, showing that the selection of the music was not casual. **Johann Christoph Pepusch** composed an overture for the work, as well as supplied basses for the melodies.

BALLETT. The ballett in England represents an adaptation of the ensemble dance song associated with Giovanni Gastoldi. The naturalization of the style is much the fruits of **Thomas Morley**, who described the ballett in his *A Plaine and Easie Introduction to Practicall Musicke* (1597):

> There is another kind [of music] more light than this which they term Balletti or dances, and are songs which being sung to a ditty may likewise be danced. These, and all other kinds of light music (saving the **Madrigal**) are by a general name called "airs."
>
> There be also another kind of Balletts commonly called "Fa las." The first set of that kind which I have seen was made by Gastoldi; if others have labored in the same field I know not, but a slight kind of music it is and, as I take it, devised to be danced to voices.

The Gastoldi model establishes dancelike character, prominent use of homophony, fa-la refrains, and bipartite construction. In Morley's *The First Booke of Balletts to Five Voyces* (1595)—a work significantly published in both English and Italian versions—the relationship to Gastoldi can be parodistic (see for example, the well-known "Sing We and Chaunt It" and Gastoldi's "A lieta vita"). However, Morley seems to reject this as music for dancing and accordingly enriches the fa-la refrains. As Kerman (1962) notes: "This expansion of the ballet is the most characteristic feature of the English variety and immediately sets it above its Italian model." In some balletts Morley took the model of the canzonet, not the Italian balletto, with more complicated texture and counterpoint the result.

BALLS (BALES), ALPHONSO (?–1635) AND RICHARD (d. 1622). Lutanists and singers. Both Bales were London **waits** and entered into the service of Charles Stuart during his years as Prince of Wales; Alphonso was also in service to Charles after he ascended the throne. The ornamented song,

"Chloris Sigh'd" is attributed to "Mr. Balls," and its survival in six manuscripts speaks to its popularity.

BALTZAR, THOMAS (1631?–1663). German violin virtuoso and composer. The early stages of Baltzar's career find him performing in Sweden and in his native Germany; however, he began to perform in England in 1655 and worked there until his untimely death, playing in the theater (including **Sir William Davenant**'s landmark *The Siege of Rhodes*), Oxford music meetings, and from 1661 at court as a member of the King's **Private Musick**. Along with other foreign virtuosi like **Nicola Matteis**, he was responsible for establishing the violin in England as a solo instrument of high regard. And considering technique, **Sir John Hawkins** specifies he was instrumental in introducing "shifting and the use of the upper part of the finger-board" to the English.

Early historians like **Charles Burney** and Hawkins, the diarist **John Evelyn**, and the Oxford antiquary **Anthony Wood** all were enthusiastic in their accounts of Baltzar's playing. Evelyn, for instance, much taken with his dexterity, perfection, and "ravishing sweetnesse," said, "I stand to this houre amaz'd that God should give so greate perfection to so young a person." His virtuoso abilities brought him into competition with Davis Mell, a competition that we can imagine nurtured his celebrity.

Both Hawkins and Burney observe that Baltzar drank heavily, and Hawkins attributes his early death, in part, to these excesses.

BANASTER, GILBERT (ca. 1430–87). Composer and poet. Banaster was appointed gentleman of the **Chapel Royal** in 1468, and perhaps had been a chorister there as well. He became master of the choristers in 1478. His compositions survive in only small quantity and include an antiphon in the **Eton Choirbook** (possibly commemorating the pregnancy of Elizabeth Tudor in 1486) and a Passion **carol**, "My feerfull dreme," in the **Fayrfax Manuscript**.

BANDORA (ALSO PANDORA). The bandora is described by Michael Praetorius as "an English invention of the **lute** type. It is rather like a large **cittern**, and is strung with brass and steel strings each of one, two, three, four, or even more strands." Characteristic details of its construction include a scalloped body with flat belly and back. Its invention can be traced to John Rose, the elder, in 1562.

A bass-register instrument, it was one of the standard members of the so-called **English consort**, in which it provided both harmonic realization as well as lower octave doubling of the bass **viol** line. Following one of the most famous collections of this repertory by **Thomas Morley**, the tuning is C D G c e a, although the number of courses and tuning was subject to variation.

In addition to its role in the English consort, it was used in the theater and also claimed a solo repertory of pieces by composers such as **Antony Holborne, Alfonso Ferrabosco**, and **John Dowland**. Although an English invention, it was also used on the Continent as a continuo instrument. Filippo Bonanni in his *Gabinetto Armonico* tellingly called it a *cetera tedesca*.

BANISTER, JOHN (1624/25–79). Violinist, composer, and flageolet soloist. Banister received an appointment to the royal violin band late in 1660 and soon thereafter studied in France. The Francophilic taste of the court owed much to Charles II's continental exile during the Commonwealth; Banister was among the first of the young king's musicians to study there, anticipating **Pelham Humfrey**'s more noted trip by several years. In 1662, likely showing the influence of the French *La Petite Bande*, Banister established and led a small select ensemble at court. In addition to activity at court, Banister was also much involved in theater music, a telling example of the overlapping of personnel in various London venues.

Banister fell from grace in the mid-1660s. In part this was due to the ascendancy of the Frenchman **Louis Grabu** as **Master of the King's Music** (1666), who asserted his own leadership of the violin band, and in part the result of accusations of embezzlement. In contemporary comment, **Anthony Wood** also noted that the king was angry with Bannister for "some saucy words."

In the wake of his eclipse at court, Banister became a key figure in the promotion of **public concerts** in London. The *London Gazette* advertised his daily afternoon concerts in "White Fryers" in December 1672. And **Roger North** (1959) described them in detail:

> The first attempt [at public concerts] was low: a project of old Banister, who was a good violin, and a theatricall composer. He opened an obscure room in a publik house in White fryars; filled it with tables and seats, and made a side box with curtaines for the musick. . . . Here came most of the hack-performers in towne, and much company to hear; and divers musicall curiositys were presented, as, for instance, Banister himself, upon a flageolet in consort, which was never heard before nor since, unless imitated by the high manner upon the violin.

Holman (1993) has drawn attention to a surviving wordbook from a concert of odes titled "Musick: or a **Parley of Instruments**" from 1676. The wordbook documents not only the large scale of the undertaking, but also, through an address to the reader, that Banister ran a school that offered instruction in music, dance, painting, foreign languages, and mathematics, inter alia.

His son, John, was also a violinist and composer, succeeding his father in the King's Violins. Another Banister in the royal violin band, Jeffrey, may have been the elder John's brother.

BANTOCK, SIR GRANVILLE (1868–1946). Composer, editor, conductor, and adjudicator. After studies at **Trinity College of Music** and the **Royal Academy of Music (2)**, Bantock worked as an editor of the *New Quarterly Musical Review* and conducted numerous ensembles, including dance bands and touring musical companies. He was appointed principal of the Birmingham and Midland School of Music in 1900 and became the second Peyton Professor of Music at Birmingham University (succeeding **Sir Edward Elgar**), a position he held from 1908 to 1934. Bantock was a prolific composer, working within all of the idioms of the **English Musical Renaissance**: besides successful compositions for the great **musical festivals**, such as the highly popular secular **cantata** *Omar Khayyám* (1906–9), Bantock composed numerous programmatic compositions for orchestra, works for brass band, and a handful of **operas**. Bantock's style was tonal, leaning to chromaticism, and heavily melodic. There was a decline in interest in his work after World War I. In his teaching and conducting careers, he was a great promoter of British music. Bantock was knighted in 1930.

BARBIROLLI, SIR JOHN (ALSO GIOVANNI BATTISTA; 1899–1970). Conductor and cellist. Early studies at **Trinity College of Music** and the **Royal Academy of Music (2)** prepared him for a dual career, and for a time starting in 1916 he predominantly played cello and conducted on the side. Starting from 1928, he received several important guest-conducting appointments, including for the British National Opera Company and at **Covent Garden**. A guest conductorship with the New York Philharmonic Orchestra in 1936 turned into an appointment as conductor from 1937 to 1942. His longest association was with the **Hallé Orchestra**, where he was appointed conductor in 1943; Barbirolli remained associated with this ensemble for the remainder of his life, while also conducting the Houston Symphony Orchestra (1961–67) and guest conducting the Berlin Philharmonic Orchestra (1961–70). Barbirolli had a wide repertoire of instrumental music, but was most famous for his recordings of **Sir Edward Elgar**, **Ralph Vaughan Williams**, and some **Benjamin Britten** (his recording of Elgar's Cello Concerto, op. 85, is particularly and justly famous), but, possibly because of the jealousy of **Sir Thomas Beecham**, he never cultivated conducting **opera** after his early stint at **Covent Garden**. Barbirolli was knighted in 1949 (KB); he became a CH in 1969.

BARNARD, JOHN (fl. 1641). Music editor and composer. Barnard is best known for his publication *The First Book of Selected Church Musick, consisting of Services and Anthems, such as are now used in the Cathedrall and Collegiate Churches of this Kingdome* (London, 1641), a significant anthology of English liturgical music from the late 16th and early 17th centuries. The anthology includes works by **Thomas Tallis, Elway Bevin, Orlando Gibbons, William Mundy, Thomas Morley, Richard Farrant, Adrian Batten, William Byrd, Robert Whyte**, and **Thomas Weelkes**. As none of the composers represented were alive at publication, the anthology in many cases documents the persistence of older repertory in church practice. A second collection in manuscript (GB Lrcm mss. 1045–51) also survives, including two of his own works.

BARNBY, SIR JOSEPH (1838–96). Composer, conductor (primarily choral), educator, and organist. Barnby was known throughout his professional career for championing the music of Charles Gounod and Johann Sebastian Bach, for introducing lavish choral **services** into the churches where he worked, and as a popular composer and conductor on the provincial **musical festival** circuit (through works such as his **oratorio** *Rebekah* [1870]). After training as a chorister at York Minister, Barnby attended the **Royal Academy of Music (2**; where he won the first **Mendelssohn Scholarship**) and took a series of organist positions in and around London, including prestigious ones at St. Andrew's, Wells Street (1866–71), and St. Anne's, Soho (1871–1886), and was precentor of Eton College (1875–92). He was the principal of the **Guildhall School of Music** from 1892 until his death in 1896. Barnby founded the **London Musical Society** choir (1878–87), conducted choirs sponsored by publishing firm **Novello & Co.**, and was the conductor of the **Royal Choral Society** (1873–96). He was knighted in 1892.

BARNETT, JOHN FRANCIS (1837–1916). English composer, pianist, and occasional conductor. He studied at the **Royal Academy of Music (2)** and then in Leipzig with Julius Rietz and Ignaz Moscheles, among others. His career in England was split between writing dramatic choral works for **musical festivals** (including those at Birmingham, Brighton, Leeds, and Norwich) and choral societies, teaching piano students, and editing an edition of Franz Schubert's "Unfinished" Symphony.

BARRETT, JOHN (ca. 1676–1719?). Composer and organist. Barrett was trained in music as a chorister in the **Chapel Royal** under the mastership of **John Blow**. He later held London posts at the church of St. Mary-at-Hill and Christ's Hospital. His work is largely theatrical—he wrote incidental music for 17 plays—although diverse keyboard pieces and a trumpet sonata also survive. He is anthologized by **Thomas Durfey** in *Pills to Purge Melancholy* and also adapted in *The Beggar's Opera*. **Sir John Hawkins** describes Barrett as a "skilful musician."

BARRETT, WILLIAM ALEXANDER (1834–91). Writer and singer. Barrett wrote musical criticism for the *Morning Post* and edited most of the major music periodicals of the second half of the 19th century, including the *Monthly Musical Record*, the *Orchestra*, and the *Musical Times*. He was a professional lay clerk at Magdalene College, Oxford, and at St. Paul's Cathedral in London. Aside from his duties as a lay clerk and an editor, he was also for a time the assistant inspector of schools for music (working with **John Hullah** and **Sir John Stainer**), and he wrote on topics as diverse as **glees**, **madrigals**, folk song, **music festivals**, and church musicians.

BARSANTI, FRANCESCO (1690–1772). Composer, flautist, oboist, and viola player of Italian origin. He arrived in London in 1714 and, except for occasional trips back to Lucca, remained in Great Britain for the rest of his life. He initially played oboe in the orchestra of the Italian Theatre and gained a reputation in London as an excellent player and composer. He left London for Edinburgh for eight years in 1735, where he married and worked under the patronage of Scottish nobility. When he settled back in London in 1743, he did not regain his earlier fame and played viola in various orchestras within the city. His output included liturgical music but was primarily focused on solo sonatas and concerti.

BARTHÉLEMON, FRANÇOIS-HIPPOLYTE (1741–1808). French-born violinist, composer, and orchestra leader. Fanny Burney, daughter of the historian **Charles Burney**, immortalized him in her book *Evelina; or the History of a Young Lady's Entrance into the World* as "a player of exquisite fancy, feeling, and variety." After early work in various Parisian orchestras, Barthélemon settled in London in 1764 and played violin for most of the **opera** orchestras, playhouses, and **pleasure gardens** of the time. He was well connected to the London musical scene, being friends with and the musical associate of **Johann Peter Salomon**, **Franz Joseph Haydn**, **Johann Christian Bach**, and **Carl Friedrich Abel**, among others. He married the famous singer **Polly Young** in 1766. Aside from several trips to Ireland and the Continent, he remained in England for the rest of his life. He composed a number of **operas**, an **oratorio**, dramatic **cantatas**, and numerous ballets, as well as violin sonatas. No work of his—aside from the hymn "Awake my soul"—survives in the modern repertoire.

BARTLET, JOHN (fl. 1606–10). Composer. Bartlet enjoyed the patronage of Sir Edward Seymour, Earl of Hertford, who received the dedication of his only publication, the *Booke of Ayres with a Triplicitie of Musicke* (London, 1606). The dedication praises Seymour's "singular skill and exquisite knowledge [of music]." As was typical of many **lute** ayre publications, the *Book of*

Ayres offered songs in both monophonic and four-part versions. Spink (1974) suggests that here the four-part versions may constitute the original form.

BASSANO. A family of wind instrumentalists and instrument makers active through several generations in England from the middle of the 16th century well into the 17th. The musical family descends from Jeronimo, a musician in Venice, possibly a wind player in service to the Doge in the first part of the 16th century. Five of his sons—Alvise, Gasparo, Zuane, Antonio, and Baptista—received appointments as musicians at the court of Henry VIII as trombone and recorder players. Four of the five are listed as playing both; Baptista's appointment is as a recorder player, though references in the Seymour accounts from the 1530s may suggest that he, like his brothers, also played trombone (Ashbee and Lasocki, 1998).

The family's activity as instrument makers was extensive and multigenerational. Their workshop produced highly regarded wind instruments (recorders, cornetti, crumhorns, inter alia) as well as **lutes** and **viols**.

BATES, JOAH (1740–99). Organist, impresario, and conductor. Bates was the husband of the singer Sarah Bates and one of the greatest experts on **George Frideric Handel** during the second half of the 18th century. With his family, he organized an early choral society in Halifax (The Messiah Club) and an early local festival of Handel's **oratorios** nearby; conducted the **Concerts of Ancient Music** from 1776 to 1793; and was one of the major organizers—along with his patron, John Montagu, Fourth Earl of Sandwich—of the great **Handel Commemoration** festival in Westminster Abbey in 1784. He was Montagu's private secretary for some years starting in 1771 and before that likely the singing tutor of Montagu's mistress, Martha Ray, and their children.

BATESON, THOMAS (1570/75?–1630). Organist and composer. Bateson was appointed organist at Chester Cathedral in 1599 and by 1609 had taken up an appointment at Christ Church Cathedral, Dublin. He is known chiefly for his two publications of **madrigals**, appearing in 1604 and 1618. Kerman (1962) underscores his musical indebtedness: "Bateson is . . . a derivative composer, though his writing is pleasing enough. From [**Thomas**] **Morley** he takes his basic style and some characteristic narrative subjects; from [**John**] **Wilbye** a delicacy, sometimes successful, that is an advance over Morley's writing, and an occasional tendency to take a poem quite seriously, though with varying success."

BATHE, WILLIAM (1564–1614). Irish writer and priest. While a student at Oxford, Bathe authored a nonextant music treatise, *A Brief Introduction to the True Art of Musicke*. Its publication in 1584 makes it the first musical textbook to appear in English (Rainbow, 1982). A second undated version appeared under the title *A Brief Introduction to the Skill of Song* (1596).

Sir John Hawkins is dismissive of the work and critical of the author's temperament: "They say of this William that he was of a sullen saturnine temper, and disturbed in his mind that his family was fallen from its ancient splendour." Elsewhere he notes that **Anthony Wood** "says of him that he had a most ardent zeal for the gaining of souls; and that though of a temper not very sociable, he was much esteemed by those of his own persuasion for his extraordinary virtues and good qualities."

The work of Bernarr Rainbow (1982; *NG*, 2001) underscores the innovative nature of Bathe's method for teaching one to read music. Bathe systematized a seven-note mixolydian scale (ut re mi fa sol la fa) that was transposable. Thus he could avoid the complexity of mutation in solmization and offers a pre-echo of modern "moveable doh" sight-singing.

Bathe seems to have abandoned musical interests when he undertook theological training abroad and entered the Society of Jesus in the mid-1590s. His subsequent language treatise, *Janua Linguarum* (1611) was highly regarded. On the basis of the new directions his career took in the 1590s, Rainbow argues for a date of ca. 1587–90 for the revision of his musical treatise.

BATTEN, ADRIAN (1591–1637). Composer. Batten can be identified as a student of John Holmes, which suggests that he was a chorister at Winchester Cathedral, where Holmes was a lay vicar. In 1614 Batten became a lay vicar at Westminster Abbey; in 1626 he became a **vicar-choral** at St. Paul's Cathedral (London) and can be documented there until 1635.

He was prolific in the composition of **anthems** and **services**, though modern comment faults his harmonic conservatism. **Charles Burney** planted the seeds of this view: "He [Batten] seems to have jogged on in the plain, safe, and beaten track, without looking much about him, nor if he had, does he seem likely to have penetrated far into the musical *terra incognita*."

The "Batten Organbook" (GB Ob Ten 791) is a major source of church music from ca. 1630; its attribution to Batten is, however, not secure.

BATTISHILL, JONATHAN (1738–1801). Composer, keyboardist, and singer. Known for the **anthem** "Call to Remembrance," he was the organist at St. Clement Eastcheap and St. Martin Orgar (1764) and Christ Church, Newgate (1767). However, aside from a few pieces in the sacred vein, his compositions largely reflect work for **Drury Lane**, **Covent Garden**, and the London **pleasure gardens** (an **opera**, a pantomime, and several collections of songs). His education was at St. Paul's Cathedral under William Savage (starting in 1747), and he frequently deputized for **William Boyce** at the

Chapel Royal. By the mid-1750s his rise into London musical society began with an appointment as conductor at **Covent Garden**, as well as membership in the **Madrigal Society**, the **Royal Society of Musicians**, and the **Noblemen and Gentlemen's Catch Club**. Most of his secular compositions were published in the fertile period between 1760 and 1775. After this period, Battishill became dissolute through drink, possibly caused in part by his wife—the singer and actress Elisabeth Davies—abandoning him.

BAX, SIR ARNOLD (1883–1953). Composer, poet (many of his writings were published under the pseudonym Dermot O'Byrne), and adjudicator. Bax was considered to be one of the most important composers of the 1920s. He composed several film scores for the Ballets Russes when they were resident in England. The popularity of Bax's music declined in the 1930s but enjoys a revival today, thanks in part to the efforts of the scholar Lewis Foreman. He is remembered primarily for his symphonies and film scores, though he touched upon most British genres of his day, save for **opera**. Bax had early private lessons on piano and was later trained at the Hampstead Conservatory by **Cecil Sharp** and later at the **Royal Academy of Music (2; 1900–1905)**. A wide reader, Bax was early inspired by the Irish Literary Revival (especially the work of William Butler Yeats) and translations of Nordic literature—which matched his early enthusiasm for Wagerian opera—and Russian music and literature. As Bax was born into an upper-middle-class family and had no need of a private income, he was able to travel widely; he lived for a time in Ireland and had significant trips to Russia and Germany. His personal life was tumultuous; he left his wife Elsita Sobrino for the pianist Harriet Cohen and for a time maintained a relationship with both Cohen and Mary Gleves. Though his music was no longer popular, Bax was knighted in 1937 (KB; he was made a KCVO in 1953) and made **Master of the King's Music** in 1942.

BBC. *See* BRITISH BROADCASTING CORPORATION.

BEDFORD, ARTHUR (1668–1745). Priest and writer. Bedford was a central figure in promoting the cause of "ancient music," in this case the music of Elizabethan composers, as part of a campaign of moral reform. In his *The Great Abuse of Music* (London, 1711), dedicated to the Society for the Propagation of Christian Knowledge, he characteristically laments that "[N]othing is admired [today] but what is new, and nothing hath the Air of a *new composition*, but what is *profane* or *lewd*." His concern with the connection between modern music and licentiousness found an echo in his criticism of the theater as well, as developed in his *The Evil and Danger of Stage Plays* (Bristol, 1706).

BEECHAM, SIR THOMAS (1879–1961). Conductor, impresario, and writer. In his time Beecham was one of the best-known English conductors and did a great deal to professionalize British institutions by forging regular seasons and rehearsal schedules. Until the early 1920s, Beecham could count on a personal fortune to help him finance his conducting and promotional activities; after this time, he was able to push most of his artistic endeavors through networking and his reputation. He was the founder of the Beecham Symphony Orchestra (1909), the Beecham Opera Company (1915), and the **London Philharmonic** (1932). Beecham conducted **opera** at both **Covent Garden** and **Drury Lane**, and was a conductor, artistic director, or guest conductor for many of the major orchestras and opera companies in Great Britain, including the **Hallé Orchestra**, the **Royal Philharmonic Society**, and others. He worked internationally as well, with a North American tour in 1928 that set the stage for his conducting the Seattle Symphony Orchestra (1941–43) and the Metropolitan Opera in New York City (1942–44). His funding was key in bringing the Ballets Russes to London in the 1910s. His repertoire was wide-ranging, and he was especially known for his championing of **Sir Frederick Delius**, as well as his interpretation of operas by Hector Berlioz and Wolfgang Amadeus Mozart. He recorded widely, and many of his interpretations are still available at the time of writing.

THE BEGGAR'S OPERA. See BALLAD OPERA; GAY, JOHN; PEPUSCH, JOHANN CHRISTOPH.

BELSHAZZAR'S FEAST. Dramatic **cantata** or short **oratorio** for baritone soloist, chorus, and orchestra by **Sir William Walton**, premiered at the Leeds Triennial **Musical Festival** in 1931. The composition's subject is the Babylonian captivity from the Old Testament. Osbert Sitwell compiled the libretto from the Bible. The commission came from the **British Broadcasting Corporation** and was originally meant to be a work for a soloist, a small chorus, and a chamber orchestra, appropriate for broadcasting. Like many of Walton's works of the 1930s, *Belshazzar's Feast* has a strong rhythmic contour and borrows from jazz and popular music. *Belshazzzar's Feast* established Walton as one of the leading British interwar composers.

BENEDICT, SIR JULIUS (1804–85). Composer, conductor, teacher, and pianist of German origin. Benedict arrived in London in 1835, after long apprenticeships in Germany and Austria (studying at times with Johann Nepomuk Hummel and Carl Maria von Weber) and Italy, where he conducted two **opera** theaters in Naples. Once in England, Benedict conducted at most of the opera houses in London, including the **Lyceum Theatre** (1836–38), **Drury**

Lane (1838–48), and Her Majesty's Theatre, **Haymarket**, and **Covent Garden**. He composed English operas for these venues (the most famous was *The Lily of Killarny* [1862]), most of which were produced on the Continent as well. He was also the director of the Norwich **Musical Festival** (1845–70), for which he composed a number of **cantatas**; his sole **oratorio**, *St. Peter* (1870), which influenced **Sir Edward Elgar**'s works *The Apostles* and *The Kingdom*, was premiered at the Birmingham Musical Festival.

Benedict was well known as both a teacher (his obituary in *MT* stated, "As a teacher he was at the head of his profession for many years. To be able to write 'Pupil of Sir Julius Benedict' was an honour coveted by almost every young musician.") and an accompanist in his own time, so much so that he was the conductor and accompanist for **Jenny Lind** on her tour of North America between 1850 and 1852. With **Henry Thomas Smart** he founded the **Vocal Association** (1855–65), a large choir that performed regularly at the **Crystal Palace**. He was knighted in 1871.

BENNETT, JOSEPH (1834–1911). Music critic, writer, librettist, adjudicator, and organist. As a critic, Bennett wrote for numerous publications, including the *Sunday Times*, the *Daily Telegraph*, *Musical Standard*, *Musical World*, *Lute*, and *MT*. He was also one of the best-known **music festival** librettists of his day, contributing to **Sir Alexander Campbell Mackenzie**'s *The Rose of Sharon* and **Sir Arthur Sullivan**'s *The Golden Legend*, as well as compositions by **Sir Herbert Brewer**, **Frank Bridge**, **Sir Frederic Hymen Cowen**, and C. Lee Williams (longtime organist of Gloucester Cathedral and **oratorio** composer). His books include volumes of biography on Hector Berlioz, Frederic Chopin, and Gioachino Rossini, as well as an epistolary report from Bayreuth and a history of the Leeds Triennial Musical Festival.

BENNETT, SIR WILLIAM STERNDALE (1816–75). Composer, conductor, pianist, and teacher. The Leipzig circle of **Felix Mendelssohn** and Robert Schumann also held Bennett in great regard, and composers of the **English Musical Renaissance** considered him to be one of the most important mid-19th-century figures, as evidenced by the ample appreciations and tributes in 1916, the centenary year of his birth. Bennett's initial training came as a chorister in Cambridge followed by attendance at the **Royal Academy of Music (2)** starting in 1826 (he would teach piano there from 1837 to 1858, and became the principal of the institution in 1866). He composed his first successful instrumental works in the early 1830s and had a successful career as a concert pianist (he played at the **Royal Philharmonic Society** concerts regularly until 1848 and held his own series of chamber music concerts between 1842 and 1856 at the **Hanover Square Rooms**). He spent time with Mendelssohn and Robert Schumann in Leipzig on several visits between 1836 and 1842, which coincided with his greatest period of creativity.

From 1849 until his death, he was engaged with almost every aspect of the English musical infrastructure. Bennett was a founding member of the **Bach Society** (1849) and conducted the English premiere of the *St. Matthew Passion* in 1854, conducted the Philharmonic Society Concerts (as a guest in 1855 but as its conductor from 1856 to 1866), conducted the **musical festival** at Leeds in 1858, and was appointed Professor of Music at Cambridge (1856). His music was well regarded in his own time: his symphonies were performed by both English orchestras and the Gewandhaus Orchestra in Leipzig, and he had important choral works that appeared at the musical festivals (*May-Queen* at Leeds in 1858 and *The Woman of Samaria* at Birmingham in 1867). He was knighted in 1871.

BERKELEY, SIR LENNOX (1903–89). Composer, teacher, and writer on music. As Malcolm Williamson notes in Berkeley's *MT* obituary, the composer was "the most inconvenient to place or position" within 20th-century English music, as he was a "cosmopolitan" composer and not a "nationalist" one. Berkeley's initial education occurred in England (he took a BA from Merton College, Oxford), but his musical training took place largely in France, under the influence of Maurice Ravel via studies with Nadia Boulanger (1926–32). A lifelong friendship with **Benjamin Britten** began in 1936; the two lived together for a time, set music to some of the same poets, and collaborated on occasion. He was a professor of composition at the **Royal Academy of Music (2)** between 1946 and 1968. Like many of Boulanger's students, his compositions show influence from *Les Six* and Igor Stravinsky's neoclassical works; he also began working with expanded twelve-tone techniques in the 1960s. He composed in every available genre, from chamber works to grand **opera**. He was named a CBE in 1957 and knighted in 1974.

BERNERS, LORD (GERALD TYRWHITT; 1883–1950). Composer, writer, and painter. Berners came from an aristocratic family and after his initial education spent a great deal of time abroad. He traveled widely in France, Germany, and Italy in the 1900s and became an honorary attaché of the Foreign Service between 1909 and 1920; under these auspices he spent time in Constantinople and Rome. His early work was humorous, modernist, and followed the model of Erik Satie; his cosmopolitanism can be seen in the many works that have non-English titles and texts. From the 1920s forward, his music became less modernist and more exoticist, focused at first on **opera** and ballet (such as *The Triumph of Neptune* [1926] and *A Wedding Banquet* [1936], which Stravinsky admired), as well as film scores. In addition to music, he was a prodigious painter and published a number of novels and plays.

BEVIN, ELWAY (ca. 1554–1638). Welsh composer and organist. Described by **Charles Burney**, perhaps exaggeratedly, as a "man of genius," to be numbered among the "musical luminaries," Bevin was a **vicar-choral** at Wells (1579), followed by a long tenure as master of the choristers (1585) and organist (by 1589) at Bristol Cathedral. His dismissal from that post close to the end of his life perhaps derives from recusancy. He was also appointed gentleman extraordinary to the **Chapel Royal** in 1605.

In addition to Anglican **service** music and **anthems**, Bevin was prolific in the composition of canons, an enthusiasm reflected in his tutorial, *Briefe and Short Instruction in the Art of Musicke* (1631).

BIRMINGHAM MUSIC FESTIVAL. *See* MUSICAL FESTIVALS.

BISHOP, SIR HENRY RAWLEY (1786–1855). Composer, conductor, impresario, and editor. Bishop was one of the most important musicians of his day, involved in most contemporary institutions. Thomas Panchon, the racehorse owner, sponsored his musical training in harmony by Francesco Bianchi, but otherwise Bishop was largely self-taught. He served from 1810 to 1824 as the musical director of **Covent Garden** and at **Drury Lane** from 1824. He directed music at the **pleasure gardens** at **Vauxhall** from the 1820s to 1840, was the principal conductor of the **Concerts of Ancient Music** from 1840 to 1848, held the Reid Professorship at Edinburgh University from 1841 to 1843, and was Professor of Music at Oxford from 1848 until his death. Bishop was the composer of over 80 dramatic works and pastiches for the London stage, many songs, and **glees**. While extremely popular in his own life, he is all but forgotten today, save for the song "Home, Sweet Home." Bishop was knighted in 1842, the first musician recognized for his talent and musical services to the realm.

BLAGRAVE, THOMAS (ca. 1620–88). Cornettist, violinist, composer, and singer. Blagrave's career is marked by versatility. His initial appointment at the court of Charles I was as a wind player (1637), the colleague and later successor to his father, Richard, in the **cornett** and **sackbut** ensemble. Later under Charles II he held appointments as a wind player, a member of the court violin band, and a member of the **Chapel Royal**. From 1664 to 1670 he was master of the choristers at Westminster Abbey.

BLISS, SIR ARTHUR (1891–1975). Composer, conductor, pianist, and teacher. After initial studies at Pembroke College, Cambridge, Bliss studied conducting for a year at the **Royal College of Music**. His early compositions were cosmopolitan in nature, showing the influence of contemporary French composers, Igor Stravinsky, and Arnold Schoenberg; later, he would adopt a more romantic idiom more in line with **Sir Edward Elgar**. His compositions were premiered both in British institutions, like the Three Choirs and Norwich **musical festivals** and **Covent Garden**, and internationally, by the Philadelphia Orchestra and at the New York World's Fair of 1939. Bliss served as the conductor of the Portsmouth Philharmonic Society (1921), taught at the University of California at Berkeley (1931–41), and was the music director of the **British Broadcasting Corporation** (1942–44). He was knighted in 1950 and named both a KCVO (1969) and a CH (1971). In 1953 he was named **Master of the Queen's Music**.

BLITHEMAN, JOHN (ca. 1525–91). Organist and composer. Blitheman, a gentleman of the **Chapel Royal** from 1558, is best known for his keyboard compositions, which appear in both the **Fitzwilliam Virginal Book** and the **Mulliner Book**. Some are liturgical **organ** works to be performed *in alternatim*, such as his verses to the chant *Aeterne rerum*. Others, though chant-based, are not tied to the liturgy, such as his several settings of the *In nomine* (*Gloria tibi trinitas*). In these settings Blitheman shows a penchant for virtuosic passagework, a trait echoed in the music of his pupil, **John Bull**. Blitheman's epitaph documents this teacher-student relationship, as well as his membership in the **Chapel Royal** and his ability on the organ:

> Of Princes Chappell Gentleman
> Unto his dying day;
> Whom all tooke greate delight to heare
> Him on the Organs play.

BLOW, JOHN (1648/49–1708). Composer. Blow's musical career well positioned him to be one of the most prominent musicians of the Restoration, holding appointments twice as organist of Westminster Abbey (the second time followed the death of **Henry Purcell**, who himself succeeded Blow there in 1679), several positions within the **Chapel Royal** (gentleman, master of the choristers, organist, and composer), and also master of the children at St. Paul's. His long tie to the Chapel Royal began even earlier as a chorister under Captain **Henry Cooke**, who likely recruited him from his hometown of Newark in 1661. The Chapel Royal in the early years of the Restoration was in a stage of rebuilding, but the formidable talents of a number of the boy choristers like **Pelham Humfrey** and Blow made it the seedbed of the new **anthem** style born of Charles II's continental tastes. In the account of **Thomas Tudway**, Blow is described as "one of the brightest and forwardest children of the chapel" to whom fell the composition of anthems in the royally favored style.

Blow's prominence emerges with the greatest clarity in his large body of church music, which includes a number of **services** and an impressive quantity of anthems in both the full and verse style. Significantly, as Blow was one of its progenitors, the Restoration symphony anthem—a verse anthem with ample independent participation of instrumental forces—also reached its greatest proportions in his work, along with that of Purcell. The 1685 coronation of James II occasioned several anthems from the pair; Blow's "God spake sometime in visions" extends the dimensions and scoring to create a work on a monumental scale.

Blow's secular music includes a body of songs, many of which were anthologized in his *Amphion Anglicus* of 1700, harpsichord dances and grounds, and **organ** voluntaries. In contrast to Purcell, his interest in theater seems relatively small, though the court **masque** *Venus and Adonis* is important as one of the first fully sung English music dramas. Performed at court (likely in 1683), it was also performed at Josias Priest's school in Chelsea, a circumstance that links it with Purcell's *Dido and Aeneas*, and a circumstance that also suggests that Purcell's work may similarly have been performed at court and at Chelsea, though a court performance remains only speculative.

The evaluation of Blow's work has frequently focused on what seems either his harmonic boldness and individuality or a degree of harmonic incompetence. **Charles Burney** was one of the first to underscore the issue: "I am as sorry to see, as to say, how confused and inaccurate a harmonist he was; but as it is necessary to speak of an artist so celebrated and honoured by his cotemporaries, to dissemble his faults would surpass candour, and incur the censure of ignorance and partiality."

BONONCINI, GIOVANNI (1670–1747). Composer and cellist. Born into a musical family, Bononcini was musically accomplished at a young age, being both a published composer and active in Bologna's Accademia Filarmonica and San Petronio while still in his teens. In the 1690s he was active in Rome and later worked at the Viennese court.

Bononcini's first major impact on London came in the form of his **opera** *Il Trionfo di Camilla* (1696), first performed at **Drury Lane Theatre** in an English translation in 1706; an impressive 63 performances would follow through 1709. The impact of *Camilla* may be gauged through an anonymous account in *A Critical Discourse upon Operas in England*:

[B]efore this every man that had the least smattering in music undertook to compose an opera, but upon the appearance of *Camilla* all their projects vanished into nothing: . . . at least six or seven embryos of operas that had no being but in the airy conceptions of their pretended composers became abortive, and everyone joined in the admiration of *Camilla*.

That it was performed in English translation underscores a transitional attitude toward Italian opera in the decade after the death of **Henry Purcell**.

Bononcini came to London in 1720 to be one of the composers for **George Frideric Handel**'s opera company, the **Royal Academy of Music (1)**, and in this close theatrical proximity the perception of rivalry between the composers was a marked one. The rivalry was lampooned by John Byrom in a contemporary epigram:

> Some say, compar'd to Bononcini,
> That Mynheer Handel's but a Ninny;
> Others aver, that he to Handel
> Is scarcely fit to hold a candle:
> Strange all this Difference should be
> 'Twixt Tweedle-dum and Tweedle-dee!

Bononcini was a member of the **Academy of Ancient Music** from 1726, though in 1731 he was embroiled in a case of plagiarism there. He left London in 1733.

BOOK OF COMMON PRAYER. Liturgical book giving texts, structures, and rules for the liturgy of the Church of England. Thomas Cranmer, the archbishop of Canterbury under Henry VIII, was the leading architect and author of the first *Book of Common Prayer* of 1549. Cranmer sought to establish a liturgy in the vernacular and a liturgy that might simplify and reform the complexities of late medieval worship. The vernacularism of the 1549 *Book* had a number of precedents: the Creed, Our Father, and the Decalogue had been recited in English since 1538; Cranmer's Litany was published in 1544; in 1547 the Epistle and Gospel were recited in English; and in the next year, vernacular communion texts were introduced. Thus, when the 1549 *Book* appeared, the ground was well prepared.

In composing the *Book of Common Prayer*, Cranmer drew on a number of liturgical sources familiar to the English church—the missal, breviary, and primers, among them—as well as continental, Reformed material. Its contents are comprehensive, containing liturgies of Morning and Evening Prayer, Holy Communion, Baptism, Confirmation, Matrimony, Burial, and Visitation and Communion of the Sick, as well as a calendar, lectionary, collects, and epistle and gospel readings for Holy Communion.

In the *Book of Common Prayer*, Cranmer's contribution is not only liturgical but literary to a degree, providing devotional language of great beauty that has been notably long lived. Gordon Jeannes observes that "while Cranmer could produce the most majestic phrases and seem to imply much by them, he could also be deliberately vague. At times his language resembles a kind of verbal incense that offers an attractive religious haze but no clarity of meaning. This may have contributed to the way in which the Prayer Book has served as a vehicle of prayer and worship over many centuries and in many cultures" (Hefling, 2006). A musical companion to the first prayer book by **John Marbeck**, *The Book of Common Praier Noted*, appeared in 1550.

Given the religious turbulence of England in the 16th and 17th centuries, it is no surprise that the Prayer Book would see significant revision with editions in 1552, 1559, 1604, and 1662. The 1662 *Book* endures as the liturgical standard of the Church of England to the present day. Significantly, however, liturgical reform has seen the appearance of several alternate liturgies authorized for use: the *Alternative Service Book* of 1980 and its successor, the several volumes of *Common Worship*, begun in 2000.

The constituent churches of the Anglican Communion manifest their communal bonds in allegiance to the notion of a *Book of Common Prayer*, though as autonomous churches, each has its own Prayer Book.

BOUGHTON, RUTLAND (1878–1960). Composer, writer, pianist, and impresario. Boughton's music and writings on music frequently included a political agenda. In writings such as *The Death and Resurrection of the Music Festival* (1913), he positioned communal music as a way to purify and ennoble society. Boughton also, in the periodical the *Sackbut*, assaulted both modernism (as being too removed from humanity) and his contemporary British composers (for not finding a proper musical language to reach the ordinary individual). His own musical style was at times simple to extremes, but always approachable. Accessibility and the musical education of society were always his aims, be it during his time teaching at the Midland Institute School of Music (1905–11) or in his organization of the Glastonbury Festivals (1914–26), which combined music-dramatic performances, chamber concerts, lectures, and exhibitions. It was for this festival that he planned a British response to Richard Wagner's *Ring* cycle, a series of **operas** on Arthurian stories. Boughton retired from active music organizing in the 1930s to complete his cycle of Arthurian dramas and write about music. His best-known composition is the music drama *The Immortal Hour*, premiered at the first Glastonbury Festival of 1914.

BOULT, SIR ADRIAN CEDRIC (1889–1983). Conductor. With **Sir John Barbirolli**, **Sir Thomas Beecham**, and **Sir Malcom Sargent**, Boult was a long-standing champion of British music and premiered and recorded many important works. Education at both the Westminster School (1901–8) and Christ Church, Oxford (1908–12; BMus), allowed him to hear many concerts and perform a great deal of music. He studied at Leipzig Conservatory from 1912 to 1913, being particularly taken with the work of Arthur Nikisch. He took a DMus from Oxford in 1914 and began working with various ensembles, including **Covent Garden** in that year. He taught conducting at the **Royal College of Music** from 1919 to 1930 and again from 1962 to 1966, and became music director of numerous ensembles, including the **City of Birmingham Symphony Orchestra** (1924–30; 1959–60), the **Bach Choir** (1928–31), the **British Broadcasting Corporation** (BBC) Symphony Orchestra (1930–50; he was also music director of the BBC from 1930 to 1942); and the **London Philharmonic Orchestra** (1950–57). Boult raised each of these ensembles to a high standard of performance and presented adventurous programs including a great deal of contemporary British and continental music. After 1957, Boult guest conducted many ensembles and began a series of important recordings of English music, including the symphonies of **Sir Edward Elgar** and **Ralph Vaughan Williams**. His final public appearance occurred in 1978. Boult wrote articles on a variety of musical subjects, two books on conducting (*The Point of the Stick* [1920] and *Thoughts on Conducting* [1963]), as well as an autobiography (*My Own Trumpet* [1973]). Boult was knighted in 1937 and named a CH in 1969.

BOWEN, JEMMY (ca. 1682–AFTER 1701). Singer. Bowen sang in a number of **Henry Purcell**'s theater works, including *Abdelazer* and *Indian Queen*. He has been anecdotally immortalized in Purcell's famous defense of his youthful ability. To those who would instruct him in ornamentation, Purcell reputedly said, "O let him alone . . . he will grace it more naturally than you, or I, can teach him."

BOWMAN, JOHN (ca. 1660–1739). Singer and actor. Bowman was appointed to the Royal **Private Musick** in 1684 as a bass singer, a position he held into the 18th century. His theatrical career was notably as both an actor and a singer, appearing in London productions from 1677. He is particularly known for several important **Henry Purcell** roles, including Grimbald in *King Arthur* and Cardenio in *Don Quixote*. In the latter role his performance of the famous **mad song**, "Let the Dreadful Engines Roar," would seem to suggest an accomplished degree of versatility (Spink, 1974).

BOYCE, WILLIAM (1711–79). Composer and organist. Boyce was one of the most prominent English musicians in the mid-18th century, despite his developing deafness, and a composer of numerous **anthems, odes**, music for the theater, and instrumental ensemble music. As a chorister at St. Paul's Cathedral, London, he forged a long-lasting relationship with the organist **Maurice Greene**, with whom he studied both during his years in the choir and afterward; in 1755 he succeeded Greene as **Master of the King's Music**.

He was appointed a composer to the **Chapel Royal** in 1736, at which time he also took on some of the organist's duties as well. A contemporaneous reference notes: "whereas the place of Organist has much more duty and attendance belonging to it than the place of Composer . . . , I the said William Boyce do promise and agree that so long as I shall continue in the place of Composer, I will perform one third part of the duty and attendance belonging to the Organist . . . ," a revealing glimpse of hierarchy and duty in the chapel. In 1758 Boyce was formally appointed as one of the organists.

His success was clear with works like the serenata *Solomon*, the 1743 publication of which had an impressive number of subscribers, and at the end of the decade he received a Cambridge DMus, followed by a two-day festival devoted to his works. In the 1740s, as well, he brought out a collection of 12 trio sonatas (1747) that reveal his debt to Corelli. His musical interests and procedures characteristically bear the stamp of this kind of historical bent. **Charles Burney** makes this explicit in his description: "There is an original and sterling merit in his productions, founded as much on the study of our own old masters, as on the best models of other countries." Boyce's historical activity is most notable as the compiler of *Cathedral Music* (1760–73), an anthology of church music from the 16th into the 18th centuries. It was a collection that had not only practical value but, significantly, musicological value as well. Burney, for instance, in writing his own history of music, makes rich use of it as a resource and reference. Additionally, *Cathedral Music* bears the stamp of Boyce's relationship with Greene, for Boyce inherited the project from his own teacher.

BRACEGIRDLE, ANNE (1671–1748). Actress and singer. Between 1688 and 1707 Bracegirdle was an actress on the London stage, developing a career of great prominence as a member of the United Companies; in 1695 she became, along with Thomas Betterton and Elizabeth Barry, one of the leading figures in the new company formed at **Lincoln's Inn Fields**; the last year of her professional life (1706–7) was spent at the Queen's Theatre, **Haymarket**. Her ability to sing was praised by **John Dryden**, and she performed only music written by **John Eccles** (Price, 1984). Her following was ardent. Colley Cibber remarked that "her Youth and lively Aspect threw out such a Glow of Health and Chearfulness, that on the Stage few Spectators that were not past it could behold her without Desire." Such desire had dire consequences in 1692 when, in the wake of an unsuccessful attempt at her abduction, one of her stalkers—Captain Richard Hill—murdered the actor-singer Will Mountfort, whom he believed to be her lover. The situation was doubly freighted given that Bracegirdle's public persona was celebratedly virginal.

BRADE, WILLIAM (1560–1630). Violinist and composer. Brade left his native England in the 1590s to develop a career in Germany and Scandinavia, a move that placed him in the company of other English musicians like **John Dowland.** He held appointments at courts in Berlin, Copenhagen, and Bückeburg, and also was active in Hamburg. He was a prolific composer of dance music.

BREWER, SIR HERBERT (ALSO ALFRED HERBERT; 1865–1928). Organist, conductor, and composer. After being a chorister and organist at various institutions, Brewer was trained at the **Royal College of Music** under **Sir Walter Parratt.** His most important post was as the organist of Gloucester Cathedral, a position he held from 1896 until his death, and he was heavily involved in the Three Choirs **musical festival.** Many of his compositions were either for the festivals, such as his **oratorios** *Emmaus* (1901) and *The Holy Innocents* (1904), or for Church of England **services.** Brewer was knighted in 1926.

BRIAN, HAVERGAL (ALSO HAVERGAL WILLIAM; 1876–1972). Composer, critic, and organist. Brian had working-class origins, little formal training, and—apart from a half-year teaching job at the **Royal College of Music**—did not fit into the usual infrastructure of English music during the first half of the 20th century. His career ran hot and cold with the British public. At times he had the encouragement of important parts of the musical establishment, including **Sir Edward Elgar, Sir Frederick Delius**, and **Sir Granville Bantock**, and even several years' support from a patron, so he would not have to find teaching work. Early fame in his home region of Staffordshire from shorter choral works written for the **competition festivals** was followed by success with a concert at the **Queen's Hall Proms** in 1907. After moving to London in 1913, Brian worked in a variety of capacities, including as the assistant editor of *Musical Opinion* (1924–40), and published smaller compositions. Brian lost some popularity in the 1930s, but his audience returned in the late 1940s. From this point until his death, Brian composed numerous symphonies (he wrote 32 in all) and a number of dramatic works as well. While some late honors came to him (he was named composer of the year by the Composers' Guild of Great Britain in 1972), few complete performances of his works occur at the time of writing.

BRIDGE, FRANK (1879–1941). Composer, violist, conductor, and teacher. Bridge attended the **Royal College of Music** (1899–1903) and studied with

Sir Charles Villiers Stanford. He was in demand throughout most of his career as a violist, performing with the English String Quartet between 1906 and 1915, and a conductor, leading, at times, the **Savoy Theatre** (1910–11) and **Covent Garden** (1913), deputizing for **Sir Henry Wood** at the **Proms**, and guest conducting other orchestras. He is best known today for his chamber music, though he wrote widely in many genres, and for his tutoring of **Benjamin Britten**.

BRIDGE, SIR FREDERICK (1844–1924). Organist, composer, adjudicator, teacher, and writer. As an organist, Bridge served at Holy Trinity Church, Oxford (1865–69), Manchester Cathedral (1874–75), and at Westminster Abbey (deputy organist, 1875–82; organist, 1882–1918). His compositions concentrated on church and choral works; the most famous of these, *The Repentance of Nineveh* (Three Choirs **Musical Festival**, 1890), included Wagnerian touches and was called "quite modern" by *MT*. As an establishment musician, Bridge contributed music to the jubilees of Queen Victoria in 1887 and 1897, as well as to the coronations of Edward VII (1901) and George V (1910). Bridge was interested in elements of performance practice, and at the request of **Sir George Grove**, he studied the manuscript score of **George Frideric Handel**'s *Messiah* in order to return to a smaller orchestration. He used this version while conducting the **Royal Choral Society** (1896–1922). Bridge also organized commemorative concerts at Westminster Abbey for **Orlando Gibbons** (1907). He held several teaching positions, including the Gresham Professor of Music, and the King Edward Professor at the University of London; taught at the National Training School for Music and at the **Royal College of Music**; and was chairman of **Trinity College of Music** for a time. He held both a BMus and a DMus from Oxford University (and led the fight, contra **Sir John Stainer**, against a residency requirement there) and was an FRCO. He was knighted in 1897 and named an MVO in 1901 and a CVO in 1910.

BRITISH BROADCASTING CORPORATION (BBC). Britain's state-sponsored media outlet began broadcasting via radio in 1922 and television in 1936. Along with a national service, the BBC has long maintained various regional services and has become one of the premier media platforms for international news and arts coverage via its broadcast, satellite, and cable channels. Aside from a broadcasting unit, the BBC has also been a thorough patron of the arts since its origins, through commissions (such as **Sir Edward Elgar**'s Third Symphony); support of ensembles such as the BBC Singers (1924), the BBC Symphony (1930), the BBC Philharmonic Orchestra (formerly the Northern Wireless Orchestra), and the BBC Northern Orchestra (1931); and sponsorship of various **musical festivals** and concerts, most notably the London **Proms** since 1927.

BRITISH LIBRARY (BRITISH MUSEUM). The British Library is one of the premier resources in the world for the study of music, English and otherwise. Initially part of the British Museum (founded 1753), the British Library became its own institution in 1973. The collection includes reference works, prints, manuscripts, and sketches. Even as early as the 18th century, the curators of the museum collected selections of composers' musical autographs. It has also acquired numerous other reference libraries to build up its collection, notably the National Sound Archive (founded 1955; incorporated with the British Library in 1983) and the Royal Music Library (indefinite loan in 1911; given to the library in 1957).

BRITTEN, BENJAMIN (1913–76). Composer, writer, and conductor. With **Sir Edward Elgar** and **Ralph Vaughan Williams**, Britten is considered one of the leading English composers of the 20th century and is much more frequently studied by contemporary musicologists and music theorists than the others. Britten is best known internationally for his **operas**, such as *Peter Grimes* (1944–45), *Billy Budd* (1950–51), *Turn of the Screw* (1954), and *A Midsummer Night's Dream* (1959–60), but he also scored a great many films, wrote pieces for choirs and orchestras of all abilities, and realized scores of historical works, such as **John Gay** and **Johann Christoph Pepusch**'s *The Beggar's Opera* and **Henry Purcell**'s *The Fairy Queen*. Britten's musical language depends on long, spun-out melodies (at times, like Vaughan Williams, borrowing elements of folk melodies) and consonant tonality, but with a greater proportion of dissonance than the older composer, and his rhythmic structures are freer, frequently controlled by neoclassical and exoticist tendencies, such as ostinato.

Britten had early musical training through composition lessons with **Frank Bridge** and had some compositions published while studying at Gresham's, an English public school. He attended the **Royal College of Music** between 1930 and 1932. In 1935, he joined the General Post Office Film Unit, where he met the poet W. H. Auden, and came to terms with his own left-leaning political ideals (including his pacifism) and his homosexuality. He met his lifelong partner, the tenor Peter Pears in 1937, while there. With Pears he visited America between 1939 and 1942, where he composed his first opera, *Paul Bunyan*, with a libretto by Auden. When Britten and Pears returned to England in 1942, Britten began to work furiously within opera, completing works for **Sadler's Wells**, the English Opera Group, the Glyndebourne English Opera Company, and eventually, the Aldeburgh Festival (founded 1948). Success in these ventures brought him additional commissions, including for the 1951 **Festival of Britain**, which premiered *Billy Budd* (libretto by E. M. Forster). Pears and Britten visited Asia in 1955–56, where Britten heard as much music as he could, including Japanese *Noh* opera and both the Balinese and Javanese gamelans.

With the death of Vaughan Williams in 1958, Britten became the de facto center of English composition, as seen in his commission to compose the *War Requiem* for the consecration of Coventry Cathedral (1961). For the next 15 years, Britten continued to compose and travel (Venice, America, and India, the latter for a year) and solidified his position as the public face of British music. Britten declined a knighthood but was named a CH in 1953 and a life peer in 1976.

BRITTON, THOMAS (1644–1714). Concert producer. Britton was a charcoal dealer in London whose business premises became the venue for a long-running series of weekly **public concerts**. He opened his business in Clerkenwell in 1677 and in the next year began to indulge his interest in music by sponsoring music meetings in the long, narrow room above the ground-floor business space. One entered, apparently awkwardly, from an external staircase, and the room offered little amenity besides the music. **Sir John Hawkins** notes that "in every respect [the site was] so mean, as to be a fit habitation for only a very poor man." Yet, until Britton's death, concerts were held there that attracted people of quality and musicians of considerable note, such as **George Frideric Handel** and **Johann Christoph Pepusch**. Hawkins enthusiastically tries to claim for the concerts the palm of primacy—"the first meeting of its kind and the undoubted parent of some of the most celebrated concerts in London"—although **John Banister**'s concerts, begun in 1672, would have preceded those of Britton.

BROADSIDE BALLAD. *See* BALLAD.

BROADWOOD, LUCY (1858–1929). Folk music collector and editor, amateur singer, and adjudicator. Broadwood was one of the major intellectual figures in the collecting and publishing of English folk music in the first half of the 20th century, working within the **English Folk Dance and Song Society**. She served variously as its secretary (1904), editor (1906), and president (1928); she was also a patron of numerous pianists (including Fanny Davies) and helped found the Leith Hill Music Festival. For the early part of her career, her publications of folk music were collaborative acts, including the reissuing of her uncle John Broadwood's 1843 *Old English Songs* as *Sussex Songs* (1890; with piano harmonizations by H. F. Birch Renayrdson) and *English Country Songs* with J. A. Fuller-Maitland (1893). She later published *English Traditional Carols and Songs* (1908).

Broadwood was born in Scotland and lived on the Surrey-Sussex border before moving to London in 1894. In London she continued to edit folk songs and began writing on collecting while frequently maintaining a salon of contemporary singers and pianists. Some of her collected songs and songs composed to emulate folk songs became standard fare for singers in the first decade of the 20th century.

BROWNE, JOHN (fl. ca. 1480–1505). Composer. Little is known of Browne's life, though he seems to have had an as-of-yet unspecified tie to Oxford; Bowers (NG, 2001) suggests he may have been chaplain to John de Vere, Earl of Oxford. His antiphons are prominent in the **Eton Choirbook**, where his compositions open the manuscript, a sign of both the extent of his contribution and the high regard in which he was held. It is also likely that he is the "Browne" represented in the **Fayrfax Manuscript** (GB Lbl Add. 5465) with three vernacular settings, including the Passion **carols** "Woffully araid" and "Jhesu, mercy." The modern assessment of his works has, at times, been exuberant. Harrison (1963) notes that "Browne's technical command, the deeply penetrating quality of his imagination, and his capacity for strikingly dramatic expression place him among the greatest composers of his age."

BROWNING. The popular melody associated with the text **"The Leaves be Green"** or "Browning my dear" was often the basis of instrumental settings by composers such as **William Byrd** and **Elway Bevin**, and the settings were known as "Brownings." The melody is given in a canonic form in **Thomas Ravenscroft**'s *Deuteromelia* of 1609. Many settings employ the tune as the foundation of continuous variations and allow the melody to migrate from voice to voice. As with settings of *In nomine*, the popularity of Brownings confirms the prominence of preexistent melody in consort practice.

BULL, JOHN (1562/63?–1628). Composer and keyboard virtuoso. Bull was a prolific composer of keyboard music, including plainsong-based works, fantasias, grounds, variations, and dances, and the degree of technical demand in many of them—his "customary figurative exuberance" (Neighbour, *NG*, 2001)—suggests his own virtuosic ability. He was a chorister at Hereford in 1573; in the next year he appears as a chorister in the **Chapel Royal**. He returned to Hereford in 1582 as organist, becoming master of the choristers as well in the next year. In 1586 he was appointed a gentleman of the Chapel Royal. He held music doctorates from both Cambridge and Oxford.

At the recommendation of Queen Elizabeth, Bull was appointed the first public reader in music at Gresham College (London) in 1597. His duties required him to give two "solemn" lectures a week, with the content divided between theoretical and practical matters (the latter by "concert of voice or of instruments.")

In 1613 Bull left England for the Low Countries, working under the patronage of the Austrian Archduke Albert and later as organist of the cathedral at Antwerp. His relocation to the Continent placed him in the company of other English musicians—notably **Peter Philips**—who had gone there as Roman Catholics seeking religious tolerance. Bull would avow that this was his motivation as well; although, as he was at the time being prosecuted for adultery in England, his motivation must have been mixed at best. His degree of disrepute in the scandal is clear in the remarks of the archbishop of Canterbury, George Abbott: "The man hath more music than honesty and is as famous for marring of virginity as he is for fingering of organs and virginals." Situated in the Low Countries, he was a strong link in the connections between the English and Dutch styles.

BURDEN. The refrain of a **carol** is known as a burden. In its classic 15th-century form it was marked not only by the repetition of music and text at the end of stanzas, but also by a shift from two-part writing to three-part and a change from solo singing in the verses to choral singing in the refrain. Some carols, famously the Agincourt carol, have two burdens, one in two and three parts respectively.

BURNEY, CHARLES (1726–1814). Writer of music history, composer, keyboardist, and impresario; father of the novelist Fanny Burney. Burney's initial musical training occurred at Chester Cathedral under the organist Edmund Baker. He was apprenticed to **Thomas Arne** from 1744 to 1748, who introduced him to a wide network of London musicians and institutions; he met **George Frideric Handel** in 1745 and played regularly at **Drury Lane** and the **pleasure gardens** at **Vauxhall**. In 1748 Fulke Greville purchased Burney's remaining period of apprenticeship from Arne, and Burney briefly became Greville's personal musician and companion. Greville released him from obligation in 1749, and Burney found work as an organist at St. Dionis Backchurch and in the theaters and concert series in London. From 1751 to 1760 Burney was the organist at St. Margaret's in King's Lynn (relocating there because of health reasons), where he also taught music to local families. He returned to London in 1760, reestablished himself within musical life (especially within the theater), and began studying and writing about music. He was appointed organist at the Oxford Chapel in 1773 and at Chelsea Hospital in 1783.

Burney's accounts of long travels on the Continent in the early 1770s, *The Present State of Music in France and Italy* (1771) and *The Present State of Music in Germany, the Netherlands, and the United Provinces* (1773), became the basis of his great work, *A General History of Music from the Earliest Ages to the Present Period* (1776–89). Burney's music writings were rivaled only by those of his contemporary **Sir John Hawkins**. In the last years of his life, he received an annual pension from the Crown. His large collection of music books was sold on his death to the **British Museum**; they became the core of the music collection of the **British Library**.

BUSH, ALAN (1900–1995). Composer, pianist, teacher, and conductor. Bush was known throughout his career as a composer who integrated his left-wing and communist politics into his music. As a consequence, many of his **operas** were more widely performed in the German Democratic Republic than in Great Britain. *Wat Tyler*, for instance, was completed in 1951, premiered in Leipzig in 1953, and had a run of more than a dozen performances in its first season and numerous revivals there before being given its British professional premiere in 1974 at **Sadler's Wells**. Bush received early training in composition and piano at the **Royal Academy of Music** (2; RAM; 1918–22) and studied composition further with **John Ireland** (1921–27) as well as musicology and philosophy at the University of Berlin (1929–31). He taught composition at the RAM from 1925 until 1978. In the years before World War II, he avidly mixed music and politics by conducting the London Labour Choral Union (1929–40), joining the Communist Party (1935), founding and chairing the Worker's Music Association in 1936 (he was named its president in 1941, a position he retained until his death), and conducting the London String Orchestra (1938–51). He was also central to the creation of large classical-music events for the working class, such as the *Pageant of London* (**Crystal Palace**, 1934) and a staging of **George Frideric Handel**'s **oratorio** *Belshazzar* as an opera with the London Co-Operative Society (Wembley Stadium, 1938), among others.

Bush's politics did not always suit the British musical establishment; the **British Broadcasting Corporation** banned performances of his music between March and June 1941 because he signed the People's Convention. During the war he was a reception clerk for the Royal Army at the Millbank Military Hospital in London, where he organized an army choir. His music— which includes several operas, four symphonies, and a great deal of chamber music—is marked by an engagement with serial techniques (he was an early admirer of Arnold Schoenberg), but within a tonal context and often using folklike materials.

BUTLER, CHARLES (ca. 1560–1647). Cleric and man of learning. In addition to his priestly vocation, Butler studied bees, philology, and music, writing treatises on all three. His musical treatise, *The Principles of Musik* *in Singing and Setting: with the Two-fold Use thereof, Ecclesiasticall and Civil* (London, 1636), was dedicated to Charles I and discusses rudiments, church music, instruments, and matters of composition and performance. His work was highly regarded by both **Sir John Hawkins** and **Charles Burney**. Hawkins described the *Principles* as a "very learned, curious, and entertaining book." Burney noted that "the book contains more knowledge, in a small compass, than any other of the kind, in our language."

Butler's work on bees, *The Feminine Monarchie* (Oxford, 1609), includes musical transcriptions of apiarian buzzing.

BUTTERWORTH, GEORGE (1885–1916). Composer, folk dancer, folk song and dance collector, and teacher. Butterworth became—primarily because of his early death in World War I—frozen as an example of the pastoral school from the second generation of the **English Musical Renaissance**. Much of his existing music has been constructed in what Frogley refers to as "a ruralist and often Elegiac vision of 'Englishness'" (*DNB*). His most famous surviving works are a handful of orchestral pieces based on English folk songs and 18 songs, many of them set to the rural paeans of A. E. Housman.

Butterworth had a privileged background, attended Ayrgath, Eton, and Trinity College, Oxford (at the latter he was the President of the University Music Club for a season); his family wished him to be a solicitor. Leaving Oxford in 1908, he abandoned his family's plans and worked briefly on the music staff of the *Times* and taught at Radley before enrolling at the **Royal College of Music** (1910–11). His interest in folk music and dance had already manifested itself by this point; he joined the **English Folk Song Society** in 1906, was a founding member of the English Folk Dance Society in 1911, collected morris and sword dances with **Cecil Sharp**, and was an intimate friend of **Ralph Vaughan Williams**. He destroyed a good deal of his juvenilia, and most of the music that survives was published and premiered between 1910 and 1914, including the rhapsody *A Shropshire Lad* (Leeds Triennial **Musical Festival**, 1913) and the idyll *The Banks of the Green Willow* (1913). He enlisted in the army at the end of August 1914 and was killed in action in July 1916 at Pozières, France.

BYRD, WILLIAM (ca. 1540–1623). Composer. Byrd's prominence in Elizabethan music is unrivaled, and in this world he emerges as a prolific composer of **consort songs**, the leading voice in shaping the English verse **anthem**, the fount of the so-called English **virginal** school, a master figure in giving the late 16th-century Latin motet its English accent, and an icon of English Romanism and recusancy.

Much of Byrd's life was spent in association with the **Chapel Royal**, where he had perhaps been a chorister—the implications of his being identified as a student of **Thomas Tallis** makes this likely—and where he was appointed "Gentleman" in 1572, remaining in that appointment until his death some 50 years later. Prior to coming to London, he held an appointment at Lincoln Cathedral (1563–70), and tellingly, after his move to London, Lincoln continued in a contractual arrangement with him so that he might continue to send compositions to the cathedral. This early acknowledgment of his value as a composer was amply echoed in his long tenure at court, where, one feels certain, his musical gifts trumped any official difficulty with his illegal practice of Roman Catholicism.

Byrd's religious faith had a number of musical manifestations, both explicit and implicit. His patrons, such as Thomas, Lord Paget, and the Petre family of Essex, were leaders in the often-underground Catholic community, and Byrd's relocation to Essex in the later years of his life (1593) suggests he was involved in providing music for the covert liturgies. Additionally, late in his life he took on the composition and bold publication of explicit Roman forms: three masses from the 1590s and two volumes of polyphonic mass propers, the *Gradualia* (1605, 1607). The *Gradualia* has been recently identified with Jesuit contemplative practice (McCarthy, 2007), and this mystical dimension is resonant with the composer's remarks in the preface about the power of the holy words themselves:

> Moreover in these words, as I have learned by trial, there is such a profound and hidden power that to one thinking upon things divine and diligently and earnestly pondering them, all the fittest numbers occur as if of themselves and freely offer themselves to the mind which is not indolent or inert.

And much of Byrd's music seems to offer poignant comment on the state of Roman Catholics in England at the time. His song "Why Do I Use My Paper, Ink, and Pen" addresses the execution of the Jesuit Edmund Campion. And the profusion of penitential, lamentative Latin motets, especially those employing exilic Psalm texts, seems also to express the plight of his own religious exile. It may be, of course, that this also reflected a degree of temperament. Henry Peacham in 1622 noted that Byrd was "naturally disposed to gravity and piety."

Byrd's Romanism seemed no impediment to his important contributions to Anglican liturgical and devotional repertories, much of which he wrote while at Lincoln. He is one of the principal shapers of the verse anthem, with works like "Christ rising again" an important example. Similarly, his impressive "Great Service" draws on the verse principle of accompanied solo passages in alternation with choral tuttis to achieve a stunning array of textures, here amplified by the alternation of *cantoris* **and** *decani*. His full anthems can be tinged with a madrigalistic approach to the text, as in the exuberant "Sing Joyfully."

Latin motets figured on both sides of church divisions, and the Latin motet had the blessing of the ceremonially minded Queen Elizabeth, most famously in accepting the dedication of Byrd and Tallis's 1575 *Cantiones Sacrae*. Byrd's motets here draw in part on the model of the instrumental fantasia— "Laudate pueri," for instance, exists in an earlier instrumental version—and in all seem to bring an English accent to mainstream contrapuntal procedures, evident in richness of sonority and the use of the so-called **English cadence**. In the preface to the volume, the authors, in fact, offer a fervent salute to the strength of English composition:

> British Music, already contemplating battle, saw that she, who yields to none of the nine Muses in art, could safely proceed by one course: if the Queen would declare herself her patron, and if she could include as her own such distinguished authors who if they would compose would astonish the rest of the multitude. Therefore, blessed with the patronage of so learned a Ruler, she fears neither the boundaries nor the reproach of any nation. Proclaiming Tallis and Byrd her parents, she boldly advances where no voice has sung. (trans. Monson, 1977)

Byrd's prolificity in writing **consort songs** provided a distinctively English repertory, and one that easily influenced both the verse anthem and polyphonic ensemble singing. Much of his ensemble vocal music, as in the 1588 *Psalmes, Sonets, & Songes* . . . , are versions that supply text to earlier instrumental lines. This permeability of medium surfaces in Byrd's instrumental music as well, where fantasias and dance music appear in collateral keyboard and consort versions.

Byrd's keyboard music presents fantasias, song variations, grounds, and dance music (chiefly Pavans and Galliards), much of which was collected in the retrospective *My Lady Nevells Booke* (1591), a collection that also includes programmatic keyboard music, such as "The Battell." To this body of writing, one may also add several cantus-firmus **organ** works from Lincoln.

C

CAIUS CHOIRBOOK. GB Cgc 667 is one of the principal surviving sources of early 16th-century English liturgical polyphony. Copied in the 1520s, it contains five- and six-part Masses and Magnificats by **Robert Fayrfax, Nicholas Ludford,** and **William Cornysh,** inter alia. The source bears the inscription of "Ex dono et opere Edwardi Higgons," a confirmation that it, like the **Lambeth Choirbook,** a similar source from the same scribe, was commissioned by Edward Higgons. The Caius Choirbook was likely intended for St. Stephen's, Westminster Palace, though Salisbury Cathedral, a later owner, is also a possibility.

CAMPION, THOMAS (1567–1620). Poet and composer. Campion was a prolific author and composer of **ayres** as well as an important contributor to the early 17th-century court **masque.** Though not a professional musician—he studied law in the 1580s and received a medical degree at Caen in 1605—Campion emerges as a significant figure both literarily and musically, theoretically and artistically.

His ayres, settings of his own poetry, are generally straightforward, tuneful, and unencumbered by artifice. The unsigned preface to his collaborative collection with **Philip Rosseter** (1601) is presumably of his authorship and brings into focus the qualities he sought in writing ayres:

> What Epigrams are in Poetrie, the same are Ayres in musicke, then in their chiefe perfection when they are short and well seasoned. . . . [T]here are some, who to appeare the more deepe, and singular in their judgement, will admit no Musicke but that which is long, intricate, bated with fuge, chaind with syncopation, and where the nature of everie word is precisely exprest in the Note. . . . But such childish observing of words is altogether ridiculous, and we ought to maintaine as well in Notes, as in action a manly carriage, gracing no word, but that which is eminent, and emphaticall.

Unsurprisingly from a poet-composer, he sought a close relationship between word and music, but did not find madrigalistic text-painting a fruitful route to this end. Interestingly, one ayre, "Come let us sound with melody," engages quantitative measure on the model of *musique mesurée*, echoing his own concerns with classical scansion in his literary treatise, *Observations in the Art of English Poesie* (1602). Campion was the author of an influential musical treatise as well, *A New Way of Making Fowre Parts in Counter-Point* (1613–14).

Campion contributed text and music to several masques, including that for Lord Hayes (1607), the Lords' Maske (1613), and a masque celebrating the wedding of the Earle of Somerset and Lady Frances Howard (1614). Significantly, these works are documented by his published descriptions.

CANTATA (ALSO DRAMATIC CANTATA, SACRED CANTATA, SECULAR CANTATA, ETC.). Composition for voice or voices and accompaniment. In the first half of the 18th century, English composers began essays in the genre by copying Italian solo cantatas, alternating recitative and aria structures, setting music to pastoral texts (e.g., **Henry Carey**'s *Cantatas for Voice and Accompaniment* [1724]). By the 1740s the nymphs and shepherds of the first half of the century were joined by texts celebrating hunting and drinking. In the second half of the century, the cantata became one of the major genres heard in the **pleasure gardens**; such cantatas had larger accompaniments (often small orchestras) and featured a more fluid presentation of recitative and aria styles. Composers of such cantatas include **Johann Christian Bach**, **James Hook**, and **John Worgan**.

In the 19th century the English cantata began to track the **oratorio** in its style and construction. Cantatas might be classed as "sacred" or "secular," but the groups that produced them and the audiences that heard them remained largely the same: they were performed at the many **musical festivals** extant throughout the century, as well as by local amateur choral societies. The 19th-century cantata was a work for soloists, chorus, and orchestra; if secular, it might have a poetic text, such as **Sir Hubert Parry**'s *Blest Pair of Sirens* (1887) or a dramatic one, such as **Sir Edward Elgar**'s *King Olaf* (1896). If sacred, it might be based on either *lauda*-type texts (texts of purely a prayerful/praising nature instead of texts that were narrative; see, for instance Thomas Adams's *The Immortal Hope* [1892]), or they might be narrative texts that were shorter than the typical oratorio, like **Sir Arthur Sullivan**'s *The Martyr of Antioch* (1877). Cantatas reflected all of the major stylistic innovations of the century, such as emulation of **Felix Mendelssohn**, like **Sir William Sterndale Bennett**'s *The May Queen* (1858), and a passion for exoticism, as found in **Frederic Clay**'s *Lalla Rookh* (1877) and **Samuel Coleridge-Taylor**'s *Scenes from the Song of Hiawatha* (1898–1900), or nationalism, heard within Elgar's *Caractacus* (1898).

British composers in the 20th century gradually turned away from the named genre of the cantata itself, but its elements may be found in many like works, such as **Gustav Holst**'s *Hymn of Jesus* (1917), **Ralph Vaughan Williams**'s *Five Tudor Portraits* (1936), and **Benjamin Britten**'s *Cantata Academica* (1960). Like their 19th-century predecessors, these are works for soloists (usually), choir, and orchestra. *See also* BANTOCK, SIR GRANVILLE; *BELSHAZZAR'S FEAST*; BENEDICT, SIR JULIUS; CHORLEY, HENRY FROTHERGILL; CURWEN PRESS; DELIUS, SIR FREDERICK; GAUL, ALFRED R.; GIBBS, CECIL ARMSTRONG; HANDEL, GEORGE FRIDERIC; HEAP, CHARLES SWINERTON; HILES, HENRY; LLOYD, CHARLES HARFORD; MACFARREN, SIR GEORGE ALEXANDER; MACKENZIE, SIR ALEXANDER CAMPBELL; MAD SONGS; NOVELLO & CO.; ODE; ROSEINGRAVE, THOMAS; SCOTT, CYRIL; *A SEA SYMPHONY*; SILAS, EDOUARD; SMART, HENRY THOMAS; SOMERVELL, SIR ARTHUR; STANLEY, JOHN; THOMAS, ARTHUR GORING; WESLEY, CHARLES (2).

CANTICLE. Generally a biblical song, not one of the Psalms, used as a prescribed part of the liturgy, as for example, the Magnificat at Vespers or the Nunc Dimittis at Compline. The Magnificat enjoyed particular cultivation in the late 15th and early 16th centuries in England, as evidenced by the **Eton Choirbook**. With the reform of the English Church and the development of the *Book of Common Prayer*, canticles from the monastic daily office were incorporated for use at Morning and Evening Prayer. Thus, the vernacular Magnificat and Nunc Dimittis follow the lessons at Evening Prayer. The modern prominence of **evensong** has seen these canticles achieve particular attention.

The use of the *Te Deum* as a canticle at Morning Prayer is a significant exception to the canticle's typical reliance on biblical text.

CANTIONES SACRAE. Three volumes of late 16th-century Latin polyphony were published under this title in 1575, 1589, and 1591 by **William Byrd**, the first of which was a collaborative venture with **Thomas Tallis**. Byrd and Tallis, both Gentlemen of the **Chapel Royal**, were granted a monopoly on the printing of music in 1575; *Cantiones Sacrae I* is their first venture under that patent. Dedicated to Queen Elizabeth in the 17th year of her reign, it has become traditional to see the 17 motets of each composer in the collection as a numerical salute to the monarch. Significantly, the royal dedication allows one to infer the acceptability of Latin works in certain circumstances at a date when the *Book of Common Prayer* would have enshrined vernacular texts.

*CANTORIS **AND** DECANI.* These terms refer to the two sides of a divided choir. Cantoris, that is, "of the precentor," is the side of the choir on the liturgical north, and decani, "of the dean," is the side of the choir on the liturgical south. The division was manifest both in the antiphonal recitation of psalms—verses alternating from side to side—and also in the subdivision of the ensemble in 16th-century liturgical polyphony.

CAREY, HENRY (1687–1743). Composer and librettist. **Sir John Hawkins** called Carey a "man of facetious temper," a "musician by profession, and one of the lower order of poets." Modern opinion continues to note the problem of quality: he was "a butterfly figure of charm but little substance, who left his mark on the London theatres in surprisingly varied ways" (Fiske, 1986). Among those varied ways is his significant pro-English satire of the Italian **opera**. In verse this could be quite pointed, as in his "Satyr on the Luxury and Effeminancy of the Age":

> I hate this Singing in an unknown Tongue,
> It does our Reason and our Senses wrong;
> When Words instruct, and Music cheers the Mind,
> Then is the Art of Service to mankind:
> But when a Castrate Wretch, of monstrous size,
> Squeaks out a Treble, shrill as Infant cries,
> I curse the unintelligible Ass,
> Who may, for ought I know, be saying Mass.

His libretto to *The Dragon of Wantley*, set by John Frederick Lampe (1737), brought the lampooning of the Italian opera to the stage and was both successful and influential on public taste. Carey had also attempted to promote serious English opera with two librettos, *Amelia* and *Teraminta*. He was a prolific song composer, generally setting his own texts.

CARL ROSA OPERA COMPANY. Operatic company founded in 1867 as the Parepa-Rosa Grand Opera Company by the conductor Karl August Nikolaus Rosa and the soprano Euphrosyne Parepa in America. When the company came to Great Britain in 1873, Parepa was too ill to sing, and the company was renamed the Carl Rosa Opera Company. From 1873 until its final dissolution in 1960, the company presented **operas** in English (both originally composed in English or translated from their original languages). The repertoire included both premieres and operas from repertoire. Following long provincial tours, the company would usually give seasons in London, Manchester, and Liverpool. Besides Rosa (who died in 1889), many famous conductors in England were associated with the company, including **Sir Eugene Goossens**, Walter van Noorden, **Sir Thomas Beecham**, and **Sir Henry Wood**. The company commissioned a number of operas from English composers, including **Sir Charles Villiers Stanford** (*The*

Canterbury Pilgrims, 1884), **Sir Alexander Campbell Mackenzie** (*Colomba*, 1883), and **Sir Frederic Hymen Cowen** (*Pauline*, 1879).

CAROL. English song genre. In early 15th-century England, the carol, a genre with likely roots in the French round-dance song, the *carole*, took the classic form of a strophically set song whose verses are punctuated by a repeating refrain, the **burden**. Textural distinctions also help demarcate the structure, with two-voice solo verses and three-voice choral burdens typical. The texts are vernacular, Latin, or macaronic (a combination of the two) and often address celebrative occasions, with the tie to Christmas being the most enduring and best known. Carols from the later 15th and early 16th centuries in sources like the **Fayrfax Manuscript** focus on the Passion of Jesus, sometimes with a significant amount of affectivity in both text and music, as in **William Cornysh**'s "Woffully araid." Other texts skirt devotion and address political events, as in the famous "Agincourt Carol," celebrating the victory of Henry V over the French forces of Charles VI in 1415.

In terms of use, some carols may well have been used liturgically in processions—the formal similarity to processional **hymns** is compelling—or as substitutes for Office Antiphons like the "Benedicamus." Others in Harrison's (1963) memorable phrase were "moral and convivial," with usage at banquets and the like.

Formal elements may have been defining, but themselves show variability. The "Agincourt Carol," for instance, is one of many with two burdens; carols in the Fayrfax Manuscript extend to four voices, have burdens that may or may not recur, and can be through-composed. By the late 16th century, carols had grown more rare, though not without some formal echoes of the earlier style persisting. **William Byrd**'s "From Virgin's Womb" (1589), for instance, is set as a **consort song**, though preserving a refrain, which is sung with the angelic scoring of high voices.

The Puritan ascendancy in the 17th century saw the neglect of the carol, unsurprisingly so for its ties to the suspect observance of Christmas. And while at the Restoration popular forms of the carol were published in broadsides, the composed tradition remained in a state of decline. Rejuvenation of the carol emerged under the influence of High Church Anglicans in the 19th century, a group that often looked to the medieval church and in that look would also have glimpsed both a richer sense of the celebration of Christmas and the carol's role in it. Significantly, the rise of this Tractarian movement also coincided with Charles Dickens's much-heralded "rediscovery" of Christmas in works like *A Christmas Carol* (1843).

The modern enthusiasm for carols draws on an international Christmas repertory in diverse styles, but one in which the English have maintained a leading voice, especially as arrangers, with the works of Sir David Willcocks, Reginald Jacques, and John Rutter particularly influential. The Service of Nine Lessons and Carols begun at King's College, Cambridge, in 1918 has also in itself become an icon of the modern Christmas celebration and the model for services worldwide. *See also* BANASTER, GILBERT; BROAD-WOOD, LUCY; CONSORT SONG; "GREENSLEEVES"; HESELTINE, PHILIP; *MUSICA BRITANNICA*; PASSION; RITSON MANUSCRIPT; STAINER, SIR JOHN.

CARVER CHOIRBOOK. An early 16th-century manuscript source (GB En 5.15) perhaps associated with the Scottish Chapel Royal. It includes liturgical works by Robert Carver (1484/87–after 1567), one of the leading Scottish musicians of the early 16th century, who was an Augstinian canon associated with Scone Abbey. It also includes English works from ca. 1500, as well as Netherlandish compositions, including a mass on *L'homme armé* by Guillaume Dufay. The Netherlandish works help document the close ties between Scotland and the Continent.

CASE, JOHN (ca. 1539–1600). English philosopher. Case was a fellow at St. John's College, Oxford, described by **Anthony Wood** as "the most noted disputant and philosopher that ever set foot in that college." His musical writings, in continuity with various writers of antiquity, focus on the relationship of music, civil life, and virtue. This discourse appears in both *Sphaera Civitatis* (1588) and *Apologia Musices* (1588). The anonymous *The Praise of Musick* (1586) has traditionally been attributed to Case, in part buttressed by the Thomas Watson/**William Byrd madrigal** "A Gratification unto Mr John Case, for his Learned Booke, Lately Made in the Praise of Musicke," though recent writing (Binns, *NG*, 2001) has called the attribution into question.

CATCH. Canonic vocal form. The catch is a round sung by male voices, typically in taverns and similar settings, with humorous, often bawdy, text. The collections by **Thomas Ravenscroft**, *Pammelia* (1609), *Deuteromelia* (1609), and *Melismata* (1611), show the catch at an early stage; later collections, such as **John Hilton**'s *Catch That Catch Can* (1652), which extended into numerous editions, well document the catch's popularity. Moreover, it attracted the attention of notable composers; **Henry Purcell**, for instance, wrote over 60 catches and in doing so extended the vocal demands beyond the typical amateur. By the late 18th century, the catch's low humor had become problematic, and its popularity declined. The signature gesture of the catch is the contrapuntal juxtaposition of innocent words and phrases whose new polyphonic proximity reveals a risqué expression.

CATCH CLUB. *See* NOBLEMEN AND GENTLEMEN'S CATCH CLUB.

CAUSTUN, THOMAS (ca. 1520/25–1569/70). Composer. Caustun was a member of the **Chapel Royal** from as early as 1553 and was active there until his death in 1569 or 1570, whereupon **Richard Farrant** succeeded to his place as Gentleman. As a composer he contributed both to **John Day**'s *Mornyng and Evenyng Prayer* (1565)—he was the largest contributor, in fact—and to *The Whole Psalmes in Foure Parts* (1563). Some of his music, in the severity of its style, well exemplifies the Edwardian Protestant ethos of the middle of the century.

CAVENDISH, MICHAEL (ca. 1565–1628). Composer. Cavendish's songs and **madrigals** appear in his 1598 printed collection, *14 Ayres in Tabletorie*, where his **ayres** show the influence of the **consort song**. One of his madrigals in the collection, "Come gentle swains," is an early instance of the refrain "Then sang the shepherds and nymphs of Diana, long live fair Oriana," a refrain that would a few years later become the signature motive in the madrigal collection *The Triumphs of Oriana* (1601). "Come gentle swains" appears in a revised version in this latter collection.

CELLIER, ALFRED (1844–91). Composer, conductor, and organist. Cellier was in the orbit of his fellow **Chapel Royal** choirboy **Sir Arthur Sullivan** for most of his viable career. While he was an organist at All Saints, Blackheath; St. Albans, Holborn; and (for a brief period) in Ireland, he is best known as a composer and conductor of operetta. He held conducting appointments at the Court Theatre (London), the Prince's Theatre (Manchester), the Criterion, and St. James's Theatre, and was long associated with the **D'Oyly Carte Opera Company** as their conductor both in England and for touring abroad in North America. He contributed overtures to Sullivan's *H.M.S. Pinafore* and *Pirates of Penzance*. One of his operettas, *Dorothy* (1886), held the record for the longest running operetta of its time (931 performances). He wrote several works with libretti by **Sir William Schwenck Gilbert**, including *Topsyturveydom* (1874) and the posthumously produced *The Mountebanks* (1892).

CEREMONIAL MUSIC. The formal public life of both church and state was musical in varying degrees. Although functional at its root—music for processions, music to accompany ritual actions, fanfares to summon attention, etc.—the degree of elaboration that ceremonial music might attain was a powerful element in rendering the ceremony itself impressive. Particularly prominent examples include **Henry Purcell**'s "Funeral Music for Queen

Mary" and **George Frideric Handel**'s coronation **anthem** "Zadok the Priest." *See also* CORONATION MUSIC.

CHANGE RINGING. Change ringing is a method of sounding multiple bells—typically rope-pulled tower bells—in a variety of sequences that explore the permutations of order offered by that particular number of bells. Control of the sequence is in part derived from systems that see a bell move directly through the succeeding positions (the so-called plain hunt). Change ringing was first theorized in the 17th century in two sources, *Tintinnalogia* (1668), perhaps by Richard Duckworth with contributions by Fabian Stedman, and *Campanologia* (1677) by Fabian Stedman. **Anthony Wood**'s remark that the sound of church bells offered "the music nighest bordering upon heaven" suggests something of the 17th-century taste for the bell music from the tower.

One of the most widely known literary evocations of the cult of change ringing is Dorothy L. Sayers' 1934 mystery novel *The Nine Tailors*, in which not only the bell tower and a memorable ring figure prominently in the plot, but also a key alphabetic cipher is solved on the basis of its likeness to a peal. Sayers is exuberant in her enthusiasm for change ringing in her foreword:

> From time to time complaints are made about the ringing of church bells. It seems strange that a generation which tolerates the uproar of the internal combustion engine and the wailing of the jazz band should be so sensitive to the one loud noise that is made to the glory of God. England, alone in the world, has perfected the art of change-ringing and the true ringing of bells by rope and wheel, and will not lightly surrender her unique heritage.

CHAPEL ROYAL. The Chapel Royal is the body of clerics and musicians attached to the court to supply the liturgical needs of the monarch. Although there were earlier forms, the Chapel Royal was first incorporated under Edward IV in 1483 as the "Royal Free Chapel of the Household," at which time the chapel was comprised of 24 chaplains and gentlemen clerks as well as eight choristers. These numbers would vary over the years, although the division of personnel into choristers, gentlemen of the chapel, and clerics is long standing. And at various times, the musical personnel would include the master of the children (almost all of whom were drawn from the ranks of the gentlemen of the chapel), organist, bell ringer, lutanist, and violist. Choristers in the premodern era were recruitable by impressment. Since the early 17th century the dean of the chapel has generally been in Episcopal orders, and since the early 18th century this office has almost always been the prerogative of the bishop of London. Musical supervision has traditionally been the purview of the office of subdean.

In addition to musical duties, children of the chapel have at times also been called upon to act in dramatic productions, notably at the Blackfriars Theatre during the reign of Elizabeth I.

It is important to stress that the Chapel Royal is a body of people rather than a dedicated liturgical building, although in the 19th century, internal power struggles suggest that this was sometimes misunderstood. The chapel is a mobile ensemble; however, when Queen Anne located her court at St. James in 1702, the chapel at St. James in Colour Court became and has remained in effect the home of the chapel. The Chapel Royal Choir School was established in 1886; prior to this time choristers had traditionally lodged with the master of the children. The school closed in 1923, after which time the choristers have studied at the City of London School.

Appointment to the Chapel Royal has been a sign of distinction, and gentlemen and masters have included many of England's most well-known composers, such as **Samuel Arnold, Thomas Attwood, John Blow, William Boyce, William Byrd, William Croft, Orlando Gibbons, Henry Lawes, Thomas Morley, Henry Purcell, Sir Arthur Sullivan, Thomas Tomkins**, and **Samuel Sebastian Wesley.** *See also* ABELL, JOHN; ALEYN, JOHN; AMNER, JOHN; BANASTER, GILBERT; BARRETT, JOHN; BATTISHILL, JONATHAN; BEVIN, ELWAY; BLAGRAVE, THOMAS; BLITHEMAN, JOHN; BULL, JOHN; CAUSTUN, THOMAS; CELLIER, ALFRED; CHILD, WILLIAM; CHOIRBOY PLAYS; CLARKE, JEREMIAH; CLUB ANTHEM; COOKE, HENRY; CORNYSH, WILLIAM; CORONATION ANTHEM; EDWARDS, RICHARD; FARRANT, RICHARD; FAYRFAX, ROBERT; GATES, BERNARD; GIBBONS, CHRISTOPHER; GILES, NATHANIEL; GLEE; GOSTLING, JOHN; GREENE, MAURICE; HEATHER, WILLIAM; HINGESTON, JOHN; HOOPER, EDMUND; HUMPHREY, PELHAM; IMMYNS, JOHN; ISAACK, BARTHOLOMEW; KENT, JAMES; LLOYD, CHARLES HARFORD; MUNDY, WILLIAM; NARES, JAMES; ODE; PARSONS, ROBERT; PORTER, WALTER; PURCELL, DANIEL; RANDALL, JOHN; RIMBAULT, EDWARD FRANCIS; ST. CECILIA'S DAY OBSERVANCE; SHEPPARD, JOHN; SMART, SIR GEORGE THOMAS; SMITH, JOHN STAFFORD; TUDWAY, THOMAS; TURNER, WILLIAM; TYE, CHRISTOPHER; WELDON, JOHN; WILSON, JOHN; WISE, MICHAEL.

CHAPPELL & CO. Music publishing and instrumental sales firm, founded in 1810. It was bought by Philips in 1968 and then acquired in 1987 by Warner Communications. As a company, Chappell was heavily involved in the growing infrastructure of 19th-century English music. Its influence helped create the **Royal Philharmonic Society** (1813), the **Musical Antiquarian**

Society (1840), and the Monday and Saturday Popular Concerts at **St. James's Hall** (1858), and it organized the **Proms** at **Queen's Hall** from 1915 to 1926. Early on, the firm took an active role in publishing antiquarian music and folk music, especially under the auspices of William Chappell, son of one of the firm's founders. The firm also took an early interest in publishing lighter music and published most of the operettas of **Sir William Schwenck Gilbert** and **Sir Arthur Sullivan** in the 19th century and the works of artists such as Noël Coward and Ivor Novello in the 20th. It began to sell pianos in 1812, manufacturing them by 1840, and did so until the Chappell Piano Company became an independent entity in 1919. Like many large publishing concerns, by the end of the 19th century, Chappell had offices in both North America and Australia.

CHARITY FESTIVALS. *See* MUSICAL FESTIVALS.

CHILD, WILLIAM (1606/7–97). English composer and organist. Child is described as a pupil of **Elway Bevin** by **Anthony Wood**. In 1630 he was elected clerk of St. George's Chapel, Windsor, and succeeded John Mundy (son of **William Mundy**) as organist of the chapel in 1632. He served in this capacity until 1644 when the Civil War saw the disbanding of the chapel. His last composition before leaving Windsor was a setting of verses from Psalm 79, whose references to the inheritance of the heathen become especially poignant in this context.

At the Restoration, Child resumed his duties at Windsor and also took up royal appointments as organist of the **Chapel Royal** as well as composer of the Wind Musick and cornettist. Active as a composer both before and after the interregnum, his music is stylistically diverse, including conservative imitative counterpoint and also music that reflects the modern Italian advances of the 17th century. His publication *First set of Psalmes of III voices fitt for private chappells, or other private meetings with Continuall Base, either for the Organ or Theorbo, newly composed after the Italian way* (1639; reissued as *Choise Musick* in 1650 and 1656) is explicit in its stylistic orientation.

Child's friendship with the Restoration diarist **Samuel Pepys** is well documented, and on at least one occasion (26 February 1665/66) he was a gracious host to both him and his wife on a trip to Windsor, treating them to a performance by the choir. Additionally, **Sir John Hawkins** records several instances of his charitable bent.

Child was admitted to the BMus at Oxford in 1631 and the DMus in 1663. The Faculty of Music at Oxford houses an anonymous painting of him in doctoral dress.

A CHILD OF OUR TIME. **Oratorio** by **Sir Michael Tippett**, written between 1939 and 1941 and premiered in London on 19 March 1944. *A Child* *of Our Time* was Tippett's first attempt to harness his political beliefs into a large, abstract musical structure. Tippett drew the story from contemporary events: the 1938 murder of German diplomat Ernst vom Rath by teenage Polish refugee Herschel Grynszpan. The oratorio is patterned after **George Frideric Handel**'s *Messiah* (a three-part structure) and the Passions of Johann Sebastian Bach (substituting African American spirituals for chorales). Since its premiere, *A Child of Our Time* has been a regular feature at **musical festivals**.

CHILMEAD, EDMUND (1610–54). Oxford musician and man of letters. Chilmead spent much of his short life at Oxford, taking the BA (1628) and MA (1632) and holding a chaplaincy at Christ Church. He was also for a time a clerk at Magdalen College. A classicist, he compiled a catalogue of Greek manuscripts at the Bodleian Library as well as being active as a translator. The political and religious upheavals of the 1640s caused him to leave Oxford, from whence he located in London. There he was active in setting up weekly music meetings in Aldersgate, "deriving from the profits thereof the means of a slender subsistence" (**Sir John Hawkins**).

CHM. *See* ROYAL COLLEGE OF ORGANISTS.

CHOIRBOY PLAYS. During the reign of Henry VIII on into the 17th century, boy choristers from various chapels, including the **Chapel Royal**; St. George's, Windsor; and St. Paul's, London, were engaged as actors in entertainments at court and theaters such as Blackfriars. Their musical talents within these entertainments gave rise to the **consort song**, with examples by **Robert Parsons, Richard Edwards,** and Nathaniel Patrick especially associated with the choirboy plays. **William Shakespeare** confirms the fashionability of the boy actors in *Hamlet* (II/ii): Rosencrantz says, ". . . but there is, sir, an aery of children, little eyases, that cry out on the top of question, and are most tyrannically clapped for't: these are now the fashion."

CHORAL FESTIVALS. *See* MUSICAL FESTIVALS.

CHORAL HARMONISTS SOCIETY. Amateur concert-giving group active between 1833 and 1851. Like many amateur groups active in the first half of the 19th century, the Choral Harmonists Society met not in a concert hall or rehearsal rooms, but in drinking establishments: either the New London Tavern on Bridge Street, Blackfriars, or the London Tavern on Bishopsgate Street. The Society's conductors included at times **Vincent Novello**, Charles Lucas, Charles Neate, and Henry Westrop. It presented a varied repertoire within its concerts, featuring works like **Henry Purcell**'s *King Arthur*, and including perhaps the first performance of the Credo from Johann Sebastian Bach's Mass in B minor in Great Britain and the first public performance of Ludwig van Beethoven's *Missa Solemnis*, op. 123, in Great Britain.

CHORLEY, HENRY FROTHERGILL (1808–72). Writer, librettist, and critic. While a novelist, playwright, and poet of some ability, Chorley is remembered for his music criticism for the *Athenaeum* (he began writing articles for them in 1830 and was a member of the staff there from 1834 to his retirement in 1868) and the *Orchestra*, which were frequently reprinted in other contemporary music magazines. He wrote or translated **opera** and **cantata** libretti for figures as diverse as Daniel-François-Esprit Auber, **Sir William Sterndale Bennett**, Domenico Cimarosa, Christoph Willibald von Gluck, Charles Gounod, and **Sir Arthur Sullivan**, though his original libretti never became popular.

CHURCH CHORAL SOCIETY. *See* TRINITY COLLEGE OF MUSIC.

CITTERN. A plucked string instrument, generally with four courses of strings strung in metal, and played with a plectrum. A flat back, narrow sides, and fixed frets are all characteristic of the Cittern. Much has been made of its availability in barbershops for the amusement of the clientele, but it was an instrument with higher attainments as well. It was an integral member of the so-called **English consort** (or "broken consort"), playing strummed harmonies, and it also claimed a solo literature as seen in two English publications: **Antony Holborne**'s *The Cittharn Schoole* (1597) and Thomas Robinson's *New Citharen Lessons* (1609).

CITY OF BIRMINGHAM SYMPHONY ORCHESTRA (ALSO CITY OF BIRMINGHAM ORCHESTRA; CBSO). Symphony founded in 1920 by Appleby Matthews. Early performances of the CBSO occurred in the Birmingham Town Hall; the ensemble moved to Symphony Hall in 1991. The orchestra became a full-time ensemble in 1944. Numerous important conductors have served as the orchestra's director, including **Sir Adrian Boult** (1924–30 and 1959–60), **Sir Andrzej Panufnik** (1957–59), and Simon Rattle (1980–98).

CLARKE, JEREMIAH (ca. 1674–1707). Composer and organist. Clarke was brought up in the **Chapel Royal**, documented as a chorister there as early as 1685. He emerges later as organist at Winchester College, followed by an appointment as **vicar-choral** at St. Paul's, London, where he also officially assumed the position of master of the choristers in 1704. In 1700 he was named a gentleman extraordinary of the **Chapel Royal**, where he also assumed the duties of organist in 1704.

Clarke's works include theater pieces—the 1700 anthology *A Choice Collection of Ayres for Harpsichord* identifies him in association with the Theatre Royal at **Drury Lane**—church music, odes, and keyboard works. **Sir John Hawkins** notes that "his **anthems** are remarkably pathetic, at the same time that they preserve the dignity and majesty of the church style." A bent for pathos may have been typical, for Hawkins relates that he died by suicide, having "a hopeless passion for a very beautiful lady in a station of life far above him."

In the modern day he is best known as the composer of the piece that "**Henry Purcell** didn't write"—the so-called "Trumpet Voluntary"—which has long been standard fare as a bridal march.

CLARKE, REBECCA (1886–1979). Composer and violist. Clarke was a groundbreaking composer and performer in the first four decades of the 20th century. She attended the **Royal Academy of Music (2)** from 1903 to 1905 and the **Royal College of Music** (RCM) from 1907 to 1910, where she was one of **Sir Charles Villiers Stanford**'s first female composition students, and she studied the viola with Lionel Tertius. After leaving the RCM, she performed in chamber ensembles and joined the formerly all-male **Queen's Hall Orchestra** in 1912 at the invitation of **Sir Henry Wood**. Between 1916 and 1924 she lived in America and performed chamber music with the cellist May Muckle (long associated with the British women's suffrage movement). During her last period in England (1924–39), she was once again a solo and ensemble viola player, being one of the founding members of the quartet the English Ensemble (1927). She moved permanently to America in 1939, and her composition slowed considerably. Clarke is best known today for her early chamber music, such as the Viola Sonata (1919), her Piano Trio (1921), and a number of important songs.

CLAY, FREDERIC (1838–89). Composer. Clay was known primarily as a melodist and composer of operetta, and is famous today for having introduced **Sir William Schwenck Gilbert** to **Sir Arthur Sullivan** at a rehearsal of his composition *Ages Ago* (1869; libretto by Gilbert). His operettas were performed at both **Covent Garden** and the Alhambra Theatre, and his **cantatas**, such as *Lalla Rookh* (Brighton, 1877), at **music festivals**.

CLAYTON, THOMAS (1673–1725). Composer and violinist. Clayton is an important figure in the history of **opera** in England, especially in the transition to Italianate fully sung forms in the early 18th century. In 1705 his *Arsinoe*, a fully sung musical pasticcio to an Italian libretto (Tommaso Stanzani) translated by Peter Motteux, was given at **Drury Lane**. Popular in its day—Price (1979) calls it "the first work without spoken dialogue to achieve such success on the London stage"—it nonetheless received pointed critical scorn by later generations. Price postulates that the fact that it was performed on a shared bill with parts of other stage works may have contributed to its success by rationalizing the performance of the opera.

Arsinoe was followed in 1707 by *Rosamond* to a libretto by Joseph Addison; the production was famously unsuccesful. One might reasonably speculate that Addison's satirical view of Italian opera in the *Spectator* (6 March 1711) is colored by this failure.

CLEMENTI, MUZIO (1752–1832). Composer, virtuosic pianist, conductor, instrument manufacturer, and publisher of Italian birth. Clementi was a giant in the London music scene, though his compositions were frequently out of fashion with the public, particularly after **Franz Joseph Haydn**'s two visits to London. Born and trained in Italy, he was brought to England and indentured in Dorset for seven years by the family of Peter Beckford. He moved to London in 1774 and began to slowly make a name for himself as a solo pianist and teacher; during this period he also conducted (from the keyboard) at King's Theatre, **Haymarket**. Aside from the 1783–84 season, he spent 1780–85 abroad touring. He returned to London in 1785, when he performed at the **Hanover Square Rooms** as a soloist (until 1790) and conducted his symphonies (until 1796). During this time, his reputation as a teacher also grew; John Field became one of his students. Aside from teaching and performing, he also began active participation in the music publishing and instrument manufacturing fields; when he returned to the Continent in extended tours from 1802–10, 1816–17, and 1822, he frequently represented the firm of **Clementi & Co.** In the last period of life, he continued composing but was more known for his business acumen and as a conductor, such as at the **Royal Philharmonic Society** (conducting from the keyboard between its 1813 founding and 1824) and the Concerts of Ancient and Modern Musics (founded in 1824; not to be confused with the **Concerts of Ancient Music**). He composed several symphonies (now forgotten), over 100 keyboard works, and pedagogical works still in use today.

CLEMENTI & CO. Shorthand name for a publishing firm active in London between 1798 and 1832 owned and managed by the composer **Muzio Clementi** and a number of other individuals. Clementi & Co. originally took over the premises of the defunct company Longman & Broderip in Cheapside, but in 1806 it became one of a number of music publishers with quarters on Tottenham Court Road. The firm built and sold pianos, and published the virtuosic music of Clementi, Ludwig van Beethoven, and **Franz Joseph Haydn**'s *The Seasons*. Upon Clementi's death, the firm was renamed Colliard & Colliard.

CLUB ANTHEM. A setting of "I Will Alway Give Thanks," composed jointly by three choristers of the Restoration **Chapel Royal**—**Pelham Humfrey**, **John Blow**, and **William Turner**. Significantly, as confirmed by the account of **Thomas Tudway**, the forging of a new style of **anthem** during the Restoration was the fruit of choristers' compositional activities and the king's interest in them.

COATES, ERIC (1886–1957). Composer, conductor, and violist. Coates was a prolific composer who eagerly embraced new technology and new musical styles. Aside from his songs and works for orchestra, he wrote for radio, television, and film, including the march from *The Dam Busters* (1955) around which Leighton Lewis composed the rest of the film's music. Coates was trained in viola and composition at the **Royal Academy of Music (2)** from 1906 to 1910. He was a member of **Sir Henry Wood**'s **Queen's Hall Orchestra** from 1910 to 1919 and was principal violist for the last seven years of this period. His waltz "By the Sleepy Lagoon" is still used to introduce the **British Broadcasting Corporation** radio program *Desert Island Discs*.

COLERIDGE-TAYLOR, SAMUEL (1875–1912). Composer, conductor, adjudicator, and teacher. Coleridge-Taylor was one of the finest and best-regarded composers of his generation, and one of the individuals actively promoted by August Jaeger of **Novello & Co.** His achievement is extremely impressive given the prejudice he faced daily in turn-of-the-century England because of his mixed-race heritage (his father was from Sierra Leone and his mother from England). He studied at the **Royal College of Music** from 1890 to 1897, starting out as a violinist, but increasingly working on composition, studying with **Sir Charles Villiers Stanford** by 1892. Success as a composer came early through publications by Novello & Co., commissions from **musical festivals** (starting in 1898), and the genre-shifting premiere of *Hiawatha's Wedding Feast* (1898), part of a trilogy of **cantatas** entitled *Scenes from the Song of Hiawatha* (1900). This cantata became immensely popular among choral societies and was eventually presented with costumes and scenery at the **Royal Albert Hall** between 1928 and 1939.

Coleridge-Taylor was active as a conductor, directing the Westmorland Musical Festival (1901–4) and the **Handel Society** (1904–12); he also taught composition at **Trinity College of Music** and the **Guildhall School of Music**. Aside from his cantatas and festival works, Coleridge-Taylor also had an avid interest in promoting African themes within his music, which stemmed in part from his meeting with the American poet Paul Laurence Dunbar and his trips to the United States (1904, 1906, and 1910), where he also met the composer and singer Henry Burleigh.

COLLEGE OF CHURCH MUSIC, LONDON. *See* TRINITY COLLEGE OF MUSIC.

COLLEGE OF ORGANISTS. *See* ROYAL COLLEGE OF ORGANISTS.

COMMUNITY SINGING. *Community singing* was the name given to organized, public, audience-participation singing during the middle of the 1920s. The phenomenon started in London and seems to have originated in the demise of the music halls, where audience participation had been a regular feature. Cinemas, concert halls (including the **Royal Albert Hall**), and other large buildings were opened for singing, led by a conductor and accompanied by either **organ** or piano and, on rare occasions, orchestras. The Community Singers Association was formed in 1925 to promote the movement; by 1926 large newspapers, such as the *Daily Express*, sought to capitalize on it, publishing songbooks for use by community singers. The songs sung at such events were limited to national songs, **hymns**, and songs about World War I. The Australian-born violinist turned choir director Gibson Young was associated with the movement.

COMPETITION FESTIVALS. *See* MUSICAL FESTIVALS.

CONCERT ROOMS. Using advertisements from the *London Gazette*, **Sir John Hawkins** constructs a helpful overview of **public concert** venues in the late 17th century, including concerts at White Fryers, Shandois-street (Chandos Street; Covent Garden)—a concert every evening except Sundays—the Academy at Little **Lincoln's Inn Fields**, the Musick School in the Essex buildings (the Strand), Bow Street (Covent Garden), and the York Buildings (Villiers Street). Many of these venues were associated with the concerts of **John Banister**; **Roger North** noted that "he [Banister] opened an obscure room in a publik house in White fryars; filled it with tables and seats, and made a side box with curtaines for the musick," a description that documents the tavernlike setting of the early concerts.

A long-standing series of concerts was given by the small-coal merchant **Thomas Britton** in rooms above his coal shop in Clerkenwell, accessed with difficulty via an external staircase. Hawkins records it was a long and narrow room with a low ceiling, and "the house itself was very old and low-built, and in every respect so mean, as to be a fit habitation for only a very poor man. Notwithstanding all, this mansion, despicable as it may seem, attracted to it as polite an audience as ever the **opera** did."

Not all the early concert venues were tavernlike or ill-suited to "sober recreation" (Hawkins). The York Buildings in Villiers Street offered a venue specifically constructed for music, described by North as a "great room." *See also* HANOVER SQUARE ROOMS; HICKFORD'S ROOM; PANTHEON.

CONCERTS OF ANCIENT MUSIC (ALSO CONSERTS OF ANTIENT MUSIC; CONCERTS OF ANCIENT MUSICK; CONSERTS OF ANTI-ENT MUSICK). A London concert society founded by a group of noblemen in 1776, sometimes referred to as the "King's Concerts." The concerts presented music that was 20 years old or older. While usually conducted by a professional (or at least an extremely talented amateur), the programs were organized by the amateur members of the board of directors, in rotation. Musicians associated with the concerts included **Joah Bates** (director, 1776–79), **Thomas Greatorex** (director, 1779–1831), **Sir George Smart**, and **Sir Henry Bishop** (director, 1843–49). The concerts were held first in the Queen's or West London Theatre (1776–95) and later at the **Hanover Square Rooms** (1804–49). The Concerts of Ancient Music ended in 1849, though efforts were made to revive them in 1867 and 1870. *See also* COOKE, TOM; CRAMER, JOHN BAPTIST; DRAGONETTI, DOMENICO; HANDEL COMMEMORATION; MENDELSSOHN, FELIX; PUBLIC CONCERTS; SMART, HENRY.

CONSORT SONG. A setting of vernacular, strophic poetry for solo voice or voices and an accompanying consort of instruments, generally assumed to be viols. The consort song (or "concerted song," as Wulstan [1985] proposes) arose in the 1580s with antecedents in the **choirboy plays**, the popularity of **viol** consorts, and flexible attitudes toward modes of performance. A number of composers are associated with the genre, include **Richard Farrant** and **Robert Parsons**, but it is chiefly with **William Byrd** that the consort song finds its richest development. Byrd's consort songs are typically contrapuntal with the sung voice part, but one strand in an imitative weave. As imitation assumes an equality of voice parts and as attitudes toward scoring were decidedly flexible, this meant that the instrumental parts were also ripe for singing as well, transforming the consort song into a vocal ensemble piece. This relationship is made explicit in collections like Byrd's 1588 anthology

Psalmes, Sonets, & Songs of Sadnes and Pietie, where the composer explains that many of the five-part texted works originated in versions for one voice and instrument. Additionally, he singles out the original vocal line as the "first singing part."

Consort songs with choral sections—the repetition of the last line of a stanza, for instance, or a concluding coda, as in the **carol** "From Virgin's Womb"—show the close relationship between the consort song and the verse **anthem**. *See also* CAVENDISH, MICHAEL.

COOKE, BENJAMIN (1734–93). Organist and composer. Cooke was from a family of musicians (his father, also named Benjamin, was a London music publisher, and his son, Robert, was a somewhat successful organist). He is remembered today primarily for his **Service** in G as well as a number of **glees**, which won prizes from the **Catch Club**. As a child he sang under **Johann Christoph Pepusch** at the **Academy of Ancient Music**. His positions included master of the choristers at Westminster Abbey (1757) and its organist (1762), and organist at St. Martin-in-the-Fields (1782); he held all three positions until his death. He was also widely involved in the contemporary London musical infrastructure, being conductor of the Academy of Ancient Music from 1752 to 1789 and a member of the **Society of Musicians**, the **Madrigal Society**, and the **Noblemen and Gentlemen's Catch Club**; he was also the assistant director of the 1784 **Handel Commemoration**.

COOKE, HENRY (ca. 1615–72). Singer, composer, lutanist. Although Cooke held a number of positions in the Royal Music, he is chiefly known as the master of the choristers of the **Chapel Royal** at the time of the Restoration until his death in 1672. In this position, Captain Cooke—"Captain" by virtue of his service in the Royalist Forces during the Civil War—trained notable musicians of the next generation, including **Pelham Humfrey** and **John Blow**, advanced the verse **anthem**, became a catalyst for musical Italianism, and rebuilt the chapel choir after years of forced inactivity, especially a problem with respect to treble voices.

Writers of the day noted his abilities with the Italian style, perhaps reflecting the influence of **Walter Porter** in the Chapel Royal of Charles I, in which Cooke was a chorister. **John Playford** goes so far as to refer to him as the "Orpheus of our time," a significant anticipation of **Henry Purcell**'s appellation as the "Orpheus Britannicus." **Samuel Pepys**, though impressed with his singing, disparaged his degree of vanity and called him a "vain coxcomb." (Pepys did not tolerate the vanity of musicians easily, as his description of Cooke's son-in-law, Humfrey, also demonstrates.) **John Evelyn**, in describing being entertained by Cooke, notes that he did so "with his voice and **theorbo**," likely a reference to self-accompaniment.

Outside the activities of the Chapel Royal, Cooke participated in important theatrical ventures including **Sir William Davenant**'s Rutland House Entertainment and *The Siege of Rhodes*. Humfrey married Cooke's daughter, Katherine, in 1672, and succeeded him as master of the choristers.

COOKE, TOM (ALSO THOMAS SIMPSON; 1782–1848). Tenor, instrumentalist, composer, and teacher of singing of Irish birth. Cooke arrived in London in 1813 after having trained as a violinist and composer in Dublin and fallen into singing. He sang at the **Lyceum Theatre** in 1813, and by 1815 he was heard regularly at **Drury Lane**, where he became the principal singer and orchestral leader for some years (he could play more than six instruments with great facility). Most of his compositions and arrangements were for the theater, though he did write a number of **glees** and **catches**, particularly for **pleasure gardens** at Vauxhall (where he served as one of the musical managers between 1828 and 1830) and the **Noblemen and Gentlemen's Catch Club**, where he was named a professional member in 1821. He was a member of the **Royal Philharmonic Society** and was the last director of the **Concerts of Ancient Music** (1846–48).

COPRARIO, JOHN (ca. 1570/80–1626). Violist and composer. Coprario, whose name is an Italian transformation of "Cooper" or "Cowper" that the composer had adopted by 1601, composed in a variety of genres, including two volumes of **lute ayres** (1606, 1612) that "contain duets and solos of a passionate gravity that finds no exact parallel in the songs of the period" (Caldwell, *OHEM*, vol. 1). However, his chief contribution lies in the innovation and development of the so-called **fantasia-suite**, or "set." The fantasia-suites were popular at the court of Charles I, blessed by royal participation; **John Playford** notes that the king "could play his Part exactly well on the Bass-**Viol**, especially of those Incomparable Phantasies of Mr. Coperario to the Organ." Scored for one or two violins, bass viol, and **organ**—the organ part is sometimes independent—the fantasia-suites consisted of a contrapuntal fantasia movement followed by two dances (Almain and Galliard). His consort fantasias for five and six players survive with Italian titles, suggestive of the notion that they were for vocal and/or instrumental performance.

Coprario was a composer-in-ordinary to Charles I and also the teacher of both **William** and **Henry Lawes**.

CORBETT, WILLIAM (ca. 1675–1748). Violinist and composer. Corbett, a onetime leader of the orchestra at the **Haymarket** Theatre prior to the advent of **George Frideric Handel**, is best known as a collector of music and instruments and the composer of *Le Bizzarie universali* (1728), 35 concertos (without concertino) written to evoke national and place-specific styles. His collection was amassed during a long residence in Italy and caused **Sir John Hawkins** to report he was involved in espionage: "Those who . . . were otherwise at a loss to account for his being able to lay out such sums as he was observed to do in the purchase of books and instruments, confidently asserted that besides his salary he had an allowance from the government, and that his business at Rome was to watch the motions of the Pretender [James Francis Edward Stuart]." **Charles Burney** refers to him as a "worthy professor"; Hawkins describes him as "a good composer, and a great collector of music and musical instruments."

CORDER, FREDERICK (1852–1932). Teacher, conductor, keyboardist, writer, and composer. Corder studied at the **Royal Academy of Music (2; RAM**; 1873–75) and won the prestigious **Mendelssohn Scholarship**, which allowed him to travel to Cologne (1875–78, where he studied with Ferdinand Hiller) and Milan (1878–79). For most of the 1880s, he attempted a career as an **opera** composer; *Nordissa*—his most successful work—was premiered in 1887 by the **Carl Rosa Opera Company**. During this period, he also took on numerous jobs as a conductor (of the Brighton Aquarium [1880–82] and the Devonshire Park Theatre in Eastbourne), organist, and music writer. He is perhaps best known as a teacher; he joined the staff of the RAM as a composition professor in 1888 and remained there until retirement in 1924 (**Sir Arnold Bax** was one of his students). He wrote articles for the first edition of *A Dictionary of Music and Musicians*, edited by **Sir George Grove**, translated the libretti of Richard Wagner's operas and music dramas, and wrote occasional pieces for the *Musical Quarterly* and the *Musical Times*. He was one of the founders and an early chairman of the Society of British Composers.

CORNELYS, THERESA (BORN TERESA IMER; ALSO MADAME TRENTI; 1723–97). Singer and impresario of Italian birth. As a singer, Cornelys toured much of Europe from her debut in Verona in 1741 until 1759, when she settled permanently in England. Arriving in London, she began organizing a series of concerts; from 1760 these concerts were held in Carlisle House in Soho Square. In 1765–67 part of this series was directed by **Johann Christian Bach** and **Carl Friederich Abel**. On the departure of Bach and Abel to Almack's and eventually the **Hanover Square Rooms**, **Felice Giardini** and Mattia Vento directed the concerts at Carlisle House. Due to bankruptcy, she lost control of Carlisle House in 1772 but continued to organize concerts there until 1778. In addition to concerts, Cornelys also mounted masquerades at Carlisle House, sometimes attracting more than 2,000 guests. She had a daughter with Giacomo Casanova.

CORNETT. Wind instrument of wood with fingerholes, played with a cup-shaped mouthpiece. The cornett was made in three sizes: treble (in G), tenor (in C), and a descant form (*cornettino*) in C or D. In England, as elsewhere, the treble cornett was frequently used as the soprano member of the trombone consort, both in secular repertories and as a voice-doubling instrument in church. Its purity of tone and vocal quality is attested by **Roger North** (1742), who wrote: "What can yield a tone so like an eunuch's voice as a true cornet pipe?" Though North also observes that it is "seldom well sounded," this likely reflects the instrument in a period of decline. **John Evelyn** (21 December 1662) observed with regret the replacing of the solemn wind music in the **Chapel Royal** with French-styled violin music: "This was the first time of change, and now we no more heard the cornet which gave life to the organ: that instrument quite left off in which the English were so skilful."

English music specifying cornetts includes **John Adson**'s *Courtly Masquing Ayres* (1621), two **fantasia-suites** by **John Hingeston**, and **Matthew Locke**'s "[Music] ffor his Majesty's Sagbutts & Cornetts" and "5 partt things ffor the cornetts."

CORNYSH, WILLIAM (?–1523). Composer and dramatist. Cornysh was active as a gentleman of the **Chapel Royal** during the reigns of both Henry VII and Henry VIII and was master of the children of the Chapel Royal from 1509. In addition to his musical duties, he was active as a dramatist and actor in court entertainments as well. His **partsong** contributions to the **Fayrfax Manuscript**, where he is identified as "William Cornyssh Junior," are notable both for their expressive quality and their extension of the medieval **carol**. Several liturgical works in the **Eton Choirbook** have been assumed to be his, works that show a range of style from the impressively florid to simpler textures. Recent work by David Skinner (1997) suggests these liturgical works, on the grounds of maturity of style and archival evidence, may be by the elder William Cornysh (d. ca. 1502), *informator choristarum* at Westminster (1479–91) and likely the father of the younger composer.

CORONATION MUSIC. As tradition plays a strong part in the formation of the coronation rite, it is unsurprising that certain texts and musical settings have much continuity in the crowning of the English monarch. For example, "I Was Glad" has been traditionally sung at the monarch's entry into Westminster Abbey since the coronation of Charles I in 1626; "Zadok the Priest" has been sung at the anointing since the 10th century, with **George Frideric**

Handel's setting, written for the coronation of George II in 1727, being particularly long-lived. Handel's expatriate status was no impediment to his role in defining the English royal idiom. That he was asked to provide music for George II's coronation, though not a member of the **Chapel Royal** nor appointed to Westminster Abbey, amply documents his celebrated status. And the use of the "Hallelujah" from *Messiah* at the coronations of George IV (1821) and Victoria (1838) speaks to the way his music had become royally iconic.

As iconic as the music for these two 19th-century coronations was, it was also entirely—save for Handel's donation—homegrown. The music at Victoria's coronation (1838) included English music from only the 18th and 19th centuries: works by **Thomas Attwood, William Boyce, William Knyvett,** and **Sir George Smart** alternated with Handel's "Zadok the Priest," the "Hallelujah" chorus, and the *Occasional Overture.* In the first half of the 20th century, coronation music became an increasingly broad statement about England's place within the cultural and political world, and, as a consequence, much more music was included in the ceremonies, and a great deal of it was commissioned explicitly for the occasion—and not only from British composers. Edward VII's coronation (1902) included commissioned marches from **Sir Alexander Campbell Mackenzie,** Camille Saint-Saëns, **Sir Frederic Hymen Cowen,** and Percy Godfrey, along with previously written marches by **Sir Edward Elgar,** Charles Gounod, Pytor Il'ych Tchaikovsky, and Richard Wagner. The music took in a much broader historical sweep, as well, with **Thomas Tallis** and **Orlando Gibbons** rubbing shoulders with **Sir Hubert Parry, Sir Charles Villiers Stanford, Sir Arthur Sullivan,** and **Samuel Sebastian Wesley** within the coronation service itself. George V's coronation (1911) followed suit: new marches by Mackenzie and Elgar for the processionals vied with new service music by Walter Alcock, **Sir Frederick Bridge,** Elgar, Parry, and Stanford, as well as the reintroduction of **Henry Purcell**; the marches before the service included music by many non-English composers. George VI's coronation (1937; Edward VIII abdicated before his coronation) included more before-service music by non-English composers, as well as a new *Coronation March* by **Sir William Walton.** Only with Elizabeth II's coronation in 1953 did the coronation music retreat to all English (plus Handel); Walton's specially composed *Orb and Sceptre March* and *Te Deum* were heard along with English music from the 15th century forward, much of which had been written for the coronations from 1902, 1911, and 1937. At the very point when Great Britain was beginning to become a truly multicultural nation, it presented a ceremonial face of a long-standing tradition—which, to that point, existed nowhere else, save in the creation of that tradition itself.

COSTA, SIR MICHAEL (1808–84). Conductor and composer of Italian birth. Costa was one of the most important conductors in mid-19th-century England. He brought to his ensembles a sense of discipline and worked within the **opera** theaters he conducted to eliminate as much of the deputy system (where members of the ensemble would send a deputy to rehearsal, but play for the performance themselves, thus destroying any hope of cohesion) as he could. Costa was trained in Naples and arrived in England in 1829 to conduct a **cantata** by his teacher Niccolò Antonio Zingarelli at the Birmingham **Musical Festival**. He remained in England and quickly established himself as a leading conductor, moving from a keyboardist employed by the King's Theatre, **Haymarket**, in 1830 to the director and conductor there (1833–46; by the time he left the institution, it had been renamed Her Majesty's Theatre). He founded the Royal Italian Opera at **Covent Garden** in 1847 and conducted it until 1868, returning to conduct at Her Majesty's Theatre, Haymarket, between 1871 and 1882. He was also well known for his choral conducting, as the director of the **Sacred Harmonic Society** from 1848 to 1882, the Handel Festivals at the **Crystal Palace** between 1857 and 1880, and the Birmingham Musical Festivals from 1849 to 1882, among others. He was also conductor of the **Royal Philharmonic Society** from 1846 to 1854.

Costa's compositions, while few in number, were mostly dramatic or choral. In his own time, his best-known works were the **oratorios** *Eli* (1855) and *Naaman* (1864), both of which premiered at the Birmingham Musical Festival. He was knighted in 1869.

COSYN, BENJAMIN (ca. 1580–1653). Organist and composer. Cosyn held several **organ** posts, the longest and last of them at Charterhouse (1626–43), brought to an end by the Puritan curtailment of organs in church. He was a significant anthologizer, as seen in the "Cosyn Virginal Book" (GB Lbl R.M. 23.L.4) from 1620, a collection of works by **Orlando Gibbons**, Cosyn, and others, and a 1652 collection (F Pc Rés 1185) containing likely autograph fair copies of music by **John Bull** and others.

COUNTERTENOR. A mature male voice generally singing in the alto register. Etymologically an Anglicization of "contratenor," "countertenor" often has the implication of a falsettist, though historically in the 17th century it may likely have referred to tenors singing in their high range. Purcellian countertenors included John Freeman and **John Pate**, the latter of whom **Samuel Pepys** lauded in superlative tones.

The English cathedral practice of an all-male choir with men, not boys, on the alto part has given the countertenor a particularly long-lived English identity, though the emergence of the modern countertenor soloist is deeply indebted to the career of Alfred Deller (1912–79), whose concerts and recordings beginning in the 1940s were important in the revival not only of early repertories but of the voice type itself. Although some will make a distinction between the choral falsettist and the soloist, it is important to note that Deller himself was a member of the cathedral choir at Canterbury.

The modern repertory for countertenor most notably includes the role of Oberon in **Benjamin Britten**'s *A Midsummer's Night Dream*, originally written for Deller. In the modern day, as well, countertenors have had some notable success in singing some of the operatic castrato roles.

COUNTRY DANCE. A body of dances and associated tunes that represent rustic dance traditions translated into genteel and aristocratic settings. The most famous collection of English country dance is **John Playford**'s *The English Dancing Master: or, Plaine and Easie Rules for the Dancing of Country Dances, with the Tune to each Dance* (1651). Reprinted well into the 18th century, the collection presents both choreography and melodies, many of which are **ballad** tunes. In the prefatory material Playford underscores the refinement of the pursuit, claiming that dancing is "excellent for recreation, after more serious studies, making the body active and strong, gracefull in deportment, and a quality very much beseeming a Gentleman."

COVENT GARDEN THEATRE. Opera house, ballet theater, and dramatic theater in London, known variously throughout its history as the Royal Italian Opera (1847–92) and the Royal Opera House (1892–present). The original Covent Garden Theatre was built in 1732 and used for a mixture of theatrical, operatic, and ballet performances. Fires destroyed the theater in 1808 and 1856; it was rebuilt each time. A major renovation of the space occurred between 1996 and 2000, and Covent Garden now seats 2,238 people. **George Frideric Handel** conducted operas and **oratorios** there between 1735 and 1759, **Sir Henry Bishop** was a music director there between 1810 and 1824, **Sir Michael Costa** directed the Royal Italian Opera there from 1847 to 1868, **Sir Thomas Beecham** used the theater frequently in the 1920s, and the **Carl Rosa Opera Company** staged works there between 1921 and 1924. It also briefly housed the Royal English Opera (1858–64). *See also* ARNOLD, SAMUEL; BARBIROLLI, SIR JOHN; BATTISHILL, JONATHAN; BENEDICT, SIR JULIUS; BLISS, SIR ARTHUR; BOULT, SIR ADRIAN CEDRIC; BRIDGE, FRANK; CLAY, FREDERIC; DIBDIN, CHARLES; ELLA, JOHN; FARINELLI; FISHER, JOHN ABRAHAM; GALLINI, GIOVANNI ANDREA BATTISTA; HOOK, JAMES; JULLIEN, LOUIS ANTOINE; LOCK HOSPITAL; MACCUNN, HAMISH; MAZZINGHI, JOSEPH; *MESSIAH*; RANDEGGER, ALBERTO; SHIELD,

WILLIAM; SMART, HENRY; STANLEY, JOHN; WEBBE, SAMUEL; WESLEY, SAMUEL; YOUNG, POLLY.

COVERDALE, MILES (1488?–1569). Cleric and translator. Best known for his edition of the English Bible (1535), the first English version in print, Coverdale also published a Lutheran-influenced anthology of *Goostly Psalmes and Spiritual Songes* (ca. 1635) that contained a number of **metrical psalms** set to unharmonized melodies.

COWARD, SIR HENRY (1849–1944). Choral conductor, teacher, writer on music, and composer. Largely self-taught, Coward became one of the greatest proponents of his age for sight-singing, especially using **Tonic Sol-fa**, and one of the best regarded choral conductors of his time. He began teaching Tonic Sol-fa to singers in the Sheffield area when he was 17 and founded several choirs in the area while working as a schoolteacher and then a headmaster. When his school closed in 1888, he decided to turn to music as a full-time profession, consequently taking degrees at Oxford (MusB in 1889 and MusD in 1894). From this point forward, he conducted most of the major choral associations in the north of England as their conductorships opened, including ones at Sheffield, Huddersfield, Barnesley, Preston, and Newcastle-on-Tyne, among others. He founded and was the choral conductor of the Sheffield Musical Union (1876) and the Sheffield **Musical Festival** (1896), and took 200 voices on a tour of North America in 1911 with the composer **Sir Edward Elgar**. In the 1920s Coward became a frequent contributor to the *Musical News and Herald*, the house magazine of the **Curwen Press**; within it, he continued to promote singing but also frequently criticized jazz in a racist way. He was the president of the **Tonic Sol-fa College** from 1926 until his death. Coward was knighted in 1926.

COWEN, SIR FREDERIC HYMEN (1852–1935). Conductor, composer, pianist, and writer on music. During his life, Cowen was most famous as a conductor, but well known for his Symphony no. 3 in C minor ("The Scandanavian"; 1880, London) and the **oratorio** *Ruth* (1887, Three Choirs Festival). While he was a regular contributor to the **musical festival** circuit until 1910, most of his works are forgotten today. Private study in England was followed by training in Leipzig (nominally under the teachers at the conservatory there, though he was not enrolled) and at the Stern Conservatory in Berlin. His parents funded concerts in London that were his first forays into piano performance and composition, starting in 1869. Aside from conducting his own compositions, he began regular work as a conductor in 1880, conducting the **Proms**, the **Royal Philharmonic Society** (1888–92 and 1900–1907), the **Hallé Orchestra** (1895–99), the Liverpool Philharmonic Society (1896–1913), the Bradford Festival Choral Society (1897–1915), the Scottish Orchestra (1900–1910), the Cardiff Festival (1902–10), and the Handel Festival (1903–23; his last appearance as a conductor was at this festival in 1923). He was the author of several books, including autobiographical works and studies of **Franz Joseph Haydn**, Wolfgang Amadeus Mozart, Gioachino Rossini, and **Felix Mendelssohn**. Cowen was knighted in 1911.

CRAMER, JOHN BAPTIST (ALSO JOHANN BAPTIST; "GLORIOUS JOHN"; 1771–1858). Pianist, publisher, teacher, and composer of German birth. Cramer's family was active in the London musical scene. His father, Wilhelm Cramer, was a prominent London violinist, associated with **Johann Christian Bach** and **Carl Friedrich Abel** and founder of the **Professional Concert**; his brother, François Cramer, was **Master of the King's Music** from 1837 to 1848 and was the leading violinist of the **Concerts of Ancient Music** for several decades. John Cramer was well known as a pianist, especially for his performances of the works of Johann Sebastian Bach, Wolfgang Amadeus Mozart, and Ludwig van Beethoven (he introduced many of Beethoven's piano works to the London public). According to Ferdinand Ries, Beethoven considered Cramer to be the best contemporary pianist and thought Cramer's pedagogical method, *Studio per il pianoforte* (2 vols., 1804 and 1810), to be excellent preparation for the performance of Beethoven's works. Cramer toured the Continent on several occasions, meeting all of the major composers of his day.

Cramer invested in publishing ventures beginning in 1805. The third iteration of Cramer's publishing firm, J. B. Cramer and Co., existed from 1824 to 1964, when it was taken over by Kemble & Co. He was one of the founding members of the **Royal Philharmonic Society** (1813—where his piano concertos were heard with some frequency) and the **Royal Academy of Music** (2; 1822). His farewell concert in 1829 included appearances by **Domenico Dragonetti**, **Felix Mendelssohn**, and **Ignaz Moscheles**.

CRANFORD, WILLIAM (d. ca. 1645). Singer and composer. Cranford was a **vicar-choral** at St. Paul's Cathedral, London, from 1624 or likely earlier. **Sir John Hawkins** describes him as a "singing man of St. Paul's, the author of many excellent rounds and **catches** in [**John**] **Hilton**'s and [**John**] **Playford**'s Collections." The catches may show a light side; he is, however, also the composer of verse **anthems** and a number of consorts, which may accord better with Lord North's description: "Mr. Cranford, whom I knew, a sober plain-looking Man: his pieces mixed with Majesty, Gravity, Honeydew Spirit and Variety."

CROFT, WILLIAM (1678–1727). Composer and organist. Croft emerged as one of the leading English composers in the first part of the 18th century— significantly, a time when foreign importation was ascendant. Brought up in the **Chapel Royal** under **John Blow**, his tie to the elder composer would echo in his succeeding him as composer and master of the children of the Chapel Royal as well as organist at Westminster Abbey in 1708. Croft received the DMus at Oxford in 1713 upon the submission of two **odes** ("With Noise of Cannon" and "Laurus Cruentas"). A composer in a number of genres, he is best known for his church music, published in a two-volume collection, *Musica Sacra* (1724). Although his verse **anthems** may be seen to develop the form, they also show the influence of the Restoration style, as in, for instance, solo writing over an ostinato.

Croft composed several **hymn** tunes still in use today, none more popularly so than "St. Anne" (familiarly sung to the text "O God Our Help in Ages Past"). First published anonymously, there are later ascriptions to Croft, buttressed by the fact that he was at one time the organist of St. Anne's, Soho.

Charles Burney's description of his character suggests an admirable array of qualities: "We hear of no illiberal traits of envy, malevolence, or insolence. He neither headed nor abetted fiddling factions; but insensibly preserving the dignity of his station, without oppressing or mortifying his inferiors by reminding them of it, the universal respect he obtained from his talents and eminence in the profession seems to have been blended with personal affection."

CROSS, LETITIA (1682–1737). Actress and singer. Cross, notably early in her teenaged years, came to prominence on the London stage in productions that featured the late works by **Henry Purcell**. Songs that she first sang include "I Attempt from Love's Sickness to Fly" (*Indian Queen*) and the demanding **mad song** "From Rosy Bowers" (*The Comical History of Don Quixote*).

CROTCH, WILLIAM (1775–1847). Composer, teacher, organist, and painter. Crotch was one of the most famous musicians of his own time, both as a lecturer on music and as a composer. His **oratorio** *Palestine* (1812) was performed frequently in London and at provincial **musical festivals** for several decades before falling out of favor. (**Sir Michael Costa** revived it somewhat successfully in 1874, but it, like most of Crotch's music, is now largely forgotten.)

Crotch was a child prodigy; in his early years he toured throughout Great Britain to show off his prodigious talents at sight-reading and keyboard performance. He was named an assistant (1786–88) to **John Randall**, music professor at Cambridge, and then continued his musical studies at Oxford, involving himself in the musical infrastructure of that city, where he became organist of Christ Church in 1790, took degrees (BMus in 1794; DMus in 1799), and taught from 1797 until his death as the Heather Professor of Music. In the early years of his Oxford professorship, Crotch's talents as a lecturer on music history, theory, and aesthetics became well known. He delivered similar lectures at the Royal Institution in London between 1805 and 1807. By 1807 Crotch resigned his Oxford organist positions and settled permanently in London. (Since there were no residentiary duties for the Oxford Professor of Music at this time, he retained that post.)

While not greatly active as a performer, Crotch composed and continued lecturing on music. He was named the principal of the **Royal Academy of Music (2)** on its founding in 1822 and taught harmony, counterpoint, and composition there until 1832. He frequently directed the **Royal Philharmonic Society** and conducted his works at **musical festivals**. His last public appearance was as organist of the **Handel Commemoration** in Westminster Abbey in 1834, though he continued to write on music and other subjects. His most influential books in the 19th century were the *Elements of Musical Composition* (1812; reprinted twice) and *The Substance of Several Courses of Lectures* (1831; drawn from his musical lectures starting in the 1800s).

CRYSTAL PALACE. London exhibition and performance venue. The Crystal Palace was built in 1851 in Hyde Park as part of the Great Exhibition. It was moved to Sydenham and enlarged in 1854. It had two performance venues that were in use for concerts of all varieties until it was destroyed by fire in 1936. Initially, the ensemble housed a military-style wind band; when **Sir August Manns** took over the direction of the ensemble in 1855, it was gradually turned into an orchestra that presented 10 concerts per week. Manns introduced many English composers to the public at these concerts, as well as continental composers such as Pytor Il'ych Tchaikovsky. A prominent feature of these concerts were the analytical programs written by **Sir George Grove** between 1856 and 1894, who was for a time the secretary of the company that ran the building. Manns continued these concerts until 1900. The building also became a venue for large competitions, celebrations, and **musical festivals**. The London **Handel** Festivals used the Crystal Palace as its performance venue from 1857 until their dissolution in 1926. The **Tonic Sol-fa Association** frequently held gigantic exhibition concerts and choral contests there, directed by such stalwarts as Joseph Proudman and **Henry Coward**. Brass bands, temperance choral organizations, and others held yearly contests. It was also the location for the 1911 Festival of Empire. *See also* BENEDICT, SIR JULIUS; BUSH, ALAN; COSTA, SIR MICHAEL; EXETER HALL; HANDEL COMMEMORATION; MACCUNN,

HAMISH; MCNAUGHT, WILLIAM GRAY; PROUT, EBENEZER; SA-
CRED HARMONIC SOCIETY; STANFORD, SIR CHARLES VILLIERS;
VOCAL ASSOCIATION.

CURWEN, JOHN (1816–80). Writer, publisher and propagator of the **Tonic
Sol-fa** sight-singing notation and system; father of **John Spencer Curwen**.
Curwen initially trained to be a Congregationalist minister and held a degree
from Wymondly Independent College (later Coward College) of the University of London. Long interested in children's pedagogy, he created a reading
method called "Look and Say" and wrote a moral instructional children's
book titled *The History of Eleanor Vanner* (1841).

While not a musician himself, he was charged by the Congregational
Church in 1841 to find a method to teach children congregational psalmody.
Research led him to a book by **Sarah Glover** describing a Sol-fa system
(later called the "Norwich Sol-fa") that he adapted (without her permission)
into Tonic Sol-fa. Curwen published numerous method books on the notation, starting in the 1840s, and founded institutions to promote it, including
the **Tonic Sol-fa Association** (1851), the **Tonic Sol-fa College** (1869), and
a publishing company, the Tonic Sol-fa Agency (later called J. Curwen and
Sons and the **Curwen Press**) to provide method books and music and a
magazine, the *Tonic Sol-fa Reporter* (with two issues published in 1851 and
a regular run starting in 1853), to publicize it. Until 1864, Curwen worked on
Tonic Sol-fa in tandem with his Congregationalist ministry; in that year, he
turned to music promotion full time.

Within Curwen's work, music was always of secondary importance. The
focus of his activities at all times was to use music to improve the morals of
the individual and to aid moral philanthropic causes, including church music,
temperance, missionary work, children's education, the antislavery movement, and many others. He continually noted the use of Tonic Sol-fa by such
philanthropic movements, and he frequently provided subventions for them,
so long as they would use Tonic Sol-fa notation. He modeled his promotion
of Tonic Sol-fa notation on the temperance movement, including publiciz-
ing it through large, traveling evangelical-style meetings and demonstrations
that created local classes and societies to study and sing from the notation in
their wake and the issuing of pledgelike certificates denoting various levels
of certificates of Tonic Sol-fa "proficiency." Curwen believed in the power
of music to aid in the moral reform or the moral decay of the individual, and
consequently he used his growing publishing apparatus to produce music
that would reflect his dissenting, philanthropic values while "improving" the
taste of the individual. Tonic Sol-fa methods would thus begin with **hymns**,
simple songs about patriotism, hard work, and the beauty of the country, and

work toward the **oratorio** choruses of **George Frideric Handel** and **Felix Mendelssohn**.

By the end of Curwen's life, the popularity of Tonic Sol-fa eclipsed all of the other rival sight-singing systems in Great Britain (including those of **John Hullah** and **Joseph Mainzer**); the *Reporter* claimed that hundreds of thousands of British subjects had been trained using the system, and its use spread far beyond the island to missionary fields touched by British organizations (including Australia, China, India, Japan, Madagascar, New Zealand, South Africa, and many other territories), as well as being used in North America by members of the Church of Jesus Christ of the Later-Day Saints and throughout the world by the **Salvation Army**.

CURWEN, JOHN SPENCER (1847–1916). Composer, musician, writer, and publisher; propagator of the **Tonic Sol-fa** sight-singing notation system; son of **John Curwen**. While throughout his career as Tonic Sol-fa's primary propagator, John Curwen treated music as a means to a moral and philanthropic end, he realized that the various branches of the Tonic Sol-fa organization needed the imprimatur of a professional musician, in order to explain, defend, and promote the sight-singing notation to the British musical establishment. Consequently, Spencer Curwen attended the **Royal Academy of Music** (2; RAM), taking lessons from **Sir George Alexander Macfarren**, **Sir Arthur Sullivan**, and **Ebenezer Prout**. He began writing articles and editorials for the *Tonic Sol-fa Reporter* in 1870 and was named a fellow of the RAM in 1879. At this point, the apparatus of the **Tonic Sol-fa Association** and the **Curwen Press** was too large to be controlled by a single individual. Spencer Curwen therefore became the de facto head of the Tonic Sol-fa movement upon his father's death in 1880, editing the *Reporter* and heading the **Tonic Sol-fa College**, while his brother, Joseph Spedding Curwen (?–1919), took over the day-to-day aspects of running the business and publishing company.

Spencer Curwen's interests were always in the improvement of the individual's musical tastes, whether or not those tastes were aided by Tonic Sol-fa. Throughout his career as publisher of the Curwen Press magazines, he gradually turned them from catering to especially philanthropic-minded musicians to amateur musicians in general, by increasingly including articles on items of general interest, such as discussions of the **musical festivals** and laudatory descriptions of modern composers. About the time he renamed the *Reporter* to the *Musical Herald* (1889), he began to distance the journal from dissenting philanthropic causes, including temperance and missionary work (though the Curwen Press would remain prominent publishers of temperance music and would fund a prize at temperance choir contests well into the 1910s). In spite of these reforms, under his control, the journal and publishing company remained firmly committed to the amateur singer, and not the instrumentalist. He was an early supporter of competition festivals for amateur musicians (he sometimes erroneously claimed to be their founder) and used them as a way of encouraging an excellent standard of choral music—though through promoting a relatively conservative repertoire of **oratorios**, **cantatas**, and partsongs.

CURWEN PRESS (ALSO THE TONIC SOL-FA AGENCY; CURWEN & SONS). Music publishing firm. The company was initially incorporated in 1863 and existed until 1984. It was the major printer of **Tonic Sol-fa** notation throughout the 19th century and published the journals associated with the **Tonic Sol-fa Association**, including the *Tonic Sol-fa Reporter*, the *Musical Herald*, and the *Musical News and Herald*. In its first decades the Curwen Press printed pedagogy books, **oratorio** and **cantata** scores (both the classics, such as **George Frideric Handel**'s *Messiah* and works specifically written in Tonic Sol-fa notation), and Tonic Sol-fa journals almost exclusively under the aegis of founder **John Curwen** and his sons **John Spencer Curwen** and Joseph Spedding Curwen. In the first decades of the 20th century, the press published many well-known figures of the second generation of the **English Musical Renaissance**, such as **Ralph Vaughan Williams**, **Philip Heseltine**, and **Dame Ethel Smyth**, releasing a mixture of vocal and instrumental music. In 1908, the press also began limited printings of high-quality books.

CUTTING, FRANCIS (?–1596). Lutanist and composer. Cutting's compositions, including dances, divisions, and arrangements of keyboard works, appear prominently in William Barley's 1596 anthology, *New Booke of Tabliture*, alongside works by **John Dowland**.

D

D'OYLY CARTE OPERA COMPANY. Organization founded by the impresario and composer Richard d'Oyly Carte, principally for the promotion of operettas by **Sir William Schwenck Gilbert** and **Sir Arthur Sullivan**. The company existed as an entity from 1879 to 1982, held as a private, forprofit venture until 1961 and a charitable trust from 1961 to 1982. While it celebrated its centenary in 1975, this was more to mark the anniversary of the collaboration of Richard d'Oyly Carte, Gilbert, and Sullivan for *Trial by Jury*, which was presented in a theater managed by d'Oyly Carte. The D'Oyly Carte Opera Company followed a shorter venture organized by Richard d'Oyly Carte to promote Gilbert and Sullivan, the Comedy Opera Company (1877–79), which produced *The Sorcerer* (1877) and *H.M.S. Pinafore* (1878). When the company formed in 1879, it promoted London productions of Gilbert and Sullivan operettas and touring companies in the British provinces and North America, and licensed other companies to tour the works on other continents.

The company built the **Savoy Theatre** (1881) especially for the production of operetta, and the English Opera House for the production of grand **opera** in English. The Savoy survived, flourished, and still exists today; the English Opera House had one successful production (Sullivan's *Ivanhoe*, 1891) before being sold. After Richard d'Oyly Carte's death, the company was run by his widow, Helen Lenior d'Oyly Carte (1901–13), Rupert d'Oyly Carte (1913–48; a son by a previous marriage), and Bridget d'Oyly Carte (Richard's granddaughter). Aside from Gilbert and Sullivan, the Company employed such composers and conductors as **Alfred Cellier**, **Sir Edward German**, **Sir Alexander Campbell Mackenzie**, and Edward Solomon. An attempt was made to revive the company in 1988, but the new version of the organization folded in 2003.

DANNREUTHER, EDWARD (1844–1905). Pianist, impresario, Wagnerian, writer, teacher, and composer of German origin. Dannreuther, along with **William Ashton Ellis**, was one of the most important Wagnerians living in England in the second half of the 19th century. His translations and emendations of Richard Wagner's prose works, as well as his articles on Wagner for **Sir George Grove**'s *Dictionary of Music and Musicians* and his reading of a Ludwig van Beethoven/Wagner axis, influenced his writing in *The Oxford History of Music* (1905 edition) and powered the Anglophonic reading of music history for decades. In a series of concerts at his Orme Square home (1876–93), Dannreuther introduced English intellects and musicians to the chamber music of Johannes Brahms, Pytor Il'ych Tchaikovsky, Richard Strauss, **Sir Charles Villiers Stanford**, and **Sir Hubert Parry**. He was also a noted pianist and presented English premieres of a number of English and continental piano concertos.

Dannreuther was born in Germany, though he moved with his family to Cincinnati in 1846. He attended the Conservatory at Leipzig from 1860 to 1863. The American Civil War halted his family's ability to support him, and consequently, he left Lepzig in 1863 for London, under the sponsorship of **Henry Frothergill Chorley**. Aside from concert tours, he spent the remainder of his life in England. On his arrival, he quickly began to organize fellow Wagnerians, through being part of the so-called Working Men's Society (founded in 1867), which played through most of Wagner's music dramas; being a founder of the London Wagner Society (1872; president, 1895–1905); promoting the London Wagner Festival in 1877 (hosting Wagner in his home); and writing and lecturing. He was also a piano professor at the **Royal College of Music** (1895).

DARTINGTON INTERNATIONAL SUMMER SCHOOL. Summer school and **musical festival** for music and the arts held at Dartington Hall in Devon. It began as the Bryanston Summer School in 1948 and moved to Dartington Hall in 1953. Notable teachers in residence at the school include Luciano Berio, Nadia Boulanger, Elliot Carter, Aaron Copland, Georges Enescu, Paul Hindemith, **Imogen Holst**, and Luigi Nono. William Glock, sometime conductor of the **British Broadcasting Corporation Proms**, directed the school between 1948 and 1979. Peter Maxwell-Davies directed it from 1980 to 1984, succeeded by Gavin Henderson.

DAVENANT, SIR WILLIAM (1606–68). Dramatist and poet. Davenant figures prominently in the establishment of **opera** in England in the 1650s. In 1656 his *The First Dayes Entertainment at Rutland-House by Declamations and Musick: after the manner of the Ancients* was performed; its nature, as Dent (1967) describes it, was as a "lecture-recital in costume," a format that would allow it to gratify operatic taste while subverting Puritan bans on stage productions. Later that same year he produced *The Siege of Rhodes . . . a Representation by the Art of Perspective in Scenes . . . the Story sung in Recitative Musick*. This might properly be seen as the first English opera, though none of the music by **Henry Lawes**, **Henry Cooke**, **Matthew Locke**, Charles Coleman, and George Hudson survives. Following the Restoration, Davenant turned his attention to semi-operatic adaptations of **William Shakespeare**.

As a royalist, he fled England in the 1640s and went abroad to France, where he would have been exposed both to Roman opera as well as to French operatic works. Davenant was knighted in 1643.

DAVIES, SIR (HENRY) WALFORD (1869–1941). Composer, organist, teacher, writer, and radio broadcaster. As a composer, his most popular work during his own life was the **oratorio** *Everyman* (premiered 1904 at the Leeds **Musical Festival** and performed for the next two decades throughout Great Britain); his best-known work today is the "RAF March Past," as orchestrated by **Sir George Dyson**. Davies received early training as a chorister and **Sir Walter Parratt**'s pupil assistant at St. George's Chapel, Windsor. He attended the **Royal College of Music** (1890) and was named teacher of counterpoint there in 1895, where one of his students was **Rutland Boughton**. During his time in London, he was organist for a number of churches, before taking an appointment at the Temple Church as organist and choirmaster (1898–1919). He also conducted the **Bach Choir** (1903–7). After the war, he was Professor of Music at Aberystwyth University in Wales (1919–26), the Gresham Professor of Music at the University of London (1924–39), organist at St. George's Chapel in Windsor (1927–32), and the voice of a popular **British Broadcasting Corporation** educational radio series titled *Music and the Ordinary Listener* (1926–39). He was knighted in 1922 and was **Master of the King's Music** from 1934 until his death.

DAVIS, MARY (MOLL) (ALSO DAVIES; ca. 1650–1708). Singer, actress, dancer, royal mistress. Davis's performances brought her to royal attention and favor; she became a mistress of Charles II around 1667. She was the mother of the king's youngest child, Lady Mary Tudor, who appeared with her in **John Blow**'s *Venus and Adonis*, the mother singing the role of Venus and the daughter the role of Cupid. She married the recorder player and composer **James Paisible** in 1686.

DAVY, RICHARD (ca. 1465–1538). Composer. Davy is associated with Magdalen College, Oxford, as organist and *informator choristarum* in the early 1490s. Attempts to locate him after 1494 are speculative, although a time as a **vicar-choral** at Exeter or as a singing-man at Fotheringhay are possible. Davy is best known for his contributions to the **Eton Choirbook**, which include an incomplete four-voice responsorial setting of the Matthew **Passion**, the first Passion setting by a named composer.

DAY, JOHN (1522–84). Printer. Day's musical printing made a rich contribution to the dissemination of the **metrical psalm** and the development of reformed devotional and liturgical music. His *The Whole Book of Psalmes* was first issued in 1562, giving unharmonized melodies for the metrical texts of the Sternhold and Hopkins psalter. In 1563 Day published harmonized tunes (the melody generally in the tenor) in *The Whole Book of Psalmes in Foure Partes*. His *Certaine Notes set forthe in Foure and Three Parts*, first fully printed in 1565 as *Mornyng and Evenyng Prayer and Communion, set forthe in foure partes*, comprises **anthems** and liturgical material.

THE DEATH OF MINNEHAHA. See *THE SCENES FROM THE SONG OF HIAWATHA.*

DELIUS, SIR FREDERICK (1862–1934). Composer, born and buried in England, who spent most of his intellectual and musical life outside that country, though he became immensely popular there in the last years of his life. Delius grew up in a musical family of German descent, but his father meant him to enter the family's wool business. When, in 1884, it became apparent Delius would not take to this, he left England only to return for the occasional concert and for a brief period at the beginning of World War I. He spent a few years in America, where he was educated in Florida by Thomas F. Ward, a local organist, before moving briefly to Virginia and New York. He had 18 months of study in Leipzig, where he met Edvard Grieg, who became a champion of his works. He settled permanently in France in 1888.

Recognition of Delius's talents in England was slow to develop. He organized and funded a successful concert of his works in London in 1899 and was championed by **Sir Henry Wood** (in a concert of his Piano Concerto in 1907) and then by **Sir Thomas Beecham**, who premiered Delius's *Mass of Life* (composed 1904–5; London public premiere in 1909); this, along with the **cantata** *Sea-Drift* (premiered on the Continent in 1906; presented in England at the Sheffield **Musical Festival** in 1908), became his most popular choral piece. Beecham conducted a festival of six concerts dedicated to Delius in 1929 at the **Queen's Hall**. His popularity in England (mostly due to Beecham's festival) is seen in the large crowd that witnessed his interment in a small church graveyard at the Surrey village of Limpsfield. He was named a CH in 1929.

DENT, EDWARD J. (1876–1957). Musicologist, teacher, translator, composer, and critic. Dent holds the curious position of being one of the most respected as well as the most reviled critics of his time. His negative interwar statements about Ludwig van Beethoven and **Sir Edward Elgar** (including his references to *The Dream of Gerontius* as "Gerry's Nightmare" and his harsh condemnation of the composer and his music in Guido Adler's *Handbuch der Musikgesichte* [1924]), which led to public outcries, are balanced against his great professional success in encouraging English musicians to embrace pre-19th-century repertoire for performance.

Dent was educated at Eton and Cambridge and was a member of what Brett refers to as "the queer set in that haven for homosexuals at the turn of the century" (2002). From 1902 to 1918, and again from 1926 to 1941, he was a fellow of King's College, Cambridge, and the Professor of Music there in the later period. In his time there, he reorganized the requirements and expectations of the MusB degree, creating a program that catered to the intellectual professional musician. He was active as a music writer and critic in London between 1918 and 1926, and spent his last two decades in London after he left Cambridge. He was particularly active in the field of **opera**—both as a libretto translator and as a scholar—and was active in the intellectual infrastructure of English music, being the president of the International Society for Contemporary Music (1923–38), the International Musical Society (1931–49), and the **Royal Musical Association** (1928–35).

DERING, LADY MARY (1629–1704). Composer. A pupil of **Henry Lawes** from 1648, Dering was an accomplished composer, earning the praise of her teacher: "[You] are yourself so good a *Composer*, that few of any sex have arriv'd to such perfection." Lawes dedicated his 1655 anthology, *Select Ayres and Dialogues*, to her and included several of her songs in the collection.

DERING, RICHARD (ca. 1580–1630). Composer and organist. Dering took the BMus at Oxford in 1610. His conversion to Roman Catholicism is resonant with both his time spent in Italy and also the necessity to work as an expatriate abroad, as he did as organist of an English convent in Brussels from 1617. In 1625 he returned to England as a royal musician to both Charles I and his queen, Henrietta Maria, whose Roman Catholic Chapel would presumably prove spiritually congenial.

Dering's Italianate music with basso continuo unsurprisingly includes Latin motets that ironically were favored by Oliver Cromwell. His English music includes two examples of "cries"—*City Cries* and *Country Cries*—that popularly combine contrapuntal viols with vocal evocations of vendors' calls and the like.

DIALOGUE. Seventeenth-century declamatory settings that feature exchanges between singers in character. Significantly, the dialogue sees the notion of recitative develop in England and also nurtures the development of dramatic musical scenes. Early examples of the dialogue appear in the music of **Alfonso Ferrabosco the younger**, but with more declamatory maturity mid-century with composers like **Nicholas Lanier** and **Henry Lawes**. The subjects of the dialogues are often conventionalized, with the pastoral nymph-and-shepherd trope common, as was the Charon dialogue, an exchange between the boatman of the River Styx and a variety of passengers to the underworld. More dramatically hefty were biblical and mythological dialogues by **John Hilton** (the younger) and **Robert Ramsey**, works that Spink (1974) likens to "small-scale **opera** and **oratorio**." Ramsey's setting of the Biblical story of Saul and the Witch of Endor ("In Guilty Night") found a later echo in **Henry Purcell**'s setting of the same text.

DIBDIN, CHARLES (1745–1814). Composer, dramatist, poet, novelist, actor, and entertainer. Dibdin was largely self-taught as a composer, though he did have **organ** lessons from **James Kent** and Peter Fussell, the successive organists at Winchester Cathedral. Between 1760 and 1781 he composed **operas**, pastorals, and afterpieces for most of the major venues in London, including **Covent Garden**, **Sadler's Wells**, and **Drury Lane**. None of these compositions remain in the repertory. During this time, he also composed music for (and occasionally managed the music at) the Ranelagh **pleasure gardens**. From 1781 to 1784 Dibdin entered into a partnership with Charles Hughes to create the Royal Circus, an entertainment complex that featured horseback riding tricks and music sung by children.

After a stint in debtors' prison, Dibdin began a provincial tour to raise money for a planned emigration to India. He did not make the voyage but used the idea of "table entertainments" developed from this tour (a combination of singing topical songs and monologues) and presented them in London from 1789 to 1805. These entertainments became so successful that Dibdin built two small theaters to house them: one off the Strand, and one in Leicester Square. Both were named the Sans Souci Theatre. His songs were successful with both the public and the government; William Pitt the Younger offered a pension of £200 per year for Dibdin to compose patriotic songs during the Napoleonic Wars. (The pension was later revoked.) Dibdin left the stage in 1805 and continued to write songs for a London publisher until he suffered a debilitating stroke. He composed more than 300 songs, of which "Tom Bowling" and "Tight Little Island" may be the best known today.

DIDO AND AENEAS. A fully sung dramatic work composed by **Henry Purcell** to a libretto by Nahum Tate, later to become poet laureate. The fully sung nature of the work is rare both for Purcell and for the Restoration stage, and though it is tempting to see it as an **opera**, its short duration relative to continental models suggests that it is closer perhaps to a **masque**. The libretto freely adapts Virgil, with the story as follows: Aeneas, a warrior prince, sets out to found a new Troy on the banks of the river Tiber. A storm blows him to Carthage and to Queen Dido, with whom he falls in love. Witches—a sorceress and her coven—conjure up a false Mercury to call Aeneas back to his original goal; this is a trick calculated to devastate Dido who, abandoned, dies.

The original performance history of the work is cloudy. A printed epilogue by **Thomas Durfey** is dated 1689 and cites that the "Opera of Dido and Aeneas" was "perform'd at Mr. Preist's [Josias Priest's] Boarding School at Chelsey." However, whether this performance at a school for young gentlewomen was the first is open to question, especially as a sister work, **John Blow**'s *Venus and Adonis*, was performed both at court and in Chelsea, a double-venue model that is tempting to posit for *Dido* as well. Scholars have proposed various earlier dates, including 1684 (Wood and Pinnock, 1992) and 1687 (Walkling, 1994).

The libretto is richly prone to allegorical interpretation and, dependent on chronology, may be seen to offer comment on the reign of William and Mary (Buttrey, 1967/68) or James II and the Declaration of Indulgence (Walkling, 1994).

The music has a propensity both for dances—a French theatrical influence—and for ground basses. Dido's lament at the end of the opera, sung over a lachrymal descending chromatic tetrachord, is justly revered as one of Purcell's most moving compositions.

DOLMETSCH, (EUGÈNE) ARNOLD (1858–1940). Instrument builder, music editor, and violinist. Dolmetsch was one of the major figures in the early 20th-century revival of historical instruments and period-music practices. His studio for building copies and refurbishing original instruments, founded in Haslemere, Surrey, in 1920 became a leading center for the study of early music and its performance, and the Dolmetsch Foundation (established 1928) continues this work today. The Haslemere Festival, begun in 1925 by Dolmetsch, also became a well-known location for the performance of early music.

Dolmetsch came from a family of instrument makers. After private study with Henri Vieuxtemps at the Brussels Conservatory, Dolmetsch studied at the **Royal College of Music** (1883–85). From 1885 to 1889 he taught violin at Dulwich College. From 1889 forward he began building his first copies of early instruments, including **lutes**, clavichords, and harpsichords; he also worked with **viol** consorts and later, recorders. From 1904 to 1914 he spent time working for instrument firms in the United States of America and Paris, but returned to London in 1914 before moving permanently to Haslemere in

1917. Aside from editing manuscripts of early music, some of which were in long use at the early music festival in Haslemere, Dolmetsch was also the author of *The Interpretation of Music in the XVII and XVIII Centuries Revealed by Evidence* (London, 1915), one of the first major texts in the burgeoning historical performance movement.

DORSET GARDEN THEATRE. Designed by Christopher Wren, the Duke's Theatre at Dorset Garden was built in 1671 for the company of players under the direction of **Sir William Davenant**, one of two theater companies under royal patent in the early years of the Restoration. The other, the King's Company, was under the direction of Thomas Killigrew at the Theatre Royal in **Drury Lane**. In addition to regular plays, the Duke's Theatre produced operatic entertainments (i.e. **semi-operas**) and was the venue for Davenant's operatic **William Shakespeare** adaptations in the 1670s, **John Dryden** and **Louis Grabu**'s unsuccessful *Albion and Albanius* (1685), **Henry Purcell**'s *King Arthur* (1691) and *Fairy Queen* (1692), and the 1701 settings of Congreve's *Judgment of Paris* by **Godfrey Finger**, **John Eccles**, **Daniel Purcell**, and **John Weldon**.

The music room for the instrumentalists was located above the proscenium arch. However, in Shadwell's publication of *The Tempest* (1676) he notes "The Front of the Stage is open'd, and the Band of 24 Violins, with the Harpsicals and Theorbo's which accompany the Voices, are placed between the Pit and the Stage."

DOWLAND, JOHN (1563–1626). Lutanist and composer. Widely regarded as the leading **lute** figure of his day, it is ironic that he was not appointed to an English court position until 1612, long after his career was well established and 18 years after the first likely opening appeared. Unsurprisingly, he thus spent a significant time abroad in the service of the ducal court at Wolfenbüttel and the Danish court of Christian IV (1598–1606). Early in his career he also enjoyed the patronage of Sir Henry Cobham in Paris, and it was there that he took up Roman Catholicism, a politically problematic move that he subsequently rejected in 1595.

As a composer, Dowland's contribution to the lute-song repertory (*see* AYRE) not only gives a large number of its most familiar examples, but also nurtures the genre's growth from the strophic dance-air to the more modern, through-composed song, with new degrees of declamation and harmonic expressivity, as seen in works like "In Darkness Let Me Dwell." His solo lute works, dances in the main, are likely a mirror of his own performance abilities and show in their florid diminutions an impressive level of virtuosity.

Much has been made of the association of Dowland and melancholy. One of his most famous and widely disseminated works is his *Lachrimae* pavan, a work that also coexists as the song "Flow My Tears" and is the basis for his stunning cycle of pavans, *Lachrimae or Seaven Teares* (1604). The lachrymal title, echoed in the falling-tear motive of the pavan's opening tetrachord, seems iconic of the composer whose song texts could be notably dark and who famously titled a pavan "Semper Dowland Semper Dolens" (Ever Dowland, Ever Sad). It is tempting to read these works as autobiographical, and perhaps they are, but given the ubiquity of the cult of melancholy among the Elizabethans, it is also possible that artistic persona and personal reality significantly diverge.

Dowland modeled the notion of a "learned" musician, especially in rendering his translation of Andreas Ornithoparcus's Latin 16th-century treatise, *Micrologus*, which he published in 1609. Learnedness, admittedly of a basic sort, also figures in his preface to *A Pilgrimes Solace* (1612), where he is critical of those who are "merely ignorant, even in the first elements of Musicke, and also in the true order of the mutation of the Hexachord in the Systeme," the type of musicians he feared gained favor while his own advancement was enmired in frustration.

DRAGHI, GIOVANNI BATTISTA (ca. 1640–1708). Composer and keyboard player. Draghi came to London in the 1660s to join a nascent Italian **opera** company under the direction of the **Albrici** brothers. The diarists **Samuel Pepys** and **John Evelyn** both praise his abilities, and he became well established as both a teacher and a keyboard player, including appointment as organist in the Roman Catholic chapel of Catherine of Braganza. A measure of his regard emerges in his participation in an **organ**-builders' competition between **Renatus Harris** and **Bernard Smith**, both vying for the contract to build an instrument for the Temple Church; Harris selected Draghi as his demonstrator.

A manuscript discovery in the 1990s brought to light a collection of **Henry Purcell**'s keyboard works in autograph that also includes 17 works by Draghi.

DRAGONETTI, DOMENICO (1763–1846). Double bass virtuoso and composer of Italian origin. Dragonetti's contemporaries considered him the finest bass player of his time, and he could command enormous fees for performance, even within an orchestra. As an example, his salary of £47 6s. at the Chester **Musical Fetival** of 1821 was the third highest in the orchestra, and far higher than the string players' average fee of £6 6s. Dragonetti received his early training and held his first substantial employment in Venice. He moved to England in 1794 on a purported two-year leave from the instrumental ensemble of San Marco but made London his home for the remainder of his life, aside from trips to the Continent in 1799 and 1808–14. He was frequently heard at most of the contemporary musical festivals as well as all of the London venues, including the King's Theatre, **Haymarket**; the **Concerts of Ancient Music**; and the **Royal Philharmonic Society**. He was great friends with the cellist **Robert Lindley** and was often seen at festivals and concerts in the company of his dog, Carlo. His compositions and arrangements were mostly for his instrument and remain a staple of the double bass repertoire today.

DRAMATICK OPERA. "Dramatick opera" is **John Dryden**'s term for **semi-opera**, used in reference to his 1691 *King Arthur*.

THE DREAM OF GERONTIUS. **Oratorio** by **Sir Edward Elgar** to a text by John Henry Cardinal Newman, first performed at the Birmingham **Musical Festival** on 3 October 1900. The work, along with the op. 36 *Variations on an Original Theme* (**"Enigma"**), made Elgar famous. *Gerontius* describes the journey of a man from his last hours on earth to his entrance in Heaven as a Soul and features evocative writing in a Wagnerian vein; August Jaeger wrote a Hans von Wolzogen–style guide to the Leitmotivs within it. The Birmingham premiere was not a great success, mostly due to lack of rehearsal time for the chorus. Yet, in spite of its Catholic nature (the main subject of *Gerontius* is the forgiveness of sins, and Gerontius/the Soul is sent to Purgatory at the end of the work), the work succeeded greatly in its first decade, with performances throughout Germany and North America. The work was banned in Gloucester Cathedral until 1910 and admitted only after the more "Catholic" elements of the text were removed from the libretto. *Gerontius* was particularly championed by musical festivals and choral societies, becoming a close rival to both **George Frederick Handel**'s *Messiah* and **Felix Mendelssohn**'s *Elijah*, and remains Elgar's most popular choral work in Great Britain today, though it is rarely heard outside that country.

DRURY LANE THEATRE. The Theatre Royal at Drury Lane opened under Thomas Killigrew in 1663 and was rebuilt in 1674, at which time it competed with the Duke's Company at **Dorset Garden**. Although **Henry Purcell**'s **semi-operas** were performed at Dorset Garden, his association with the Theatre Royal was long—from 1680 until the year of his death in 1695—being the venue for much of his stage music.

In the early 18th century, the Theatre Royal was particularly influential in nurturing the taste for Italianate **opera** productions with performances of **Thomas Clayton**'s *Arsinoe* (1705) and **Giovanni Bononcini**'s *Camilla* (1706). The early 18th century also saw the Theatre Royal in a complicated competitive relationship with the Queen's Theatre at the **Haymarket**. In the

1706–7 season Drury Lane held the monopoly on operas, while the Haymarket had no musical productions at all; the year 1708 would then reverse this situation with Drury Lane presenting plays only and the Haymarket exclusively operas; the 1709–10 season saw plays with music at Drury Lane and Italian operas and plays with music at the Haymarket.

From the mid-18th century forward, Drury Lane continued to present mixed entertainment, with spoken theater and opera performances presented within the same seasons. David Garrick managed Drury Lane from 1747 to 1776. Under his auspices, Drury Lane introduced **oratorio** evenings during Lent in 1762; though these were somewhat sporadic, **Thomas Linley** (the elder) managed them between 1774 and 1786. Garrick also employed **Charles Dibdin** to manage the music at the theater from 1768 to 1775. The theater was demolished in 1791 and rebuilt by 1794 by Richard Brinsley Sherridan, who managed it from 1776 to 1809. Sherridan's rebuilt theater included 3,600 seats. Throughout the tenure of both Garrick and Sherridan, and long into the 19th century, Drury Lane presented arrangements of continental opera and the occasionally commissioned English opera. For instance, 1794 saw the production of **Steven Storace**'s *The Cherokee*. Drury Lane had a disastrous fire in 1809 and was rebuilt again by 1812 with 3,060 seats. This is the building that survives today.

Throughout the 19th century, Drury Lane hosted the famous and the not-so-famous; **Sir Henry Bishop** was music director for a time starting in 1824. **Louis Antoine Jullien** presented some of his promenade concerts there; he also engaged Hector Berlioz to conduct a season of opera (1847). The **Carl Rosa Opera Company** had seasons there from 1883 to 1885, and **Sir Thomas Beecham** conducted Russian operas at Drury Lane in 1913–14. The theater also presented the first staged performance of an opera by Richard Wagner in England: *Die fliegende Hollander*, translated into Italian as *L'Olandese Dannato* (1870).

A refurbishment in 1922 decreased the number of seats in the theater to 2283, and from the 1930s forward Drury Lane became a theater for musicals and lighter entertainment—first presenting works by Noël Coward and Ivor Novello, and then, after the end of World War II, long-running American and British musicals. *See also* ABRAMS, HARRIET; ARNE, THOMAS AUGUSTINE; BABELL, WILLIAM; BALFE, MICHAEL WILLIAM; BATTISHILL, JONATHAN; BENEDICT, SIR JULIUS; BONONCINI, GIOVANNI; BURNEY, CHARLES; CLARKE, JEREMIAH; CLAYTON, THOMAS; COOKE, TOM; ECCLES, JOHN; FINGER, GODFREY; HOOK, JAMES; LINLEY, THOMAS (THE YOUNGER); LOCK HOSPITAL; LYCEUM THEATRE; NORRIS, THOMAS; ORATORIO; PEPUSCH, JOHANN CHRISTOPH; PUBLIC CONCERTS; RANDEGGER, ALBERTO;

RUSH, GEORGE; SMART, SIR GEORGE THOMAS; SMART, HENRY; STORACE, STEPHEN; WEBBE, SAMUEL.

DRYDEN, JOHN (1631–1700). Poet and dramatist. Dryden, poet laureate from 1668 to 1689, figures significantly in the development of English operatic works, especially in his association with **Henry Purcell**. His first substantial operatic work is *Albion and Albanius*, an allegorical work originally intended as a prologue to *King Arthur*. Set as a fully sung work in the French style by **Louis Grabu**, the work was unsuccessful in its 1685 performance, owing to an unfortunate coincidence with Monmouth's Rebellion and the turbulence of the political circumstance underlying the work's allegory.

The choice of Grabu as composer reflected the poet's lack of confidence in the English musical establishment: "When any of our countrymen excel him [Grabu], I shall be glad, for the sake of old England, to be shewn my errour." Dryden was indeed shown his error with Purcell's successful **semi-opera** *Dioclesian*, which he acknowledged both implicitly in collaborating with him in music for the play *Amphytrion* and explicitly in that work's dedication. Subsequently, their grandest collaboration was the semi-opera *King Arthur* (a revised version for 1691), which Dryden described as a play "Written in blank Verse, adorn'd with Scenes, Machines, Songs, and Dances," an admirable description of the semi-opera form itself.

DUNSTAPLE (DUNSTABLE), JOHN (ca. 1390–1453). Composer. Dunstaple emerges not only as the most eminent of the English composers of the early 15th century but also as a defining figure of the early Renaissance style. Johannes Tinctoris, for instance, observes around 1476 (*Proportionale Musices*) that "the possibilities of our music have been so marvelously increased that there appears to be a new art [the Renaissance style] . . . whose fount and origin is held to be among the English, of whom Dunstable stood forth as chief." And his influence in the transmission of this style to Burgundian composers is confirmed in Martin le Franc's famous reference (*Le Champion des dames*) to Guillaume Dufay and Giles Binchois "wearing the English guise."

Dunstaple's style is one favoring full triadic vertical sonorities, triadic melodic mottos, a dissonance control that approaches pan-consonance, frequent hemiolas, both vertical and horizontal, and the sweet sound of successive 6-3 sonorities. Some of his works, like the early "Veni Sancte Spiritus," embrace medieval structures like isorhythm; others, like the motet "O quam pulchra es," are progressive in their declamatory elements, preserving both the audibility of the text as well as its natural accentuation.

Bent (1981) judged Dunstaple "probably the most influential English composer of all time and one of the few who can be ranked internationally as a great figure." Significantly, both his epitaph and several written sources also document his interest in astronomy, a manifestation of the unity of the quadrivial arts.

DURFEY, THOMAS (ca. 1653–1723). Poet and dramatist. Durfey is best known for his large collection of poems with tunes entitled *Wit and Mirth, or Pills to Purge Melancholy* (1719–20). He is also the author of the printed epilogue to **Henry Purcell**'s *Dido and Aeneas*. Attempts to associate him with the stuttering poet in Purcell's *Fairy Queen* have been compellingly challenged by Price (1984).

DUSSEK (DUSÍK), JAN LADISLAV (1760–1812). Pianist, teacher, composer, and music publisher. Dussek was born in Cáslav, outside Prague (in what was then part of the Austrian Empire and now part of the Czech Republic), and spent the first three decades of his life gaining a reputation throughout the Continent as a gifted pianist and teacher. In 1789, after several years in France in the service of the Berlin ambassador, but playing frequently for the French aristocracy, he fled to London ahead of the French Revolution. For the next decade, he became a fixture of London musical life: his lessons were extremely popular, he performed at the **Hanover Square Rooms**, he made frequent guest appearances at **Johann Peter Salomon**'s concerts, and he entered into a partnership with his stepfather to form the Corri, Dussek & Co. music publishing company, which also acted as selling agents for Broadwood pianos in Scotland. When bankruptcy threatened, Dussek fled to the Continent in 1799, where he spent the rest of his life, likely never seeing his wife or daughter again.

DYKES, JOHN BACCHUS (1823–76). Clergyman and amateur composer. While studying classics at Cambridge, Dykes had **organ** lessons from T. A. Walmisley, sang in a **madrigal** society, and was president of the Cambridge Musical Society. From 1849 to 1862, he was the precentor and a minor canon at Durham Cathedral, where he wrote many of the **hymns** for the 1861 edition of *Hymns Ancient and Modern*, including "Nearer My God to Thee." He was a frequent lecturer on church music and was given the honorary MusD by Durham University in 1861.

DYSON, SIR GEORGE (1883–1964). Composer, teacher, writer on music, and organist. Dyson was best known for large choral and **musical festival** compositions during his lifetime, including *The Canterbury Pilgrims* (1931), though these are mostly unknown today. He attended the **Royal College of Music** (RCM) from 1900 to 1904 and won the **Mendelssohn Scholarship**, which allowed him to travel to Florence, Rome, Vienna, and Berlin between 1904 and 1907. He served in a variety of posts upon his return to England, including being the director of music for the Royal Naval College at Osborne (1907), music master at Marlborough College (1911), and professor at the RCM (1921). He enlisted twice during World War I, first in the Royal Fusiliers in 1914 and then in the Royal Air Force in 1916. He completed the MusD from Oxford in 1918. Dyson served as the director of the RCM from 1938 to 1952 and was knighted in 1941.

E

EAST, MICHAEL (ca. 1580–1648). Composer. East, the nephew of the music publisher **Thomas East**, was for a time a lay clerk at Ely, but by 1618 he had become master of the choristers at Lichfield. Much of his music was printed, including **madrigals**, large-scale **anthems**, and consort music. He contributed "Hence Stars, too Dim of Light" to **Thomas Morley**'s *The Triumphs of Oriana*.

EAST, THOMAS (ca. 1540–1608). Music publisher. East, the uncle of the composer **Michael East**, was one of the leading music printers of his day, publishing works by **William Byrd** as well as important collections like *Musica Transalpina* and *The Triumphs of Oriana*. He is especially well known for his harmonized metrical psalter, *The Whole Booke of Psalmes . . .* (1592 et seq.).

ECCLES, JOHN (ca. 1668–1735). Composer. In the years following the death of **Henry Purcell** in 1695, Eccles emerged as the leading theater composer in London. Writing for the United Companies at **Drury Lane** as early as 1693, Eccles began a long relationship with **Anne Bracegirdle**, who after that time sang his music exclusively, including the notable **mad song** from *Don Quixote*, "I Burn, I Burn." The demise of the United Company led to the formation of a new company at **Lincoln's Inn Fields** in 1695 under the direction of Thomas Betterton, and Eccles was much in evidence there as company composer. His large-scale **dramatick opera**, *Rinaldo and Armida*, was performed there in 1698 and featured one of his best-known airs, "The Jolly Breeze." The librettist of *Rinaldo and Armida*, John Dennis, innovatively insisted on the dramatic integrality of the music with the drama, extending the principle of integrality even to the instrumental act tunes, which sadly do not survive.

In 1701 Eccles was one of the participants in the *Judgment of Paris* competition, winning second prize for his setting of William Congreve's text. A few years later Eccles took on Congreve's *Semele*, intended most likely for the opening of the **Haymarket** Theatre in 1705. However, Eccles was slow in the completion of the score, not finishing it until 1707, and it never gained a public performance. A fully sung **opera**, *Semele* pointed a way for English music drama to develop in the 18th century, but in the face of the popularity of Italian opera, it remained unpursued.

EDWARDS, RICHARD (1525–66). Composer, poet, and dramatist. Edwards was appointed gentleman of the **Chapel Royal** at the end of Mary Tudor's reign; in 1561 he became master of the children of the chapel, an appointment that well positioned him to further the **choirboy plays**, including his own *Damon and Pithias* (1564). Some of his poetry was posthumously published in *The Paradyse of Daynty Devises* (1576).

ELGAR, SIR EDWARD (1857–1934). English composer, conductor, violinist, and lecturer on music. Many consider Elgar to be the most important English composer of his time, if not of all time. Elgar successfully composed in every English genre available save for **opera** (he left an incomplete score for one, *The Spanish Lady*, at his death). His **oratorios** and **cantatas**, especially *The Dream of Gerontius* (1900), were frequently performed in his own lifetime at all of the major **musical festivals** and by most English choirs; performances of his symphonies and concertos far outstripped those of his contemporaries.

The traditional narrative presents Elgar achieving stratospheric success with the premiere of his op. 36 *Variations on an Original Theme* (**"Enigma"**) in 1899; in truth, Elgar had spent most of the 1890s gradually gaining experience and acceptance as a composer and conductor in Birmingham, Worcester, Hereford, and Gloucester. He was largely self-taught, though did take some violin lessons with Adolf Pollitzer, and relied on the books and scores at his father's music shop in Worcester to fill in the gaps of his education. Additional early experience included being the organist at St. George's Roman Catholic Church in Worcester, playing violin in various festival orchestras, conducting a band at a local asylum, and teaching privately as well as at a girl's school in Malvern. Aside from a short period in London in 1889 after his marriage to Alice Roberts, Elgar spent most of the time in his early career in Western England, living in Malvern, Worcester, and Hereford.

After the success of the "Enigma" Variations and *Gerontius*, Elgar's fame became international, and the premieres of his compositions—such as *The Apostles* and *The Kingdom* (Birmingham Musical Festival, 1903 and 1906, respectively)—were major public events, and he and his music were in great demand. The trio section of his first **"Pomp and Circumstance"** march was turned first into a segment of the *Coronation Ode* for 1902 and then into a stand-alone vocal piece, as **"Land of Hope and Glory"** became in effect a second national anthem—particularly during World War I. During this time, Elgar was named Peyton Professor of Music at the University of Birmingham (1905–8) and conductor of the **London Symphony Orchestra** from 1911 to 1912.

Elgar moved to London in 1912; in the next few years, his compositions took on a more dramatic bent, including the tone poem *Falstaff* (1913), ballet scores, music for various charities and commemorations during World War I, the late chamber music, and the Cello Concerto (1919). He spent the years from 1923 until his death in Worcester but traveled frequently to conduct concerts of his own works. As a late Romantic composer, his music was accessible to a wide audience; his **British Broadcasting Corporation** broadcasts and early recordings for H.M.V. ensured this. In the years since his death, much of Elgar's music has remained popular and used by many to forward a nostalgic agenda of a conservative England. Elgar was knighted in 1905, named MVO in 1911 and KCVO in 1928, created First Baronet of Broadheath in 1931, named GCVO in 1933, and named **Master of the King's Music** in 1924. He received numerous honorary doctorates from institutions in Great Britain, on the Continent, and in North America. *See also* CORONATION MUSIC; ENGLISH FOLK DANCE AND SONG SOCIETY; ENGLISH MUSICAL RENAISSANCE; *FANTASIA ON A THEME BY THOMAS TALLIS*; HALLÉ ORCHESTRA; LONDON CHORAL SOCIETY; ODE; RICHTER, HANS; SHAKESPEARE, WILLIAM; SHAW, GEORGE BERNARD.

ELIJAH. **Oratorio** by **Felix Mendelssohn**, premiered at the Birmingham **Musical Festival** on 26 August 1846. The two-part oratorio is based on the biblical stories of the prophet Elijah found in 1 and 2 Kings. These include various trials and miracles Elijah brings upon the people of Israel in the name of God and culminate in Elijah's removal to heaven in a fiery chariot. Partly because of Mendelssohn's great popularity in England, and partly because of the immense power of the composition, *Elijah* quickly became the second most important oratorio in England, and few could imagine a musical festival without it. In the words of the *Yorkshire Post* (3 October 1895), it was the "mutton" to the "beef" of **George Frideric Handel**'s *Messiah*. Cheap scores were quickly made available, both in staff notation and in **Tonic Sol-fa**, and it was featured frequently by choral societies throughout the land.

ELLA, JOHN (1802–88). Impresario, music critic, and violinist. Ella came from a trade family in Leicester, and was apprenticed to be a baker, but early violin lessons sparked a lifelong interest in music. In London by the early 1820s, he studied harmony and was a subprofessor of violin at the **Royal Academy of Music (2)** and worked for the **Royal Philharmonic Society**, the **Concerts of Ancient Music**, and the Royal Italian Opera at **Covent**

Garden. He also wrote music criticism for the *Morning Post* (1826–42) and the *Athenaeum* (1830-34), as well as occasional pieces for the *Musical World* and *Court Journal*. Some material from these critical pieces, as well as descriptions of his musical travels abroad, may be seen in *Musical Sketches, Abroad and at Home* (1869). He organized a number of concert societies, including the Musical Winter Evenings (1852–55) and the Musical Union Soirées (1857–59), but is best known for his direction of the **Musical Union,** an organization dedicated to presenting exemplary chamber music concerts; he directed it from 1845 until 1880. He was a lecturer (from 1855) and a professor of music (from 1871) at the **London Institution** and the director of the Musical Union Institute from 1860 to 1868. The latter organization presented concerts and had a music library.

ELLIS, WILLIAM ASHTON (1852–1919). Wagnerian, writer, and translator. Ellis was one of the best-known English Wagnerians at the end of the 19th century; his translation into English of *Richard Wagner's Prose Works* (1892–99), though seen as flawed today, was highly influential on figures such as **Sir Edward Elgar** and **George Bernard Shaw.** Ellis was originally trained as a doctor and worked for some years as one, but following exposure to Wagner in the 1870s, he became a lifelong devotee and partisan. He edited the *Meister*, a journal of all things Wagnerian, between 1888 and 1895 and, besides the *Prose Works*, published a six-volume biography of Wagner (1900–1906). He returned to medicine in 1915 but continued throughout the first years of World War I to defend the performance of Wagner's music.

ENGLISH CADENCE. A cadential idiom arising in Elizabethan polyphony and persisting through the 17th century that features harmonic cross-relation. Specifically, a tone resolving upward by a half-step will appear simultaneously or in close proximity with a flattened version of that tone, descending in another voice. **Thomas Tallis**'s "O nata lux" offers one of many memorable examples. Although we tend to hear it as harmonically eventful, it was likely not intended to be an expressive device but rather simply the fruits of good linear voice leading. In the 17th century, with the establishment of tonal harmony, its presence asserts a tension between older horizontal principles and new vertical priorities.

ENGLISH CONSORT. Mixed ensemble of six instruments, specifically **lute, bandora, cittern,** bass **viol,** treble viol or violin, and flute. Arising perhaps out of the tradition of treble-ground lute duets (Nordstrom, 1976), the ensemble featured florid divisions on the lute with harmonic reinforcement from the cittern playing strummed patterns with a plectrum and the bandora;

the bass viol rendered a structurally inclined bass line, while the flute played an inner harmony line or the melody; the treble viol or violin was used both melodically and for divisions. This ensemble is particularly enshrined in **Thomas Morley**'s 1599 collection, *The First Booke of Consort Lessons*. It is also shown in the famous anonymous painting of "Henry Unton—feast and **masque**" in the National Portrait Gallery, London.

The ensemble is unusual in claiming a specific instrumentation at a time in which instrumentation was more generally casual and is unusual in being a "broken," i.e. mixed, consort at a time in which full, homogeneous consorts enjoyed great popularity.

ENGLISH FOLK DANCE AND SONG SOCIETY (ALSO ENGLISH FOLK DANCE SOCIETY; ENGLISH FOLK SONG SOCIETY; FOLK DANCE SOCIETY; FOLK-SONG SOCIETY). Organization dedicated to the preservation, publishing, and performance of English folk music and dance. It was amalgamated in 1932 from the Folk-Song Society (founded in 1898) and the English Folk Dance Society (founded in 1911). Each society brought its own journal that published songs, dances, and contextual information; these were also combined to create the *English Folk Dance and Song Society Journal*, renamed in 1965 as the *Folk Music Journal*. The collecting of folk music in England began as an antiquarian interest in the mid-19th century, under the auspices of William Chappell in works such as *Collection of National English Airs* (1838–40).

At the end of the century, works on folk music began to appear with some regularity: **Lucy Broadwood** republished a collection of Sussex folk tunes, **William Alexander Barrett** published a book of folk songs in 1891, and others followed. Many of the eminent composers of the day were involved in the founding of the Folk-Song Society, including **Sir Edward Elgar**, **Sir Charles Villiers Stanford**, and **Sir Hubert Parry**, but their involvement was far surpassed by that of **Cecil Sharp**, **Ralph Vaughan Williams**, **Maud Karpeles**, **Percy Grainger**, and others who preserved folk song and dance, created an infrastructure for its continued performance, and even used such material as a basis for new composition. The organization and its library (named for Vaughan Williams) reside in Cecil Sharp House, in Camden Town (London). *See also* BUTTERWORTH, GEORGE; CHAPPELL & CO.; MORRIS DANCE; NEAL, MARY.

ENGLISH GUITAR. **Cittern**-like instrument popular in the second half of the 18th century. The so-called English guitar was strung in metal with six courses, tuned c-e-g-c'-e'-g', with metal frets on the neck. It was popular with dilettantes—Baines (1966) notes it was "intended chiefly for the feminine amateur"—and as a way of simplifying its technique, it sometimes was made with finger levers on the table of the instrument which, when depressed, activated hammers to strike the strings.

ENGLISH MUSICAL RENAISSANCE (ALSO EMR; SECOND ENGLISH MUSICAL RENAISSANCE; BRITISH MUSICAL RENAISSANCE). Descriptive name given to the period between roughly 1840 and 1940 when British critics were self-consciously aware of a new excellence in indigenous composition and musical training. The name *Renaissance* was first applied to the period by **Joseph Bennett** in 1882; the first use of the phrase "English Musical Renaissance" seems to have occurred in a set of lectures by Morton Latham, delivered at Cambridge University in 1888; these were collected and published in a volume titled *The Renaissance of Music* in 1890. For most of the late 19th and early 20th centuries, the "origin" of the movement was thought to be the premiere of **Sir Hubert Parry**'s **cantata** *Prometheus Unbound* on 1 September 1880; however, in the second half of the 20th century, the dates of the movement were moved further back into the 19th century to encompass the founding of the National Training School for Music (1876; shortly to become the **Royal College of Music**) and the rise of sight-singing methods like **Tonic Sol-fa** and choral societies; no two critics agree on a precise date range for the "Renaissance." Use of the term *Renaissance* by contemporary critics often implied that British music was coming out of a "dark age" where no good indigenous music was to be had. While it is tempting to imagine that the stratospheric national and international careers of **Sir Alexander Campbell Mackenzie**, Parry, **Sir Charles Villiers Stanford**, **Sir Arthur Sullivan**, **Sir Edward Elgar**, **Gustav Holst**, and **Ralph Vaughan Williams**, among others, were unique, this is not the case; indigenous music and composition by the likes of **Samuel Sebastian Wesley**, among many others, was excellent and well regarded.

ENGLISH NATIONAL OPERA. *See* SADLER'S WELLS.

ENGLISH OPERA HOUSE. *See* LYCEUM THEATRE.

ENGLISH SLIDE TRUMPET. In the late 17th-century manuscript devoted to musical instruments (GB Och 1187), **James Talbot** describes the "flat trumpet" as one having a "2d crook [bow] placed near [the] left Ear & by it you draw out the Inward yards." Thus the flat trumpet expanded its length of tubing by sliding the back bow of the instrument (the bow closest to the player) in and out, and in so doing, allowed the player to play chromatically, as Talbot's note chart confirms. **Henry Purcell** made use of flat trumpets in his music for *The Libertine*, music that he more familiarly reused in the "Funeral Music for Queen Mary."

No examples of flat trumpets survive. However, in its 19th-century mechanized form, the English slide trumpet was ubiquitous. Invented by John Hyde ca. 1790, it featured the same expansion via the back bow of the instrument; however, it also had a clock-spring mechanism for returning the slide. The persistence of this instrument into the valve era may be attributed to the strength of its chief exponents, Thomas Harper (1786–1853) and his son, Thomas Harper Jr. (1816–98).

"ENIGMA" VARIATIONS. *See* VARIATIONS ON AN ORIGINAL THEME ("ENIGMA"), OP. 36.

ETON CHOIRBOOK. Copied between 1490 and 1502, the Eton Choirbook (GB WRec 178) is an important collection of liturgical polyphony—**votive antiphons**, Magnificats, and a **Passion** (Davy)—by composers such as **John Browne**, **Richard Davy**, Walter Lambe, **Robert Wylkynson**, **William Cornysh**, and **Robert Fayrfax**. It survives incomplete, though with an original index that shows 93 pieces. The prominence of the votive antiphon reflects both the strength of the cult of Mary and also the College Statutes that required an antiphon to be sung daily before an image of the Virgin.

Many of the works are unusually sonorous with a notably expanded treble range. And large, full sonorities, as in Wylkynson's nine-voice "Salve regina," are frequently placed in contrast with reduced textures where floridity and a decorative rhythmic complexity are characteristic.

EVELYN, JOHN (1620–1706). Diarist. Like his contemporary **Samuel Pepys**, Evelyn was fond of music, and his diary (discontinuous from 1641 until his death) contains significant observations of musical life in Restoration England. He was present at important public occasions—Charles II's coronation, for instance—and records details of the event, but he also encountered music in more intimate, private settings and offers occasionally rich description. For instance,

> After supper, came in the famous Trebble Mr **[John] Abel [Abell]** newly return'd from Italy, and indeede I never heard a more excellent voice, one would have sworne it had ben a womans it was so high, and so well and skillfully manag'd. (27 January 1682)

Or in another home:

> I visited Sir Rob. Reading, where after supper we had musique, but none comparable to that which Mrs. Bridgeman made upon the Gittar, which she master'd with such extraordinary skill, and dexterity, as I hardly ever heard any **lute** exceede for sweetnesse. (10 January 1684)

By his own account he had studied the "rudiments of music" and "afterwards ariv'd to some formal knowledge," but with regard to performance skills he confessed that he had "small perfection of hand because I was so frequently diverted, with inclinations to newer trifles."

EVENSONG. The Anglican service of sung evening prayer according to the order of the *Book of Common Prayer*. Evensong is generally a daily offering in English cathedrals and university chapels with choral foundations. The major musical elements of the liturgy comprise psalmody, the Magnificat and Nunc dimittis, and an **anthem**.

EXETER HALL. London lecture and concert hall, built in 1831 and demolished in 1907. For a time, the hall was associated especially with Nonconformist causes and organizations. The hall had two auditoriums: one that could seat about 1,000, and another about 4,000. From 1836 to 1880, Exeter Hall was the home of the **Sacred Harmonic Society**, which performed a series of regular choral concerts, usually featuring **oratorios**. Beginning in the 1870s, the Hall hosted numerous choral competitions, including the Ragged School Union, the Church of England Temperance Society, and the **Tonic Sol-fa Association**, among others; the larger of these moved to the **Crystal Palace** in the 1880s, but smaller ones remained. In 1880 the Young Men's Christian Association bought the hall and prohibited oratorios there, calling their performance "improper." Recitals resumed in the 1890s. Various individuals and organizations gave lectures and demonstrations in the Hall, including **John Hullah** and **John Curwen**, who each presented their methods of sight-singing there. *See also* CONCERT ROOMS; PUBLIC CONCERTS.

F

FABURDEN. Fifteenthth-century method of improvising polyphony on a plainsong. In faburden, as described in the anonymous "The Sight of Faburdon" (GB Lbl Lansdowne 763), associated with Waltham Abbey, three-voice polyphony is derived from the plainsong by having one voice replicate the chant at the interval of an upper perfect fourth, while another voice sings lower thirds and fifths to the chant. In this lower voice, the "faburden voice," the lower thirds and fifths can alternate at will, though not with two fifths in succession. The result is thus a harmony that often produces parallel 6-3 chords, the same sweet sonority that characterizes the continental practice of fauxbourdon. In deriving the faburden voice, a system of "sights" was employed, through which the singer envisioned a note either in unison or a third above the chant, yet pitched the voice so that it sounded a fifth lower (creating the lower fifth and third). In this way the mental image of the faburden voice was kept within the bounds of the plainchant staff. Tudor organists also used faburden voices as the basis for contrapuntal **organ** pieces.

FANTASIA-SUITE (ALSO FANTASY SUITES). Seventeenth-century, multimovement instrumental form. The fantasia-suite, following the model of **John Coprario**'s early examples, is a three-movement form, consisting of a contrapuntal movement (the "fantasia") followed by two dance movements, almaine and galliard, which were sometimes nominally "**ayres.**" Though typically for violin(s) with bass **viol** and **organ**, some examples, notably two by **John Hingeston**, replace the violin and viol with **cornett**(s) and trombone. Other composers of fantasia-suites include **William Lawes**, **John Jenkins**, and **Christopher Gibbons**.

FANTASIA ON A THEME BY THOMAS TALLIS (ALSO "Tallis" Fantasia). Variations by **Ralph Vaughan Williams** for double orchestra and string quartet on the **hymn** "Why Fumeth in Fight" (an anti-Catholic hymn) by **Thomas Tallis**. The theme is presented in both full and fragmentary forms, capitalizing on antiphonal effects of the three ensembles. The *Fantasia* premiered at the Gloucester meeting of the Three Choirs Festival on 6 September 1910, heard just before a performance of a bowdlerized version of **Sir**

Edward Elgar's *Dream of Gerontius*, perhaps to "Anglicize" the Cathedral before the performance of an overtly Catholic **oratorio**. The composition remains one of Vaughan Williams's most popular.

FARINELLI (ALSO CARLO BROSCHI; 1705–82). Castrato. Farinelli, richly lauded by **Charles Burney** for his unrivaled "power, sweetness, extent, and agility" of voice, came to London in 1734 to join the so-called **"Opera of the Nobility,"** the company at the King's Theatre in the **Haymarket** in fierce rivalry with **George Frideric Handel**'s company at **Covent Garden**. Celebrated and lavishly rewarded, Farinelli, according to a 1737 newspaper account, earned at least £5,000 per annum. He left London in 1737, taking up a position at the Spanish court and living in Spain until 1759. His musical abilities were well-described by Quantz:

> Farinelli had a penetrating, full, rich, bright and well-modulated soprano voice, whose range extended at that time from a to d′′′. . . . His intonation was pure, his trill beautiful, his breath control extraordinary and his throat very agile, so that he performed even the widest intervals quickly and with the greatest ease and certainty. Passage-work and all varieties of melismas were of no difficulty whatever for him. In the invention of free ornamentation in adagio he was very fertile.

FARNABY, GILES (ca. 1563–1640). Composer. Farnaby was professionally a joiner, as was his father and his cousin, Nicholas, described also as a **virginal** maker. However, despite his profession, he took the BMus at Oxford in 1592. He contributed a number of settings to **Michael East**'s *Whole Booke of Psalmes*; he is best known for his substantial body of keyboard works, the vast majority of which appear in the **Fitzwilliam Virginal Book**. Caldwell (1973) colorfully notes, "The predominant impression created by this music is of considerable technical difficulty of a somewhat unrewarding nature, combined with a rather eccentric musical personality, which is not, however, without its own quaint charm."

FARRANT, RICHARD (ca. 1525/30–80). Composer. Farrant was a longtime member of the **Chapel Royal** who, for a period in the 1570s, assumed some of the duties of the master of the children. He left the Chapel Royal for a time in order to become master of the choristers at Windsor but returned to maintain both posts in the last decade of his life. His historical significance is as one of the earliest progenitors of the verse **anthem**, as seen in his "When as We Sat in Babylon." He is also notable for his strong ties to the **choirboy plays**; from the mid-1560s the Windsor boys were active in annual dramatic performances at court, sometimes in collaboration with the boys of the Chapel Royal. His full **anthem**, "Call to Remembrance," has a long popularity.

FAYRFAX, ROBERT (1464–1521). Composer. Fayrfax was a gentleman of the **Chapel Royal** from 1497 until his death in 1521, a member whose esteem found him named Knight of the King's Alms of Windsor in 1514. He held the MusB from Cambridge (1501) as well as DMus from both universities (Cambridge, 1504; Oxford, 1511). On the basis of several patronal works like the *Missa Albanus*, as well as his being buried there, it is likely he held an appointment at St. Alban's Abbey.

As a composer his work in developing the large-scale cyclic mass is especially significant. Cohesion in these large-scale works is furthered by the use of head-motives and, in most cases, common cantus firmus, both techniques that had emerged earlier in English mass composition. Especially notable is that the *Missa O bone Iesu* and an associated Magnificat are both developed from a common polyphonic antiphon, adopting the so-called parody technique. The *Missa O quam glorifica* is atypically complex, perhaps owing to its use as his doctoral exercise at Cambridge.

FAYRFAX MANUSCRIPT. One of the three major songbooks of the early Tudor Court. The Fayrfax Manuscript (GB Lbl Add. Ms. 5465), along with the Henry VIII Manuscript (GB Lbl Add. 31922) and the **Ritson Manuscript**, is among the chief sources of vernacular song from early Tudor composers. The Fayrfax Manuscript—so called because it includes music by **Robert Fayrfax** as well as his heraldic arms—contains both love lyrics and devotional **carols** by composers such as **Richard Davy**, **John Browne**, and **William Cornysh**. The devotional carols are a rich manifestation of contemporary **Passion** culture, and Cornysh's "Woffuly araid" is an affective masterpiece. It and its sister Passion **carols** are emotive, personal expressions of striking intensity.

FELIX NAMQUE. Marian offertory chant popularly used as the cantus firmus for keyboard settings in the 16th century. Examples include settings by **John Redford**, Thomas Preston, and **Thomas Tallis**.

FERRABOSCO, ALFONSO (THE ELDER; 1543–88), AND FERRABOSCO, ALFONSO (THE YOUNGER; ca. 1575–1628). Father (composer) and illegitimate son (composer and violist) are the two most prominent members of a family of musicians active in Italy and England. Ferrabosco the elder was a gentleman of the Privy Chamber from 1562. He wrote in a variety of genres, including Latin sacred works, instrumental fantasias, and Italian **madrigals**, the latter of which were well regarded in England, performed both in "Englished" and instrumental versions. The late 1570s were problematic for him with accusations of murder, robbery, and secretive attendance at mass; abroad he was suspected of espionage and also imprisoned for a while by the pope.

Ferrabosco the younger also held royal appointment as **viol** player, composer, and instructor to the royal children. From 1617 he was also musician to Charles, Prince of Wales. His viol consort music is significant, characterized by "skilful deployment of vigorously conceived melodic lines" and "bold sweep of his harmonic and tonal conceptions" (Caldwell, *OHEM*, vol. 1). He also made strong contributions to the **masque**, including works like the "Masque of Blackness," "Hymenaei," and the "Masque of Augurs." His vocal music significantly moved English song in an Italianate, declamatory direction; manuscript sources themselves underscore this connection, such as GB T Mss. 1018–9, which contains a number of works by Giulio Caccini as well as monodic-styled works by Ferrabosco.

FESTING, MICHAEL CHRISTIAN (1705–52). Violinist and composer. Festing was a prominent figure in London musical circles. A member of the King's Musick from 1726, he performed in various London **concert rooms**, was a member of the **Academy of Ancient Music** and the Apollo Academy, was the orchestra leader at the King's Theatre and Ranelagh **pleasure gardens**, and was one of the founders of the "Fund for the Support of Decay'd Musicians and their Families," a forerunner of the **Royal Society of Musicians**.

As a violinist Festing was trained by Richard Jones and **Francesco Geminiani**, the latter's influence being strong in the Italianate concertos that Festing composed. But despite this Geminiani pedigree, Festing's abilities as a performer were disparaged by both **Charles Burney** and **Sir John Hawkins**. Hawkins called him "a very elegant composer," but "as a performer" he was "inferior to many of his time." Burney is more exacting:

> This performer, with a feeble hand, little genius for composition, and but a shallow knowledge in counterpoint, by good sense, probity, prudent conduct, and a gentleman-like behaviour, acquired a weight and influence in his profession, at which hardly any musician of his class ever arrived. . . . [A]nd yet there is not a ripieno player on the violin at the opera now, whose hand and abilities are not superior to those of Festing upon that instrument.

FESTIVAL OF BRITAIN. National culture festival, including a **musical festival**, held for five months beginning in May of 1951. Festival events focused on London, but celebrations occurred in many other British cities as well. Meant initially to celebrate the centenary of the Great Exhibition of

1851, the Festival of Britain was nationalistic in nature, celebrating British contributions to culture, science, and technology. The "cultural" aspect of the celebration included innumerable choral, orchestral, chamber, and solo concerts, especially under the rubric "London Season of the Arts," featuring music by British composers, including specially commissioned works, such as **Sir George Dyson**'s "Song for a Festival" (with words by Cecil Day Lewis) for unison children's choir, and works composed for Festival competitions, including **Alan Bush**'s opera *Wat Tyler*. The festival also featured the opening of the **Royal Festival Hall** in London. Festivals at other cities also included music within their celebrations. *See also* BRITTEN, BENJAMIN.

FESTIVALS. *See* MUSICAL FESTIVALS.

FINGER, GODFREY (ALSO GOTTFRIED; ca. 1660–1730). Violist and composer. A Moravian musician, Finger was in London by 1687 to occupy a post in the chapel of James II and remained in England following the Glorious Revolution. His 1690 collection of sonatas was fundamental in establishing the solo sonata in England. In its dedication he notes the "humour of them [the sonatas] is principally Italian: A sort of Music which thô the best in the world, yet is but lately naturaliz'd in England." If the sonatas spoke in an Italian accent, Moravian echoes were also discernible, as for instance in his music for trumpet.

Following the 1695 reorganization of the London theaters, Finger contributed to dramatic works for both Betterton's company at **Lincoln's Inn Fields** and Christopher Rich's company at **Drury Lane**. It was likely theater music that led to his leaving England for the Continent in the first years of the 18th century: a competitor in the famous contest involving William Congreve's *Judgment of Paris*, his fourth-place finish behind **John Weldon, John Eccles**, and **Daniel Purcell** proved the ultimate dispiritment.

FINZI, GERALD (1901–56). Composer, writer on music, adjudicator, and conductor. Finzi is known as one of the most sensitive text setters of the first half of the 20th century; his harmonically approachable style makes his music—particularly for amateur choirs—still accessible today. Finzi studied privately, first under Edward Farrar, then under **Sir Edward Bairstow** in York (1917–22), and finally he studied counterpoint under R. O. Morris. After a short time in London, culminating with working at the **Royal Academy of Music (2)** from 1930 to 1933, he moved to the country, first to Aldborne in Wiltshire and finally to Ashmansworth in Hampshire, where he lived simply on a small farm, composing and writing. He founded the Newbury String Players in 1940, an amateur group that performed a great deal of new music.

Finzi's works were performed on the **musical festival** circuit, particularly in the 1940s and 1950s, including *Intimations of Immortality* (1939, meant to be premiered at the Three Choirs festival but canceled because of the war). Finzi published numerous editions of 18th-century music and presented three Crees lectures in 1954 on the subject of text setting.

FISHER, JOHN ABRAHAM (1744–1806). Violinist, composer, and theater manager. Fisher's compositions were mostly for the theater (pastiches, pantomimes, incidental music for plays, etc.), especially at **Covent Garden**, where he led the orchestra from 1768 to 1778, and songs for the **Vauxhall pleasure garden**, where he led the orchestra from 1769. By marriage he had a share in Covent Garden and took some administrative duties there from 1772. In 1777 he earned a BMus and a DMus from Magdalen College, Oxford, and spent much of the 1780s touring the Continent. He settled in Dublin from 1787, giving lessons and presenting the occasional concert until his death. Compositions noted during his own time were the **oratorio** *Providence*, composed for his Oxford doctoral exercise and performed in Oxford and London, and his music for the opening of the New Freemasons' Hall in London in 1776.

FITZWILLIAM VIRGINAL BOOK. The largest collection of English **virginal** music. The manuscript Fitzwilliam Virginal Book (GB Cfm32.g.29) contains close to 300 works by **John Bull**, **William Byrd**, **Giles Farnaby**, **Orlando Gibbons**, **Thomas Morley**, **Peter Philips**, and others. The pieces include dances, voluntaries, fantasias, cantus-firmus pieces, and variations on popular melodies. J. A. Fuller Maitland and William Barclay Squire, in their 1899 edition, advanced the view—now regarded as tenuous—that Francis Tregian the younger copied the manuscript while incarcerated in Fleet Prison. The presence of a number of works by Peter Philips, an English Catholic abroad in the Netherlands, and by Jan Pieterszoon Sweelinck, the most prominent of the Dutch keyboardists of the day, is resonant with the recusancy of the Tregian family.

FLAT TRUMPET. *See* ENGLISH SLIDE TRUMPET.

FOLK DANCE SOCIETY. *See* ENGLISH FOLK DANCE AND SONG SOCIETY.

FOLK-SONG SOCIETY. *See* ENGLISH FOLK DANCE AND SONG SOCIETY.

FORCER, FRANCIS (1649–1705). Organist and composer. Forcer was trained as a chorister at Durham and held **organ** positions at Dulwich College; St. Giles, Cripplegate; and St. Sepulchre's, Holborn. He also contributed theater music to productions at **Dorset Garden** and **Lincoln's Inn Fields**. Additionally, he was one of the managers of **Sadler's Wells**. That his five-part consort ground was included in the same manuscript with **Henry Purcell**'s Fantasias (US NYpl Drexel 5061) speaks well of its regard; modern comment on Forcer's many songs, however, is disparaging: "There is . . . little to say in favour of Francis Forcer, whose numerous songs are among the feeblest written by any composer of the period" (Spink, 1974).

FORD, THOMAS (?–1648). Composer and violist. Ford was in royal service from 1611, first in the retinue of Prince Henry and then in service to Charles as prince and monarch, holding appointments both as composer and violist. Although a composer of consort music (fantasias and lyra **viol** duets), Ford was most prolific and significant as a composer of **lute ayres** and **partsongs**. His 1607 *Musicke of Sundrie Kindes* reveals a fine capacity for melodic craft, as in the richly contoured and memorable ayre "Since First I Saw Your Face."

FORESTER SONG. A text type featuring hunters, often rich in erotic double entendre. There are several examples in the Henry VIII Manuscript (GB Lbl Add. 31922), such as "I have been a foster" and "I am a joly foster"; **William Shakespeare** offers an example, "What shall he have that kild the Deare?" in *As You Like It*.

FOULDS, JOHN (1880–1939). Composer, conductor, writer, and cellist. Foulds was for a time one of the most celebrated composers of theater music in London, and his *A World Requiem* (completed 1921) was a prominent part of London Armistice Day celebrations from 1923 to 1926. Foulds was from a musical family but largely self-taught. From 1900 to 1906 he played cello in the **Hallé Orchestra** under **Hans Richter** but left to pursue composition in London. In London he began a long collaboration with the stage actor and director Lewis Casson; he also became the music director of the Central YMCA in 1918 and the London University Musical Society. Foulds spent the last part of the 1920s on the Continent, returning to London from 1930 to 1935, where he wrote his examination of contemporary music, *Music To-day* (1934). In 1935 he moved to India to study music there; he worked in radio to support himself up to his death in 1939.

FOUNDLING HOSPITAL. London charity hospital, founded in 1739 for the benefit of orphans. **George Frideric Handel** was associated with the Foundling Hospital from 1749 until his death; he presented charity concerts of his music there annually and eventually gave the hospital his score to *Messiah* (performed there every year under his direction save 1749). A tradition of performing this work at the hospital chapel to raise funds continued until 1777.

FRANKFURT GROUP. English composers who studied with Iwan Knorr and at the Hoch Konservatorium in Frankfurt at various times in the late 19th century. The group included **Henry Balfour Gardiner**, **Percy Grainger**, Norman O'Neill, **Roger Quilter**, and **Cyril Scott**.

FREEMEN'S SONGS. A vague term in use to describe certain vernacular songs in the 16th and 17th centuries. **Thomas Ravenscroft**, for instance, in his *Deuteromelia* (1609) includes amid "Pleasant Roundelais" and "such delightfull Catches" a group of pieces that were "*K.H. mirth, or* Freemens Songs," with "We Be Three Poor Mariners" a familiar example. Various references suggest it was used interchangeably with "three men's" songs, one term as a corruption of the other; many examples are, in fact, three-voiced pieces, though problematically this is not invariably the case. Duffin (2002) compellingly makes the case that "free" could refer to "free of a company," and thus the freemen's songs were those of tradesmen.

FRICKER, PETER RACINE (1920–90). Composer, educator, and administrator. Fricker was one of the best-known dissonant composers in the years after World War II. While not wholeheartedly embracing twelve-tone methods, his music turned away from the folk-derived pastoral school of **Ralph Vaughan Williams** and the neoclassical tendencies of **Benjamin Britten**. He attended the **Royal College of Music** from 1937 to 1941 and took classes as well at Morley College, where **Sir Michael Tippett** was the music director. After wartime service in the Royal Air Force, he returned to Morley College to study with **Mátyás Seiber** (1946–48). Fricker's music began to receive critical acclaim in this period; in the space of a few short years, he won the A. J. Clements Prize (1947), the Koussevitsky Prize (1950), and the Arts Council of Britain Prize (1951). He succeeded Tippett as music director of Morley College in 1952. In 1964 he was visiting professor of composition at the University of California, Santa Barbara; he remained at that institution for the rest of his life. He worked in most major genres save **opera**.

FRYE, WALTER (?–BEFORE 1475). Composer. Frye was a member of the London Guild of St. Nicholas (admitted in 1456/57) and in the employ of Anne of Exeter in the 1460s and 1470s. Anne's sister, Margaret of York, was the wife of the Burgundian Charles the Bold, a connection that may help to explain the composer's works surviving almost totally in continental sources. His several mass settings, using tenor cantus firmus and motto, further the English development of the unified mass cycle. One mass, *Summe Trinitati*, is also isorhythmic. His motet "Ave regina celorum" enjoyed particularly wide circulation. His vernacular songs include both English ballades and French-texted rondeaux.

FUND FOR DECAYED MUSICIANS. *See* ROYAL SOCIETY OF MUSICIANS.

G

GALLIARD, JOHN (JOHANN) ERNST (?–1747). Oboist and composer. A German musician from the court orchestra at Celle, Galliard came to London in 1706 in the service of Prince George of Denmark. As oboist at the Queen's Theatre, he played the prominent solo parts in **George Frideric Handel**'s *Teseo*, and likely in works like *Silla* and *Amadigi di Gaula* as well. His theater works include several English **operas**, such as *Calypso and Telemachus*, *Circe*, and *The Happy Captive*, the latter of which significantly incorporates an intermezzo. With Lewis Theobald he wrote a number of successful pantomimes for **Lincoln's Inn Fields** as well. His translation of Tosi's *Opinioni de' cantori antichi e moderni* (*Observations on the Florid Song* [London, 1742]) is a valuable guide to vocal performance practice.

Sir **John Hawkins** pointed to the naturalness and elegance of his style, while **Charles Burney** was dismissive: "I never saw more correctness or less originality in any author, that I have examined, of the present century, Dr. [**Johann Christoph**] **Pepusch** always excepted." Modern comment echoes Burney. Of the music of *Calypso*, Dean and Knapp (1987) underscore that it "is solid, worthy, and quite dull enough to account for its failure to capture the town."

GALLINI, GIOVANNI ANDREA BATTISTA (1728–1805). Choreographer, dancer, and impresario of Italian origin. After training and work in Italy and Paris, Gallini came to London in 1757. Until 1766 he and his choreographic work appeared frequently on London stages. In the years following, he was a popular dancing-master, was the proprietor of the **Hanover Square Rooms** (where concerts run by **Johann Christian Bach** and **Carl Friedrich Abel** were held, along with the **Academy of Ancient Music**), and managed **opera** at King's Theatre, **Covent Garden**, and Little Theatre, **Haymarket**. With **Johann Peter Salomon**, he enticed **Franz Joseph Haydn** to London in the 1790s.

GARDINER, HENRY BALFOUR (1877–1950). Composer and impresario. Gardiner is best known today for his composition "Evening Hymn" (1908), used frequently in Anglican **services** as an **anthem**, and for his championing of English composers in a series of concerts at the **Queen's Hall** in 1912 and 1913. He was one of the composers of the so-called **Frankfurt Group**; Gardiner studied with Iwan Knorr at the Hochschule für Musik from 1894 to 1896 and frequently in summers and on school vacations in the years thereafter. He attended Charterhouse and New College, Oxford (from 1896), and studied conducting in Sondershausen (1901). Since he was privately wealthy, he did not amass the typical collection of academic and professional posts of his contemporaries, though he did collect folk songs in Hampshire between 1905 and 1907 and taught briefly at Worcester College. Highly self-critical, Gardiner withdrew and destroyed many of his own compositions (especially instrumental ones), and more remained unpublished during his lifetime. He stopped composing in 1925.

GATES, BERNARD (1686–1773). Bass and composer. Gates was trained as a chorister in the **Chapel Royal** from 1697 to 1705 and was closely tied to the chapel in subsequent years as gentleman, master of the children, and tuner of the regals and **organs**. He also held appointments at Westminster Abbey, including master of the choristers. Gates's accomplishments as a singer are confirmed in solo assignments for **George Frideric Handel**, including the Utrecht and Dettingen *Te Deums*. And he surfaces as a pivotal figure in several important contexts. For instance, in the **Giovanni Bononcini–Academy of Ancient Music** scandal, it was he who discovered that Bononcini's "In una siepe ombosa" had earlier appeared in print by Lotti. In the history of the **oratorio** in England he is also significant in giving the genre its first London airings with three performances of Handel's *Esther* at the Crown and Anchor Tavern in 1732. Significantly, these performances were staged, a welcome confirmation of their essentially theatrical nature and intent.

GAUL, ALFRED R. (1837–1913). Composer, organist, conductor, and teacher. During his lifetime, Gaul was best known for a series of **cantatas** that were frequently performed on the **musical festival** circuit. *The Holy City* (premiered at the Birmingham Festival of 1882) was perhaps the most popular cantata of its day (the publisher **Novello & Co.** sold 162,000 copies of it by 1914). Gaul was trained as a chorister and articled pupil at Norwich Cathedral (1846) and worked as an organist first at Fakenham (1854) before taking positions at St. John's, Ladywood (1859), and finally St. Augustine's, Edgbaston (1868). He earned a MusB from Cambridge in 1863. Aside from composing and being an organist, Gaul taught harmony and counterpoint at the Birmingham and Midland Institution and at the King Edward High School for Girls, and was conductor for a time of the Wallsall Philharmonic Society, starting in 1887.

GAY, JOHN (1685–1732). Playwright and poet. Gay is the inventor of the **ballad opera**, a popular and tuneful foil to the reigning aristocratic Italian *op-*

era seria of the 1720s. *The Beggar's Opera* (1728), first of Gay's offerings, was hugely successful; its sequel, *Polly* (1728), was banned from the stage by a touchy Sir Robert Walpole and his administration, although it was successful in its print subscription. Traditional interpretations of *The Beggar's Opera* as satirical criticism of both Walpole and the Italian opera may be exaggerated (Hume, *NG*, 2001), although the fact that *Polly* was pulled from the stage suggests that the administration found Gay problematic.

GEMINIANI, FRANCESCO (1687–1762). Violinist and composer. Geminiani came to London in 1714 amid the popularity of musical Italianism, as seen most vividly in the advance of the *opera seria*. A pupil of Arcangelo Corelli, his playing was described by **Sir John Hawkins** as exquisite— "where in a short time he so recommended himself by his exquisite performance, that all who professed to understand or love music, were captivated at the hearing him"—though his concert appearances were reputedly infrequent. He relied on the largesse of patrons like Baron Kilmansegge, chamberlain to George I, and on teaching and composing. His works include sonatas and concerti grossi as well as concerto grosso arrangements of Corelli's Op. 5 solo sonatas. Geminiani is the author of several treatises, including *A Treatise of Good Taste in the Art of Musick* (1749) and *The Art of Playing on the Violin* (1751), the latter of which **Charles Burney** praises as "a very useful work in its day."

GENTLEMEN'S CATCH CLUB. *See* NOBLEMEN AND GENTLEMEN'S CATCH CLUB.

GERHARD, ROBERTO (1896–1970). Composer, writer, and lecturer on music of Catalan birth. Gerhard, though occasionally ignored within his own time, was one of the major compositional figures of the 20th century. His fusion of folk music and serial styles, his use of electronics for incidental music, and his adaptation of post-serial techniques put him at the vanguard of musical styles throughout his life. His early studies with Felipe Pedrell (until 1922) were followed by several years as an assistant to and pupil of Arnold Schoenberg (1923–28). He began writing about music in the late 1920s, balancing this with composition and teaching at the Escola Normal de la Generalitat until 1938.

In exile after the Spanish Revolution, Gerhard obtained a one-year fellowship at King's College, Cambridge (1939–40), and settled in that city for the rest of his life. For the next few decades, Gerhard cultivated relationships with the **British Broadcasting Corporation** (for which he wrote incidental music as well as being a musical journalist and commentator) and dramatic groups, including the Shakespeare Memorial Theatre at Stratford-upon-Avon (from 1949). From the late 1950s until his death, he was increasingly recognized for his nondramatic music, leading to appointments as a visiting professor of composition at the University of Michigan (1960) and teaching at Tanglewood (1961). He was made a CBE in 1967 and presented with an honorary doctorate from King's College, Cambridge, and a fellowship at University College, London, in 1968.

GERMAN, SIR EDWARD (ALSO EDWARD JONES GERMAN; 1862–1936). Composer and conductor particularly known for his incidental music and his operettas. German attended the **Royal Academy of Music (2)** from 1880 and was subprofessor of violin there between 1884 and 1887. He played for a number of theater orchestras in London and was appointed music director at the Globe Theatre in 1888. For the next 15 years, he wrote a great deal of incidental music for the plays of **William Shakespeare** and others, which he turned into popular suites, including music for *Henry VIII*, *Much Ado about Nothing*, and *Romeo and Juliet*. He also received commissions from numerous **musical festivals** during this period. Work for the **Savoy Theatre** completing **Sir Arthur Sullivan**'s *Emerald Isle* (1901) led him to operetta, and he composed the well-known *Merrie England* (1902) using elements of an antique style. He stopped composing in the early 1920s but continued to conduct at festivals until the end of the decade. German was knighted in 1928.

GIARDINI, FELICE (1716–96). Violinist, composer, conductor, and impresario of Italian origin. Giardini was hailed by **Charles Burney** and others as the finest violinist of his day. He was also somewhat successful as an **opera** composer. After typical training and work in Italy in an opera orchestra, playing solo, and teaching, Giardini settled in London in 1751 via a continental tour. He stayed in London until 1784, taking on various roles in the public and private musical life there. He organized a concert series in the Great Room, Dean Street, in 1751–52, repeating it in 1753 and 1755; was long associated with **Lock Hospital** as a performer, concert organizer, and governor (1752–80); led the orchestra of the Italian Opera at King's Theatre, **Haymarket**, in the mid-1750s, 1776–77, and 1782–83; acted as impresario there for the 1756–57 and 1782–83 seasons; and often led the orchestra at the **Pantheon** Concerts in Oxford Street between 1774 and 1779. He was music master to the Duke of Gloucester (1767), the Duke of Cumberland (1767), and the Prince of Wales (1782). Giardini also organized the annual concert of **George Frideric Handel**'s *Messiah* at the **Foundling Hospital** from 1769 to 1774. He left England for Italy in 1784 but returned, briefly, from 1790 to

1792, when he led the orchestra at **Haymarket**. After leaving England a final time, his precise whereabouts are unknown, though he died in Russia. Aside from numerous pastiches and instrumental works, he was best known in his own time for an **oratorio** he composed with **Charles Avison**, *Ruth* (1763).

GIBBONS, CHRISTOPHER (1615–76). Organist and composer. Gibbons was the son of **Orlando Gibbons**, under whose direction he was likely trained in the **Chapel Royal**, though the death of the father in 1625 probably saw the son come under the care of his uncle, Edward, at Exeter. In 1638 he was appointed organist at Winchester; in the 1640s, however, the effects of the **Puritan** ascendancy prompted him to relocate in London, where he taught, was organist to Sir John Danvers, and performed in works like *The Siege of Rhodes*. In 1660 he was appointed organist of the Chapel Royal, a post once held by his father; for a time he was also organist and later master of the choristers at Westminster Abbey. At the king's behest, he received the DMus from Oxford in 1664. Zimmerman (1983) considers circumstantial evidence that suggests an intimate acquaintance between Gibbons and **Daniel** and **Henry Purcell**'s family, including the fact that both families at different times had lived in the same house.

GIBBONS, ORLANDO (1583–1625). Composer and keyboardist. Gibbons emerges as one of the most eminent of the Jacobean musicians, highly esteemed for his keyboard abilities, and the composer of works that seem to define the Jacobean style. He was trained as a chorister at King's College, Cambridge, under the direction of his brother, Edward (Master there from 1592 to 1598). He was appointed organist of the **Chapel Royal** in 1604/5, took the BMus at Cambridge in 1606, was named virginalist to the Privy Chamber in 1619, and in 1623, organist at Westminster Abbey. Tradition puts forth a DMus from Oxford in 1622, although the recent work of Harley (1999) calls this into question, noting among other things the way Gibbons is styled on his monument and the absence of doctoral reference to him in contexts where others were clearly so designated. Gibbons died dramatically while traveling with the new Caroline court to Canterbury to receive Queen Henrietta Maria.

Gibbons's inclusion as one of the three composers in *Parthenia* along with **William Byrd** and **John Bull** confirms his rank as a keyboard composer. In his writings for the church, the verse **anthems**, such as the enduringly fine "This Is the Record of John" or "See, See, the Word Is Incarnate," are especially significant in their masterful combining of declamatory elements in polyphonic contexts; Wulstan (1985) describes the former as an example of Gibbons's "uncanny ability . . . to unfold a declamatory voice part within a fully worked-out contrapuntal texture, uniting the *prima* with the *seconda prattica*." His **madrigal** "The Silver Swanne" is justly praised for its memorable melody.

GIBBS, CECIL ARMSTRONG (1889–1960). Composer, adjudicator, and conductor. Gibbs was a well-known competition adjudicator for **musical festivals**, and much of his composition reflects the needs of the amateur choir. His entrée into the competition festival movement was as the conductor of the Danbury Choral Society (a post he held from 1919); he was also vice president of the British Federation of Music Festivals for a time (1937–52). Gibbs's early education at Winchester College was followed by a BA at Trinity College, Cambridge, in history (1911) and a MusB (1913). After several years as a music master at public schools, he studied at the **Royal College of Music** for a year (1920) and then taught composition there (1921–39). He took the MusD degree from Cambridge in 1931. Aside from songs and **cantatas** for competition festivals, Gibbs was known in his own time for incidental music such as *Midsummer Madness* (1924), for a play by Clifford Bax, or light music such as *The Blue Peter* (1923), to a libretto by A. P. Herbert.

GILBERT, SIR WILLIAM SCHWENCK (W. S.; 1836–1911). Librettist and dramatist. Gilbert was in his own time and remains today a household name, particularly for his satirical operetta collaborations with **Sir Arthur Sullivan**. With their incredible coincidences, biting social satire, and memorable turns of phrase, these operettas became famous throughout the English speaking world, and as promoted by the **D'Oyly Carte Opera Company**, they were heard throughout Great Britain, North America, Australia, and elsewhere. Gilbert was educated at King's College, London, and after early work in the civil service worked as a barrister. He began to write satirical verse in the 1860, working as a journalist as well. By the end of the 1860s, Gilbert wrote librettos for dramatic entertainments with music, as well as operatic parodies and burlesques.

The 15-work collaboration with Sullivan started in 1871 and lasted, with some ruptures, until 1896. Some of the most memorable works of the 19th century came from this union, including ***H.M.S. Pinafore*** (1878), ***The Pirates of Penzance*** (1879), and ***The Mikado*** (1885). Aside from Sullivan, Gilbert wrote libretti for the composers Frank Osmund Carr, **Alfred Cellier**, **Frederic Clay**, **Sir Edward German**, and George Grossmith. Gilbert was knighted in 1907.

GILES, NATHANIEL (ca. 1558–1634). Composer and organist. Giles was likely trained at Worcester under John Colden, whom he succeeded at the

Cathedral in 1569. In 1585 he became master of the children and organist at St. George's, Windsor, the same year in which he received the BMus from Oxford. He was appointed master of the children of the **Chapel Royal** in 1597, a post that he maintained along with his duties at Windsor. His time in the Chapel Royal coincides with tensions arising out of the so-called **choir-boy plays**, in which some feared that choristers were brought into the chapel more for their theatrical than their musical talents. Giles received the DMus from Oxford in 1622.

GLEE. Secular vocal genre similar to the **partsong**. While the term occurs as early as the 1650s (**John Playford** uses it in his third set of *Ayres and Dialogues* [1659]), the glee flourished primarily between 1750 and 1914, when tens of thousands were composed. The glee was a short vocal piece in no specified form, usually meant to be sung a cappella, but occasionally with instrumental accompaniment. The social history of the glee matches that of choral singing: in the 18th century, it was an activity for upper-class males supplemented by paid professional singers from theaters, churches, cathedrals, and even the **Chapel Royal**, as were glees sung by the **Noblemen and Gentlemen's Catch Club**. Such glees were usually in ATB, TTB, or ATTB vocal arrangements. In the 19th century, the glee became a mixed-sex amateur genre sung by hundreds at a time in the great choral societies and **musical festivals** (especially those featuring competitions), often for SATB or SSATB arrangements.

Subjects of glees were classed either "cheerful" or "serious" (both were annual prize categories at the Noblemen and Gentlemen's Catch Club); they featured drinking, love, and pastoral themes, though they were generally less bawdy than the **catch**, making them appropriate for female participation, especially in the 19th century. This did not, however, stop Evangelical philanthropists such as **John Curwen** from condemning many 18th-century works as unfit for singing in the 19th century, calling their words "suited to the immoral age in which [they were] composed."

Like **madrigals**, glees frequently set different sections of text to alternating textures, and might include quick changes of tonality or meter depending on the texts set. **Sir Henry Bishop**'s "Sleep, while the Soft Evening" is a typical example; homophonic sections alternate with brief solo lines in simple counterpoint, with the occasional poignant harmony before a structural cadence. The text describes an extended farewell before bedtime. Most of the major composers of the 18th and 19th centuries set glees, including **John Alcock, Thomas Augustine Arne, Jonathan Battishill, Benjamin Cooke, Tom Cooke, Charles Dibdin,** John Goss, **Pieter Hellendaal, Henry Hiles, James Hook, William Horsley, Thomas Linley (the elder),**

Sir George Alexander Macfarren, Thomas Norris, Stephen Paxton, William Shield, John Stafford Smith, Stephen Storace, Samuel Webbe, Charles Wesley (2), Samuel Wesley, and **Samuel Sebastian Wesley,** inter alia. *See also* ANACREONTIC SOCIETY; BARRETT, WILLIAM ALEXANDER.

GLORIA TIBI TRINITAS. Sarum antiphon for the First Vespers of Trinity Sunday, used as the cantus firmus for *In nomine* settings. The foundational setting for this repertory of pieces is **John Taverner**'s "Benedictus" from the *Missa Gloria tibi Trinitas* at the words "in nomine."

GLOVER, SARAH (1786–1867). Children's educator, inventor, and singing teacher. Using a notational system she devised, Glover taught children to sing **hymns** at the Norwich church of St. Lawrence, where her father was rector. Glover created the system by turning standard solfège syllables into notation, reducing them to capital letters for printing, substituting the syllable Ti or Te for the usual Si (to avoid confusion with Sol), and separating them with punctuation signs to show a rudimentary rhythmic system. In 1835 she published *Scheme for Rendering Psalmody Congregational*, followed in 1839 by the *Tonic Sol-fa Tune Book* to disseminate the system.

    John Curwen read the *Scheme* in 1841 and, after modifying the notation by using lower-case letters for syllables instead of capital ones, began to propagate it without her permission, using the name **Tonic Sol-fa** to do so. With his modifications, Tonic Sol-fa became one of the major notations used in Great Britain in the second half of the 19th century. While Curwen acknowledged Glover as the notation's inventor in the journal the *Tonic Sol-fa Reporter* and his numerous public lectures on the method, the two had an ambivalent relationship until her death. Glover renamed her system "Norwich Sol-fa" to separate it from Curwen's better-known Tonic Sol-fa. She devised numerous aids to teaching music, including the Sol-fa Ladder, a chart to aid visualizing transposition (which Curwen modified and used), and the Sol-fa Harmonicon, a small glockenspiel with 25 keys and dials above each one that would display solfège syllables for all major scales.

"GOD SAVE THE KING (QUEEN)." Song traditionally sung in salute to the English monarch and as the national anthem. The identification of its composer is uncertain; a posthumous attribution to **Henry Carey** remains unverified. The song came into popular usage, however, in the wake of the Battle of Prestonpans (21 September 1745), sung regularly in an arrangement by **Thomas Arne** at **Drury Lane** on behalf of George II, under threat by the Jacobite uprising in the north.

GOOSSENS, SIR EUGENE (1893–1962). Conductor and composer active in England, the United States, and Australia. Goossens was one of the most important conductors of the middle of the 20th century and was a champion of contemporary music. His 1942 commission of patriotic fanfares for the Cincinnati Symphony Orchestra included Aaron Copland's now famous *Fanfare for the Common Man*.

Goossens came from a musical family (his father and grandfather, both named Eugène, conducted the **Carl Rosa Opera Company**; his siblings were also famous musicians). After initial training at Bruges Conservatory and in Liverpool, he attended the **Royal College of Music**. He was a violinist in **Sir Thomas Beecham**'s **Queen's Hall** Orchestra from 1912 to 1915 and served as Beecham's assistant conductor for a time. In 1921 Goossens founded his own orchestra (the Goossens Orchestra) and began a long conducting career with such organizations as the Carl Rosa Opera Company. From 1923 to 1956 Goossens held positions in the United States, including the Eastman-Rochester Philharmonic Orchestra (1923–31) and the Cincinnati Symphony Orchestra (1931–46), and in Australia at the Sydney Symphony Orcestra (1946–57); he was also for a time the director of the New South Wales Conservatorium of Music. He left Australia when he was caught smuggling pornographic images into that country; he returned to England in 1956 and continued recording with British and continental orchestras. Goossens was knighted in 1955.

GOSTLING, JOHN (1650–1733). Singer and cleric. Gostling became a gentleman of the **Chapel Royal** in 1679 and a minor canon at St. Paul's, London, in 1683. He additionally served as a chaplain to William III. As a singer he was particularly noted for the profundity of his bass range, used to striking effect in verse **anthems** like **Henry Purcell**'s "They That Go Down to the Sea in Ships." **Sir John Hawkins** records that this particular anthem resulted from Gostling's presence on Charles II's royal yacht, *The Fubbs*, during a violent storm, an experience dramatic enough to send Gostling to the psalms for appropriate verses, which he took to Purcell to set. Purcell did so in a particularly text-depictive way, "adapting [the music] . . . so peculiarly to the compass of Mr. Gostling's voice, which was a deep bass, that hardly any person but himself was then, or has since been able to sing it." Gostling's presence on the yacht suggests royal favor, confirmed by the king's fabled gift to Gostling of a silver egg filled with guineas, adding that "he had heard that eggs were good for the voice."

Gostling was also active in the copying of church music, as in the Gostling Partbooks at York (GBYm15).

GRABU, LOUIS (fl. 1665–94). Violinist and composer. Grabu's appointment to royal service in 1665 coincides with the popularity of French taste at court, although resentment from English musicians like **John Banister**, whose leadership of the court violins was a casualty of Grabu's rise, was strong. Grabu was a Spaniard, Francophied in musical matters, and his Roman Catholicism saw his court position fall in the wake of the Test Act in the mid-1670s, at which time he focused his attention on theater music. The most well known of his theatrical works is the **opera** *Albion and Albanius*, to an allegorical text by **John Dryden**. Intended originally to be the prologue to *King Arthur*, its independent performance in 1685 was a failure, in part, one suspects, due to its being performed during the Duke of Monmouth's unsuccessful but dramatic attempt to gain the throne.

John Dryden's esteem of the composer is enshrined in the prefatory material to *Albion*. Conscious of having chosen a foreigner, Dryden explained: "When any of our countrymen excel him, I shall be glad, for the sake of old England, to be shewn my errour."

GRADUALIA. Two volumes of mass propers published by **William Byrd**. The later years of Byrd's life saw a number of manifestations of his Roman Catholic faith, including participation in the recusant community of John Petre and boldly publishing music for the Roman rite, including three settings of the ordinary and a large collection of mass propers for major feasts and Marian occasions. The two volumes of *Gradualia* (1605 and 1607; both reissued in 1610) are devoted to the mass propers. The dedicatory material is interestingly personal and intimate, as in this statement where the composer writes of a mystical contemplation of the words leading him to their proper setting:

> [I]n these words, as I have learned by trial, there is such a profound and hidden power that to one thinking upon things divine and diligently and earnestly pondering them, all the fittest numbers occur as if of themselves and freely offer themselves to the mind which is not indolent or inert.

GRAINGER, PERCY ALDRIGE (ALSO GEORGE PERCY; 1882–1961). Composer, pianist, and writer on music of Australian origin. Though Grainger spent a little over a decade in England (1901–14), he collected English folk songs, and they remained a staple influence of his compositional technique throughout his career. Grainger received early education and training in Australia and in Frankfurt, being one of the composers of the so-called **Frankfurt Group** who studied with Iwan Knorr at the Hochschule für Musik there. While in England, he was active mostly as a concert pianist, though Schott began publishing his compositions in 1911, and he had a concert of his own works in 1912 in London. In 1914 he moved to the United States and spent the rest of his career between the United States and Australia, returning to Europe occasionally to tour and collect folk songs. His works have remained popular, especially in wind-band arrangements.

GRAY, CECIL (1895–1951). Music critic, writer on music, and composer. Gray was one of the most powerful and provocative critical voices of the 1920s and 1930s, along with **Constant Lambert, Philip Heseltine**, and **Bernard Van Dieren**. With Heseltine, he founded the *Sackbut*, to which they both contributed material for nine controversial issues before losing control of the magazine when it was purchased by the **Curwen Press** (1920–21). Gray's books, including *A Survey of Contemporary Music* (1924) and *The History of Music* (1928), as well as volumes on Jean Sibelius, Heseltine, Don Carlo Gesualdo, and Johann Sebastian Bach, were popular though critically problematic in their own time. Little is known about his early artistic education, though he did take a degree in arts from Edinburgh University (1913) and studied privately with Healey Willan before Willan emigrated to Canada in 1913. Gray composed little but completed three **operas** (mostly unperformed) and a Symphonic Prelude (1945).

GREATOREX, THOMAS (1758–1831). Conductor, organist, teacher, composer, astronomer, and mathematician. Greatorex was one of the most highly regarded musicians of his day, both for his activities in London and for his conducting of provincial **musical festivals**. He was an **organ** pupil of **Benjamin Cooke** in London and—on the recommendation of **Joah Bates**— worked early on as an organist for the Earl of Sandwich. From 1771 to 1784 he was the organist of Carlisle Cathedral, but he made frequent trips to London, such as in 1776, when he sang in the first of the **Concerts of Ancient Music**. He studied singing with Giuseppi Santarelli in Italy and keyboard with Ignace Joseph Pleyel in Strasbourg between 1786 and 1788, whereupon he returned to various positions in London for the rest of his career: conductor of the Concerts of Ancient Music (1793 until his death), organist of Westminster Abbey (1819 until his death), and professor of organ and harmony at the **Royal Academy of Music** (2; 1822 until his death). He was a member of the **Noblemen and Gentlemen's Catch Club** and conducted musical festivals at Birmingham, Chester, Derby, and York. For his works on mathematics and astronomy, he was elected a member of the Royal Society.

GREENE, MAURICE (1696–1755). Composer and organist. Greene's appointments as organist of St. Paul's, London (1718), organist and composer of the **Chapel Royal** (1727), and **Master of the King's Music** (1735) made him a particularly prominent figure in 18th-century London musical circles, an English voice amid Handelian importations. His compositions include a large body of **anthems** in full, verse, and solo formats—many of which were published in *Forty Select Anthems* (1743)—**services, voluntaries,** and **oratorios**. Late in his life he began work collecting church music for a planned anthology, historical and contemporary. Aided by the collateral work of **John Alcock**, this material resurfaces in **William Boyce**'s *Cathedral Music*.

Greene was a pivotal player in the **Academy of Ancient Music** plagiarism scandal of 1731 involving his performance of a **madrigal** ostensibly by **Giovanni Bononcini** but in reality the work of Antonio Lotti. In the wake of this turbulence, Greene withdrew from the Academy of Ancient Music in favor of the Apollo Academy.

"GREENSLEEVES." Popular 16th-century **ballad** tune. The popularity and familiarity of "Greensleeves" is suggested in **William Shakespeare**'s two references to the melody in *The Merry Wives of Windsor*. Its modern familiarity has been sustained both by its use with the **carol** text "What Child Is This?" and in its setting by **Ralph Vaughan Williams** in his enduringly popular *Fantasia on "Greensleeves"* (1934). One reasonably expects a degree of variability in ballad tunes, particularly given the frequency of their oral transmission. Different versions of "Greensleeves" survive that, in addition to melodic variation, also proceed in different meters. The bass line generating the harmonies for "Greensleeves" conforms to familiar patterns of standard ground basses—in this case the *Passamezzo antico* and the *Romanesca*—a situation that is strongly suggestive of roots in improvisation.

GROVE, SIR GEORGE (1820–1900). Engineer, writer on music, music administrator, educator, and impresario. Grove is best remembered today for his editing of and many contributions to *A Dictionary of Music and Musicians* (1879–89), which became through various editions *Grove's Dictionary of Music and Musicians* and *The New Grove Dictionary of Music and Musicians*, often simply shortened to *Grove*. Grove worked as an engineer from 1836 to 1849 before turning to literary and cultural pursuits. He was named secretary of the Society of Arts in 1849 and secretary of the **Crystal Palace** Corporation in 1852; he began writing a series of analytical program notes for the Crystal Palace Concerts in 1854. He continued to work for the Crystal Palace until 1873, when he resigned to devote more time to the *Dictionary*, though he continued to write program notes for the Saturday concerts. He was involved from 1881 in the foundation of the **Royal College of Music** and was named its director in 1882—a post he held until 1894. Grove was a longtime contributor to the *Times* and many other newspapers and journals; wrote a monograph, *Beethoven and His Nine Symphonies* (1894), that is still in use today; and was a sought-after expert on numerous subjects, including biblical history and geography. He was knighted in 1883 and named a Companion of the Bath in 1894.

GUEST, JANE (ALSO JENNY GUEST; JANE MILES; 1762–1846). Pianist and composer, primarily of vocal and keyboard works. Guest was trained and performed early concerts in her hometown of Bath before taking lessons with **Johann Christian Bach** in 1776. She organized her own subscription series at the Tottenham Street Rooms (1783–84) and played at the **Hanover Square Rooms** and Willis's Rooms as well. Guest was also appointed by George III to be the musical instructor of Princess Amalie (1804) and Princess Charlotte (1806). Aside from salon music, she is known to have composed piano concertos.

GUILDHALL SCHOOL OF MUSIC (GSM). Musical education center that awards BMus (performance) and MMus (composition) degrees, founded by the Corporation of the City of London in 1880 from the success of the Guildhall Orchestral and Choral Society, conducted by T. H. Weist Hill (he became the school's first principal, followed, at his death, by **Sir Joseph Barnby**). The school has had three locations: Aldermanbury (1880), Blackfriars (1887), and finally the Barbican (1977). Initially, Guildhall offered students part-time courses, but began offering full-time ones in 1920. In 1935 the institution became the Guildhall School of Music and Drama when theater courses were added to its purview. *See also* COLERIDGE-TAYLOR, SAMUEL; LEHMANN, LIZA; MACCUNN, HAMISH; PROUT, EBENEZER; RUBBRA, EDMUND; SILAS, EDOUARD.

GURNEY, IVOR (1890–1937). Poet and composer, predominantly of songs. Gurney was a chorister and pupil of **Sir Herbert Brewer** at Gloucester Cathedral before studying at the **Royal College of Music** (RCM) in 1911 with **Sir Charles Villiers Stanford**. War service interrupted his education (1915–18); he was hospitalized, and contemporaries claimed he suffered thereafter from "shell shock." During this time, he began to publish volumes of poetry, including *Severn & Somme* (1917) and *War's Embers* (1919), both to some acclaim. He returned to the RCM, studying there from late 1918 to 1921 with **Ralph Vaughan Williams**. In the early 1920s, he had an extremely prolific period of songwriting, but after a short period in Gloucester around 1921, he spent the remainder of his life in various mental hospitals. Most of his publications come from the end of the 1910s and early 1920s; more of his work was published after his death, but much of it remains in manuscript.

GYFFARD PARTBOOKS. Manuscript source (GB Lbl Add 17802–5) copied in the main during the reign of Mary Tudor (1553–58), containing liturgical music by **John Taverner**, **John Sheppard**, **Christopher Tye**, **Thomas Tallis**, and **Robert Whyte**, among others.

GYMEL. The division of one vocal part into two parts of equal range. Though found earlier in continental sources, the first English source for gymel is the **Eton Choirbook**, with several examples. A late 15th-century Italian treatise by Guilielmus Monachus, *De Preceptis Artis Musicae*, describes gymel as a "modus Anglicorum" (one of two) that consists of parallel thirds and sixths. While some scholars have seen this tertian element as key, modern commentators view it as too constraining and a misapplication of the term.

H

HALLÉ, SIR CHARLES (ALSO CARL HALLE; 1819–95). Conductor and pianist of German birth, known best for his conducting of the highly disciplined **Hallé Orchestra** in Manchester and his recitals of Beethoven's piano sonatas in London. Hallé studied with Ludwig Spohr as well as in Darmstadt and Paris; he gave his first recital at the age of nine and conducted two **operas**—*Die Zauberflöte* and *Der Freischütz*—at the age of 11. Hallé settled in England in 1848, first in London, but centering his activities in Manchester late in that year. He began conducting the Gentleman's Concerts there in 1849, with an orchestra of 40; when an exhibition in 1857 required a larger orchestra, he organized this and used it as the nucleus of the Hallé Orchestra (founded 1858). Hallé was a great believer in the idea that good music led to self-improvement, and he made cheaper seats available at early concerts in the Manchester Free Trade Hall and took his orchestra on frequent tours to poorer districts without large instrumental forces. Aside from the Manchester ensemble, he was also the director of the Royal Liverpool Philharmonic Orchestra from 1883 to 1895 and the principal and piano instructor at the Royal Music College, Manchester, from 1893 until his death. Hallé was knighted in 1888.

HALLÉ ORCHESTRA. Manchester-based orchestra, founded in 1858 by **Sir Charles Hallé** and consistently considered the best (and most disciplined) instrumental ensemble in England during the second half of the 19th century. The orchestra performed regularly at the Free Trade Hall in Manchester before moving to the newly constructed Bridgewater Hall in 1996. The orchestra performed many notable premieres of English works (including **Sir Edward Elgar**'s Symphony no. 1 in A-flat major in 1908) and had as regular conductors and directors some of the most famous individuals working in England in the 19th and 20th centuries, including Hallé (1858–95), **Frederic Cowen** (1895–99), **Hans Richter** (1899–1911), as well as **Sir Thomas Beecham**, Hamilton Harty, **Sir Malcolm Sargent**, and **Sir John Barbirolli**. The Hallé Orchestra frequently toured and often made up part or all of provincial **musical festival** orchestras, including those of Bristol and Huddersfield.

HANDEL, GEORGE FRIDERIC (1685–1759). The most accomplished composer of the first part of the 18th century in England. Handel's irrefutable iconicity as an English composer is rooted in his prominence in the London musical scene, especially that of the operatic theater, but more enduringly in his contribution to the ceremonial royal style—his **coronation anthem** "Zadok the Priest," written for the coronation of George II in 1727, has not only become a fixture at succeeding coronations, but also in its grand gestures creates a long-lasting *typos* of musical regality, echoed in celebrative works like *Musick for the Royal Fireworks* (1749)—and in his creation of the English **oratorio**, a form distinct from its Italian counterpart and one that would receive long life in the English choral festival. Handel's English iconicity is not without irony.

A native Saxon whose early influences were German (Friederich Zachow in Halle and Reinhold Keiser in Hamburg) and Italian (Corelli, inter alia, in Rome), Handel did not become naturalized until 1727, long after his prominence has been established in London. As a composer whose activities in his first two decades in England are most notably devoted to Italian **opera**, he seems well to personify the invading foreigner whose cultural "victory"—the unanswerable popularity of Italian opera—led to the demise of the English musical theater. Suggestive of the extent to which native English musical theater had become moribund, the poet and opera director Aaron Hill in 1732 referred to "our Italian bondage" in a letter to Handel. But if with one hand Handel thwarted the native form, in his cultivation of English oratorio, a cultivation largely begun in the wake of the financial collapse of London opera in the late 1730s, he gave back with the other. Certainly the English form was distinctive and enduring; however, the strong imprint of Handel's own idiom in the oratorio form perhaps, also ironically, impeded the growth of later English composers in that genre.

Handel's compositional range was broad; he wrote odes, anthems, Latin psalms (including the notably challenging setting of *Dixit Dominus* from 1707), a large quantity of Italian **cantatas**, orchestral works (including concerti grossi whose form echoes Corelli and suites like the famous "Water Music"), and solo instrumental works. But his greatest attention was focused on music drama, be it opera or oratorio, and his fidelity to the theater spanned nearly all stages of his career. Opera was to be his "calling card" to London audiences when, as the new Hanoverian Kappelmeister, he traveled to England and premiered his opera *Rinaldo* (1711), a work rich in compelling arias, such as the haunting sarabande "Lascia ch'io pianga" and the bravura "Or la tromba," and a work rich in stagecraft, as satirically noted by Addison in the *Spectator*. And although Handel dutifully returned to Hanover in the summer of 1711, the success of *Rinaldo* and the professional possibilities of London prompted both his quick return and his famous extending of his leave of absence.

London opera began a new era with the establishment of the **Royal Academy of Music (1)** in 1719, an opera company financed by subscription and located at the **Haymarket** Theatre. Handel, functioning as music director, traveled to the Continent in May 1719 to hire "proper voices to sing in the opera" and to "engage Senezino [*sic*] as soon as possible to serve the said company and for as many years as may be." The interest in star singers, reinforced by the aria-driven style of the operas, would eventually bring to the Royal Academy the great castrato **Senesino** and the divas Francesca Cuzzoni and Faustina Bordoni (Hasse). A company of such luminaries fed the audience tastes for foreign singers of celebrity but also exacted a toll emotionally, as seen in the public feuding between Cuzzoni and Bordoni. The coming to blows of the two singers and their supporters during a performance of **Giovanni Bononcini**'s *Astianatte* unsurprisingly prompted contemporary comment. John Arbuthnot, for instance, opined that "it is certainly an apparent shame that two such well bred ladies should call 'Bitch' and 'Whore,' [and] should scold and fight like any Billingates." The tension between singers, the high salaries they commanded, and a shift in audience taste, seen for instance in the popularity of *The Beggar's Opera* (1728), a **ballad opera** that lampooned both the aristocracy and Italian opera, undermined the viability of the company, and it closed in 1728.

A second academy was formed in 1729, again under the leadership of Handel and **John Jacob Heidegger**. Among the challenges facing this second academy was the competition of an unprecedented second company, the **"Opera of the Nobility,"** which opened in 1733, led by **Johann Christoph Pepusch** and featuring **Senesino**, who had become estranged from Handel, and **Farinelli**. A note from the Minister of the King of Prussia describes the unrest out of which the "Opera of the Nobility" arose: "Last Saturday the opening of the new Opera-house took place, which the *Noblesse* has undertaken since they were not satisfied with the *Conduite* of the *Directeur* of the old *Opera*, *Händel*, and to abase him, planned a new one." Both the second academy and the "Opera of the Nobility" closed in bankruptcy in 1737.

In the wake of the demise of the opera companies, Handel turned to oratorio, and in so doing remained a man of the theater—oratorios, though on sacred subjects, were conceived as works to be performed in the theater. His turn to oratorio reshaped the well-established Italian genre—a genre he knew well from his early days in Rome and from his own composition of works like *La Resurrezione* (1708)—by using vernacular texts and English singers, and by giving to the chorus a newly significant role. Most of the English oratorios were based on Old Testament narratives, as in *Samson* (1741), *Israel in Egypt* (1739), and *Saul* (1739), and emerge potentially as national allegories and responses to the advance of Deism (Smith, 1995).

The most famous exception to the model is, of course, Handel's most famous work, *Messiah*, first performed in Dublin in 1742. Handel's oratorio offers a nonnarrative, contemplative consideration of the arc of Jesus's life and work, with Biblical texts compiled into a libretto by Charles Jennens. Its unflagging modern popularity may derive in no little part from its seasonal association with Christmas, although it was clearly successful at its Dublin premiere; the *Dublin Journal* noted that "words are wanting to express the exquisite Delight it afforded to the admiring crouded Audience," a sentiment that seems to be nearly timeless. But additionally, part of its popularity may rest in its strong and highly varied choruses, ranging from the intimate textures of the so-called duet choruses, based on earlier Italian duets, to the powerful anthem choruses, such as the expansive and impressively contrapuntal "Amen." *See also* ANTHEM; ARNE, MICHAEL; ARNOLD, SAMUEL; AVISON, CHARLES; BABELL, WILLIAM; BATES, JOAH; BONONCINI, GIOVANNI; BRIDGE, SIR FREDERICK; BURNEY, CHARLES; CEREMONIAL MUSIC; CORONATION MUSIC; COVENT GARDEN THEATRE; CRYSTAL PALACE; CURWEN PRESS; FOUNDLING HOPSITAL; GALLIARD, JOHN ERNST; GATES, BERNARD; GIARDINI, FELICE; HANDEL COMMEMORATION; HANDEL SOCIETY; HAWKINS, SIR JOHN; HAYES, WILLIAM; HELLENDAAL, PIETER; HICKFORD'S ROOM; MACFARREN, SIR GEORGE ALEXANDER; MUSICAL FESTIVALS; ODE; PLEASURE GARDENS; PROUT, EBENEZER; ROSEINGRAVE, THOMAS; ROYAL SOCIETY OF MUSICIANS; "RULE BRITANNIA"; SMITH, JOHN CHRISTOPHER (THE ELDER); SMITH, JOHN CHRISTOPHER (THE YOUNGER); VAUXHALL GARDENS; WALSH, JOHN.

HANDEL COMMEMORATION. Organized by John Montagu, the Fourth Earl of Sandwich, Sir Watkins Williams Wynn, and **Joah Bates**, with the **Concerts of Ancient Music** and the **Society of Musicians**, the Handel Commemoration took place between 26 May and 5 June 1784, marking the 25th anniversary of **George Frideric Handel**'s death. The five concerts (three planned, two repeated because of popularity) of the commemoration were held in Westminster Abbey and the **Pantheon** and featured more than 500 performers, conducted by Bates. The concerts featured a full performance of *Messiah* and selections from Handel's other works, especially his **oratorios**—a practice that became popular at **musical festivals** for the next 50 years. **Charles Burney** wrote a description of the commemoration in 1785, and the performances were repeated in 1785, 1786, 1787, 1790, and 1791. The large forces at these concerts were repeated in Handel festivals throughout the 19th century (especially those at the **Crystal Palace**, beginning in 1856) and became a regular feature of some musical festivals as well. *See* *also* COOKE, BENJAMIN; CROTCH, WILLIAM; NORRIS, THOMAS; PARKE, MARIA FRANCIS; PAXTON, STEPHEN; PUBLIC CONCERTS.

HANDEL FESTIVAL. *See* MUSICAL FESTIVALS.

HANDEL SOCIETY. London choir active between 1882 and 1939 dedicated to the performance of **George Frideric Handel**'s lesser-known **oratorios**. **Samuel Coleridge-Taylor** and **Ralph Vaughan Williams** both conducted it for a time. *See also* RIMBAULT, EDWARD FRANCIS.

HANOVER SQUARE ROOMS (ALSO HANOVER SQUARE CONCERT ROOMS; QUEEN'S CONCERT ROOMS). London **concert rooms** built in partnership between **Giovanni Andrea Battista Gallini**, **Johann Christian Bach**, and **Carl Friedrich Abel** in 1775 for the Bach-Abel concerts and a rival series on alternate evenings by Gallini, and used eventually by **Johann Peter Salomon** for **Franz Joseph Haydn**'s concerts in London between 1791 and 1795. Like many venues, the Hanover Square Concert Rooms became an extension of the subscribers' own drawing rooms (it had sofas surrounding the rooms), and the managers sought social exclusivity through both high ticket prices and screening potential ticket subscribers. The venue was used well into the 19th century for concerts (**Sir William Sterndale Bennett**, for instance, held occasional orchestral concerts there between 1848 and 1856), and it was also the location of the library of the **Bach Society**.

HARRIS, RENATUS (ca. 1652–1724). Organ builder. The son of Thomas Harris, an organ builder who had relocated in France during the interregnum, Renatus returned with his father at the Restoration of the monarchy, eventually succeeding the elder Harris in the family business. Renatus, described by **Charles Burney** as "an ingenious and active young man," was famously the rival of the organ builder **Bernard ("Father") Smith**. The most noted instance of the rivalry was their mutual competition for the new organ at London's Temple Church, a competition that saw each builder provide an instrument within the church and engage players to demonstrate. Smith's instrument, the ultimate victor, was played by **John Blow** and **Henry Purcell**; Harris's instrument was played by **Giovanni Battista Draghi**, an association that reflects Harris's Roman Catholicism. Among Harris's many instruments was a large organ for Salisbury Cathedral, the first in England to be configured with four manuals.

HAWKINS, SIR JOHN (1719–89). Music historian. The publication of Hawkins's *General History of the Science and Practice of Music* (1776) brought to the public one of the first two general music histories in English, the other being **Charles Burney**'s *A General History of Music*. Though both works drew on extensive research—Hawkins spent 16 years working on his history—the two works are significantly different in their views. Hawkins's orientation is more historical, with an aesthetic appreciation of music of the past, repertories that he additionally anthologized within his study. "Modern" music, however, fares less well. With Burney, the reverse obtains. The historical orientation of Hawkins may have contributed to the viability of his study in later generations (Harrison, Hood, Palisca, 1963); the *General History* was reprinted twice in the 19th century (1853 and 1875).

Hawkins's friends included prominent London musicians like **George Frideric Handel** and **John Stanley**; he was also a friend of Samuel Johnson, whose biography he published prior to the more enduring version offered by James Boswell in 1791.

Hawkins received training first as an architect and then as a lawyer; the latter was his career. He began writing in 1739 on numerous topics and gradually became more involved with the music and musicians of his time. He became a member of the **Academy of Ancient Music** sometime in the mid-1740s, joined the **Madrigal Society** in 1748, and played chamber music as an amateur. A family bequest in 1759 allowed him to pursue scholastic matters, including purchasing musical manuscripts and old prints (through these funds, he acquired **Johann Christoph Pepusch**'s library). Between 1761 and 1775, he researched *A General History* both at the **British Museum** and within his own library. Aside from *A General History*, he also published studies of **William Croft** (1775), Arcangelo Corelli (1777), and **William Boyce** (1788). Hawkins was knighted in 1772 for his work as a magistrate.

HAYDN, FRANZ JOSEPH (1732–1809). Austro-Hungarian composer, active in England between 1791–92 and 1794–95. For the first few decades of the 19th century, he was the most important composer in England after **George Frideric Handel**; his **oratorios** *The Creation* and *The Seasons* were staple works at **musical festivals**. While Bremer published some of Haydn's quartets in the early 1770s, his music did not become popular in England until the 1780s. When he visited in the 1790s, after his invitation from **Johann Peter Salomon**, he performed to popular acclaim at the **Hanover Square Rooms**; the King's Theatre, **Haymarket**; and other venues, including over 50 concerts. The compositions he completed for his English trips include Symphonies nos. 93–104 (the *London* **Symphonies**), piano sonatas, and solo songs; inspiration for *The Creation* may have come from witnessing performances of Handel's music in Westminster Abbey. *See also* ADAMS, THOMAS; ANTHEM; BARTHÉLEMON, FRANÇOIS-HIPPOLYTE; CLEMENTI, MUZIO; CLEMENTI & CO.; COWEN, SIR FREDERIC HYMEN;

GALLINI, GIOVANNI ANDREA BATTISTA; PARKE, MARIA FRAN-CIS; PROFESSIONAL CONCERT; SCHROETER, JOHANN SAMUEL; VIOTTI, GIOVANNI BATTISTA.

HAYES, WILLIAM (1708–77). Composer, conductor, organist, singer, and writer on music. Hayes was an ardent Handelian, well respected as a conductor and singer at the provincial **musical festivals**, and a longtime professor of music at Oxford. He received early education and training as a chorister at Gloucester Cathedral. Hayes's positions included being organist at St. Mary's Shrewsbury (1729) and Worcester Cathedral (1731) and as the *informator choristarum* at Magdalen College, Oxford (1735), before being appointed professor of music and organist of the University Church at Oxford (1741). He took a BMus from Oxford in 1735 and a DMus in 1749. Hayes's compositions, mostly unpublished, include an **oratorio** (*The Fall of Jericho*), **odes** (including one dedicated to **George Frideric Handel**, "O That Some Pensive Muse"), sacred music, and some instrumental selections.

HAYMARKET (ALSO HAYMARKET THEATRE; HER MAJESTY'S THEATRE; HIS MAJESTY'S THEATRE). In 1705 John Vanbrugh built the first of several theaters on the west side of London's Haymarket, where with Congreve he began the productions of **operas**; the venue, or its latter-day descendants, became the chief London theater for Italian opera well into the 19th century. Initially the Queen's Theatre, becoming the King's Theatre in 1714 with the accession of George I, the Haymarket saw the first performances of a number of **George Frideric Handel**'s operas, beginning with *Rinaldo* in 1711. The King's Theatre was home to the **Royal Academy of Music (1)** from 1719 to 1728, an operatic venture that featured the operas of Handel, **Giovanni Bononcini**, and Attilio Ariosti; in 1734 the rival **"Opera of the Nobility"** was in residence, featuring the operas of **Nicola Porpora** and the celebrated singing of the castrato **Farinelli**. The first theater was destroyed by fire in 1789 and the second built in 1791. Within this iteration, the King's Theatre saw the productions of operas by Wolfgang Amadeus Mozart, Gioachino Rossini, Vincenzo Bellini, Gaetano Donizetti, and Giuseppe Verdi; the new theater seated 3,300. The theater was renamed Her Majesty's on Queen Victoria's accession in 1837.

In the 1840s the focus of the theater changed, and French and German operas were heard alongside Italian ones. Also, for a time, the theater's ballet company was as prestigious as the opera company. A third theater was built in 1868 with a capacity of 1,900 seats; though, because of a rent dispute, it went unused until 1874. This version of Her Majesty's Theatre presented the London premiere of Richard Wagner's *Ring* cycle, among other works. It also saw the production of the last opera there, in 1889; thereafter, this theater, and the 1,319-seat fourth theater that replaced it in 1897, concentrated on drama, operetta, and, eventually, musical theater. *See also* ARNOLD, SAMUEL; AYRNTON, WILLIAM; BACH, JOHANN CHRISTIAN; BENEDICT, SIR JULIUS; BRACEGIRDLE, ANNE; CLEMENTI, MUZIO; CORBETT, WILLIAM; COSTA, SIR MICHAEL; DRAGONETTI, DOMENICO; EC-CLES, JOHN; FARINELLI; GALLINI, GIOVANNI ANDREA BATTISTA; GIARDINI, FELICE; HAYDN, FRANZ JOSEPH; HEIDEGGER, JOHN JA-COB; MAZZINGHI, JOSEPH; PEPUSCH, JOHANN CHRISTOPH; PUB-LIC CONCERTS; SACCHINI, ANTONIO; SHIELD, WILLIAM; SMART, HENRY THOMAS; STORACE, STEPHEN; VIOTTI, GIOVANNI BAT-TISTA; WEBBE, SAMUEL; YOUNG, POLLY.

HEAP, CHARLES SWINERTON (1847–1900). Conductor, organist, singer, and composer. For almost three decades, Heap was a substantial presence in the music scene of Birmingham and surrounding areas as a teacher, performer, and choral conductor. He had early training at York Minster and spent 1865–67 in Leipzig under the auspices of the **Mendelssohn Scholarship.** He earned a BMus (1871) and a DMus (1872) from Cambridge University before settling in the Birmingham region. He conducted many area choral societies and **musical festivals**, including the Birmingham Musical Union (1870–86), the Wolver-hampton Festival (1883 and 1886; the latter festival included the premiere of his **cantata** *The Maid of Astolat*), the North Staffordshire Festival (1888–99), and the Birmingham Festival Choral Society (1895).

HEATHER, WILLIAM (ca. 1563–1627). Musician and Oxford donor. Al-though Heather was both a lay clerk at Westminster Abbey (1586–1615) and a gentleman of the **Chapel Royal** (appointed 1615), his compositional abilities are called into question by his MusD submission at Oxford being in reality the music to **Orlando Gibbons**'s "O Clap Your Hands." His legacy at Oxford has been an enduring one in the form of an endowment to support both practical and theoretical music instruction in the university; the professor in the Faculty of Music is styled the "Heather Professor." The model for his generosity was his close friend, William Camden, headmaster of Westminster School, who both endowed a chair in history at the university as well as profitably made Heather the executor and a beneficiary of his estate. Several musical works were dedicated to him, including **Thomas Tomkins**'s "Music Divine" and **John Hilton's** (the younger) 1627 collection of three-voice **ayres.**

HEIDEGGER, JOHN JACOB (1666–1749). Impressario and **opera** manager. Known as the "Swiss Count," Heidegger came to London in the first decade of the 18th century where he began a long managerial career at the **Haymarket** Theatre, first as an assistant to Owen Swiney; following Swiney's absconding with the theater's funds, Heidegger became manager in 1713 and remained so until well into his old age. In this capacity he worked frequently with **George Frideric Handel** and was an important catalyst for the promotion of Italian opera in London. His promotion extended to other entertainments, as well, including profitable masquerades, as noted by both **Sir John Hawkins** and **Charles Burney**. Burney's note observes that "During his regency, *Ridottas* and masquerades were first introduced in that [the Haymarket] theatre. Dr. Arbuthnot inscribed to him a poem called *The Masquerade*, in which he seems more severe upon the count's *ugliness*, which he could not help, than on his voluntary vices." With regard to his appearance, Hawkins notes only that "he was a man of a projecting head." Winton Dean (*NG*, 1980) underscored the issue, observing that "He was notoriously ugly, and won a bet that Lord Chesterfield could not produce a more hideous face in London." One may judge for oneself from the familiar etching of Heidegger with the opera singers Francesca Cuzzoni and **Farinelli** by Joseph Goupy and Dorothy Boyle.

HELLENDAAL, PIETER (1721–99). Composer, violinist, and organist of Dutch origin. Hellendaal had early education and employment at Utrecht and Amsterdam before attending the University at Leiden from 1749 to 1751. At the end of 1751, he moved to London, where he became part of the general musical scene as a violinist (playing concerts at **Hickford's Room**, the **Foundling Hospital** under **George Frideric Handel**, and other locations). In 1760 he was appointed organist at St. Margaret's, King's Lynn, and moved permanently to Cambridge in 1762, first as organist of Pembroke Hall (1762), then at Peterhouse Chapel (1777). In and around Cambridge, he was frequently heard in concert and had many pupils. Hellendaal published works for violin or flute and keyboard, a number of canons and **glees** (including one given an award by the **Noblemen and Gentlemen's Catch Club** in 1769), and a widely used metrical psalm hymnal.

HENRY LESLIE'S CHOIR. A cappella choir famous for its generous rehearsals, musical skill, and sensitive performance of English music. The choir was first conducted by Frank Mori before being handed over to **Henry Leslie** in 1855. Leslie—who would become one of the best-known choral conductors of his era—conducted it until 1880, dissolving it, but **Alberto Randegger** reconstituted it in 1882; he conducted it until 1885, when Leslie took it over once again. The choir ceased to exist in 1887. Originally consisting of 35 handpicked members, it grew to 60, and then to 240. The repertoire it performed included Elizabethan **madrigals** and Victorian **partsongs** (**William McNaught** thought that the cultivation of this genre by contemporary composers was entirely due to the existence and excellence of the choir). For most of its existence, the choir performed its regular season at **St. James's Hall**. *See also* MACFARREN, SIR GEORGE ALEXANDER.

HER MAJESTY'S THEATRE. *See* HAYMARKET.

HERBERT, GEORGE (1593–1683). Cleric and poet. A younger son of a titled family, Herbert briefly entered politics as a member of Parliament but abandoned this for the church, receiving diaconal ordination by 1726 and priestly ordination in 1730, the year in which he became rector of Bemerton, close to Salisbury. His attachment to music was deep, as evidenced in his poetry, his regular trek to Salisbury Cathedral where he found the music a "Heaven upon Earth," and his participation in private music meetings. His poem "Church-musick," from the collection *The Temple* (1633), is a poignant hymn to church music's transcendant power in which he observes of this "sweetest of sweets" that "if I travel in your companie, You know the way to heavens doore." His poetry was set to music by a number of 17th-century composers, including **Henry Purcell**; **Ralph Vaughan Williams**'s 1911 setting of the *Five Mystical Songs* is widely known.

HESELTINE, PHILIP (ALSO PETER WARLOCK; 1894–1930). Composer, music editor, and writer on music. Heseltine was infamous in the 1920s as both musician and libertine; he was caricatured by authors such as D. H. Lawrence (*Women in Love*, 1920), Aldous Huxley (*Antic Hay*, 1923), and Osbert Sitwell (*Those Were the Days*, 1938). As a composer, he excelled in smaller forms like songs and **carols**. His best-known work is *The Curlew* (1922), a song cycle set to the poetry of William Butler Yeats. Heseltine was perhaps more famous in his day as a transcriber of early English music (with some 570 works edited) and a music writer and critic, along with his intimates **Cecil Gray** and **Bernard Van Dieren**.

Heseltine's musical education was sporadic. He attended Eton, where he was introduced to the music of **Sir Frederick Delius**, and briefly both Oxford (1913–14) and the University of London (1914), before taking a job for a few months as music critic at the *Daily Mail* (1915). Between 1915 and his death, Heseltine lived variously in Wales, Dublin, Eynsford, and London. He supported himself through transcription of Elizabethan music, publication of both songs as well as books on music (nine in all), reviews, and articles. From 1920 to 1921, he edited, with **Cecil Gray**, the *Sackbut*, imbuing it with controversial pieces on the contemporary state of music, until it was bought out by the **Curwen Press**.

HIAWATHA'S DEPARTURE. *See THE SCENES FROM THE SONG OF HIAWATHA.*

HIAWATHA'S WEDDING FEAST. *See THE SCENES FROM THE SONG OF HIAWATHA.*

HICKFORD'S ROOM (ALSO HICKFORD'S GREAT ROOM). London **concert room** active between 1697 and 1789. Hickford's was one of the most important concert rooms of the 18th century. Originally organized as a dancing academy by John Hickford (sometime dancing master to Queen Anne), Hickford's was an early site for subscription and benefit concerts. Many of the most influential musicians performed or organized concerts there, including **Carl Friedrich Abel, Johann Christian Bach, Michael Christian Festing, Francesco Geminani, George Frideric Handel**, Wolfgang Amadeus Mozart, and **John Christopher Smith**, among others. Hickford's first existed on James Street but moved to an enlarged room (50 feet by 30 feet) in 1739. The concert room gradually lost prestige throughout the 18th century and was almost entirely supplanted when the **Hanover Square Rooms** opened in 1775. Hickford's was renamed Rice's Great Rooms in 1789. *See also* HELLENDAAL, PIETER; PUBLIC CONCERTS; SMITH, THEODORE; WESLEY, CHARLES; WESLEY, SAMUEL.

HICKSON, WILLIAM EDWARD (1803–70). Music education philanthropist and writer on music. For much of his life, Hickson championed the teaching of singing to poor students in the same way as **John Curwen, Sarah Glover, John Hullah,** and **Joseph Mainzer**. His family's business was shoe and boot manufacturing, which provided him the wealth to retire in 1840 to devote his time to philanthropic causes. He published numerous books both promoting singing and pedagogy, including *The Singing Master* (1836), *The Use of Singing as Part of the Moral Discipline of Schools* (1838), and *Instructions for Teaching in Schools and Families* (1840). From 1840 to 1852 he owned and edited the *Westminster Review*, which he used as an organ to promote Reform causes.

HILES, HENRY (1826–1904). Educator, conductor, composer, and organist. Hiles was most famous for his work in and around Manchester, both with local choral societies at Knutsford, Blackburn, Preston, and Warrington, among other places, and with various educational institutions—lecturer in music at Owens College (1876) and Victoria University (1879) and professor of harmony at the Royal Manchester College of Music (now known as the **Royal Northern College of Music**; 1893–1904). He studied **organ** initially with his brother, John Hiles (1810–82; an organist with a reputation for good pedagogy), before filling organist positions at Bury Parish Church (1845) and Bishop Wentworth (1847). From 1851 to 1857 he lived in Australia, failing as a gold prospector. He returned to London and won a post at St. Michael's, Wood Street, in 1859, keeping it for only three months before accepting work in Manchester at Henshaw's Blind Asylum. Later, he was organist at the Parish Church of Bowdon (1861) and St. Paul's Church in Hulme (1863–67). Hiles wrote several textbooks on harmony and the somewhat famous *Grammar of Music* (1879), edited the *Quarterly Music Review* between 1885 and 1888, and composed **glees**, **cantatas**, and **oratorios** for local choirs and **musical festivals**. The most famous of these, *The Patriarch* (1866), sold well in an expensive edition in the 1870s; his cantata *The Crusaders* (1873) was briefly popular in America.

HILTON, JOHN (1599–1657). Organist and composer. Hilton was the son of John Hilton, the organist of Trinity College, Cambridge (d. before 1609). The son's appointment as organist of St. Margaret's, Westminster, in 1628 thus echoed his father's path, though his composition of a variety of vocal music proves distinctive. The *Ayres or Fa-las* (1627) and his contributions to *Catch That Catch Can* (1652) represent a lighter repertory, while the **dialogues** of GB Bl Add. Ms. 11608 are devoted to biblical and mythological subjects (the Judgment of Solomon, the Temptation of Job, and the Judgment of Paris). The dialogues on biblical themes are especially notable for furthering the development of the English **oratorio**. Among Hilton's sacred songs is his moving setting of John Donne's witty "Hymne to God the Father," a setting perhaps composed at the poet's behest.

HINGESTON (HINGSTON), JOHN (ca. 1606–83). Organist, composer, and violist. Hingeston was a chorister at York Minster and later a pupil of **Orlando Gibbons**. In the north he enjoyed the patronage of the Earl of Cumberland until 1645. Hingeston was in the south of England during the interregnum, active as Oliver Cromwell's organist and leader of his musical retinue. At the Restoration he was retained by the royal court, both as a member of the **Private Musick** and as curator of the royal musical instruments. In this latter capacity he was assisted by **Henry Purcell**, who was appointed assistant in 1673 following his voice change and subsequent dismissal from the **Chapel Royal** choir. Purcell would take over the position upon Hingeston's death. The majority of Hingeston's music is consort pieces, many of which further the genre of **fantasia-suite**. In this category are two examples for **cornett**(s) and **sackbut**, unusual examples of contrapuntal music explicitly scored for these instruments.

HIS MAJESTY'S THEATRE. *See* HAYMARKET.

H.M.S. PINAFORE, OR THE LASS THAT LOVED A SAILOR. Operetta in two acts by **Sir William Schwenk Gilbert** and **Sir Arthur Sullivan**, premiered in London in 1878; its initial run was 571 performances and was the duo's first major international hit. The plot turns on a case of mistaken identity: Capitan Cochrane (baritone) wishes his daughter Josephine (soprano) to marry Sir Joseph Porter (baritone). When it is revealed that Cochrane was switched at birth with Ralph Rackstraw (tenor), Josephine can marry her true love, Rackstraw.

HOLBORNE, ANT(H)ONY (ca. 1545–1602). Composer. Holborne is chiefly known for two published collections, *The Cittharn Schoole* (1597) and *Pavans, Galliards, Almains . . .* (1599), the latter collection marketed as being playable on **viols**, violins, or wind instruments. The flexible scoring is typical of contemporary attitudes; many of the works also survive in versions for plucked strings. Holborne's brother, William, contributed several vocal works to the 1597 collection.

HOLBROOKE, JOSEPH (ALSO Josef; 1878–1958). Composer, conductor, and pianist. Holbrooke was a prolific composer during his life with an easily accessible style; his music fell into neglect after World War I, around the time he started to become deaf. He studied with **Frederick Corder** at the **Royal Academy of Music** (2; 1893–96) and entered into the life of an itinerant musician shortly after. Holbrooke's large-scale compositions were frequently heard in concerts conducted by **Sir Henry Wood** and **Sir Thomas Beecham** until the beginning of World War I, both in London and at provincial **musical festivals**. From 1908 he secured the patronage of Lord Howard de Walden (T. E. Ellis), which allowed him to complete a trilogy of **operas**, *Cauldron of Annwn* (1910–20), earning him the nickname "The Cockney Wagner." De Walden also funded early recording of Holbrooke's music. A revival of his music through new recordings began at the 50th anniversary of his death in 2008.

HOLST, GUSTAV (ALSO VON HOLST; 1874–1934). Composer, teacher, conductor, and trombonist; father of **Imogen Holst**. Because of the fame he gained after the 1918 premiere of *The Planets* (1914–16)—still his most recognizable work today—Holst became during his time one of the most famous living British composers. In his lifetime, the only serious rival to the popularity of *The Planets* was his choral work *Hymn of Jesus* (1917), heard frequently at interwar **musical festivals**. Holst came from a musical family, and he learned piano from his father and studied counterpoint privately before studying with **Sir Charles Villiers Stanford** and **Sir Hubert Parry** at the **Royal College of Music** (RCM; 1893–98), where besides composition, he studied trombone. He met his lifelong friend **Ralph Vaughan Williams** there in 1895. While at the RCM, Holst began what would become the second half of his life's work outside of composition: teaching music to youth and amateurs. He was named the conductor of the Hammersmith Socialist Choir in 1896. Following his graduation, he worked as an orchestral trombonist in both the **Carl Rosa Opera Company** (1898–1900) and the Scottish Orchestra (1900–1903) before taking a teaching position at James Allen's Girls School in Dulwich (1903–5).

Holst's longest-running position was as head of music at the St. Paul's Girls' School in Hammersmith (1905–34), an appointment he held jointly at times with being Director of Music at Morley College (1907–24), teaching at the RCM and University College, Reading, and even being a visiting lecturer in composition at Harvard University (1932). Holst also organized the Whitsun Festival for amateur and professional musicians in Thaxstead, Essex (1916–34), and, during World War I, worked as a bandleader for the Young Men's Christian Association, entertaining troops in Salonica (now Thessaloniki) and Constantinople. Holst's early compositional influences—Richard Wagner, Walt Whitman, and William Morris—were gradually replaced by his mutual work with Vaughan Williams, his studies of the Hindu religion and Sanskrit, and English folk music. His style was always accessible, even if it did not always correspond to the strong melodic and rhythmic features the audience expected of him following the great success of *The Planets*.

HOLST, IMOGEN (1907–84). Writer on music, conductor, and composer; daughter of **Gustav Holst**. Imogen Holst had early training under her father at St. Paul's Girls' School in Hammersmith before attending the **Royal College of Music** (1926–31), where she studied piano and composition with **Sir George Dyson**, Gordon Jacob, and **Ralph Vaughan Williams**. She won the Cobbett Prize while there for a string quartet in 1928. Holst worked mostly as a freelance pianist in the 1930s but also wrote the first edition of a biography of her father (published 1938). During the 1940s she worked as an organizer of rural amateur music under the Council for the Encouragement of Music and the Arts and was named musical director of Dartington Hall in 1942, a school for the advancement of the arts.

In 1952 Holst met Peter Pears and **Benjamin Britten** and began a long association with the Aldeburgh Festival; she was its artistic director from 1954 to 1977. From the 1950s forward, she published and edited a steady stream of volumes on British music, including works on her father, Vaughan Williams, Britten, **Henry Purcell**, and others, as well as a book on conducting and an introductory primer for music theory. For the last few years of her life, Holst concentrated on recording the music of her father, though she continued to produce compositions regularly. She was named a CBE in 1975.

HOOK, JAMES (1746–1827). Composer, keyboardist, and teacher. Hook was a major force during his time and a prolific composer. Through his idiomatic compositions, he advanced keyboard playing in England from harpsichord to the fortepiano. Hook was a prodigy, performing public concerts by the age of six and studying with Thomas Garland, organist of Norwich Cathedral. He was frequently heard in and around Norwich in concert during his teenage years before moving to London by 1764. In London he quickly established himself as one of the leading keyboardists of the day at benefit concerts and began a long career within the **pleasure gardens** there: he was organist at White Conduit House in Pentonville (1764), the organist and composer at the pleasure gardens at Marylebone (1768–73), and keyboardist and composer at those at **Vauxhall** (1774–1820). In all of these locations, he composed songs (over 2,000 of them), light dramatic works, concertos, and other music. His **operas** and stage works were frequently performed at **Drury Lane** and **Covent Garden** in his lifetime, and he composed **oratorios**, keyboard works, and chamber music that were all popular during his own life. Little of his music survived his death.

HOOPER, EDMUND (ca. 1553–1621). Organist and composer. Trained as a chorister at Exeter, Hooper was active in London by 1582 when he joined the choir at Westminster Abbey. A few years later (1588) he was appointed organist and master of the choristers there, to be followed by an appointment as gentleman of the **Chapel Royal** in 1604; by 1615 he had also been appointed organist of the Chapel Royal, along with **Orlando Gibbons**. Modern commentators have underscored the tonal propensities in his church music. Little instrumental music by him survives, though of his Alman in the **Fitzwilliam Virginal Book**, Le Huray (*NG*, 2001) observes that it "shows him to have been an adventurous and very individual composer for the keyboard."

HORNPIPE. English dance. Curt Sachs (1965) included the hornpipe among the dances of the "squat-fling" type, in the company of the Spanish *charrada*, the French *rigaudon*, and the Irish **jig**. The dancing of the hornpipe took varied forms, including a solo version, a round-dance version, and a country-dance version (as seen in **John Playford**). Much as the forms varied, so too did the meter, though 3/2 time with syncopations was characteristic in the late

17th century. References from the late 18th century forward have nurtured a maritime association with the dance.

HORSLEY, WILLIAM (1774–1858). Composer, organist, teacher, and writer on music. Horsley was best known during his own life for his composition of **glees** and his conservative tastes regarding text setting and compositional rules. Early study in London was followed by positions as organist of Ely Chapel, Holborn (1794–98), organist at the Asylum for Female Orphans (1798–1802), and musical director there (from 1802). He later served as the organist at Belgrave Chapel (1812–37) and Charterhouse (from 1838). He was in the position to judge others' works as one of the committee that awarded the Gresham Prize; he was also well connected within the musical infrastructure of his day, being a member of the **Royal Society of Musicians** and one of the founders of the Philharmonic Society in 1813 (now known as the **Royal Philharmonic Society**). From 1818 to 1828 he wrote anonymous musical criticism for the *Quarterly Musical Magazine and Review* and wrote two music theory texts as well.

HOWELLS, HERBERT (1892–1983). Composer, teacher, adjudicator, writer on music, and organist. Howells, most famous today for his church music, particularly *Hymnus Paradisi* (1938; revised 1950) and the **anthem** "Take Him, Earth, for Cherishing" (1964), was until the end of the 1920s considered to be one of the great composers of his day and was well known for his instrumental music and songs. He was extensively championed as a composer in the 1910s by both **Sir Charles Villiers Stanford** and **Sir Hubert Parry**, but he later turned much of his attention to teaching and adjudicating. His early studies were with **Sir Herbert Brewer** at Gloucester Cathedral, where he was an articled pupil with **Ivor Gurney** and Ivor Novello; he entered the **Royal College of Music** (RCM) on an open scholarship in 1912. Work as Sanford Terry's assistant from 1917 to 1920—sponsored by the Carnegie United Kingdom Trust—awakened his interest in Tudor music, which became a lifelong influence for his compositions. He taught composition for over 60 years at the RCM starting in 1920, succeeded **Gustav Holst** as the director of music at St. Paul's Girls' School in Hammersmith (1936–62), and was the King Edward VII Professor of Music at London University (1954–64). He was named a CBE in 1953 and a CH in 1972.

HULLAH, JOHN (1812–84). Educator, composer, and organist. Hullah's seminal work was the promotion of sight-singing and music in English schools throughout the middle of the 19th century; his importance was only dimmed by his methods' eventual eclipse by its rival, **Tonic Sol-fa**; his work

The Village Coquette (1836; with a libretto by Charles Dickens) was extremely successful. While he started investigating sight-singing methods by 1837, it was the patronage of James Kay that placed him firmly on the path of vocal pedagogy. In 1840 Kay (later Sir James Kay-Shuttleworth) commissioned Hullah to create a sight-singing method for teaching music in English schools; Hullah adapted a continental one by Guillaume Louis Bocquillon Wilhelm, published as *The Grammar of Vocal Music* in 1843. Kay also hired Hullah to teach vocal music at the experimental school of St. John's College, Battersea. His success here led him to start a class for teaching singing pedagogy—based on a fixed-doh sight-singing system—to school teachers. He began this at **Exeter Hall** in 1841 and continued it at **St. Martin's Hall**, Long Acre, in 1849. His growing fame as a teacher brought additional appointments, including professor of vocal music at King's College, London (1844–74), government inspector of Music in Schools (1872–84), organist at Charterhouse (1858–84), and numerous lectureships. Hullah was the author of numerous books on music and pedagogy. He was given an honorary doctorate by Edinburgh University in 1876.

HUME, TOBIAS (ca. 1579–1645). Violist, composer, and man of arms. In the preface to his 1605 *First Part of Ayres*, Hume clarifies that music is but his avocation, soldiering his vocation, and also makes strong claim for the **viol**'s musical potential:

> I doe not studie Eloquence, or professe Musicke, although I doe love Sence, and affect Harmony. My Profession being, as my Education hath beene, Armes, the onely effeminate part of me, hath beene Musicke; which in mee hath beene always Generous, because never Mercenarie. . . . From henceforth, the statefull instrument *Gambo Violl*, shall with ease yeelde full various and as devicefull Musicke as the **Lute**. For here I protest the Trinities of Musicke, parts, Passion, and Division, to be as gracefully united in the *Gambo Violl*, as in the most received Instrument that is.

Hume's music is richly associated with the lyra viol, a designation that may refer to a smaller form of the bass viol, but assuredly to a style of playing favoring chordal polyphony and often intabulated. Modern comment has sometimes painted Hume as eccentric (Boyd, 1962) and fanatic (Matthew Spring in *Blwl*, 1992).

HUMFREY, PELHAM (1647/48–74). Composer and lutanist. Humfrey joined the choir of the **Chapel Royal** as a chorister at the Restoration of Charles II, one of several choristers of note that included **John Blow**, **Michael Wise**, and **William Turner**. The new monarch's French tastes led to compositional opportunities for talented boys in the chapel, and as a measure of Humfrey's youthful success, five of his **anthem** texts appear in Clifford's *The Divine Services and Anthems* (1664). Upon leaving the chapel in 1664, Humfrey was sent to study in France and Italy, bankrolled by Secret Service funds. His study abroad gave him a strong command of continental style, and he would become a major conduit for nurturing the Lullian style at the English court.

Hunphrey is frequently mentioned in **Samuel Pepys**'s diary, with the 15 November 1667 entry a pointed comment on the continental airs he had assumed since his return to England: Humfrey "is an absolute Monsieur, as full of form and confidence and vanity, and disparages everything and everybody's skill but his own." During his time abroad, he received several royal appointments, including gentleman of the Chapel Royal in 1667. In 1672, following his marriage to Captain **Henry Cooke**'s daughter, Katherine, Humfrey succeeded his father-in-law as master of the children of the Chapel Royal, in which position he would have taught the young **Henry Purcell**. Although he died at the tragically young age of 27, his contributions to Restoration music were significant, especially in the development of the symphony anthem and the transmission of French and Italian idioms. His compositions are chiefly church music, but he also contributed to Shadwell's 1674 operatic adaptation of *The Tempest* (*The Masque of the Devils* and *The Masque of Neptune*). *See also* LUTE.

HYMN. A strophic religious song, generally sung congregationally in the context of liturgy. There is also a tradition of the hymn in use as part of private devotions. In the 17th century, for instance, Thomas Ken instructed the students at Winchester College to "be sure to sing the Morning and Evening Hymn in your chamber devoutly" (1674). Collaterally, the **metrical psalm** had an extensive domestic use among **Puritans**.

The history of the English hymn might be seen to have a rich beginning in the metrical psalters of the Reform era, including the collections of Thomas Sternhold (1558, 1560), John Hopkins (1562), Sternhold and Hopkins (1562), **Thomas East** (1592, 1594), and Nahum Tate and Nicholas Brady (1696). The tunes "Winchester Old," "Dundee," and "Southwell' are representative and enduring examples of this tradition. Eighteenth-century English hymns are particularly associated with the development of Methodism and its espousal of robust congregational singing. **Charles Wesley** (1707–88), brother of **John**, the founder of Methodism, contributed a number of important hymn texts, such as "Come, Thou Long Expected Jesus" and "Lo! He Comes"; Charles's grandson, **Samuel Sebastian** (1810–76), was an important cathedral musician whose hymn tune "Aurelia" has been especially popular.

Nineteenth-century English hymnody is represented by the compositions of composers like **John Bacchus Dykes** ("Nicaea," "Melita") and, in the wake of the Oxford Movement, a large body of medieval hymn translations by John Mason Neale and Percy Dearmer, the latter a general editor of the 1933 edition of *The English Hymnal*. The 19th century also saw the first edition of *Hymns Ancient and Modern* (1861), an enduring work in numerous editions that has sought to provide a common repertory for the Church of England. Twentieth-century composers from the "mainstream" have been prominent voices in modern English hymnody, none more so than **Ralph Vaughan Williams**. As a folk song collector, he was able to adapt a number of traditional tunes for uses as hymns, such as "Forest Green" and "King's Lynn." His many original hymn tunes, such as "King's Weston," "Salve Festa Dies," "Down Ampney," and "Sine Nomine," are among the finest and most beloved in the modern repertory. Additionally, Vaughan Williams, along with Martin Shaw and Percy Dearmer, was the editor of *Songs of Praise*, a successful attempt to provide a "national" hymnal.

English hymnody has at various times been an adaptive repertory, taking melodies from composed choral works and redrafting them as congregational songs. **Henry Purcell**'s **anthem** "O God Thou Art My God" provides the melody "Westminster Abbey," for instance, and **George Frideric Handel**'s *Judas Maccabeus* is the source of "Maccabeus." *See also* SALVATION ARMY.

I

IMMYNS, JOHN (1724–64). Amateur musician and lawyer. Immyns was largely self-taught as a musician, learning to play the **lute** from a 17th-century method book. His skill became great enough that he was named lutanist of the **Chapel Royal** in 1752. He also founded the **Madrigal Society**, was a member of the **Academy of Ancient Music**, and was a copyist for both it and **Johann Christoph Pepusch**.

IN NOMINE. A cantus-firmus based genre of fantasia, arising ca. 1530, with examples through the end of the 17th century. *In nomines* were written for keyboards, **lute**, and consort, with the latter scoring the most prominent. The cantus firmus on which these fantasias is based is the antiphon *Gloria tibi trinitas*, from the second Vespers of Trinity Sunday. The nominal reference "In nomine" derives from the polyphonic Benedictus (including the text phrase "in nomine") from **John Taverner**'s *Missa Gloria tibi Trinitas*, which was transcribed for instruments, likely the first example of what would become an important instrumental genre. *See also* ALWOOD, RICHARD; BLITHEMAN, JOHN; *BROWNING*; PARSLEY, OSBERT; TALLIS, THOMAS; TYE, CHRISTOPHER; VIOL; WARD, JOHN; WHYTE, ROBERT.

IRELAND, JOHN (1879–1962). Composer, pianist, teacher, organist, and choirmaster. During his life, Ireland was known mostly for his piano works; he also wrote excellent songs such as the popular "Sea Fever" and a few choral and orchestral works. Ireland had early training at the **Royal College of Music** (RCM), where he studied piano (1893–97) and composition with **Sir Charles Villiers Stanford** (1897–1901). He earned an FRCO in 1895 and a BMus from Durham University in 1905. He supported himself through school with various jobs, including as organist at Holy Trinity, Sloane Street, and St. Jude's, Turk's Row; Ireland was later organist and choirmaster at St. Luke's, Chelsea (1904–26), and taught composition at the RCM (1920–39), where his students included **Benjamin Britten**, **Alan Bush**, and others. Early success in composition came with winning a Cobbett Prize in 1912; in the late 1910s and early 1920s, his reputation grew, especially in London. Following his retirement from the RCM, he gradually stopped composing, living the remainder of his years quietly in West Sussex.

ISAACK, BARTHOLOMEW (1661–1709). Singer, organist, composer. Isaack was trained as a chorister in the **Chapel Royal** in the mid-1670s, at which time he may also have sung in John Crowne's court **masque** *Calisto* (1674/75). He was in Ireland for a time, holding appointments at both Christ Church Cathedral, Dublin (1684), and St. Patrick's Cathedral, Dublin (1685–87). He reemerged in the English musical scene in 1705 as organist at Southwark. The career of his brother, Peter (d. 1694), was interestingly parallel, including training in the Chapel Royal and Irish appointments at both Dublin cathedrals. Peter returned to England to take up appointment at Salisbury Cathedral (1687), but he returned to Dublin in 1692.

J

JACKSON, WILLIAM (1; 1730–1803). Composer, organist, and writer. Known mostly today for his **Service** in F and a version of the *Te Deum* still in use within the Church of England, Jackson was a well-known regional composer during his life in Exeter and its vicinity, famous for his songs and his **operas** performed in London, such as *Lord of the Manor* (1781). His early training likely came from musicians in Exeter Cathedral and in the city; he also studied for two years in London (1746–48). Jackson worked as an independent musician in Exeter from 1748 until being hired as an organist and choirmaster at Exeter Cathedral (1777)—a position he held until his death. His works, aside from being heard in Exeter and London, were also championed by **Thomas Linley (the elder)** in Bath, and his writings were important enough to be poorly reviewed by **Charles Burney**, including the *Present State of Music in London* (1791), which Burney took to be an attack on **Franz Joseph Haydn**.

JACKSON, WILLIAM (2; 1815–66). Composer, organist, and choirmaster. Jackson was known throughout his life as a self-taught composer; his work, especially in Bradford and its vicinity, involved conducting the choir and composing **oratorios** for the Bradford **Musical Festival**, among other jobs. Jackson was born in Masham, and he taught himself the rudiments of music and instrument repair. While working as first organist at the church in Masham (1832–52), he also worked in various trades. He dedicated himself entirely to music in 1852, moving to Bradford, presenting his oratorio *The Deliverance of Israel from Babylon* at the Leeds Musical Festival, and taking a job as organist at St. John's, Bradford (1852–56). Later, he was appointed organist at the Horton Lane Independent Chapel (1856–66). He was the conductor of the Bradford Choral Union, as well as the Bradford Festival Choral Society, and composed several oratorios for Bradford and London. His long experience with teaching singing led him to be suspicious of sol-fa systems, and to the publication of *A Singing Class Manual* (1849), which was eclipsed by the sight-singing systems of **John Hullah** and **John Curwen**.

JENKINS, JOHN (1592–1678). Violist, theorbist, and composer. In the history of the English **viol**, Jenkins emerges with unusual prominence as its most prolific composer in the 17th century. Echoing Jenkins's famous student, **Roger North**, **Charles Burney** described him as "a voluminous composer of Fancies for viols"; the number of his works ran to around 800.

Jenkins's early patrons included the families Derham and L'Estrange, both of Norfolk, though by the 1650s on into the next decade, he is associated with the North family, whose son, Roger, was his pupil and later would write of him at length. Jenkins was also named to the King's **Private Musick** at the Restoration as a theorbist.

Jenkins's large number of works are often fantasias in which he revealed an "unsurpassed lyrical inventiveness and outstanding gifts for tonal organization" (Ashbee, *NG*, 2001). North described the fantasias as "full of airy points, grave and triple movements, and other variety," and also noted the influence of Jenkins's performance skills on his composing: "[I]t must be owned that being an accomplished master on the viol, all his movements laid fair for the hand, and were not so hard as they seemed." Jenkins's penchant for the viol and the fantasia represented a conservative element in tension with the modern advances of the violin and the Italianate sonata. This is also suggestive of a degree of insularity, manifest for instance, in Jenkins's having spent the years of the interregnum in the country homes of the aristocracy, while others in the royal circle fled to the Continent where modern musical influence was strong. *See also* THEORBO.

"JERUSALEM." **Hymn** by **Sir Hubert Parry** to lyrics from the poem "And Did Those Feet In Ancient Times" by William Blake, first performed as part of a Fight for Right concert on 28 October 1916. Parry later gave the hymn to the Women's Suffrage Movement, conducting it at a public rally at the **Royal Albert Hall** on 17 March 1917. The hymn has become an unofficial second national anthem and is usually the last piece sung (with audience participation) at closing night of the **Proms**.

JIG (ALSO JEG). Dance and dramatic genre. (1) Jigs, diverse in choreography and musical structure, appear in varied contexts in England, including dance suites (the last dance typically), theater music (act tunes), and country dancing. The variety of structure and style is easily seen in a work like **John Playford**'s *English Dancing Master* in which "Kemps Jeg" proceeds in a lilting, dotted, compound duple meter, while "Lord of Carnarvans Jeg" moves in a sturdy, simple duple meter.

(2) The jig was a low dramatic entertainment, comedic and farcical, sung to popular melodies, with dancing an important element. The Elizabethan and

Jacobean theater would use the jig as a foil to serious drama, presenting it as an entr'acte entertainment or a comical conclusion to serious plays. Margaret Laurie (*Blwl*, 1992) aptly describes their simple form as "hardly more than dramatized and choreographed versions of broadside ballads," but also notes a more developed form that was like "a miniature low-life **opera**." In this way it may be seen to anticipate the popular 18th-century **ballad opera**.

JOHNSON, ROBERT (?–1633). Composer and lutanist. The son of one of Queen Elizabeth's lutanists, John Johnson, Robert Johnson entered the service of Sir George Carey in 1596, advantageously coincident with Carey's taking up the office of Lord Chamberlain. Undoubtedly nurtured by Carey's position, Johnson provided music for a number of productions by the King's Men company, including works of **William Shakespeare**, Francis Beaumont, John Fletcher, and John Webster. His theater songs reveal a declamatory bent as well as a gift for programmatic touches, as in the chromatic howls of his "O let us howl some heavy note" for Webster's *Duchess of Malfi* or the representational gestures of his battle song, "Arm, arm!" for Fletcher's *The Mad Lover*.

Johnson was also employed at court from 1604, contributing music for a number of **masques**, sometimes performed by large **lute** ensembles, as is the case with the 20 lutes that added a sumptuous sound to the 1611 masque of *Oberon* (Jonson). His lute music is, in the main, dance pieces that themselves may be adaptations of ensemble works.

THE JUDGMENT OF PARIS. A **masque** by William Congreve. Greek mythology presents the story of Paris, the son of Priam, king of Troy, and his task of judging the most beautiful among Hera, Athena, and Aphrodite; famously, his choice of Aphrodite led to the Trojan War. This antique beauty contest, the subject of Congreve's masque, found a modern echo in a competition among English composers to see who in the generation after **Henry Purcell** would best set Congreve's libretto. Four submissions were performed in 1701, with **John Weldon**, the winner, followed by **John Eccles**, **Daniel Purcell**, and **Godfrey Finger**.

JULLIEN, LOUIS ANTOINE (1812–60). French conductor and composer active in England 1838–59. Though remembered today primarily for his band music and lighter dance music, Jullien conducted an important series of popular concerts at London theaters, which were accessible to the working and lower-middle classes. At these concerts, Jullien would program popular music together with more serious works, partly to amuse and partly to improve the musical tastes of the audience. He also conducted **opera** at **Drury Lane** and **Covent Garden**.

K

KARPELES, MAUD (1885–1976). Writer, collector of folk songs and dances, and folklorist. Karpeles had early musical training at the Berlin Hochschule für Musik (1905–6) in piano before turning to social work. She saw a demonstration of folk dance by **Cecil Sharp** in 1909 and devoted the rest of her life to the collecting, preservation, and teaching of folk music and dance, maintaining Sharp's educational legacy. She was also a frequent and well-regarded demonstrator of folk dancing. Karpeles's 1910 Folk Dance Club became the center of the English Folk Dance Society in 1911 (what would become the **English Folk Dance and Song Society**). She journeyed with Sharp to America during World War I to collect and lecture on folk music and dance. Following Sharp's death in 1924, she continued to revise his previous work and release unpublished collections; she also collected folk music in Newfoundland and coauthored with A. H. Fox Strangways a biography of Sharp (1933). After breaking with the English Folk Dance and Song Society in 1938, she founded the International Folk Music Council (1947), serving as its secretary from 1947 to 1963. She was named CBE in 1961.

KENT, JAMES (1700–1776). Composer and organist. Kent was known during his lifetime as a composer of church music and as the occasional assistant to **William Croft**. He trained as a chorister with Croft at Winchester Cathedral and then the **Chapel Royal**. Kent held a succession of **organ** posts, including the church at Finedon, Northamptonshire (1717); Trinity College, Cambridge (1731); and Winchester Cathedral (1738–74). While his music is mostly forgotten today, volumes of it were occasionally unearthed and discussed in 19th-century periodicals, such as *MT*. One of his famous students was **Charles Dibdin**.

KETÈLBEY, ALBERT (1875–1959). Composer, conductor, and pianist. Ketèlbey was well known during his life as a composer of light music as well as dramatic music used for silent films. In the late 1920s he was the most frequently performed composer in Great Britain, and he is known today for many compositions, including "Bells across the Meadows." Ketèlbey trained as a chorister at St. Silas's Church, Lozells, Birmingham, and at the Midland Institute School of Music before going to London to study at Fitzroy College and Trinity College (1888). He received an appointment to be organist at St. John's, Wimbledon (1891), and was at times the music director of a light **opera** company, the Vaudeville Theatre in London (1897), and the Columbia Graphophone Company. He published music under numerous pseudonyms, including Anton Vodorinski, Raoul Clifford, A. William Aston, Geoffrey Kaye, André de Basque, and Dennis Charlton. Aside from composition and recording, he also arranged the music of many composers for small orchestras.

KING, ROBERT (ca. 1660–1726?). Violinist and composer. King was a member of the royal **Private Musick** from 1680, serving under Charles II, James II, William and Mary, and Anne. He was active in contributing theater music to the United Company and subsequently, in the last decade of the century, was involved in the production of public concerts. Spink (1974) is strong in his assessment of King's songs, calling him an "agreeable melodist" and one "who must rank next below **[Henry] Purcell** as a songwriter in this period." King brought out two volumes of songs (1692, 1695?), citing that they were presently being circulated in imperfect form. He also claims Italian influence, suggesting that Italian works offer the best models for vocal music.

KING'S THEATRE. *See* HAYMARKET.

KNYVETT, CHARLES (1752–1822). Singer (alto), impresario, and organist; father of the keyboardist and composer Charles Knyvett (1773–1852) and the singer and composer **William Knyvett**. The elder Charles Knyvett was trained at Westminster School and was one of **Benjamin Cooke**'s boy choristers at Westminster Abbey. He took a position as an organist at All Hallows, Barking (1770), and was named a gentleman (1786–1822), organist (1796–1822), and composer (1806–8) of the **Chapel Royal**, but he was much better known for his singing. Knyvett specialized in the music of **George Frideric Handel** and of **glees** and **catches**, for such organizations as the **Noblemen and Gentlemen's Catch Club** and the **Anacreontic Society**. As an impresario, Knyvett organized with Samuel Harrison a series of Lenten **oratorio** concerts at **Covent Garden**, where he also served as organist (1789–92). Knyvett was a member of the **Royal Society of Musicians** (from 1778) and also edited *A Favorite Collection of Glees* (1800).

KNYVETT, WILLIAM (1779–1856). Singer and composer; son of **Charles Knyvett**. Knyvett received training from his father, as well as **Samuel Webbe** and Gianbattista Cimador in keyboards and singing. Like his father, William Knyvett was well known as a singer of the music of **George Frideric Handel** and of **glees**, performing in London for such organizations as the **Concerts of Ancient Music** and in provincial **musical festivals**. He was a gentleman (1797) and composer (1808) of the **Chapel Royal** and a sought-after conductor of the Concerts of Ancient Music (1832–40) and festivals in Birmingham (1834–43) and Yorkshire (1835). He composed a number of glees, as well as **coronation music** for both George IV and Queen Victoria. Knyvett also tried his hand at being an impresario, running a series called the Vocal Subscription Concerts until 1822.

L

LACHRIMAE. An emblematic melody of **John Dowland**. "Lachrimae" is Dowland's most famous melody, widely circulated, adapted to diverse settings, and emblematic of the melancholic aura of the composer, encapsulated in the title of his pavan "Semper Dowland Semper Dolens." The melody begins with a stepwise descent—pictorially the falling of teardrops—and received settings by English and continental composers, including **William Byrd**, **Thomas Morley**, **Giles Farnaby**, Heinrich Scheidemann, and Jan Pieterzoon Sweelinck. Additionally, confirming both the melancholic aura and the popularity of the melody, Dowland would sign his name "Jo: dolandi de Lachrimae."

The work appears in a number of guises in Dowland's own work, the original being a solo **lute** pavan. This was followed by a setting as vocal air to the text "Flow my tears" (*The Second Book of Songs*, 1600). This in turn was followed by an extended set of consort pieces, *Lachrimae or Seaven Teares* (1604), composed of seven "passionate" pavans, the first of which set the original melody; the subsequent pavans retain the signature head motive.

LAMBERT, CONSTANT (1905–51). Composer, conductor, critic, and writer on music. While known today mostly for his conducting of various British ballet company orchestras, Lambert was a musical force in the late 1920s and early 1930s, with a combination of well-regarded compositions, a sharp critical mind, and association with some of the other major younger critics of the 1920s and 1930s, including **Cecil Gray**, **Philip Heseltine**, and **Bernard Van Dieren**. Lambert's musical education included study of composition, piano, and conducting at the **Royal College of Music** starting in 1922. His early musical interests were wide, including Franz Liszt, Igor Stravinsky, and jazz; later, he would also include broad neoclassicism as one of his inspirations, especially in *Summer's Last Will and Testament* (1935), perhaps his most famous piece. Lambert's *Romeo and Juliet* (1925) was the first work by an English composer to be given by Sergi Diaghilev's *Ballets Russes*. In the 1930s he wrote criticism for many periodicals, including the *Nation*, the *Athenaeum*, and the *Saturday Review*, culminating in the publication of *Music Ho!* (1934), a discussion of contemporary music (Lambert favored Jean Sibelius, Van Dieren, and Ferruccio Busoni above most other composers). Lambert also began a conducting career in the 1930s, including directing the Carmargo Society Ballet (1930) and the Royal Ballet (called at the time the Vic-Wells Company; 1931–47), acting as musical adviser for the **Sadler's Wells** Ballet (1948–51), and being the orchestral conductor of the **British Broadcasting Corporation**'s Third Programme (1946–51).

LAMBETH CHOIRBOOK. The manuscript GB Llp 1 was copied in the 1520s under the aegis of Edward Higgons. In the same hand as the **Caius Choirbook**, also a work explicitly sponsored by Higgons, the Lambeth source contains motets, magnificats, and masses by composers including **Robert Fayrfax**, **Nicholas Ludford**, and Walter Lambe.

"LAND OF HOPE AND GLORY." Composition for soloist, chorus, and orchestra by **Sir Edward Elgar** with lyrics by A. C. Benson, to the trio tune of Elgar's first **"Pomp and Circumstance"** march. Initially meant for the 1902 *Coronation Ode*, to celebrate the coronation of Edward VII, the song quickly took on a life of its own, becoming an unofficial second national anthem during World War I. It is featured prominently at the last night of the **Proms**.

LANIER, NICHOLAS (1588–1666). Lutanist, singer, and composer. Lanier, the most prominent member of a musical family active at court, was named a royal lutanist in 1616; he became **Master of the King's Music** under Charles I in 1625, a post he filled as an old man under Charles II as well. Although his official posts at court were musical, his apparently keen artistic eye made him valuable in art procurals, including parts of the Gonzaga collection from Mantua.

Lanier's collaboration with Ben Jonson in *Lovers Made Men* (1617) is a landmark in introducing and furthering the Italian dramatic style. Jonson writes that "the whole Maske was sung (after the Italian manner) stylo recitativo by Master Nicholas Lanier, who ordered and made both the scene and the Musicke." As the music to the **masque** does not survive, one is left to guess at its content, but the notion of a declamatory score in theatrical context is suggestive of early "operatic" activity.

LAWES, HENRY (1596–1662). Composer and singer. Lawes, the elder brother of the noted **viol** composer **William Lawes**, was possibly trained as a chorister at Salisbury. He entered the **Chapel Royal** in 1626 and the king's **Private Musick** in 1631; following the Restoration he also was appointed a composer in the Private Musick. He was a prolific composer of songs and as such was involved in theater productions of various sorts, including **Sir**

William Davenant's landmark *First Dayes Entertainment at Rutland House* and *The Siege of Rhodes* (1656). He was instrumental in the commission of John Milton's **masque**, *Comus*, to which he contributed several songs and in which he performed. In 1648 Milton penned a salutatory tribute to Lawes in the form of a descriptive sonnet.

Although his song style is varied, it is his embrace and nurture of declamatory principles that is most significant. Spink (1974) is strong in his assessment: "His [Lawes's] sensitivity to nuances of diction and feeling in a poem result in a richness compared with which the style of the others [his contemporaries] seems arid. It is he, really, who defines the declamatory **ayre**, and against whom the rest are measured."

LAWES, WILLIAM (1602–45). Composer, violist, theorbist, and man of arms. Like his older brother **Henry Lawes**, William may have been a chorister at Salisbury, where their father was a **vicar-choral**. A 17th-century biographical account (Thomas Fuller) states he was a pupil of **Coprario**. He was appointed to the King's **Private Musick** in 1635. Amid the growing conflict of the English Civil War, he enlisted in the Royalist Forces and, despite being given a relatively safe assignment—a measure of the esteem in which he was held—he was killed at the Siege of Chester in 1645.

Lawes's compositions are diverse, but his voice emerges with the most distinction in his consort fantasias. Therein he engages a modernly expressive idiom, rich in gesture and license. David Pinto (*NG*, 2001) has underscored the "wilful angularity" and free use of dissonance as especially distinctive.

L.C.C. CHORAL UNIONS (ALSO LONDON COUNTY COUNCIL CHORAL UNIONS). Competitive choirs in and around the London Metropolitan area, drawn from amateur singers who trained in evening music classes. The L.C.C. Choral Unions began by 1907 and continued for several decades.

"THE LEAVES BE GREEN." A popular 16th-century song that was frequently the basis for consort variations in which the melody might function in melodic quotation or as a ground bass. Sometimes these settings were known as *Brownings*, a term derived from the songs' associated text: "The leaves be green, the nuts be brown / They hang so high, they will not come down."

LEHMANN, LIZA (1862–1918). Composer, singer, and teacher. For a time, Lehmann was the most famous living British composer throughout the English-speaking world because of the great popularity of her song cycle *In a Persian Garden* (1896). Her songs—like those of her friend and fellow composer **Maude Valérie White**—were always popular within her own lifetime. She studied voice with **Jenny Lind** and **Alberto Randegger** in London and composition with Niels Raunkilde in Rome, Wilhelm Freudenberg in Wiesbaden, and **Hamish MacCunn** in London. She had a nine-year career as a professional recitalist (1885–94), in which she introduced the public to many of the songs of **Henry Purcell**, **Thomas Arne**, and **James Hook**, as well as her own music. She retired, after marriage, to pursue composition; she also became a well-known music teacher, eventually taking a post at the **Guildhall School of Music**. Aside from her songs, she also wrote choral works for the **musical festival** circuit (such as *Young Lochinvar*, first heard at the Kendall Festival in 1899), musical theater and light opera, an **opera** (*Everyman*, 1915), and a handful of chamber and orchestral works. She was the author as well of *Practical Hints for Students of Singing* (1913) and *The Life of Liza Lehmann* (1918), an autobiography.

LEMARE, IRIS (1902–97). Conductor, concert organizer, and adjudicator. Lemare was one of the first women to conduct major ensembles in Great Britain (including the **British Broadcasting Corporation**'s Orchestra [1936] and the Oxford Chamber Orchestra). She was also a founder, with **Elisabeth Lutyens** and **Anne Macnaghten**, of the **Macnaghten-Lemare Concerts** (1932–40). She studied at both the Dalcroze Eurythmics School in Geneva and the **Royal College of Music**, taking **organ** and conducting with **Sir Malcolm Sargent** and **Sir Adrian Boult**. As the director of the Pollards Opera (1935–39), she was responsible for the first revival of **George Frideric Handel**'s *Serse* in almost two centuries (1935), and as the founder and director of the Lemare Orchestra (1945), she performed at many of the postwar **musical festivals**.

LESLIE, HENRY DAVID (1822–96). Choral conductor, composer, and impresario. Leslie was one of the most important choral conductors of the second half of the 19th century. Aside from a reputation as an exacting and highly musical conductor, Leslie promoted the performance of British music. He was originally trained as a cellist and performed in concerts of the **Sacred Harmonic Society** on that instrument. He was named the honorary secretary of the Amateur Musical Society in 1847 and conducted it from 1853 to 1861. He is best known for his work with **Henry Leslie's Choir** (1855–80 and 1885–87), a London vocal ensemble known for its general excellence. In addition to conducting this choir, Leslie was also the principal of the short-lived National College of Music (1864–66), which included on its faculty **Sir Arthur Sullivan**, **Sir Julius Benedict**, and **Sir George Alexander Macfarren**. He was the conductor of the Herefordshire Philharmonic Society (1863–69), founder of the Guild of Amateur Musicians (1874), and founder of the Oswestry School and Oswestry Festival (1880), which was one of the major early competition festivals.

Leslie wrote hundreds of **partsongs** for his choirs, larger choral works for the **musical festivals** (such as *Judith*, which premiered at Birmingham in 1858), and worked avidly as a pedagogue, publishing books such as *The Elementary Manual of Music* (1872) and editing *Cassell's Choral Music* (1854). He was an avid promoter of the **Tonic Sol-fa** sight-singing system and a friend and inspiration to **Mary Wakefield**, among many others.

LEVERIDGE, RICHARD (1670–1758). Singer and composer. Leveridge was "possessed of a deep and firm bass voice" (**Sir John Hawkins**) and came to prominence in the role of Ismeron in *Indian Queen*, singing **Henry Purcell**'s impressive conjuration song, "Ye twice ten hundred deities." In addition to his work as a singer, Leveridge was also active as a composer, contributing to the 1698 *Island Princess* and 1702 *Macbeth*. The advent of Italian **opera** in London redirected his performances to the playhouse, where he had a long association with the theater at **Lincoln's Inn Fields**.

Hawkins wrote of his singing that it had "no notion of grace or elegance . . . ; it was all strength and compass," and described him as "being a man of rather coarse manners, and able to drink a great deal, he was by some thought a good companion."

LINCOLN'S INN FIELDS. London theater, 1661–1744. Originally a tennis court, the theater at Lincoln's Inn Fields opened in 1661 under the direction of **Sir William Davenant**, whose company was active there until 1671, followed by Thomas Killigrew's company from 1671 to 1674. The company formed by Thomas Betterton in 1695, a "breakaway" company from the United Company (for whom **Henry Purcell** wrote), was in residence there from its formation until 1705, with **John Eccles** as its music director. Although hampered by the size of the theater, Betterton and Eccles were able to mount **dramatick opera** successfully there, as in the performances of Eccles's *Rinaldo and Armida* (1698). In 1714 Christopher Rich and later his son, John, oversaw a grand renovation of the theater. In its new form it was the venue for the very successful **ballad opera** *The Beggar's Opera* by **John Gay** (1728). Lincoln's Inn ceased to function as a theater in 1744. *See also* BABELL, WILLIAM; BRACEGIRDLE, ANNE; CONCERT ROOMS; FINGER, GODFREY; FORCER, FRANCIS; GALLIARD, JOHN ERNST; LEVERIDGE, RICHARD; "OPERA OF THE NOBILITY"; *A PARLEY OF INSTRUMENTS*; PEPUSCH, JOHANN CHRISTOPH; PUBLIC CONCERTS.

LIND, JENNY (1820–87). Soprano of Swedish birth. Lind made her London debut in 1847 and settled permanently there in 1858. By this time, she had retired from the theatrical stage but continued to sing recitals and **oratorios**, particularly for **musical festivals** and charity. When she retired from singing in 1883, she also became a professor of voice at the **Royal College of Music**. In an era when musicians could easily become famous figures and household names, Lind towered above them all, famous throughout both Europe and America. *See also* BALFE, MICHAEL WILLIAM; BENEDICT, SIR JULIUS; LEHMANN, LIZA; MENDELSSOHN SCHOLARSHIP.

LINDLEY, ROBERT (1776–1855). Virtuosic cellist. Lindley, like his friend the bassist **Domenico Dragonetti**, was well connected into the English musical infrastructure of his time. He played frequently at the Italian Opera, the **Royal Philharmonic Society**, the **Concerts of Ancient Music**, and provincial **musical festivals**; he was named professor of cello at the **Royal Academy of Music (2)** in 1823. He is perhaps best known today for a series of concerts with Dragonetti in the 1820s, where the two played arrangements of Arcangelo Corelli's trio sonatas.

LINLEY, THOMAS (THE ELDER; 1733–95). Composer, singing-master, and impresario. Linley studied with Thomas Chilcot, organist at Bath Abbey, and in London with **William Boyce**. He managed concerts at Bath from the mid-1750s until around 1774. From 1774 to 1786 he was director of the **oratorios** at **Drury Lane** with **John Stanley** and proprietor from 1776. Linley composed music for about 30 plays, as well as pastiche **operas**, **glees**, songs, and other works. With Mary Johnson, sometime wardrobe mistress at Drury Lane, Linley had 12 children, of whom many—such as the violinist, **Thomas Linley the younger** and the singers Elizabeth Ann Linley, Maria Linley, and Mary Linley—were musically talented.

LINLEY, THOMAS (THE YOUNGER; 1756–78). Violinist (child prodigy) and composer; son of **Thomas Linley the elder**. Linley studied with **William Boyce** in London (1763–68) and studied violin with Pietro Nardini in Florence (1768–71), where he met both **Charles Burney** and Wolfgang Amadeus Mozart. He played his first concert at the age of seven in Bristol and led the Bath orchestra starting at age 12. From 1773 until his death, he led the orchestra at **Drury Lane**. One of his most famous stage works, *The Duenna*, was written with his father in 1775; he also composed an **anthem** for the Three Choirs **Musical Festival** and numerous songs and **madrigals**.

LLOYD, CHARLES HARFORD (1849–1919). Organist, composer, educator. Lloyd studied music (BMus, 1871) and theology (BA, 1872) at Magdalen Hall, Oxford, before taking the MA (1875) and DMus (1892) degrees there. While at Oxford, he was one of the founders and the first president of the Oxford Music Club (1872). Lloyd held organist posts at Gloucester Cathedral (1876–82); Christ Church Cathedral, Oxford (1882–92); and the **Chapel Royal**, St. James (1914–19), as well as teaching positions at Christ Church College, Oxford (1876–92), the **Royal College of Music (organ and composition; 1887–92), and Eton College (1892–1914). Lloyd's time at Gloucester began a long association with the Three Choirs **Musical Festival**, for which he wrote numerous secular **cantatas**.

LOCK HOSPITAL. Charity hospital to aid those who suffered from venereal diseases, founded in London in 1746 and opened to patients in 1747. Members of London's theater companies patronized the hospital, and benefit performances and concerts occurred in the 1750s for the hospital at **Drury Lane** and **Covent Garden**. For music, the Hospital is important in two aspects: First, for a series of charity concerts, begun in the Lock Hospital Chapel in 1762, which featured the performance of **oratorios** by **Thomas Arne**, **John Worgan**, and especially **Felice Giardani**, whose composition *Ruth* was performed every year there from 1768 to 1780. Second, the Lock Hospital Chapel became a prominent London Methodist establishment and was one of the first that actively encouraged its congregation both to undergo musical training and to submit to direction in rehearsals to aid the singing in the **service**. Martin Madan, the chapel's original chaplain, was a Methodist preacher, and he published a *Collection of Hymn and Psalm Tunes* to raise money for the hospital in 1769. **Charles Wesley** was organist there from 1797 to 1801.

LOCKE, MATTHEW (1622–77). Composer and organist. Locke was trained as a chorister at Exeter. He was a royalist, and there is manuscript evidence that points to his being on the Continent in 1648, a time that may have seen him in royal service and his conversion to Roman Catholicism, with which he was charged in 1654. At the Restoration he received appointments as composer to the **Private Musick** and also to the royal violin band; in 1663, perhaps with a nod to his Catholicism, he was also appointed organist to the queen, Catherine of Braganza.

Much of Locke's music is for consort, showing his trademark use of "angular and unpredictable melodic and harmonic idiom" (Holman, *NG*, 2001). He also made significant contributions to theater music, including music for the 1674 *Tempest* and the 1675 *Psyche*. In the keyboard collection under his editorship, *Melothesia* (1673), he offers instruction in keyboard continuo practice, instruction that both **Charles Burney** and **Sir John Hawkins** claim was the first published in England.

There is reason to believe that Locke was given to contention. Exeter records his fighting as a young man, and though not physical, his published dialogue of refutation with Thomas Salmon, who had offered ideas about notational reform, was volatile.

LODER, KATE (1825–1904). Composer, pianist, and teacher. Loder studied piano and composition at the **Royal Academy of Music (2; RAM)** from 1838 to 1844, winning the King's Scholarship in 1839 and 1840. She declined an offer to study with **Felix Mendelssohn** in Leipzig, instead becoming a professor of harmony at the RAM (1844) and pursuing a career in performance and composition in and around London. She performed professionally until 1854; after this, she continued to publish (primarily piano works) and teach.

LONDON CHORAL SOCIETY. Choir founded in 1903 under the direction of Arthur Fagge. The London Choral Society presented the second performance of **Sir Edward Elgar**'s *The Dream of Gerontius* in London (15 February 1904; the first occurred in Westminster Cathedral on 6 June 1903) and gave an early performance of Wagner's *Parsifal* in English. The group waned for a time around World War II but still exists as the London Chorus (renamed in 2000).

LONDON INSTITUTION. The London Institution was an educational foundation active between 1806 and 1912 dedicated to the improvement of the public. Its facilities were available on a subscription basis. It included reading rooms, a library, and—once its premises in Finsbury Circus were complete in 1815—a lecture hall that could seat 750 people. Lectures on music and music history were a regular feature of the Institution's programming, given by individuals such as **Sir Joseph Barnby**, **John Barrett**, **Arnold Dolmetsch**, **John Ella** (who was a lecturer there from 1855 and called a professor there from 1871), and Lionel Monckton.

LONDON MUSICAL SOCIETY. Chorus founded by **Sir Joseph Barnby** to promote works little performed or known in London. The choir was active between 1878 and 1887, and it presented concerts (accompanied by a professional orchestra) of several first English performances, including that of Dvorak's *Stabat Mater* (1883).

LONDON PHILHARMONIC ORCHESTRA (LPO). London orchestra founded by **Sir Thomas Beecham** in 1932. The orchestra was resident at the **Queen's Hall** from 1932 to 1941 and currently holds seasons at the **Royal Festival Hall**. An auxiliary chorus, the London Philharmonic Chorus, was formed in 1947. Conductors of the ensemble have included **Sir Adrian Boult**, Bernard Haitink, **Sir Malcolm Sargent**, and Sir Georg Solti.

LONDON PROMENADE CONCERTS. *See* PROMS.

LONDON SEASON OF THE ARTS. *See* FESTIVAL OF BRITAIN.

LONDON **SYMPHONIES.** Group of 12 symphonies (nos. 93–104) composed by **Franz Joseph Haydn** for his two trips to England and performed at **Johann Peter Salomon**'s concerts. Nos. 93–98 were all written for the 1791–92 trip, and Haydn composed nos. 99–104 for his 1794–95 visit.

LONDON SYMPHONY ORCHESTRA (LSO). London ensemble, founded in 1904, partly in response to **Sir Henry Wood**'s abolishment of the deputy system in the **Queen's Hall** orchestra. Principal conductors have included **Hans Richter**, **Sir Edward Elgar**, **Sir Thomas Beecham**, **Eric Coates**, and Arthur Nikisch, among others, and the ensemble is particularly well regarded for its many recordings.

LUDFORD, NICHOLAS (ca. 1490–1557). Composer. Ludford can be documented in London from the early 1520s from his membership in the Fraternity of St. Nicholas (1521) and his appointments at the Chapel of St. Stephen at Westminster Palace, including an appointment as verger there in 1527. His works are exclusively liturgical, ranging from large-scale festal masses for five and six voices to seven smaller-scale *alternatim* masses for three voices ("Lady Masses," one for each day of the week), structurally based on **squares**. The large-scale works are in the main found in the **Caius Choirbook** and, to a lesser degree, the **Lambeth Choirbook**. His "Magnificat Benedicta" is distinctive in its use of a chant cantus firmus, the same melody that is the structural basis of his *Missa Benedicta*.

LUMLEY PARTBOOKS. The main portion of the Lumley Partbooks (GB Lbl Roy. App. 74–6) was compiled in the late 1540s, consisting of Anglican devotional and **service** music from before the first *Book of Common Prayer*, including some use of secular to sacred contrafactum technique. A later layer records instrumental dance music that may derive from the royal court. The partbooks were at one time owned by the Fitzalan family, perhaps compiled for them; only three of the original four partbooks survive, with the bass book missing.

LUPO, THOMAS (1571–1627). Composer and violinist. Lupo, the most prominent member of a Sephardic family of musicians that came to England from Venice between 1539 and 1540, joined the court violin band in 1588 and was named composer of that ensemble in 1619. Additionally, he was a musician to Prince Henry and, subsequent to the prince's untimely death, to Prince Charles. Charles's musical retinue would also include **Orlando Gibbons, John Coprario,** and **Robert Johnson**, enjoying with Lupo an environment of "innovative music-making" (Peter Holman in Ashbee and Lasocki, 1998). As a composer Lupo contributed to several court **masques**, including Jonson's *Oberon* and **Thomas Campion**'s *The Lords' Masque*, though he is best known for his **viol** fantasias where a novel range of scoring and the influence of the Italian **madrigal** are both evident.

LUTE. Fretted, plucked string instrument with ribbed and vaulted resonator, made in a variety of sizes. The chronological range of the lute is well documented from the Middle Ages into the 18th century. However, in England it had a particularly rich blossoming from the middle of the 16th century through the first decades of the 17th; indeed, the lute is virtually iconic for the lyrical propensity of the Elizabethan Age.

The prominence of the lute under the Tudors can be seen in the large number in royal possession. The inventory of Henry VIII's musical instruments (GB lbl Harl. 1419) itemizes over 20 lutes with cases at Westminster in the charge of Philipp Van Wilder. For much of Elizabeth's reign until the last quarter of the 17th century, the **Private Musick** of the monarch had between five and eight positions for lutanists, which included **Robert Johnson** (1604–33), **John Dowland** (1612–26), his son Robert Dowland (1626–41), and Jacque Gaultier (1625–42).

The queen herself was known to have been instructed on the lute and is depicted holding the instrument in a famous miniature by Nicholas Hilliard at Berkeley Castle. The meaning of such images as well as textual references to the lute were polyvalent, denoting harmony and order of various sorts — cosmic, political, and social. The lute also had the connotation of Orpheus's lyre, evoking in its sound and imagery antique resonances for a humanistically inclined society.

The lute repertory was broad, including solo works that were often dances with a reiterative style of ornamentation that not only graced the melody but also counteracted the rapid decay of the instrument's sound, and a sizeable body of lute **ayres** for solo voice and lute accompaniment. The lute also figured in ensemble practice. It was the featured solo instrument in the so-called **English Consort**, as in the consort lessons of **Thomas Morley**, and it also was played in ensembles combining multiple lutes, such as Robert

Johnson's music for the **masque** *Oberon*, performed by 20 lutes together. *See also* ALLISON, RICHARD; ATTEY, JOHN; BACHELER, DANIEL; BANDORA; BARTLET, JOHN; BASSANO; COPRARIO, JOHN; DOLMETSCH, (EUGÈNE) ARNOLD; FORD, THOMAS; HUMFREY, PELHAM; IMMYNS, JOHN; *IN NOMINE*; *LACHRIMAE*; LANIER, NICHOLAS; MACE, THOMAS; *A PARLEY OF INSTRUMENTS*; PILKINGTON, FRANCIS; PRIVATE MUSICK; WHYTHORNE, THOMAS.

LUTYENS, ELISABETH (1906–83). Composer and violist. Lutyens was one of the first major British composers to embrace the twelve-tone method of composing convincingly and successfully, though to many, she was likely better known for her film scores, written in a more approachable style. Her early training included studying in Paris for a few months in 1923 (including classes in harmony and counterpoint at the Ecole Normale), composition and viola study at the **Royal College of Music** (1926–30), and some time studying counterpoint with Georges Caussde in Paris (1931). In the early 1930s, she formed a trio with **Anne Macnaghten** and **Iris Lemare**; this trio became the nucleus of the **Macnaghten-Lemare Concerts** in the 1930s. Performances of her compositions became increasingly frequent throughout the 1930s, coinciding with her studies of the string music of **Henry Purcell** and later Arnold Schoenberg.

Lutyens began to compose music for radio and film in the 1940s. In the 1950s her style solidified, but she found it increasingly difficult to get her works heard, as they were considered too difficult for contemporary ears. She began teaching composition students during this time. Her works began to reach a wider audience again in the 1960s, when she began a series of vocal works. She was named a CBE in 1969. She completed an autobiography, entitled *A Goldfish Bowl*, in 1972.

LYCEUM THEATRE (ALSO THEATRE ROYALE; ENGLISH OPERA HOUSE; ROYAL LYCEUM THEATRE; PALAIS DU DANCE; MECCA BALLROOM). In the 19th century this West End London theater saw the premieres of **operas** by many English composers, including **John Francis Barnett** and **Michael Balfe**. Theaters existed on this site from 1765; it housed the **Drury Lane** Company between 1809 and 1812 during the rebuilding of Drury Lane, and it was rebuilt and renamed the English Opera House in 1816 by Samuel James Arnold. After a fire, the theater was rebuilt in 1834 and continued to champion English opera for a decade. From 1840 to the end of the century, the Lyceum presented a mix of concerts, such as the Promenade Concerts presented by Phillippe Musard in 1841, spoken drama, and opera, including English premieres of works by Giovanni Bottesini and Giuseppe Verdi. The Lyceum was rebuilt in 1904 to house music-hall and variety shows, converted into a ballroom for popular music presentations in 1951, and reconstructed as a theater in 1996. Since then, it has been the venue for a number of West End musical presentations, including *Jesus Christ, Superstar*, *Oklahoma!* and *The Lion King*. The theater seats 2,000.

MACCUNN, HAMISH (1868–1916). Scottish-born composer and conductor, active in London. MacCunn studied composition (with **Sir Hubert Parry**) and piano at the **Royal College of Music** from 1883 to 1886 (he did not take a diploma). After leaving, he began composing and conducting in and around London; MacCunn's first major success, the concert overture *Land of the Mountain Flood*, was premiered by **Sir August Manns** at the **Crystal Palace** in 1887; it remains his most popular work today. While a successful composer in his day, he—like most contemporary figures—had to balance composition with other pursuits, including teaching at the **Royal Academy of Music** (2; 1888–94), privately, and at the **Guildhall School of Music** (1912–16) and conducting with the **Carl Rosa Opera Company** (1898–1900) and at the **Savoy Theatre**, **Covent Garden**, and elsewhere. His choral compositions, such as *Lord Ullin's Daughter* (1887), were extremely popular with contemporary choral societies, and his **opera** *Jeanie Deans* (1894), written for the Carl Rosa Opera Company, was heard dozens of times in MacCunn's own lifetime. Many of MacCunn's early works have Scottish subjects, and he was seen by his contemporaries as a "Scottish composer"; MacCunn's popularity began to wane when the press called for him to break away from this construction, though his early "Scottish" works remained popular with audiences until his untimely death.

MACE, THOMAS (1612/13–1706?). Writer, singer, and lutanist. Mace is documented as a member of the choir at Trinity College, Cambridge, from 1635 and spent the vast majority of his life in that city. He is best known for his wide-ranging musical tome, *Musick's Monument* (1676), a work colorful in its expression and conservative in its musical views, especially in its decided preference for **viols**, consorts, and **lutes** in place of violins, guitars, and continental styles. The section devoted to the lute offers thorough instruction and "as a systematic guide for a complete beginner achieves more than any other lute tutor book ever written, and bears constant re-reading" (Spring, 2001). The colorful expression of Mace's prose drew comment early on. **Sir John Hawkins** somewhat endearingly notes that "As to the book itself, a singular vein of humour runs through it, which is far from being disgusting, as it exhibits a lively portraiture of a good-natured, gossiping old man."

MACFARREN, SIR GEORGE ALEXANDER (1813–87). Composer, teacher, conductor, and writer on music. Macfarren was one of the most prolific and well-regarded musicians of his time. As a composer, he worked in virtually every genre available to him, including **opera**, symphony, **glees**, and chamber music. He was best known for a series of dramatic works composed for the major **musical festivals**, including the **oratorios** *St. John the Baptist* (Bristol, 1873), *The Resurrection* (Birmingham, 1876), *Joseph* (Leeds, 1877), and *King David* (Leeds, 1883). In addition, he composed **cantatas** for the Bradford Festival, the Glasgow Festival, the Musical Society of London, and **Henry Leslie's Choir.**

Macfarren's early training came from his father, Charles Lucas (a noted cellist, conductor and composer), and then from 1829 to 1836 as a student of trombone, piano, and composition (under Cipriani Potter) at the **Royal Academy of Music (2; RAM).** Macfarren was a professor at the RAM from 1837 to 1847 and then again from 1851 until his death; he was appointed principal of that institution in 1875, the same year in which he succeeded **Sir William Sterndale Bennett** as Professor of Music at Cambridge University. His writings include monographs on **George Frideric Handel**, harmony, and counterpoint. He conducted frequently until 1860, when blindness prevented further activities. Macfarren was knighted in 1883, together with **Sir Arthur Sullivan** and **Sir George Grove.**

MACKENZIE, SIR ALEXANDER CAMPBELL (1847–1935). Composer, conductor, violinist, administrator, teacher, and writer on music active in London. Together with **Sir Hubert Parry** and **Sir Charles Villiers Stanford**, Mackenzie was one of the most important British composers in the generation before **Sir Edward Elgar.** In his own time, he was famous for **oratorio** and **cantata** commissions at the major **musical festivals** (such as *The Rose of Sharon*, premiered at Norwich in 1884) and for being a zealous reformer of the **Royal Academy of Music (2; RAM)** as its principal (1888–1924). His early training, after playing at a young age in his father's orchestra, was in Germany, at the Realschule in Sondershausen (1857–62), and at the RAM (1862–65), where he studied piano and harmony. He performed, taught, and conducted in Edinburgh between 1865 and 1879, when he departed for Florence to salvage his health from overwork and devoted himself to composition.

Apart from conducting the **Novello Choir** in London from 1885 to 1886, Mackenzie spent most of his time in Florence until 1888, when he returned to London for the rest of his professional life. Until his retirement in 1924,

Mackenzie was a fixture in the national music scene, conducting the **Royal Choral Society** and the **Royal Philharmonic Society** orchestra between 1892 and 1899, as well as the student orchestra at the RAM. Aside from oratorios and cantatas, his output includes programmatic orchestral works, **operas**, **partsongs**, songs, chamber music, and folk song collections. Mackenzie wrote a book of reminiscences, numerous articles on music, as well as monographs on Giuseppe Verdi and Franz Liszt. Mackenzie was knighted in 1895 and created KCVO in 1922.

MACNAGHTEN, ANNE (1908–2000). Violinist. Macnaghten was founder and leader of the Macnaghten String Quartet, which in its first incarnation (1932–40) was entirely staffed by women, including **Elisabeth Lutyens** and **Iris Lemare**; when reconstituted after World War II (1947–78), it played primarily in schools. Macnaghten was also cofounder of the **Macnaghten-Lemare Concerts**. She was named MBE in 1987.

MACNAGHTEN-LEMARE CONCERTS. Series of concerts given between 1932 and 1937 and again from 1950 to at least 1991, originally founded by **Iris Lemare, Elisabeth Luytens**, and **Anne Macnaghten**. These concerts concentrated primarily on contemporary British music and featured performances of works by **Benjamin Britten, Gerald Finzi, Elisabeth Luytens, Dame Elizabeth Maconchy, Alan Rawsthorne**, and **Sir Michael Tippett**. From 1950 forward the series was variously called the Macnaghten Concerts, the Macnaghten Music Group, the Macnaghten New Music Group, and New Macnaghten Concerts; it organized concerts of new music and commissioned new music.

MACONCHY, DAME ELIZABETH (1907–94). English composer of Irish origin. Maconchy burst onto the English scene in 1930, when her suite *The Land* premiered at the **Proms**. Maconchy was a student of **Ralph Vaughan Williams** and **Charles Wood** at the **Royal College of Music** (and a lifelong friend of the former). She studied in Prague from 1929 to 1930 on an Octavia Traveling Scholarship. Her music was featured in the **Macnaghten-Lemare Concerts** of the 1930s, and after World War II, she composed prolifically for both amateur and professional musicians, particularly in **opera** and choral music. An able administrator, she was chair of both the Composers Guild and the **Society for the Promotion of New Music**. Maconchy was named CBE in 1977 and DBE in 1987.

MAD SONGS. A popular subgenre in Restoration theater. Reinforced perhaps by the contemporary interest in the inmates of London's Bethlehem hospital ("Bedlam"), Restoration dramatists provided significant opportunity to explore madness, feigned or real, in a number of plays. The songs in which madness is explored tend toward variety of affect and musical gesture, the lack of continuity and contrast underpinning the irrationality of the character. And with the degree of variety, the mad song could take on the dimensions and form of a **cantata**, comprised of several recitatives and arias.

Three of the most striking mad songs occur in **Thomas Durfey**'s trilogy of *Don Quixote* (1694), set by **Henry Purcell** and **John Eccles**. Eccles's "I Burn, I Burn" is sung by the character Marcella in the voice of **Anne Brace-girdle**. Durfey was explicit in his praise of what the famous actress brought to the success of the song: "[It was] so incomparably well sung and acted by Mrs. Bracegirdle, that the most envious do allow, as well as the most ingenious affirm, that 'tis the best of that kind ever done before.'" Purcell's "From Rosy Bowers," the last song he wrote, is for the character Altisidora, sung by the young **Letitia Cross**, who attempts to seduce Don Quixote with "a whimsical variety, as if I were posses'd with several degrees of Passion," and in this case, the passions range from love and gaiety to melancholy and frenzy. Purcell's "Let the Dreadful Engines Roar" is for the character Cardeno, sung by **John Bowman**. Here, in contrast to Altisidora's assumed madness, the madness is a genuine insanity brought about by the loss of his beloved Lucinda.

MADRIGAL. A form of polyphonic vernacular song, through-composed and generally on the model of light Italianate forms like the *canzonetta*. **Thomas Morley**, in his *A Plain & Easy Introduction to Practical Music* (1597), described the madrigal's adherence to an aesthetic of variety, combining a succession of affective gestures and contrapuntal writing:

> The best kind of it [light music] is termed Madrigal, a word for the etymology of which I can give no reason; yet use showeth that it is a kind of music made upon songs and sonnets such as Petrarch and many poets of our time have excelled in. . . . As for the music it is, next unto the Motet, the most artificial and, to men of understanding, most delightful. If therefore you will compose in this kind you must possess yourself with an amorous humour . . . , so that you must in your music be wavering like the wind, sometime wanton, sometime drooping, sometime grave and staid, otherwhile effeminate; you may maintain points and revert them, use Triplas, and show the very uttermost of your variety, and the more variety you show the better shall you please.

The variety of which Morley writes is generally a product of text depiction, as the composer focuses on rendering individual words with musically iconic corollaries. **Thomas Weelkes**'s well-known "As Vesta Was from Latmos Hill Descending" furnishes a number of examples of these madrigalisms, where words like "descending" and "ascending" inspire the obvious musical contours, phrases like "two by two" inspire the obvious musical pairing of voices, and the longevity of the refrain, "Long live fair Oriana," receives augmentation.

Though generally lighter and less literary than the contemporary Italian madrigal, the Elizabethan madrigal's debt to Italy is made particularly clear in several collections from the end of the 16th century, in particular *Musica Transalpina* (1588 and 1597) and *Italian Madrigals Englished* (1590). The 1588 collection features four- to six-voice Italian madrigals, most by **Alfonso Ferrabosco**, underlaid with English translations of the original texts. The 1590 collection presents mostly madrigals by Luca Marenzio, some with translated texts, but others underlaid with new English poems altogether. Collections such as these prepared the way for more fully original English collections, such as Morley's *The Triumphs of Oriana* (1601), often held to be an allegorical salute to the monarch in madrigals by diverse English composers, such as Morley, **John Wilbye**, and **Thomas Tomkins**. However, even here the Italianate echo is discernible as the general structural idea of the collection is indebted to the Italian *Il Trionfo di Dori*. Recent scholarship (Jeremy Smith, 2005) associates Oriana with Anne of Denmark, rather than the queen. Several composers of the 19th and 20th centuries revisited the genre, and numerous choirs, such as the **Madrigal Society** and **Henry Leslie's Choir**, specialized in their performance as a sort of early musical nationalism. *See also* ACADEMY OF ANCIENT MUSIC; BARRETT, WILLIAM ALEXANDER; BATESON, THOMAS; CASE, JOHN; CAVENDISH, MICHAEL; EAST, MICHAEL; GIBBONS, ORLANDO; LINLEY, THOMAS (THE YOUNGER); MOERAN, E. J.; *MUSICA BRITANNICA*; *MUSICA TRANSALPINA*; PHILIPS, PETER; PILKINGTON, FRANCIS; PORTER, WALTER; RAVENSCROFT, THOMAS; WARD, JOHN; WEELKES, THOMAS; YOUNG, NICHOLAS.

MADRIGAL SOCIETY. London amateur choir founded in 1741 by **John Immyns** for the singing of music by pre-18th-century composers, including important performances of the music of **William Byrd** as well as 16th- and 17th-century English and Italian **madrigals**. Unlike many contemporary antiquarian societies, which were run by and for members of the nobility and the elite and prominently featured professional musicians, the membership of the Madrigal Society consisted of members of the working and mercantile classes, and largely featured amateur musicians. Like many singing societies of the 18th century, the Madrigal Society started as both a musical and social club, featuring suppers after singing (until the early 19th century), held meetings in public houses and taverns (usually on Wednesday evenings), and sang from manuscript partbooks (the earliest of which were copied by Immyns himself). While it languished for a time after Immyns's death in 1764, the society was refounded in 1792 and still exists. *See also* BATTISHILL, JONATHAN; COOKE, BENJAMIN; HAWKINS, SIR JOHN.

MAINZER, JOSEPH (1801–51). German composer, teacher, and author. Together with **John Curwen, Sarah Glover,** and **John Hullah,** Mainzer was responsible for the promotion of mid-century sight-singing and music for the working classes in Great Britain. Mainzer's system, like that of Hullah, was based on fixed doh and was disseminated through large classes, but it did not survive him. Mainzer was trained as a chorister at Trier Cathedral and in Darmstadt, Munich, Vienna, and Rome on a *Wanderjahr* supported by the bishop of Trier. He took orders as a priest and became singing-master at the seminary in Trier. His sympathy for local miners and political awakening caused him to give up the priesthood and flee to Paris in 1834. He established a singing class there between 1835 and 1839, free of charge to local laborers, where he developed his sight-singing system.

Mainzer made his home in Great Britain from 1841 until his death, first establishing similar singing classes in London and Edinburgh before settling in Manchester. Aside from singing classes, he was the author of *Singing for the Million* (1841), *A Treatise on Musical Grammar* (1843), and *Music and Education* (1848). In 1841, he established the *National Singing Circular*, which became *Mainzer's Musical Times and Singing Class Circular* in 1843 and, in 1844, was purchased by **Novello & Co.** to eventually become the *MT*.

MANNS, SIR AUGUST (1825–1907). Conductor of German birth. Manns had early training in Germany on strings and woodwinds. He arrived in England in 1854, working first as the assistant conductor of the orchestra at the **Crystal Palace; Sir George Grove** appointed him to the position of conductor in 1855, and he conducted the orchestra there until 1901. A feature of his Saturday Afternoon Concerts, in addition to the wide-ranging and adventurous programming, was cheap prices that members of the lower and middle classes could afford. Aside from conducting at the Crystal Palace, Manns also conducted the London Handel Festival (1883–1900), the Glasgow Choral Union Orchestra (1879–87), and numerous provincial festivals. He was knighted in 1903.

MARBECK, JOHN (ca. 1505–85?). Singer, organist, and composer. Marbeck was likely trained at St. George's Chapel, Windsor, where he spent his career as a lay clerk and organist. His Reform leanings were problematic before the accession of Edward VI, so much so that he was tried for heresy and condemned to death in 1543, although through royal intervention he was spared capital punishment—the fate of his codefendants—and he returned to the musical estabishment at Windsor.

The publication of the first *Book of Common Prayer* (1549), Thomas Cranmer's liturgical work, brought with it the need for musical settings of the new liturgy, a need met by Marbeck's publication in 1550 of *The Booke of Common Praier Noted*. Marbeck's settings, still in use in modern Anglican practice, were both monophonic and syllabic, aiming at the text intelligibility espoused by the reformers and explicitly advocated by Cranmer in his publication of the English Litany.

"THE MARCH OF THE WOMEN." Suffrage song by **Dame Ethel Smyth** with lyrics by Cicely Hamilton (1872–1952), composed in 1911 and used especially by the Women's Social and Political Union.

MARSH, JOHN (1752–1828). Composer, violinist, impresario, and writer on music. Marsh's importance is not as a composer (though he was one of the most prolific of his time) but (for his contemporaries) as an organizer of subscription concert series in the various towns in which he lived and (for scholars today) as an avid diarist of musical life from 1796 until his death. Marsh had two years of violin lessons in Rosport, but learned music mostly by himself, becoming proficient on the spinet, viola, cello, and **organ**. At Romney (1773), Salisbury (1776), and Canterbury (1783), he became a visible local musician, often both leading and successfully reorganizing local subscription concerts. He did the same at Chichester, where he settled in 1787 and remained for the rest of his life, retiring from **public concerts** in 1813. His skill was such that he was a sought-after orchestral leader, an able **organ** deputy for local parishes and on occasion provincial cathedrals, and a published composer of symphonies, **Anglican chant**, and numerous **anthems**.

MARYLEBONE GARDENS. *See* PLEASURE GARDENS.

MASQUE. A lavish, celebratory entertainment that features scenic spectacle, verse, music, and both social and choreographed dancing by masked performers, as well as the courtly audience, all thematically unified by royal allegory and myth. The "golden age" of the masque was under the early Stuarts, James I (1603–25) and Charles I (1625–49), and productions drew on the collaborations of poets like Ben Jonson and **Thomas Campion**, stage craftsmen like Inigo Jones, and composers such as **John Coprario** and **Nicholas Lanier**. Lanier's contributions document the English awareness of declamatory style; for instance, he notes that the entire 1617 masque *Lovers Made Men* (Jonson) was "sung after the Italian manner, stilo recitativo." *Lovers Made Men* would seem to have essayed a continental operatic style, but as the music does not survive, this remains speculative. The basic template for the Jonsonian masque alternated song or speech with dance in the following form:

Antimasque (danced by professionals, often featuring grotesquerie)
Discovery
First song or speech
First entry
Second song or speech
Main entry
Third song or speech
Revels (social dancing that combined the fantasy world of the masque with
    the real world of the audience.)
Fourth song or speech or second antimasque
Terminal dance or third entry

See also ARNE, THOMAS; BLOW, JOHN; FERRABOSCO, ALFONSO (THE YOUNGER); HUMFREY, PELHAM; ISAACK, BARTHOLOMEW; JOHNSON, ROBERT; *THE JUDGMENT OF PARIS*; LANIER, NICHOLAS; LAWES, HENRY; LUPO, THOMAS; PAISIBLE, JAMES; PURCELL, HENRY; "RULE, BRITANNIA"; STAGGINS, NICHOLAS; VAUGHAN WILLIAMS, RALPH; *VENUS AND ADONIS*.

MASS PAIRS. In early 15th-century English sources, notably the so-called **Old Hall Manuscript**, movements of the mass ordinary were linked in pairs—the Gloria with the Credo, the Sanctus with the Agnus—through various devices, including common cantus firmus, a common liturgical source for different melodies used as a structural voice, motivic similarity, and recurrent textural patterns. The pairing of mass movements in this way represents a preliminary step toward the advent of the fully cyclic mass, which the English first advanced, as well, in works like **Leonel Power**'s *Missa Alma Redemptoris Mater*.

MASTER OF THE KING'S (QUEEN'S) MUSIC (ALSO MUSICK). Created in 1625, the position is one historically charged with the oversight of the court's musical establishment. In the modern day, however, the post is largely an honorific one, awarded to a composer of national distinction and particular prominence. Until the present incumbent, who holds the appointment for a 10-year term, appointments have been for life. The last word of the title was changed from "Musick" to "Music" during **Sir Edward Elgar**'s tenure. Holders of the title:

Nicholas Lanier (1625–49; 1660–66—Lanier's time is split because the
post was abolished during the Commonwealth)
Louis Grabu (1666–1674)
Nicholas Staggins (1674–1700)
John Eccles (1700–1735)
Maurice Greene (1735–55)
William Boyce (1755–60)
John Stanley (1779–86)
William Parsons (1786–1817)
William Shield (1817–20)
Christian Cramer (1829–30)
Franz Cramer (1834–37)
George Frederick Anderson (1848–70)
Sir William Cousins (1870–93)
Sir Walter Parratt (1893–1924)
Sir Edward Elgar (1924–34)
Sir (Henry) Walford Davies (1934–41)
Sir Arnold Bax (1941–52)
Sir Arthur Bliss (1952–75)
Malcolm Williamson (1975–2003)
Sir Peter Maxwell Davies (2004–present)

MATTEIS, NICOLA (?–AFTER 1713). Virtuoso violinist, guitarist, and
composer. The Italian Matteis came to England around 1670 and as a virtuoso violinist had great impact on advancing both the cause of the violin and
the Italian repertory over against the **viol** and consort music. His distinctive
manner of playing was impassioned and florid, as attested in the writings of
Roger North. North writes, "His manner was singular, but in one respect
excelled all that had bin knowne before in England, which was the arcata. His
staccatos, tremolos, devisions, and indeed his whole manner was surprising,
and every stroke of his was a mouthful." Telling evidence of his prominence
is that his manner of performance and composition was echoed across the
boundaries of genre; **John Weldon**'s "When Perfect Beauty" is styled "A
Song on a Lady in Imitation of Mr. Nicola's Manner," and this takes the form
of extended coloratura passagework.

Matteis was also an accomplished guitarist who published an important
continuo treatise for that instrument, *Le false consonanse della musica*
(1680), with an English translation in 1682.

MATTHAY SCHOOL OF MUSIC. *See* ROYAL NORTHERN COLLEGE
OF MUSIC.

MAZZINGHI, JOSEPH (1765–1844). Composer and arranger. Mazzinghi, born in England, came from a Corsican musical family. His father was a sometime violinist at the Marylebone **pleasure gardens**, and one aunt (on his mother's side) was a regular contralto soloist for **oratorio** performances. His early training came from lessons from **Johann Christian Bach** and an apprenticeship as copyist and musical assistant to Leopoldo De Michele of the King's Theatre, **Haymarket** (1779), until he was named harpsichordist there (1784). For the remainder of the 18th century, he was either a house composer at the King's Theatre (1786–89) or the **Pantheon** (1790–92) or a composer-for-hire at **Covent Garden**; at all three theaters, he both composed his own music and arranged that of others into **opera** pasticcios. During this time he was also in demand as a ballet composer. Mazzinghi withdrew from theater composition by 1810 and continued until his death as a sought-after teacher; he was music master for a time to the Princess of Wales (later Queen Caroline). He organized the Concerts of the Nobility, was a member of the **Royal Society of Musicians** from 1787 until his death, and superintended the concerts at both Carlton House and the Royal Pavilion in Brighton.

MCNAUGHT, WILLIAM (1883–1953). Music critic, editor, and adjudicator; son of **William Gray McNaught**. McNaught, who was educated at the Westminster College School and Worcester College, Oxford, never took a music degree but was initiated into a great love of music and musicians (including **Tonic Sol-fa**, adjudicating at competition **musical festivals**, and criticism) by his father. Based in London for his entire adult life, he wrote for many publications as a London music critic, including the *Morning Post*, the *Manchester Guardian*, the *Glasgow Evening News*, the London *Evening News*, and *Radio Times*. For a short time, he edited *School Music Review* and edited the *MT* from 1944 until his death.

MCNAUGHT, WILLIAM GRAY (1849–1918). Educator, journalist, editor, and adjudicator; father of **William McNaught**. His early musical experiences included learning **Tonic Sol-fa** in a school classroom and singing in concerts for the **Tonic Sol-fa Association** at the **Crystal Palace**. While working for a coffee importer, he taught himself violin and conducting and began to teach music classes in his spare time. Leaving business, he studied harmony, singing, violin, and piano at the **Royal Academy of Music (2;** 1872–76) and devoted himself professionally to music education, both as an ardent supporter of Tonic Sol-fa (leading several choirs) and as the Assistant Inspector of Music in Schools and Training Colleges under **Sir John Stainer** (1883–1901). In 1892 he founded the *School Music Review* (which he edited until his death), and he edited *MT* from 1910 until his death. Among his books are the influential *School Music Teacher* (1889) and *Hints on Choir Training for Competition* (1896).

MEAN. Voice range designation. Analogous to "medius," the mean is historically understood to have been the middle voice in three-part textures, although by the 17th century, some writers equate it with the alto or **countertenor** (Jander, *NG*, 2001). Bowers (1995) asserts that means were as frequently boys as adult singers and that in the post-Reformation years "mean" might also generically refer to the boy's voice in the way that later generations have adopted the word "treble." Bowers's assertion about both boys and men singing the mean, however, is shaped by his strong skepticism regarding the so-called high-**pitch** theory that would transpose much 16th-century polyphony upward.

MENDELSSOHN, FELIX (1809–1847). German composer, conductor, pianist, and educator. Between 1829 and 1847, Mendelssohn made ten trips to Great Britain, during which he conducted at or performed with most of the major London ensembles (including the **Concerts of Ancient Music**, the **Royal Philharmonic Society**, and the **Sacred Harmonic Society**). He was a frequent guest of the Birmingham **Musical Festival**, at which he conducted the premiere of his **oratorio** *Elijah* in 1846. Mendelssohn's importance to English music in the 19th century cannot be overestimated. Interest in *Elijah* rivaled that of **George Frideric Handel**'s *Messiah*, and musical festivals for the remainder of the 19th century programmed both works. Mendelssohn's death at a young age allowed him to enter English musical discourse as a tragic hero, and the middle classes celebrated him as such throughout the remainder of the 19th century. He also helped raise the status of English musicians from servant to professional status, since he refused to be treated like a servant while in England.

MENDELSSOHN SCHOLARSHIP. Fund, set up by **Jenny Lind** in 1849 in memory of **Felix Mendelssohn**. The purpose of the scholarship was initially to send an English composer to the Leipzig Conservatory or elsewhere for training. Winners of the scholarship include **Sir Joseph Barnby**, **Frederick Corder**, **Sir George Dyson**, **Charles Swinnerton Heap**, **Sir Arthur Sullivan**, and **Maude Valérie White**, among others.

MESSIAH. **George Frideric Handel**'s most famous composition, an **oratorio** that received its first performance on 13 April 1742 in Dublin at the New Music Hall in Fishamble Street. A setting of a biblical libretto compiled by Charles Jennens, the oratorio is unusual in its lack of narrative and dramatic construction, presenting instead a contemplative treatment of Christian salvation in the life and work of Jesus. Though its first performance was in Dublin, it was possibly composed with a London performance in mind (Burrows, 1991). Its first London performances at **Covent Garden** in 1743 took place amid discussion of the propriety of sacred subject matter in the theater. Its popularity as a charity performance for the **Foundling Hospital** echoes its use for charity benefit in Dublin; this and its frequency of performance suggest that ultimately conservative pieties were not decisive.

Messiah quickly became known throughout the English-speaking world as a compositon with a philanthropic bent, frequently presented as the aesthetic climax of many charity **musical festivals**. It was first heard at the Three Choirs Musical Festival in 1757, and scarcely a festival in the remainder of the 18th or 19th centuries could exist without its presence, usually as an opening or closing piece. Throughout the 19th century, performances of *Messiah* by festivals and professional and amateur choral societies happened weekly within Great Britain, including "monster concerts" at the **Crystal Palace** (featuring as many as 500 instrumentalists, 3,000 chorus members, and an audience in the tens of thousands), exhibition concerts of the **Tonic Sol-fa Association**, and even unaccompanied concerts by miners and other working-class groups on summer picnics. Cheap staff notation and **Tonic Sol-fa** editions of the score were ubiquitous; most journals published regular articles about the importance of *Messiah* within British culture, and arrangements of the score by Wolfgang Amadeus Mozart and **Sir Michael Costa** were frequently employed as ways to "update" the composition for 19th-century listeners.

The oratorio was somewhat overexposed by the end of the 19th century but remained a staple well into the 20th. Investigations of the score Handel left to the Foundling Hospital led to some of the first systematic investigations into performance practice of the early 18th century. The Three Choirs Musical Festival performed the work every year until 1963. *See also* ARNE, MICHAEL; ARNE, THOMAS AUGUSTINE; BATES, JOAH; BRIDGE, SIR FREDERICK; *A CHILD OF OUR TIME*; CORONATION MUSIC; CURWEN PRESS; *ELIJAH*; GIARDINI, FELICE; HANDEL COMMEMORATION; NOVELLO'S ORATORIO CONCERTS; SNOW, VALENTINE; STANLEY, JOHN.

METRICAL PSALMS. Vernacular, versified translations of the Psalter sung to strophically repeating tunes, either in harmony (often with the tune in the tenor) or monophonically, associated with 16th-century Reformed movements and in England nurtured by **Puritans**. The first complete metrical psalter arose out of Strasbourg and the circle of Martin Bucer in 1538, echoed in the next year by Calvin's *Aulcuns Psaulmes et Cantiques* and in

1562 by a complete Genevan psalter. The politics of religious exile positioned continental practice to be influential on Reform-minded Englishmen, yet significantly, several metrical psalm collections were published as early as 1549, including Robert Crowley's *The Psalter of David* (with four-part harmonizations of psalm tone melodies) and Thomas Sternhold's *Certayne Psalmes.* Sternhold's psalms from this collection and elsewhere were joined with those of John Hopkins to create a complete English metrical psalter in 1562, *The Whole Booke of Psalmes*. The preface to the collection is illuminating in that it makes reference to Elizabeth's liturgically oriented *Injunctions* of 1559, but explicitly refers to the fact that these psalms were "very mete to be used of all sortes of people privately for their solace & comfort. . . ." Thus, a private devotional usage is confirmed, as is the affective agency of the psalms to provide such things as spiritual comfort.

The 1562 Psalter provided tunes, although fewer of them than texts, implying a flexibility as regards what tune went with what text. The Psalters of **Thomas East** (1592) and **Thomas Ravenscroft** (1621) provided harmonized melodies, again with the tune in the tenor, and the fact that the melodies were harmonized is suggestive of their use with choirs, and thus in cathedrals and major chapels. Sternhold and John Hopkins's Psalter was notably long-lived; its "Old Version" was not replaced until *A New Version of the Psalms of David* by Nahum Tate and Nicholas Brady was published in 1696. Significantly, the New Version did not offer new melodies, only new texts.

THE MIKADO, OR TOWN OF TITPU. Operetta in two acts by **Sir William Schwenck Gilbert** and **Sir Arthur Sullivan** premiered in London in 1885. The most popular of Gilbert and Sullivan's operettas, its initial run at the **Savoy Theatre** was 672 performances; it has had innumerable revivals since. The story, though set in Japan, concerns social politics and manners of love and relationships that are purely English at their heart: whether or not Nanki-Poo, son of the Emperor, will be allowed to marry his true love, the soprano Yum-Yum (a woman outside his class), or be forced to marry the contralto Kaitsha. Little of the score contains the musical exoticism common during the era. In recent years, Gilbert's libretto has come under scrutiny as possibly racist for its fictionalized and stereotyped portrayal of Imperial Japan.

MILFORD, ROBIN (1903–59). Composer and educator. Milford attended Rugby and then the **Royal College of Music** (1921–26), where he studied composition with **Gustav Holst** and **Ralph Vaughan Williams**. At times within his career he worked for the Aeolian Company and taught music at both the Ludgrove School and the Badminton School. His compositions — known for their diatonic melodies and use of folk song style — achieved some fame in his lifetime, including a Double Fugue for Orchestra (which received the Carnegie Award in 1927) and his **oratorio**, *A Prophet in the Land*, which was performed at the Three Choirs **Music Festival** in 1931.

MOERAN, E. J. (ERNEST JOHN; 1894–1950). Composer of Anglo-Irish descent. Moeran was educated at the Uppingham School and then the **Royal College of Music**, where his compositional studies with **Sir Charles Villiers Stanford** (1913–14) and **John Ireland** (1920–23) were interrupted by service in World War I. Moeran was a prolific member of the "English School," inspired by both folk music (in his lifetime, he collected English folk music from East Anglia, Norfolk, and Suffolk, as well as Ireland) and **madrigals**. For a time (1925–28) he lived with **Philip Heseltine**. One of Moeran's best-known compositions during his own life was his Symphony in G minor (1924–37).

MORLEY, THOMAS (ca. 1557–1602). Composer, organist, and theorist. The dedication of Morley's treatise, *A Plaine and Easie Introduction to Practicall Musicke* (1597), to **William Byrd** identifies him as Morley's "master" and someone to whom Morley was anxious to convey a "thankful mind," both of which strongly suggest that at one time Morley was Byrd's student. He held appointments at Norwich Cathedral (1583) and St. Paul's, London, after which he was named gentleman of the **Chapel Royal** (1592). His compositional output, like Byrd's, ranges from Latin church music and Anglican **services** to instrumental works for both keyboard and consort—his *Consort Lessons* (1599) present arrangements of popular pieces that are definitive in solidifying the so-called **English** (or "broken") **Consort**.

However, his most significant activity is focused on the English **madrigal** and its derivation from Italian models, generally from lighter forms like the *balletto* or *canzonetta*, rather than from the serious Italian madrigal, per se. Some of this activity takes the form of editing, arranging, and supplying English texts to Italian works—compositions by Giovanni Francesco Anerio and Giovanni Giacomo Gastoldi, for instance, are the basis for a number of "Morley's" canzonets and ballets. Morley defined both the canzonet and **ballett** as "light"; the canzonet, he writes, is a song in which "little art can be showed," "a counterfeit of the Madrigal"; the balletts, lighter still, are songs "which being sung to a ditty may likewise be danced" (1597). And it is lightness and musical development over literary textual values that set the English madrigal apart from its Italian counterpart.

Morley's compilation anthology, *The Triumphs of Oriana* (1601), is likely the best-known collection of Elizabethan madrigals. The collection brings together madrigals by over 20 different composers in what has traditionally been seen as an allegorical salute to the monarch (Elizabeth becomes Oriana), based on the model of Croce's *Il Trionfi di Dori*. Recent scholarship (Jeremy Smith, 2005) associates Oriana with Anne of Denmark rather than the queen.

The religious complexities of Elizabethan England find an echo in Morley's own circumstance. Correspondence between Charles Paget and Sir Francis Walsingham's secretary, Thomas Phellippes (1592), suggests that Morley was a Roman Catholic, who, facing enough evidence to be hanged, repented and turned into a government spy in the ongoing rooting out of Romanism. His own Roman Catholicism, though apparently far from steadfast, suggests yet another echo of his master, Byrd. The connection to Byrd has an additional manifestation in Morley's obtaining the monopoly on the printing of music after Byrd's ownership of the monopoly expired. Unlike Byrd, Morley experienced legal difficulties with the monopoly in the form of contentious litigation with **John Day** over the publication of **metrical psalters**. In the end, the outcome was the eradication of the monopoly after Morley's term expired.

MORRIS DANCE. A folk dance, often performed by male-only troupes, who wear bells on their knees and ankles and often manually employ handkerchiefs or sticks as part of the choreography. Morris dancing has a historic association with May celebrations. Popular in the 16th and 17th centuries, its roots are earlier; tradition holds that in the 14th century John of Gaunt was influential in bringing the dance back from Moorish Spain, a connection that is echoed in the nomenclature itself, with "morris" being a cognate term for "moresca" (a Moorish dance), and also in the fact that morris dancing is sometimes done in blackface.

Cecil Sharp's legendary career as a collector of folk music was inspired in part by his 1899 experience of seeing an Oxford morris side. His own studies and publications have been influential on preserving the dance in the modern day, as have those of **Mary Neal**.

MOSCHELES, IGNAZ (1794–1870). Bohemian composer, pianist, educator, and conductor. His training occurred at the Prague Conservatory and then in Vienna, under Johann Georg Albrechtsberger and Antonio Salieri. After a period touring Europe as a virtuoso pianist, Moscheles settled in London (1825–46) teaching piano both privately and at the **Royal Academy of Music (2)**. During his time in London, he promoted the music of Ludwig van Beethoven as a conductor of the **Royal Philharmonic Society** (1832–41) and as the translator of Anton Schindler's *Life of Beethoven* (1841). He continued to compose and tour both England and the Continent during this period. In 1846 he joined **Felix Mendelssohn** in Leipzig at the conservatory there; he became head of it upon Mendelssohn's death and taught there and conducted the Leipzig Gewandhaus Orchestra until his own death.

MOTETT SOCIETY (ALSO MOTET SOCIETY). Group founded by the Scottish painter William Dyce and **Edward Francis Rimbault** to sing and publish early church music in English editions. The group was founded in 1841 and disbanded in 1857.

MUDGE, RICHARD (1718–63). Cleric and sometime amateur composer, particularly of concertos. Mudge took a BA and an MA at Pembroke College, Oxford, between 1735 and 1741. For a time, he was curate at Great Packington and Little Packington, and then rector at Little Packington, near Birmingham, under the patronage of Lord Guernsey. Some of his music may have been composed for evenings at Gurnsey's house, or perhaps for Charles Jennens (**George Frideric Handel**'s librettist), with whom Mudge was associated at this time. Mudge also spent time in Birmingham as curate at St. Bartholomew's and had a living at Bedworth. He published a set of *Six Concertos* in 1749.

MULLINER BOOK. A manuscript anthology (GB Lbl Add. Ms. 30513) of 16th-century keyboard works by **John Redford, Thomas Tallis,** and others. The anthology is in the hand of Thomas Mulliner, a musician associated with Magdalen and Corpus Christi Colleges, Oxford, and St. Paul's Cathedral, London, and contains liturgical **organ** music, dances, and vocal arrangements.

MUNDY, WILLIAM (ca. 1528–ca. 1591). Composer. Mundy was trained as a chorister at Westminster Abbey, documented there in the 1540s; his later appointments, all of them in London, include St. Martin's, Ludgate Hill; St. Mary-at-Hill; and St. Paul's Cathedral. He was appointed gentleman of the **Chapel Royal** in 1564, serving in that capacity until his death. As a composer he was both prolific and stylistically diverse, with compositions ranging from the old florid style (revived under Mary Tudor) to essays in the modern vernacular verse **anthem**. His nine-voice setting of the Magnificat and Nunc Dimittis "in medio chori" is notably elaborate, perhaps written for the Chapel Royal. The designation "in medio chori" is not unique to Mundy, although his is the only music so designated to survive complete. The designation may refer to the placing of a group of singers—soloists, perhaps—in the space between the two sides of the choir, *cantoris* **and** *decani*, for an enriched spatial effect.

Mundy's eldest son, John (ca. 1555–1630), was also a composer and organist at St. George's Chapel, Windsor, the successor to **Richard Farrant**.

MUSGRAVE, THEA (1928–). Composer and educator. Musgrave is known for her gradual move from a modal language into a serial one as well as her questioning of the basic relationship between an authoritarian or totalitarian conductor and a subservient orchestra, through compositions including the Concerto for Orchestra (1967). Musgrave studied at the University of Edinburgh, with Nadia Boulanger privately and at the Paris Conservatoire (1949–54), and at Tanglewood with Aaron Copland. She has taught at the **Dartington Summer School**; the University of London; the University of California, Santa Barbara; and as a distinguished professor at the City University of New York (1987–2002). Musgrave was made a CBE in 2002.

MUSIC ROOMS. *See* CONCERT ROOMS.

MUSICA BRITANNICA. Ongoing scholarly edition of British music published by Stainer & Bell under the auspices of the **Royal Musical Association**. Stainer & Bell published the first volume of the series in 1954, and as of this writing, 89 volumes exist. The scope of the series is broad, including music from the 15th through 19th centuries, featuring complete transcriptions of important manuscripts (such as the **Eton Choirbook** and the **Mulliner Book**), volumes devoted to genres cultivated in Great Britain (**anthems, ayres, carols**, consort music, **fantasia-suites, madrigals, services,** and songs), as well of collections of music by significant British composers (**Michael Arne, John Blow, John Bull, William Byrd, John Dunstaple, Orlando Gibbons, Maurice Greene, Sir Hubert Parry, Sir Charles Villiers Stanford**, and **Samuel Sebastian Wesley**, inter alia). In spite of its name, the series currently contains only one volume (*The Music of Scotland: 1500–1700*) that does not pertain directly to the music of England. The series concentrates on publishing British music that is not readily available in other scholarly editions, thus the music of **Henry Purcell** and **Sir Edward Elgar** have not been published in *Musica Britannica*.

MUSICA TRANSALPINA. Elizabethan anthologies of Italian **madrigals** with English texts. **Nicholas Young** edited two anthologies (1588 and 1597) of madrigals eponymously from "across the alps," i.e. from Italy, set with English texts. The first volume features pieces by **Alfonso Ferrabosco** the elder and Luca Marenzio in four to six parts. Kerman (1951) draws attention to the way *Musica Transalpina* resembles the anthologies of Pierre Phalèse in scope and structure, as well as in a significant number of concordances.

MUSICAL ANTIQUARIAN SOCIETY. Group founded in 1840 by William Chappell and **Edward Francis Rimbault** to publish early English music. The 19 volumes published by **Chappell & Co.** for the Society's subscribers included works by **William Byrd, John Dowland, Orlando**

Gibbons, **Thomas Morley**, **Henry Purcell**, and **Thomas Weelkes**, among others. The group's last formal meeting occurred in 1847, and it published its final volume in 1848.

MUSICAL ASSOCIATION. *See* ROYAL MUSICAL ASSOCIATION.

MUSICAL FESTIVALS (ALSO CHARITY FESTIVALS; CHORAL FESTIVALS; COMPETITION FESTIVALS; FESTIVALS; MUSIC FESTIVALS). Musical Festivals have existed with regularity in England since the mid-17th century, and while the focus and purpose of such festivals has changed over the last three centuries, one constant is the continual celebration of vocal and choral music. Most festivals (save ones specifically to honor **St. Cecilia**) from the mid-17th century to the end of the 18th were organized with charitable aims in mind, such as the Festival of the Sons of the Clergy (ca. 1655) and the Three Choirs Festival (ca. 1715); both raised funds for members of the clergy or their families in financial distress. The Birmingham Musical Festival (1768) raised funds for a local hospital. Repertoire included **anthems** and **services** but increasingly through the 18th century **glees**, selections from favorite **operas**, and **George Frideric Handel**'s **oratorios** as well—particularly *Messiah*, but also selections from other works and imitations of Handel by other composers. Handel received his own series of commemorative festivals at Westminster Abbey between 1784 and 1791 and in 1834; a frequent Handel Festival was held in the middle of the 19th century at the **Crystal Palace** featuring thousands of performers.

Festivals for charity continued in the 19th century and were mostly acceptable to middle-class tastes, concentrating on the performance of oratorios (*Messiah* was joined by **Felix Mendelssohn**'s *Elijah* in 1846), dramatic **cantatas**, and other works fashionable at the moment. Instrumental concerts increased in frequency at festivals throughout this century, as did the importance of the festival as a commissioner of new music. Indeed, the 19th century was the heyday of the festivals, as many more were founded in cathedral cities (Chester, Norwich, York, Chichester, etc.), as an expression of municipal pride (Bristol, Leeds, Sheffield, Wolverhampton, etc.), and as a paternalistic impulse to "improve" rural populations (Bridlington, Hovingham, etc.). In some instances, festivals were the only times that individuals in the provinces could hear the combination of an orchestra and a chorus perform locally.

From 1880 forward these charity-based festivals were joined by competition festivals, patterned after the Welsh *Eisteddfod*, organized by **Henry Leslie**, **John Spencer Curwen**, and **Mary Wakefield** but quickly emulated throughout England. Competition festivals were aimed at the working and middle classes and attempted to create a love of music and to promote music as a distraction from vice. Both charity and competition festivals were active forces throughout the first half of the 20th century and gave the composers of the **English Musical Renaissance** many commissions and promoted their fame: **Sir Edward Elgar** premiered works at the Three Choirs Festival, and his oratorios for the Birmingham Musical Festival, such as *The Dream of Gerontius*, rivaled those by Handel and Mendelssohn in popularity in the first decades of the century. **Ralph Vaughan Williams** and **Gustav Holst** also received generous exposure through festivals; all three composers also provided short test pieces and even occasional conducting and adjudication at competition festivals. In the period after World War II, the number of traditional charity and competition festivals decreased, but they continued to have a significant impact on musical dissemination beyond London and new music commissions. However, such festivals have often been eclipsed in importance because of the rise of training festivals (e.g., **Dartington International Summer School**), festivals that included other arts together with contemporary music (such as Aldeburgh, organized in part by **Benjamin Britten** and Peter Pears), or festivals devoted specifically to popular music (e.g., Glastonbury).

MUSICAL INSTITUTE OF LONDON. Organization, extant from 1851 to 1853, to promote the study of the art and science of music. The Institute included a reading room and a library and hosted paper presentations and general conversations about music. Members included **Sir William Sterndale Bennett**, **John Hullah**, **Sir Frederic Arthur Gore Ouseley**, and Ludwig Spohr.

MUSICAL UNION. A London concert society active from 1845 to 1881 that presented a series of eight afternoon concerts of instrumental chamber music each season. Like many chamber music organizations of the time, it combined high regard for the music with an attempt to educate the audience. Thus, concerts included analytical programs (complete with transcriptions of principal musical themes) circulated in advance to describe the works heard to the audience. From its foundation to 1880, **John Ella** managed the Union; the cellist Jules Lasserre managed it in its last season. Its concerts were centers of elitism; classes were stratified via differently colored chairs. The performers at concerts were a mixture of English players and foreign ones; some of the most important musicians of the day were seen at the concerts, including **Sir Charles Hallé**, Anton Rubenstein, Clara Schumann, and Henri Wieniawski. The concerts were first given in Blagrove's Small Concert Rooms but moved to Willis's Rooms in 1846 and finally to **St. James's Hall** in 1858.

NARES, JAMES (1715–83). Organist, composer, and teacher. Nares was a chorister at the **Chapel Royal** and studied as well with **Johann Christoph Pepusch**. He was an assistant organist for a time at St. George's Chapel, Windsor, before becoming organist at York Minster (1735–56). He spent the remainder of his life in various positions at the Chapel Royal, including master of the children, and as organist and composer to George III. His music is primarily sacred or keyboard oriented, and he published pedagogical works on keyboard playing (ca. 1760) and singing (ca. 1780 and 1786).

NATIONAL TRAINING SCHOOL FOR MUSIC (NTSM). *See* ROYAL COLLEGE OF MUSIC.

NEAL, MARY (1860–1944). Folk dance collector and social worker. For a period between 1905 and 1914, Neal rivaled **Cecil Sharp** for importance as a collector and disseminator of folk dance, including the **morris dance**. She began collecting and teaching folk dancing at her Espérance Club (founded in 1895 for the welfare and leisure of working women). To disseminate these folk dances throughout the country, she founded the Association for the Revival and Practice of Folk Music (later called the Espérance Guild of Morris Dancers). Whereas Sharp believed folk music and dance should be collected, catalogued, and taught only in "original" form, Neal maintained that folk music and dances had evolved and should be allowed to continue to evolve. From World War I forward, Neal withdrew from folk music and dance to concentrate on direct social charity. She was awarded the CBE in 1937.

NEW PHILHARMONIA ORCHESTRA. *See* PHILHARMONIA ORCHESTRA.

NEW QUEEN'S HALL ORCHESTRA. *See* QUEEN'S HALL ORCHESTRA.

NEWMAN, ERNEST (BORN WILLIAM ROBERTS; 1868–1959). Music critic, writer, adjudicator, and teacher. Newman was the most influential writer on music in England in the first half of the 20th century. Largely self-taught musically, he developed a penetrating analytical mind and a persuasive, fact-based critical writing style. He began writing in 1889 while working as a bank clerk in Liverpool. He published occasional articles and books over the next few years, adopting his pen name "Ernest Newman." In 1904 he taught theory and singing at the Midland Institute School of Music. In 1905 he was named music critic for the *Manchester Guardian*, and thus began his long work of introducing music and musicians to British readers. He worked at various times for the *Birmingham Daily Post* (1906–18), the London *Observer* (1919), the *Sunday Times* (1920–58), and the *Glasgow Herald*, among other papers. He published many monographs, including early biographies of **Sir Edward Elgar**, Richard Strauss, and Hugo Wolf, a four-volume biography of Richard Wagner, and many books on **opera**.

NOBLEMEN AND GENTLEMEN'S CATCH CLUB (ALSO CATCH CLUB; GENTELMEN'S CATCH CLUB). London singing institution founded in 1761. The Catch Club, as originally constituted, had a membership of 21 members of the nobility, with between 10 and 25 composers and singers as "Privileged Members" (as of 1996, this number was reduced to six). By 1762 the membership voted to give prizes of 10 and five guineas for excellent new **catches**, **glees**, or canons. Regular prizes were awarded until 1849. Prizes were occasionally awarded until 1934 at the will of the club. The club presented composers with about 200 prizes in all. To celebrate its bicentennial, the club commissioned a new work from **Sir Malcolm Arnold**, but he did not complete the composition. Privileged Members have included **Michael Arne, Jonathan Battishill, Joseph Bennett, Benjamin Cooke, Tom Cooke,** Alfred Deller, **Thomas Greatorex, Charles Knyvett, Stephen Paxton,** and **Samuel Webbe.**

NORRIS, THOMAS (1741–90). Singer, organist, and composer. Norris was trained as a chorister at Salisbury Cathedral and sang solos as a boy soprano at the Three Choirs **Musical Festivals** and at **Drury Lane** between 1761 and 1762. He settled in Oxford in 1765, taking a BMus at Magdalene College in that year. He was named organist of St. John's College in 1766, lay clerk at Christ Church in 1767, lay clerk at Magdalene College in 1771, and organist of Christ Church in 1776. As a tenor soloist, he frequently sang at musical festivals until his death, including the **Handel Commemorations** of the 1780s; as a composer, he published solo songs, **glees**, and a set of six symphonies.

NORTH, ROGER (1651–1734). Lawyer, writer, man of learning. North was born into an aristocratic family and especially benefited from the influence and patronage of his older brother, Francis, a distinguished jurist. His early years included musical study within the household, most notably with the violist **John Jenkins**. Although he matriculated at Jesus College, Cambridge, illness cut short his university career, and he subsequently took up law at the Middle Temple. His rise there would include an involvement in the famous **organ** contest between **Renatus Harris** and **Bernard "Father" Smith**, waged to see which builder would get the contract to build an organ for the Temple Church. The Whig ascendancy under William and Mary proved politically problematic for North, and in 1690 he moved to a country estate at Rougham (Norfolk) where he could more fully indulge his passions for music, mathematics, art, and architecture, inter alia.

North was a prolific writer, and his passion for music inspired much learned investigation and discourse from his pen. His writings discuss the physics of music, theoretical formulations (for instance, he anticipates Rameau's concept of chordal root), practical matters, questions of epistemology, the history of music, and also observations of the modern scene. In this latter regard, for example, he offers rich description of the violin virtuoso **Nicola Matteis**. The autobiographical *Notes of Me* is rich in musical content, joined by a number of other monographic essays that include "Cursory Notes of Musicke," *Theory of Sounds*, "An Essay on Musicall **Ayre**," and *The Musicall Grammarian*.

NORTHERN SCHOOL OF MUSIC. *See* ROYAL NORTHERN COLLEGE OF MUSIC.

NOVELLO, CLARA (1818–1908). Singer; daughter of **Vincent Novello**. Clara Novello was one of the most celebrated **oratorio** soloists in the middle of the 19th century. She was known for her pure soprano voice, great religious devotion, and excellent musicianship. Novello received initial training in Paris at the Institut Royal de Musique Classique et Religieuse (1829–30), and she frequently sang in London and at the provincial **musical festivals**. After meeting **Felix Mendelssohn** in 1837 at the Birmingham Musical Festival, she toured in Europe, starting in Leipzig. In 1839 she went to Milan to study **opera** and began performing regularly in 1841. She married Count Giovanni Baptista Gigliucci in 1843 and temporarily retired from the stage. She returned to the Italian operatic stage in 1849 and triumphantly to the English musical festivals and oratorio concerts in 1851. Her last public concert was on 21 November 1860; after which she retired to Italy with her husband.

NOVELLO, VINCENT (1781–1861). Organist, choirmaster, conductor, editor, publisher, and composer; father of **Clara Novello** and J. Alfred Novello. As an editor and publisher, Novello was largely responsible for the introduction of Catholic sacred music to the English, including works of Giovanni Pierluigi da

Palestrina, and the masses of Wolfgang Amadeus Mozart and **Franz Joseph Haydn**. He also edited and published a great deal of Anglican music, such as that by **Henry Purcell**, often at his own expense. He began publishing in 1811 and in 1830, with his son, J. Alfred, started the firm **Novello & Co.**

Novello was trained and worked within the Catholic embassy chapels, studying **organ** with **Samuel Webbe** at the Portuguese Chapel (where he would later serve as organist between 1798 and 1823). He was also organist at the Roman Catholic Chapel in Moorfields (the London procathedral) from 1840 to 1843. Novello was one of the founders of the **Royal Philharmonic Society** in 1813 and frequently conducted concerts there from the keyboard, conducted the **Choral Harmonists Society** for a time, and was a frequent guest organist at **musical festivals**. Novello retired from musical life in 1848, when he moved to Nice, France.

NOVELLO & CO. (ALSO NOVELLO, EWER, & CO.). Preeminent 19th-century music publishing firm in England, founded in 1830 by **Vincent Novello** and his son, J. Alfred Novello. Novello & Co. began publishing its vocal score "octavo editions" series in 1847 (scores not published by subscription), which supplied **musical festivals** and amateur and professional choirs with much of their music for the rest of the century. They also published dramatic choral music in **Tonic Sol-fa** notation, particularly **oratorios** and **cantatas**. Like many publishers of the 19th century, Novello & Co. sponsored ensembles (such as the **Novello Choir**) and concert series, including **Novello's Oratorio Concerts**. Novello & Co. has also been the publisher of a number of extremely important periodicals on music, including the *Musical World* (1836–91) and the *MT* (1844–present, after it was purchased from **Joseph Mainzer**).

NOVELLO CHOIR. Choir of 100 **Novello & Co.** employees begun in 1905 by **William Gray McNaught**. Harold Brooke directed it from 1912 to 1924 and re-formed the group in 1925 as the 36-singer Harold Brooke Choir. In this incarnation, it lasted until 1930. The choir began as a singing class but quickly became known for its polished and interesting programs combining early and then-contemporary English music.

NOVELLO'S ORATORIO CONCERTS. Series of concerts conducted by **Sir Alexander Campbell Mackenzie** and funded by **Novello & Co.** between 1885 and 1889. The concerts were notable for the high quality of their performances and the ambitious English and continental repertoire presented in the four seasons, including **George Frideric Handel**'s *Messiah*, **Felix Mendelssohn**'s *Elijah*, Ludwig van Beethoven's Symphony no. 9 in D minor (op. 125), as well as larger works by Mackenzie, **Sir Hubert Parry**, **Sir Charles Villiers Stanford**, and **Sir Arthur Sullivan**.

O

ODE. Celebratory, occasional works, generally written for the court. Court life was periodically graced with salutatory odes on special occasions, such as the monarch's birthday, the turning of the New Year, and the return of the monarch to London after travels. Odes to **St. Cecilia** were also a central part of the 22 November celebrations, characteristically treating themes of the affective powers of individual instruments and the harmony of the spheres. The ode came into blossom in the 17th century, with particularly notable examples by **Henry Purcell**, such as "Come Ye Sons of Art" for the 1694 birthday of Queen Mary or "Hail! Bright Cecilia" for the Cecilia Festival of 1692. **George Frideric Handel** continued the tradition in the 18th century with "Eternal Source of Light Divine" for the birthday of Queen Anne in 1713 and his setting of **John Dryden**'s Cecilian ode, "From Harmony" (1739).

In its components of chorus, orchestra, and various solo ensembles, as well as in their being performed by members of the **Chapel Royal**, it is easy to sense a kinship with the symphony **anthem**. However, distinctions are also readily apparent, such as the greater preponderance of dance music in the ode, perhaps born of its secularity.

The texts are often poor; Holman (1994) describes a pervading view that they are "inept and embarrassingly sycophantic"; Wood (1994) memorably speaks of them as "flatulent encomia." Dryden's "From Harmony," first set by **Giovanni Battista Draghi** in 1687, is a notable exception.

Between 1715 and 1820, the **Master of the King's Music** and the Poet Laureate were jointly responsible for producing birthday and New Year's odes; after this point, the tradition died out. For the remainder of the 19th century, and into the 20th, odes served two purposes: the above-mentioned celebrations of St. Cecilia (e.g., **Gerald Finzi**'s *For St. Cecilia*) and as functional music. Examples of the latter include **Sir Edward Elgar**'s *Coronation Anthem* (1902), written to celebrate the coronation of Edward VII, but not performed because of the king's illness. Other compositions called "ode," such as **Sir Hubert Parry**'s "Ode to Music" (1901) or "Ode on the Nativity" (1902), while called "ode" are better understood in the context of the contemporary **cantata**.

OLD HALL MANUSCRIPT. The major manuscript of early 15th-century English music. Now owned by the **British Library** (Add ms. 57950), the so-called Old Hall Manuscript takes its name from the previous modern owner, St. Edmund's College at Old Hall Green. The chief composer in the collection is **Leonel Power**; in the main, excepting a single contribution by **John Dunstaple**, the other composers are relatively obscure. Significantly, however, there are royal pieces by "Roy Henry"—King Henry V.

The repertory is diverse in style and chronology, including pieces from around 1370 to 1420 in the sonorous, homophonic English discant style, as well as works in various continentally influenced styles (isorhythm and canon). It is significant that the English discant pieces are notated in score, providing a compelling visual metaphor of their unified sound, while the other works, characterized by more independence of individual lines, are in choirbook format.

The majority of the collection is devoted to mass music, including **mass pairs** of movements of the Ordinary (Gloria-Credo; Sanctus-Agnus) linked by musical means, an important stage in the development of the cyclic mass. However, the arrangement of the collection by movements of a common text veils this advance.

OPERA. In the early 17th century, as Italy was developing its fully sung style of opera, the English were exploring the musico-dramatic potential of the **masque**, a hybrid aristocratic entertainment that combined poetry (sung or recited), music, lavish stagecraft, and both choreographed and social dancing. One of the chief forces in the creation of the masque was the architect Inigo Jones, who had studied and traveled in Italy. Thus, an Italianate operatic echo on the English stage, i.e., fully sung music dramas, was imaginable, but generally unrealized. However, there were significant exceptions. Ben Jonson's *Lovers Made Men* (1617)—a collaboration with Jones—was reputedly sung in "stylo recitativo" throughout, and this was identified as being after the "Italian manner." The music by **Nicholas Lanier** does not survive. **Sir William Davenant**'s *The Siege of Rhodes* (1656, though perhaps only performed later) was also fully sung to music by **Henry Lawes, Henry Cooke**, and **Matthew Locke**. This music also does not survive, and its text seems to have been intended as a spoken play, a form in which it was later performed. More prominently in view are the late 17th-century masques, *Dido and Aeneas* by **Henry Purcell** and *Venus and Adonis* by **John Blow**. The modern reception of these works has tended to view them as "operas" on a small scale; certainly their fully sung form and the emotional depth of *Dido and Aeneas* would invite the operatic label; and nationalistic composers in the late 19th and 20th centuries would attempt to emulate both within smaller chamber operas. However, in the late 17th century these were both unusual works and formally distinct from what the contemporary Englishman would know as "opera."

The late 17th-century hybrid form of **dramatick opera** or **semi-opera**, a style of music drama that featured a spoken play with elaborate, generally nonintegral musical entertainments, were the Englishman's "opera," a taste that was self-consciously made and in contrast with continental norms. The preface to **Matthew Locke**'s semi-opera *Psyche* (1675) clarifies how the distinction was one of national taste: "[I]t may justly wear the title [of opera], though all the tragedy be not in music: for the author prudently considered, that though Italy was, and is, the great academy of the world for that science and way of entertainment, England is not, and therefore mixed it with inter-locutions as more proper to our [English] genius."

The English adoption of fully sung opera as the musical dramatic norm was first realized in extent with the rise of **George Frideric Handel**. Handel's operatic invasion of London began in 1711 with his *Rinaldo*, and this paved the way for an English musical mainstream that was to be largely a foreign importation: the famous singers in the London opera were Italian castrati, like **Senesino** or **Farinelli**; the composers were foreign, like Handel and **Giovanni Bononcini**; the libretti were in Italian, often reworkings of older 17th-century texts. The exotic allure of things foreign surely helped boost opera's popularity, though not without some resentment and eventual backlash.

The style of Handelian opera is grounded in the conventions of Italian *opera seria*, wherein there is a rigorous musical and functional separation of recitative and aria: the recitative is active, the aria reflective and affective — and the da capo aria formally dominates the musical landscape, stressing the centrality of virtuosic solo singers.

Handel's London opera company, the **Royal Academy of Music**, had two incarnations: 1719–28 and 1729–37. The closing of the first can be seen against a background of shifting public taste, a shift made especially vivid in the popularity of the "democratic" and vernacular *The Beggar's Opera*; the closing of the second academy reflects the strain of competition with a second opera company, the **"Opera of the Nobility,"** and the inability or disinclination of London audiences to support them both. With the closing of the second academy in bankruptcy, Handel turned his attention to **oratorio**, a genre that continued his theatrical interests, though in a decidedly different musical form.

The nobility's continued regard for Italianate *opera seria* and the great popular success of *The Beggar's Opera* effectively framed opera in England for much of the next century and a half. Occasionally, an English composer would attempt to replicate the style and import of such Italian works, like

Thomas Augustine Arne's *Artaxerxes* (1762), an *opera seria* with typical distinction between recitative and aria, based on a libretto by Pietro Metastasio, which included castrato roles, a plot drawn from Classical mythology, and an enforced *lieto fine*. *Artaxerxes*' premiere at **Covent Garden** was a success, and it was staged numerous times in the succeeding decades in London, Dublin (1765), Edinburgh (1769), and even New York City (1828). Arne was also immediately successful with the pastiche *Love in a Village* (1762), a composition much closer in form and spirit to *The Beggar's Opera*, which contained some original music, some music recycled from Arne's older works, as well as pieces by other composers. Its first season at **Covent Garden** featured 40 performances, and the work was regularly heard in England until the 1840s.

For English composers, such successes were not the norm. Much more frequent—especially at the major London theaters of Covent Garden, **Drury Lane**, and **Haymarket**—was the avoidance of English compositions for production of Italian opera by foreign conductors, composers, and singers, including **Sir Michael Costa**, **Felice Giardini**, Giuloa Grisi, **Jenny Lind**, Giudetta Pasta, Adelina Patti, **Alberto Randegger**, and **Antonio Sacchini**, among many others. This remained constant through the 20th century, with the addition of regular performances of French operas in the 1860s and German ones shortly thereafter. *Opera* in England throughout these times frequently meant musical-dramatic works in another language. Until the late 1820s, however, such productions were frequently not premieres of new works: London audiences were happy to hear rearrangements of operas already proved successful on the Continent as well as pastiches from operas (or parts of them) already successful in London. All of the major theaters partook of such rearrangements, employing numerous English composers, such as **Samuel Arnold, Sir Henry Bishop, Charles Dibdin, Thomas Linley (the elder)**, and **Joseph Mazzinghi** to create such hybrid works. As Hall-Witt indicates (2007), these hybrid works were tolerated because the spectacle on stage was often not as interesting to society as the fashionable spectacle to be seen within the audience itself.

By 1828, following the lead of the middle class's presenting of Wolfgang Amadeus Mozart's operas in the City of London (sometimes in concert performances), Italian and Italian-language operas could be presented whole on the London stage instead of in pastiche form, as a new concern with the vitality of the work and the composer's intentions was seen. This was not the case in the presentation of opera at the provincial **musical festivals**, where piecemeal selections from current and older operas remained a constant within "miscellaneous" concert programs into the early 1860s. Until the second half of the 19th century, viable opera in the provinces either occurred at such musical festivals or through touring companies: regular companies would not be established outside of London for some time.

English composers made many attempts at opera in English through this period, some more successful (like Arne's *Love in a Village*) than others. Each generation seemed to produce a few operas that made an impression, but there was never enough momentum to create a school to rival the influence of Italian models. Some successful examples include **Henry Carey** and John Frederick Lampe's *The Dragon of Wantley* (1737), Dibdin's *The Recruiting Sergeant* (1770), *The Lord of the Manor* by **William Jackson** (1; 1780), and **Stephen Storace**'s *The Cherokee* (1794). The first half of the 19th century saw dramatically viable and successful works from the pen of Bishop, including adaptations of works by Mozart and Gioachino Rossini, as well as his own *The Maniac* (1810), numerous adaptations of **William Shakespeare**'s works, and the fully sung *Aladdin* (1826), as well as many dramas from **Michael William Balfe**, such as *The Siege of Rochelle* (1835; 73 performances in its first season) and *The Maid of Artois* (1836). Indeed, by 1834 the impresario Samuel James Arnold made one of numerous attempts to support opera by indigenous composers with the founding of the English Opera House and opera commissions for such composers as Balfe and **Sir George Alexander Macfarren**, but the organization folded in 1841. The English Opera House was resident for a time in the **Lyceum Theatre**, which continued to promote successful English works, such as Balfe's *The Rose of Castile* (1857).

Like their forebears, the composers of the **English Musical Renaissance** (EMR) had mixed success with opera. The works best known from this era are the masterful compositions of **Sir William Schwenck Gilbert** and **Sir Arthur Sullivan**: these compositions were an immense success throughout Great Britain and beyond to most English-speaking countries. Touring ensembles crossed the globe with productions of *H.M.S. Pinafore* (1878), *The Pirates of Penzance* (1879), and *The Mikado* (1885) — *Pirates* was even premiered in New York City before its London premiere. The combination of Sullivan's melodic emotionalism and Gilbert's exceedingly sharp wit and well-deployed irony was so successful that an entire industry was built to sustain it: the **D'Oyly Carte Opera Company**, besides supporting Gilbert and Sullivan, kept in its stable such conductors and composers as **Alfred Cellier**, **Sir Edward German**, and even **Sir Alexander Campbell Mackenzie** to emulate the compositions and libretti, and begat both the **Savoy Theatre** (1881) and the Royal English Opera House (1891). The former was built particularly for the production of Gilbert and Sullivan operas (the so-called "Savoy Operas"); the latter was constructed for Sullivan's hopes to move from the half-scored, half-spoken works he shared with Gilbert to fully sung grand opera on the most sublime and chivalrous of English subjects,

Sir Walter Scott's *Ivanhoe*. The 1891 opera was a popular (though not critical) success, but the D'Oyly Carte Opera Company sold the Royal English
Opera House at the completion of the 180-performance run. The venue was
renamed the Palace Theatre and featured music-hall shows and other popular
entertainments.

No contemporary composer could match the success of Gilbert and Sullivan in lighter fare, nor could they create and sustain the sort of grand opera
attempted by Sullivan with *Ivanhoe*. Numerous attempts were made from
the 1860s forward, including by the **Carl Rosa Opera Company** (founded
1867), which performed operas translated into English and written in English, such as commissioned works by **Sir Frederic Hymen Cowen** (*Pauline*,
1879), **Sir Charles Villiers Stanford** (*The Canterbury Pilgrims*, 1884), and
Frederick Corder (*Nordissa*, 1887). Poor libretti frequently marred the
composition and performance of these works, as did an unrefined sense of
dramatic pacing.

With composers in the second generation of the EMR, though, English-
language opera began to hit its stride, perhaps because composers were able
to take the best elements from the Continent unabashedly and mix them with
a fine-tuned sense of English drama. Composers like **Dame Ethel Smyth**, in
works like *The Wreckers* (Leipzig, 1906; London, 1909), and **Hamish Mac-
Cunn**, in *Jeanie Deans* (1894; written for the Carl Rosa Opera Company),
balanced out the needs of drama and text setting, using a Wagnerian-inspired
idiom but with British plots. Such an idiom could be wildly successful, as was
the case with **Rutland Boughton**'s *The Immortal Hour* (1914), which, when
revived in London in the 1920s, had a run of over 500 performances.

Other important composers of the first decades of the 20th century moved
between dramatic vocal music and instrumental music with increased fluency, if not always the same amount of success: essays in opera by both
Gustav Holst and **Ralph Vaughn Williams** met with modest success but
were—for the most part—polished, solid works. Both composed operas
based on their particular spiritual interests, though Holst's chamber work,
Savitri (1909) is perhaps more accessible than Vaughan Williams's *The
Pilgrim's Progress* (1949). The former was an early attempt by Holst, while
the latter was a decades-long *Lebenswerk* on the part of Vaughan Williams.
Both also tried their hand at setting deliberately national operas based on
Shakespeare's Falstaff: Holst's *At the Boar's Head* (1924) uses folk tunes
collected by **Cecil Sharp** as its basis, while Vaughan Williams's *Sir John
in Love* (1928) predominantly features the folkish melody **"Greensleeves."**

While perhaps not always the successes for which their composers hoped,
these works of the first few decades of the 20th century showed that modern, convincing English-language opera was possible. With the advent of

Benjamin Britten's *Peter Grimes* (1945), what had been a growing national presence for opera in Great Britain became an international one. Britten's works combined an exquisite sense of drama with an approachable score. While many of the stories in his libretti were British—*Peter Grimes* takes place in an English fishing village; *Billy Budd* (1951) is about the sea; *Turn of the Screw* (1954) takes place in a manor house—the sense of alienation they portrayed remained both topical and even universal throughout the 20th century. While other English opera composers after World War II—**Sir William Walton** and **Sir Michael Tipett**, among them—might not have been as successful internationally as Britten, by the 1950s English-language opera from Great Britain in general was second to no other national opera tradition in the 20th century. *See also* ABRAMS, HARRIET; ARNE, MICHAEL; ATTWOOD, THOMAS; BACH, JOHANN CHRISTIAN; BALFE, MICHAEL WILLIAM; BANTOCK, SIR GRANVILLE; BARTHÉLEMON, FRANÇOIS-HIPPOLYTE; BATTISHILL, JONATHAN; BENEDICT, SIR JULIUS; BONONCINI, GIOVANNI; BUSH, ALAN; CELLIER, ALFRED; CHORLEY, HENRY FROTHERGILL; CLAYTON, THOMAS; CORDER, FREDERICK; DORSET GARDEN THEATRE; DRAGHI, GIOVANNI BATTISTA; DRYDEN, JOHN; ECCLES, JOHN; FARINELLI; FESTIVAL OF BRITAIN; GALLIARD, JOHN ERNST; GRABU, LOUIS; HEIDEGGER, JOHN JACOB; HOLBROOKE, JOSEPH; HOOK, JAMES; JACKSON, WILLIAM (1); LEHMANN, LIZA; LINCOLN'S INN FIELDS; NOVELLO, CLARA; PACCHIEROTTI, GASPARO; PANTHEON; PORPORA, NICOLA; ROYAL COLLEGE OF MUSIC; RUSH, GEORGE; SADLER'S WELLS; SHIELD, WILLIAM; SMITH, JOHN CHRISTOPHER (THE YOUNGER); THOMAS, ARTHUR GORING; YOUNG, POLLY.

"OPERA OF THE NOBILITY." Opera company formed in rivalry to **George Frideric Handel**'s operatic enterprise, the **Royal Academy of Music (1)**. Born in part of the strained relations between George II and his son, Frederick, the Prince of Wales, the so-called "Opera of the Nobility" may be seen as a filial attack on the king, his composer, and his patronage. In 1733 the "Opera of the Nobility" opened at **Lincoln's Inn Fields**—they would later locate at the **Haymarket** Theatre—a new company that had drained important singers from Handel's troupe, including **Sensino** and Montagnana. Later **Farinelli** would join the "Opera of the Nobility" as well; the composer **Nicola Porpora** was the music director. The "Opera of the Nobility" enjoyed some notable successes, as for instance the 1734 production of Hasse's *Artaserse*, but London audiences were unable to support two opera companies in competition one with the other, and in 1737 both Handel's company and the "Opera of the Nobility" would close in bankruptcy.

ORATORIO. A large-scale, dramatic setting of a sacred narrative, typically performed unstaged, though often in theatrical context. Although the genre of oratorio blossomed in Italy in the 17th century under the nurture of the Roman clerical and aristocratic establishment, Protestant England showed little contemporary interest. Apart from a few sacred **dialogues**—**John Hilton**'s dialogue of Solomon and the Harlots and his dialogue of Job, God, and Satan are early examples, while **Henry Purcell**'s "In Guilty Night," a dialogue of Saul and the Witch of Endor, is the most accomplished—little survives to suggest an interest in the genre.

In the 18th century, however, the English oratorio came into blossom with **George Frideric Handel**, a situation that is somewhat ironic. Handel's turn to the oratorio in the 1730s is in part necessitated by the financial collapse of the **opera**, an Italianate establishment that effectively squelched the development of the native English music drama. However, if on the one hand Handel is seen as an "invading destroyer" of that tradition, on the other, his establishment of the English form of oratorio gives to England one of its most long-lived and resiliently national forms.

Handel's time in Italy (1706–10) schooled him in the Italian oratorio tradition, a tradition to which he contributed with works like *La Resurrezione*. However, when it came to developing the English model, Handel did not choose a simple transplant, but rather synthesized a number of stylistic elements from Italian opera, oratorio, the English choral repertory, and the **masque** tradition, among others (Smither, 1977), to create a substantially new genre, characterized by the significant part allotted to the chorus, the range of aria types, the use of English singers, and the textual focus on Old Testament narratives. Despite the often compelling nature of the narratives, the texts also had a rich allegorical potential, associating modern England with ancient Israel, and also may be considered an orthodox reply to Deism (Ruth Smith, 1995).

The sacred nature of the narratives has perhaps impeded the modern understanding of the Handelian oratorio as a theatrical and not a church work. Indeed, the early history of the Handelian oratorio suggests a staged intent, echoed by stage directions in both printed libretti and autograph manuscripts. However, in response to issues of propriety, the oratorios were generally performed in concert settings, albeit in theaters.

Messiah reigned supreme in Great Britain as the best-regarded oratorio—if not best-regarded composition—for most of the next century and a half following Handel's death. The use of the composition at the **Foundling Hospital** in annual concerts (1750–77) created a performance tradition for the oratorio, as an aid to charity, that ensured its preservation as the most important genre within English music. Quickly, **musical festivals** took it up, and performances of it in churches and cathedrals soon outstripped performances at theaters like **Drury Lane** and **Covent Garden**. English composers throughout the remainder of the 18th century created works that were Handel-like in design and purpose (such as **John Worgan**'s *Manasseh* [1766], performed at the **Lock Hospital** to raise funds for the institution) or simply pastiches of Handel's music with new texts or the music of others interpolated, including the compositions of **John Stanley** and John Brown and **Samuel Arnold**'s *Cure of Saul* (1767) and Arnold's *Omnipotence* (1774). The introduction of **Franz Joseph Haydn**'s *Creation* (1798) and *Four Seasons* (1801) might have provided a late-century counterpoise; while these oratorios were successful, they never held the critical or popular regard of *Messiah*. Into the first half of the 19th century, musical festivals and other charity concerts frequently consisted of *Messiah*; excerpts of Handel's other oratorios; oratorio premieres by other composers, such as **William Crotch**'s *Palestine* (1812), **Sir Henry Bishop**'s *The Seventh Day* (1834), and **Henry Hugo Pierson**'s *Jerusalem* (1852); and other genres popular contemporaneously.

The next major event in the history of the English oratorio was the premiere of **Felix Mendelssohn**'s *Elijah* at the Birmingham Musical Festival in 1846. Quickly, this work became the second most popular oratorio in England and provided a new model for emulation by indigenous composers, including **Sir Frederic Arthur Gore Ouseley** (*The Martyrdom of St. Polycarp*, 1854). From 1850 to the beginning of World War I, most native English composers produced one or more oratorios, and most foreign composers who worked even occasionally within England, including Antonin Dvorak, Charles Gounod, Franz Liszt, and many others, produced oratorios for English musical festivals and choral societies. Many of these works were only local successes and infrequently performed, but the list of works that were heard frequently for a decade or more is lengthy, including **Sir Arthur Sullivan**'s *The Martyr of Antioch* (1880), **Sir Alexander Campbell Mackenzie**'s *The Rose of Sharon* (1884), **Sir John Stainer**'s *The Crucifixion* (1887), and **Sir Hubert Parry**'s *Job* (1892), among others. The apogee of the English oratorio came with the masterpieces of **Sir Edward Elgar**: *The Dream of Gerontius* (1900), *The Apostles* (1903), and *The Kingdom* (1906). Each combines the didactic needs of the genre with a Wagnerian musical language (leitmotivs and chromaticism), evocatively portraying not only emotion but also physical space. During this time, the oratorio found itself at a theological crossroad: oratorios were being performed in secular spaces like town halls and concert halls throughout Great Britain, while in churches they were frequently made parts of large-scale prayer services, including litanies to be said by the congregation before and after the composition.

Elgar's works came at the height of oratorio production in Great Britain; in the years after World War I, composers turned increasingly to other choral forms and instrumental music; the surviving musical festivals and choral societies frequently commissioned compositions from other genres. The oratorio, when performed in churches, also began to lose its function as a prayer service, as churches increasingly presented concerts. As is the case with the **cantata**, numerous works can be found that approximate the oratorio, like **Benjamin Britten**'s *War Requiem* (1962): a work for soloists, a large choir, and orchestra with a sacred focus. Compositions that have kept (nominally) the genre's name have tended in the 20th century to reflect compositional— and not necessarily devotional—interests of the era, such as the satiric parody within **Sir William Walton**'s *Belshazzar's Feast*, the cool modernism of **Ralph Vaughan Williams**'s *Sancta Civitas* (1936), or the borrowing of popular styles in **Sir Michael Tippett**'s *A Child of Our Time* (1944).

With the exception of Britten's *War Requiem*, many of these compositions have not traveled well. While there was a brief fad for Elgar's *Gerontius* in Germany and North America in the decade before World War I, mostly these oratorios are kept alive by the many choral societies still extant in Great Britain. *See also* ABRAMS, HARRIET; ADAMS, THOMAS; ARNE, THOMAS AUGUSTINE; BARNBY, SIR JOSEPH; BARTHÉLEMON, FRANÇOIS-HIPPOLYTE; BATES, JOAH; BENEDICT, SIR JULIUS; BENNETT, JOSEPH; BREWER, SIR HERBERT; COSTA, SIR MICHAEL; COWEN, SIR FREDERIC HYMEN; CURWEN PRESS; DAVIES, SIR (HENRY) WALFORD; EXETER HALL; FISHER, JOHN ABRAHAM; GATES, BERNARD; GIARDINI, FELICE; GREENE, MAURICE; HANDEL COMMEMORATION; HANDEL SOCIETY; HAYES, WILLIAM; HILES, HENRY; HOOK, JAMES; JACKSON, WILLIAM (2); LIND, JENNY; LINLEY, THOMAS (THE ELDER); MACFARREN, SIR GEORGE ALEXANDER; MILFORD, ROBIN; NOVELLO, CLARA; NOVELLO & CO.; NOVELLO'S ORATORIO CONCERTS; PIERSON, HENRY HUGO; PUBLIC CONCERTS; SACRED HARMONIC SOCIETY; ST. JAMES'S HALL; SILAS, EDOUARD; SMART, SIR GEORGE THOMAS; SMART, HENRY; SMART, HENRY THOMAS; SMITH, JOHN CHRISTOPHER (THE YOUNGER); SOMERVELL, SIR ARTHUR; STANFORD, SIR CHARLES VILLIERS; STANLEY, JOHN; WESLEY, SAMUEL; WESLEY, SAMUEL SEBASTIAN.

ORGAN. The organ is strongly intertwined in the history of English music, in part owing to the fact that historically so many musicians were trained in royal, cathedral, or collegiate chapel choirs where the instrument played a fundamental role, and in part to the fact that so many prominent English musicians, ranging from **William Byrd** and **John Blow** to **Sir Edward Elgar** and **Ralph Vaughan Williams**, have been in one degree or another active as organists. Additionally, although English organ music has perhaps tended to be more at home within the parochial bounds of the Anglican **service** than in concert and recital, some works, such as Elgar's Sonata (1895), have entered the broader repertory of concert organists. Unsurprisingly, the history of the organ in England also is closely tied to extramusical forces, none more so than questions of religious reform, be it the dissolution of the monasteries in the 16th century, the ascent of Puritanism in the 17th, or battles over musical propriety in Evangelical churches and the restoration of ritualism with the Oxford Movement in the 19th. Additionally, the organ also figured importantly in the rise of secular music endeavors and venues, with the performance of **George Frideric Handel**'s organ concertos as theater interludes an important early example, but also in the inauguration of municipal concert halls in the 19th century, where large organs were installed to accommodate festival-scaled performances, as at the Birmingham Town Hall in 1834. The recent literature relating to the history of the organ in England reflects the fruitfulness of a marriage between practical experience and scholarship, as in Stephen Bicknell's monograph (1996), now the standard reference on the subject.

The most famous of the medieval organs in England is the 10th-century instrument at Winchester, built under the patronage of Bishop Alphege and described at length by the cathedral cleric, Wulfstan. In Wulfstan's description, the size and the power of the instrument are impressive, noting that its sound could be heard throughout the city. It had 400 pipes and 26 bellows, to be pumped by 70 men. There were echoes of large-scale instruments in the centuries that followed, such as the organ at Exeter, built in the early 16th century, but typically the early English organ was small, used to accompany liturgical singing.

The religious turbulence of the 16th century led to the removal or destruction of a number of instruments, with the rise of Protestant piety and politics casting a harsh shadow on both the usefulness and the propriety of the organ (and other instruments) in church. However, the resurgence of high churchmanship in the early 17th century would provide a climate that both church music and organ building would find beneficial. And the activity of builder Thomas Dallam (and later his son, Robert) well documents the reversal of the 16th-century trend. Between 1605 and 1614 Dallam built important instruments at King's College, Cambridge; Norwich Cathedral; Worcester Cathedral; and Eton College. The Worcester organ has been especially significant in the modern discussion of historical English **pitch**, as it is a transposing instrument (organ C=choir F).

Unsurprisingly, organ culture was constrained during the Commonwealth, though it would perhaps be a mistake to exaggerate the **Puritan** attitude; Oliver Cromwell himself had an organ by Robert Dallam at Hampton Court. With the Restoration, however, the new and necessary outfitting of churches saw a flurry of new instruments by builders such as Robert Dallam, John Loosemore, Thomas Thamar, Lancelot Pease, Edward Darby, and Thomas Harris at places like St. George's, Windsor, and the cathedrals at Durham, Exeter, Winchester, Peterborough Norwich, Canterbury, Chester, Lincoln, and Worcester.

The later 17th century saw the rise of two prominent builders, **Bernard "Father" Smith** and **Renatus Harris**, both of whom brought continental influence into English organ building, Smith drawing on Netherlandish ideas, and Harris, French ones. Together they famously entered into a competition for the building of the new instrument at London's Temple Church, with **John Blow**, **Henry Purcell**, and **Giovanni Battista Draghi** drawn into the fray as players. Smith emerged victorious with an instrument that interestingly employed quarter-tone keys to further the range of its meantone tuning.

The 18th-century organ favored varied colors, an "imitative variety" (Bicknell, 1996), that was heard in **voluntaries**, such as those by **John Stanley**, featuring diverse solo figuration on trumpet or cornet stop, with echoes. The 18th century as well saw the organ take on increasingly secular use, as in the theater and the **pleasure gardens**.

Nineteenth-century developments saw the essaying of very large instruments, such as the Henry Willis organ at the **Crystal Palace** (1851) and the Royal Albert Hall (1871); the desire for more volume of sound, well manifest in the use of high-pressure reeds, among other things; and a blending of sounds that allowed for impressive and smooth crescendos. This tonal ideal served English **service** music well, but the contemporary rediscovery of Johann Sebastian Bach's music and other earlier solo repertory prompted an interest in more continental tonal profiles where independence and clarity of sound were characteristic; this profile was in strong contrast to the Willis ideals and would lay the groundwork for instruments in the 20th century that sought to revive classical principles of the German instruments of Arp Schnitger and the Silbermann family.

This classical style of organ was resonant with the emerging historical performance movement, predicated on the notion that music is best served by means contemporary with its origins. And while players interested in the distinguished solo organ repertory of Johann Sebastian Bach, Heinrich Scheideman, Jan Pieterszoon Sweelinck and others would find much of interest here, traditional Anglican service playing was, and to a degree still is, wed to the ideals of the well-blended, powerful, and colorful orchestral-styled instrument. Thus, classical advances have been slower in England than on the Continent. Early examples emerged, however, especially under the advocacy of the organist and consultant Ralph Downes, notably in a Harrison & Harrison instrument at the South Bank Concert Hall (London) and a J. W. Walker & Sons instrument for the Brompton Oratory, where Downes was organist. The work of Noel Mander has been particularly significant in furthering this style of instrument, both in restoration and in new instruments built in a historical style. The division between Anglican service playing and historical solo repertory has been challenged by historically styled instruments in various English chapels, such as the 1969 Grant, Degens, and Bradbeer organ at New College, Oxford. *See also* ADAMS, THOMAS; ALEXANDRA PALACE; ANTHEM; APOLLONICON; ATTWOOD, THOMAS; BAIRSTOW, SIR EDWARD CUTHBERT; BLITHEMAN, JOHN; BREWER, SIR HERBERT; BRIDGE, SIR FREDERICK; COOKE, BENJAMIN; COSYN, BENJAMIN; FABURDEN; FORCER, FRANCIS; GREATOREX, THOMAS; GREENE, MAURICE; HILTON, JOHN; HINGESTON, JOHN; HOOPER, EDMUND; KENT, JAMES; LLOYD, CHARLES HARFORD; MULLINER BOOK; NARES, JAMES; NORTH, ROGER; NOVELLO, VINCENT; PARRATT, SIR WALTER; PURCELL, DANIEL; PURKIS, JOHN; RANDALL, JOHN; REDFORD, JOHN; ROGERS, BENJAMIN; ROOTHAM, CYRIL; ROSEINGRAVE, THOMAS; ROYAL COLLEGE OF ORGANISTS; ST. MARTIN'S HALL; SILAS, EDOUARD; SMART, HENRY THOMAS; SMETHERGELL, WILLIAM; SQUARE; STAINER, SIR JOHN; STANLEY, JOHN; TUDWAY, THOMAS; VAUXHALL GARDENS; WESLEY, SAMUEL; WESLEY, SAMUEL SEBASTIAN; WISE, MICHAEL; WORGAN, JOHN.

OSWALD, JAMES (1710–69). Scottish composer, publisher, arranger, and cellist active for a time in London. Osborne taught in Dunfermline and Edinburgh before moving to London in 1741. While there, he composed stage works, chamber music (frequently under the name Dottel Figlio), as well as Scottish tunes in the style of folk tunes, as well as arrangements of such tunes. Oswald began his own publishing company in 1747 and was named Chamber Composer to George III in 1761. He retired from public life in 1764.

OUSELEY, SIR FREDERIC ARTHUR GORE (1825–89). Church musician, educator, and composer. Ouseley was famous in his own time for championing Anglican sacred music and his attempts through such organizations as the Musical Association (later the **Royal Musical Association**) to promote the study and performance of music as a serious and respectable profession. Ouseley's father, created a baronet in 1808, encouraged his musical talent.

Ouseley matriculated at Oxford in 1843, taking a BA in 1846 and a MusD in 1854. Before his ordination in 1849, he was a lay member of the choir at St. Paul's, Knightsbridge; afterward he was a curate at St. Barnabas in Pimlico, where he supported the musical foundation at his own expense. In that year he also began organizing **St. Michael's College**, Tenbury Wells, as an institution to foster Anglican church music; when the foundation stone was laid in 1846, he became the vicar of the new parish there and the warden of the school. He was appointed precentor of Hereford Cathedral in 1855 and a canon residentiary there in 1886.

In 1855 Ouseley was also named professor of music at Oxford University; he treated this as a working post, not an honorary one, and regularly offered a course of lectures on music, as well as reforming the degree requirements and exercises. His mature music, mostly sacred in character, included church **services, anthems**, and two **oratorios**—*The Martyrdom of St. Polycarp*, his MusD 1854 degree exercise, which was both frequently performed in the middle of the century and one of the few non-Handelian oratorios before 1880 to be published in full score; and *Hagar* (Hereford, 1873, and **Crystal Palace**, 1874). He edited collections of church music from contemporaries and earlier composers, such as **Orlando Gibbons**.

P

PACCHIEROTTI, GASPARO (1740–1821). Italian singer (castrato soprano) occasionally active in London. Pacchierotti was trained in Venice and sang in Naples and most of the great Italian **opera** centers in his early career. He visited London on several occasions, including 1778–80, 1781–84, and 1791, singing at the **King's Theatre** and at the **Professional Concerts** where **Franz Joseph Haydn** heard him. **Charles Burney** and Susan Burney reported on his singing extensively; the latter noted that she was moved to tears by his performance at a benefit concert on 9 March 1780. He retired to Padua in 1793.

PAISIBLE, JAMES (ca. 1656–1721). Recorder player, oboist, and composer. A Frenchman, Paisible is first documented in England in performances of the **masque** *Calisto* in 1674/75, although it is likely he came to London with Robert Cambert in 1673. He held several court appointments, but his Roman Catholicism took him to the Continent with James II, returning to England in 1693. As a wind player at court, he was likely a channel for introducing the French modernized forms of recorder and oboe to London musicians. He was also active in theater music as a composer and performer, including documented performances on the bass and the cello, a measure of his professional diversity. He also gained prominence in theatrical "interval entertainments"—concerts between the acts of a drama—and in **public concerts** in the London music rooms. In 1686 he married the former mistress of Charles II, **Mary (Moll) Davis**.

PANTHEON. London auditorium designed by James Wyatt built in 1772. The building was initially designed for lavish public entertainments, including assemblies, balls, and subscription concerts. Aside from a large central rotunda, it included two card rooms and galleries. Some of the concerts from the **Handel Commemoration** in 1784 were held there, and **Felice Giardini** led the orchestra there from 1774 to 1779. Wyatt redesigned the Pantheon as an **opera** house to take the place of the King's Theatre, **Haymarket**, in 1791. Destroyed by fire in 1792, it reopened in 1795 as an entertainment hall once again. Redesigned as a theater again in 1811, it closed as a venue for public entertainments in 1814. The building was demolished in 1837.

PANUFNIK, SIR ANDRZEJ (1914–91). Polish conductor and composer active in England. Panufnik was trained in Poland and worked extensively there and in Paris before World War II, and in Poland thereafter as a conductor and composer. He fled Poland in 1954, settling in England. From 1957 to 1959 he was the conductor of the **City of Birmingham Symphony Orchestra**. Turning solely to composition in 1959, he rebuilt his reputation, with successful premieres in Houston, London, New York, and Chicago. He was knighted (KB) in 1991. His daughter, Roxanna Panufnik, is also a noted composer.

PARKE, MARIA FRANCIS (1772–1822). Singer, pianist, and composer. Parke was initially trained by her father, the oboist John Parke (1745–1829). She began playing keyboard in public by the age of eight and singing by the age of 14. As a soprano soloist, she was heard throughout London at the **Handel Commemorations**, **Hanover Concert Rooms**, **Johann Peter Salomon**'s concerts featuring **Franz Joseph Haydn**, and numerous benefits, as well as at most of the provincial **musical festivals**. Haydn directed a symphony at one of her benefit concerts. She composed keyboard and vocal works that were performed at the **pleasure gardens** of London. She retired from professional music-making upon her marriage in 1815. Parke is often confused with Maria Hester Park, née Reynolds (1760–1813), a noted keyboardist and teacher, especially to the Duchess of Devonshire.

A PARLEY OF INSTRUMENTS. A musical entertainment by **John Banister** in the form of three **odes** whose texts were on musical themes. The entertainment, at least the first part, was performed in 1676 at the academy in **Lincoln's Inn Fields**. The instrumental ensemble was large and varied, including **theorboes**, **citterns**, **lutes**, harps, guitars, harpsichords, flutes of various sorts, **cornetts** and **sackbuts**, oboes, violins, and **viols**.

PARRATT, SIR WALTER (1841–1924). Organist, teacher, and composer. Parratt was **Master of the Queen's Music** from 1883 until his death and used this position to influence English **organ** pedagogy and the continued revival of excellent English sacred music from **Thomas Tallis** to contemporary composition. As a prodigy, he studied with his father, Thomas Parratt (an organist at Huddersfield Parish Church), and at the choir school of St. Peter's Chapel, Cooper Street, London, and while there with George Cooper, organist of St. Sepulchre, Holborn. He held numerous organist and choirmaster positions from the age of 11 onward, including Great Witley Church, Worcestershire

(1861–68), and Wigan Parish Church (1868–72). He was organist of Magdalen College, Oxford, from 1872 to 1882 (taking a BMus in 1873) and was greatly involved in the musical activities in Oxford as a whole. Parratt was named organist at St. George's Chapel in 1882. He was the first professor of organ at the **Royal College of Music** in 1883, dean of the Faculty of Music at London University (1905), president of the **Royal College of Organists** (1905–9), and Heather Professor of Music at Oxford (1908–18). Parratt was knighted in 1892 and subsequently named MVO (1901), CVO (1917), and KCVO (1921).

PARRY, SIR HUBERT (ALSO CHARLES HUBERT HASTINGS; 1848–1918). Composer, scholar, and teacher. Parry, best known today for the **hymn** tune **"Jerusalem,"** was one of the most famous composers and English musicians of his day. The premiere of his **cantata** *Scenes from Prometheus Unbound* at the 1880 Gloucester meeting of the Three Choirs Festival is traditionally considered the beginning of the **English Musical Renaissance**. Parry was educated at Twyford and Eaton (BMus, 1866) before reading law and modern history at Exeter College, Oxford (BA, 1870). For one summer (1867), he studied with **Henry Hugo Pierson** in Stuttgart. After graduation, Parry worked at Lloyd's of London (1870–77) while studying privately with **Sir William Sterndale Bennett** and **Edward Dannreuther**.

Resigning from Lloyd's to devote himself entirely to music, Parry took up numerous academic posts, including subeditor of **Sir George Grove**'s *Dictionary of Music and Musicians* (to which he contributed 123 articles), professor of musical history at the **Royal College of Music** (RCM; 1883), *chorgas* at Oxford University (1883), director of the RCM (1895–1918), and Heather Professor of Music at Oxford (1902–8). While working on many orchestral and chamber pieces in the 1870s and 1880s, Parry was most famous in his lifetime for his dramatic choral works for major choirs and **musical festivals**, such as *Blest Pair of Sirens* (**Bach Choir**, 1887), *Judith* (Birmingham, 1888), *Job* (Gloucester, 1892), and *King Saul* (Birmingham, 1894). He was the author of several monographs, including one on Johann Sebastian Bach (1909) and published several collections of his lectures. Parry was knighted in 1898 and created a baronet in 1902.

PARSLEY, OSBERT (1511–85). Composer and singer. Parsley was a member of the choir at Norwich Cathedral for an impressive 50-year span, as confirmed in the memorial tablet to him there:

> Who here a Singing-man did spend his Days.
> Full *Fifty* Years in our Church Melody
> His Memory shines bright whom thus we praise.

His professional longevity necessitated his working in both the Latin and English rites, as his compositional output reveals. In addition, he also composed instrumental consort music, including a number of *In nomines*.

PARSONS, ROBERT (ca. 1535–71/72). Composer. Parsons was appointed a gentleman of the **Chapel Royal** in 1563, although he may be documented there from as early as 1560. His compositional output includes both Latin and English church music, as well as instrumental consorts and **consort songs**. His five-voice "Ave Maria" is likely his best-known work, notable for the elegant contours of its intertwined lines and its richness of sound. Parsons died in a drowning accident at Newark-upon-Trent and was succeeded in the Chapel Royal by **William Byrd**.

PARTHENIA. Anthology of **virginal** music. *Parthenia or the Maydenhead of the First Musicke that ever was printed for the Virginalls* appeared in 1613, commemorating the wedding of Princess Elizabeth, James I's eldest daughter, and Prince Frederick, the Elector Palatine and later King of Bohemia. The title's virginal tropes draw on the instrument, the novelty of the publishing of this repertory, and the prenuptial state of the pair, the latter made explicit in the dedication itself: "The virgin PARTHENIA (whilst yet I may) I offer up to your virgin Highnesses." The title page is also replete with the image of a young woman playing the virginals in what has become a familiar icon.

The collection contains music by **William Byrd**, **Orlando Gibbons**, and **John Bull**. In the main the pieces are dances, although there is also a contrapuntal, four-part fantasia, a reminder of the easy crossover between music for **organ** and stringed keyboards.

A companion volume, *Parthenia In-Violata*, appeared in 1624, featuring arrangements with bass **viol**. Reprints of the original collection in 1664, 1651, and 1655 attest to its popularity.

PARTSONG. Secular vocal genre, usually unaccompanied, similar to the **glee**. The partsong flourished especially in the 19th century, though it has antecedents in the 17th and 18th: it remained a small-scale, usually unaccompanied, mostly homophonic texture. The upper part frequently stood out as the most prominent. Partsongs were usually evocative of a particular mood, as is the case with **Sir Charles Villiers Stanford**'s "The Bluebird" and **Sir Arthur Sullivan**'s "The Long Day Closes"; each of which is reserved yet evocative. Such songs could be in many forms, but they were usually simple and aurally perceived, matching the expectations of the amateurs who sang them throughout the 18th and 19th centuries at home, in choral societies, and at competition **musical festivals**. *See also* FORD, THOMAS; HENRY

LESLIE'S CHOIR; LESLIE, HENRY DAVID; MACKENZIE, SIR ALEX-ANDER CAMPBELL; ROOTHAM, CYRIL; SMART, HENRY THOMAS.

PASSION. Liturgical setting of the narrative of Jesus's crucifixion. The earliest Passion settings in England are two anonymous works in the Egerton Manuscript (GB Lbl Egerton 3307), originating sometime between 1430 and 1444. These two settings, one of the text from St. Luke and the other an incomplete version of St. Matthew's account, are responsorial. That is, the evangelist's text and the words of Jesus are intoned to monophonic chant, while the "turba," the crowds and minor characters, are sung to polyphony. The **Eton Choirbook** preserves a more musically substantial responsorial setting of the Matthew Passion by **Richard Davy**.

Passion devotion comprised a rich part of premodern English spirituality, as evidenced by the number of intensely affective Passion **carols** in the **Fayrfax Manuscript** (GB Lbl Add. Ms. 5465).

PATE, JOHN (?–1704). Singer. The **countertenor** Pate was lauded by his contemporaries, the diarist **John Evelyn** going so far as to note that he was "reputed the most excellent singer, ever England had." Peter Motteux similarly praised his contribution to the *Island Princess* as giving "life to the whole entertainment." He performed solos in a number of **Henry Purcell**'s works, including *The Fairy Queen*, *The Indian Emperor*, and *Hail, Bright Cecilia*. In the manuscript of the latter, his name is given for the famous alto solo "'Tis Nature's Voice," a movement elsewhere described (Motteux) as having been sung by the composer himself.

PAXTON, STEPHEN (1734–87). Cellist and composer. Paxton came from a musical family; his brother William (1725–78) was a virtuosic cellist active around Newcastle, and his nephew George (1749–79) frequently played in London ensembles. Stephen Paxton was trained first as a chorister at Durham Cathedral and then studied with William Savage in London. He was active as a performer in London, playing at the **Handel Commemorations** in 1784. He was elected to the **Royal Society of Musicians** in 1757 and was a professional member of the **Noblemen and Gentlemen's Catch Club** (1780). His compositions included **glees**, two masses (he was a Roman Catholic), and assorted cello works.

PEOPLE'S CONCERT SOCIETY. Philanthropic concert organization dedicated to presenting concerts of classical music in London's East End, extant from 1878 to 1935. The paternal nature of the society—based on the typical Victorian belief that music could improve the morals and manners of the working and middle classes—was incorporated into the expansion of the society to give concerts to London schools and prisons. The repertoire changed over the society's existence but included a great deal of chamber music, performed primarily by middle-class amateurs. The society also organized the South Place Sunday Concerts in Finsbury (1887) and presented concerts in poorer districts throughout London.

PEPUSCH, JOHANN CHRISTOPH (1667–1752). Composer and theorist. The German Pepusch came to England close to the turn of the 18th century, supposedly disenchanted with an egregious example of Prussian injustice that he had witnessed (**Sir John Hawkins**). In London he became active in the theaters, working at various times at **Drury Lane**, the **Haymarket**, and **Lincoln's Inn Fields**. His wife, the soprano Margherita de l'Epine, was at one time also prominent on the stage. Today Pepusch's most visible contribution to theater music is his overture and bass lines to the airs in *The Beggar's Opera*, bass lines that earned **Charles Burney**'s effulgent praise: "[he] furnished the wild, rude, and often vulgar melodies with bases so excellent, tha[t] no sound contrapuntist will ever attempt to alter them." In addition to his work in the theaters, Pepusch also enjoyed the patronage of James Brydges, Earl of Carnarvon, later Duke of Chandos, and was active overseeing the duke's musical establishment.

The early historical assessment of Pepusch, perhaps overwhelmed by the glow of **George Frideric Handel**'s prominence, was not particularly enthusiastic about his compositions. Hawkins, for instance, speaks of his music as "correct, but it wanted variety of expression." However, the esteem for his theoretical investigations, especially of ancient sources, was unalloyed. Hawkins describes him as "one of the greatest theoretic musicians of the modern times." He was also a significant collector of antiquarian sources— "His admirable library, the most curious and complete in scarce musical authors, theoretical and practical" (Burney)—which reinforced his position as a founding member of the **Academy of Ancient Music**.

PEPYS, SAMUEL (1632/33–1703). Diarist. Pepys emerges as one of the most colorful observers of Restoration London. His six-volume diary, recorded from 1 January 1659/60 to 31 May 1669, provides valuable detail of English musical life, reflecting his personal enthusiasm for music. He sang, played a number of instruments, and composed. However, he was limited in his skills at harmony, calling upon various musicians to help him with basses or realizations. This limitation, however, was not the fruit of disinterest; at one time, in fact, he expressed the hope to invent "a better theory of Musique than hath yet been abroad" (20 March 1668). The diary's musical references offer significant glimpses of music-making at home, in the theater, at court, and in the church, and Pepys's broad circle of acquaintances included a number of important musicians of the day.

PERCY SOCIETY. Group founded to publish **ballads** and their accompanying music, beginning with the collections of the 18th-century collector Thomas Percy, bishop of Dromore. The society existed between 1840 and 1852. Prominent members included **Edward Francis Rimbault** (who was the society's secretary) and William Chappell, of the publishing firm **Chappell & Co.**

PETER GRIMES. **Opera** by **Benjamin Britten** to a libretto by Montagu Slater based on the short story "The Borough" by George Crabb. *Peter Grimes* premiered at **Sadler's Wells** on 7 June 1945, with Britten's longtime partner Peter Pears in the title role. *Peter Grimes* is one of the most successful 20th-century operas in the repertoire, and its premiere presaged many other excellent dramatic compositions from the pen of Britten. The story focuses on the alienation of an individual by the community and its horrific effects. At the beginning of the opera, Grimes has lost a boy apprentice, apparently to misadventure. While cleared of guilt by an inquest, he feels the weight of the community's suspicion on him, so much so that when his next apprentice dies in a tragic accident, he is convinced to commit suicide. The score is as accessible as the story is chilling.

PHILHARMONIA ORCHESTRA. London orchestra founded in 1945 by Walter Legge, also known as the New Philharmonia Orchestra between 1964 and 1977. Legge controlled the orchestra until 1964, when he attempted to disband it. Up to that date, the Philharmonia was primarily a recording orchestra; live performances by the ensemble increased greatly after this time. Prominent conductors associated with the orchestra have included Arturo Toscanini and Herbert von Karajan; music directors have included Otto Klemperer, Ricardo Mutti, Giuseppe Sinopoli, Christoph von Dohnáni, and Esa-Pekka Salonen. Since 1995 it has been in residence at the **Royal Festival Hall**.

PHILHARMONIC SOCIETY. *See* ROYAL PHILHARMONIC SOCIETY.

PHILIPS, PETER (1560/61–1628). Composer and organist. Philips trained as a chorister at St. Paul's Cathedral, London, but his Roman Catholicism caused him to leave England for the Continent in 1582. A period under the patronage of Cardinal Alessandro Farnese in Rome was followed by an itinerant period in the service of the English recusant Thomas Paget. Philips took up residence in Brussels in 1591 and remained based there for the rest of his life, including a long tenure as organist to the Archduke Albert.

Philips's compositional output is diverse, including keyboard pieces (the majority of them are in the **Fitzwilliam Virginal Book**), instrumental ensemble pieces, and a number of collections of **madrigals** and motets, the latter ranging from richly sonorous eight-voice works to intimately scored pieces for just a few singers.

PIERSON, HENRY HUGO (ALSO HENRY HUGH PEARSON; 1815–73). Composer, born in England but active predominantly in Germany. Pierson was educated at Harrow and in London, where he studied privately with **Thomas Attwood** and Arthur Thomas Corfe. He enrolled at Trinity College, Oxford, in 1836 but did not take a degree, choosing instead to leave in 1839 to study with Joseph Rinck in Darmstadt and Karl Reissiger in Dresden before moving on to Prague to work with Václav Tomásek. He was appointed the Reid Professor of Music at the University of Edinburgh in 1844 but resigned after eight months; he spent the rest of his professional life in Germany, mostly in Stuttgart. His attempts to establish himself as a composer in England ended in critical condemnation, including the **oratorios** *Jerusalem* (1852) and the unfinished *Hezekiah* (1869), both performed at the Norwich **musical festival**; the former, though panned, had several successful performances in the 1850s and 1860s. **Sir Hubert Parry** studied with Pierson in the summer of 1867, and his work was well regarded in Germany.

PILKINGTON, FRANCIS (ca. 1570–1638). Composer. Pilkington received the BMus at Oxford in 1595 and surfaces in records at Chester Cathedral in 1602, where he held appointments, including that of precentor, for the rest of his life. He took ordination in 1614 and held a number of clerical posts in and around Chester in addition to his work at the cathedral. His compositions include two collections of **madrigals** (1613/14 and 1624) and a collection of **lute ayres** (1605). Modern critical reception of the ayres has seen them as uneven and "rather turgid" (Spink, 1974). David Brown (*NG*, 2001) contextualizes the ayre collection as transitional between the style of **Thomas Campion** and the heightened expression of **John Dowland**.

PILLS TO PURGE MELANCHOLY. A six-volume collection of **ballad** texts by **Thomas Durfey** with tunes, published in 1719 and 1720 under the full title *Wit and Mirth, or Pills to Purge Melancholy*.

THE PIRATES OF PENZANCE, OR, THE SLAVE OF DUTY. Operetta in two acts by **Sir William Schwenck Gilbert** and **Sir Arthur Sullivan**, premiered in New York on 31 December 1879 (to help the **D'Oyly Carte Company** avoid rampant piracy in the United States) and in London on 3 April

1880; in the later city its initial run was 363 performances. The plot hinges on Frederic's coming of age. Mistakenly apprenticed to pirates—not pilots—by his ward, he wishes to bring the group to justice so that he may marry his beloved, soprano Mabel, with a clear conscience. The operetta contains many parodies of **opera**, including Giuseppe Verdi's "Anvil Chorus" from *Il Trovatore*.

PITCH. The question of historical pitch standards in premodern England is complex, touching on the evidence of surviving **organ** pipes, theoretical description, transposition practices, clef codes, and the constitution of the liturgical choir itself. Much of the modern discussion has centered on the relationship of the five-foot transposing organ and a so-called high-pitch choir, singing roughly a minor third higher than modern pitch. (Strong among its advocates is David Wulstan.) The transposing organ, such as that at Worcester Cathedral described in 1665 by Nathaniel Tomkins, is based (at least nominally) on a five-foot pipe activated by depressing the C key and producing an F in choir pitch, which corresponded to C a fifth lower in keyboard pitch. The five-foot pipe would sound somewhere between modern G and A-flat; thus arises the notion that the choir sang a minor third high (five-foot F→A-flat). The organist accompanying the choir would of necessity then transpose, perhaps via clefs. The transposing organ begins to disappear in the 1660s.

The extension of this 17th-century context backward into Tudor polyphony has been the subject of strong debate—counterclaims have been advanced by scholars such as Roger Bowers—and the issue strongly affects the constituent parts of the choir itself, for at high pitch, the part immediately below the top treble is generally well served by a boy treble, while at a lower pitch the adult alto functions well. Additionally, the interpretation of the material evidence itself has been the subject of recent revision. Johnstone (2003) notes that the evidence of surviving organ pipes from ca. 1630 (now at Stanford-on-Avon), nominally a five-foot organ, show longer pipes than their name would suggest and thus sound lower. In this case, instead of a minor third high, the new standard is somewhere between a half and a whole step high (A=ca. 475 Hz).

THE PLANETS. Tone poem by **Gustav Holst** composed 1914–16, premiered 15 November 1920. While evocative, the piece is a series of seven character sketches based on astrological symbols Holst read about in Alan Leo's *What Is a Horoscope and How Is It Cast?* and not a programmatic work based on Roman mythology. It was a composition without a commission, one that Holst began after hearing Arnold Schoenberg's *Fünf Orchesterstücke*. The composition became immediately popular after its premiere, and parts of it (especially the 5/4 section of "Mars, The Bringer of War" and "Uranus, The Magician") are featured frequently in motion picture trailers.

PLAYFORD, JOHN (1623–86/87). Publisher and bookseller. Following an apprenticeship with the London publisher John Benson, Playford set up his own shop "in the Inner Temple neere the Church doore." His publishing of political material during the interregnum proved problematic, though it is also at this time that he began to publish music. *The English Dancing Master* (1651), a collection of **ballad** airs, is likely the first of his musical publications, to be followed by song collections, didactic treatises—his *A Breefe Introduction to the Skill of Musick* (1654) was prominent for many years through subsequent editions—and collections of psalmody and hymnody.

The company's work positioned Playford to be the major music publisher in England for several decades. **Sir John Hawkins** observed that "with such talents as Playford possessed of, and with a temper that disposed him to communicate to others that knowledge which could not have been attained without much labour; and being besides an honest and friendly man, it is not to be wondered at that he lived upon terms of friendship with the most eminent professors of music his contemporaries, or that he should have acquired, as he appears to have done, almost a monopoly in the publication of music-books." His business passed to his son Henry (1657–1709), who also expanded its endeavors with the publication of the music periodical *Mercurius Musicus* (1699–1702).

PLEASURE GARDENS. Private parks dedicated to leisure activities, including eating, drinking, and listening to music. The first pleasure gardens were opened in the mid-17th century; the most famous were in and around London, including Marylebone (ca. 1659–1778), **Vauxhall** (1661–1859), **Sadler's Wells** (1684–1879), and Ranelagh (1742–1803). The gardens would feature daily music in the form of songs, **cantatas**, afterpieces, and chamber music; frequently they included concert halls. The pleasure gardens provided employment for many contemporary musicians, including **Thomas Arne**, **Samuel Arnold**, **Johann Christian Bach**, **George Frideric Handel**, and **James Hook**, among others. The gardens were in vogue until the 1780s; after this point, they existed, but no longer catered to the fashionable. *See also* ARNE, MICHAEL; ARNOLD, SAMUEL; BARTHÉLEMON, FRANÇOIS-HIPPOLYTE; BATTISHILL, JONATHAN; BISHOP, SIR HENRY RAWLEY; BURNEY, CHARLES; COOKE, TOM; DIBDIN, CHARLES; FESTING, MICHAEL CHRISTIAN; FISHER, JOHN ABRAHAM; HOOK, JAMES; ORGAN; PARKE, MARIA FRANCIS; PUBLIC CONCERTS; SMETHERGELL, WILLIAM; SMITH, THEODORE; WEBBE, SAMUEL; WORGAN, JOHN.

"POMP AND CIRCUMSTANCE" MARCHES. Formally titled *Military Marches, Nos. 1–5* ("Pomp and Circumstance"), **Sir Edward Elgar** composed the five marches over the course of three decades: nos. 1 and 2 in 1901, no. 3 in 1904, no. 4 in 1907, and no. 5 in 1929–30. While all remain popular today, no. 1 has been the particular favorite since its premiere. The famous trio section is used for commencement exercises throughout North America and is the basis of the English patriotic song **"Land of Hope and Glory."**

PORPORA, NICOLA (1686–1768). Italian composer. Porpora was resident in London from 1733 to 1736, where he was the composer to the so-called **"Opera of the Nobility,"** the rival company to **George Frideric Handel**'s **Royal Academy of Music (1)**. Porpora's London **operas** include *Arianna in Naxo, Enea nel Lazio, Polifemo, Ifigenia in Aulide*, and *Mitridate*.

PORTER, WALTER (ca. 1587/95–1659). Composer and singer. Porter was trained as a chorister at Westminster Abbey and later in his career became master of the choristers there in 1639; he was appointed gentleman of the **Chapel Royal** in 1617. Much has been made of his being a pupil of Claudio Monteverdi, the documentary evidence of which resides in the preface to his 1657 *Motetts* . . . . In several copies of the collection at Oxford, Porter, in his own hand, explicitly identifies Monteverdi as his "good friend and Maestro." The musical influence of Monteverdi is apparent in works like Porter's two-voiced **madrigals** and also in the declamatory and florid aspects of the **anthem** "O Praise the Lord." One may speculate that Porter's Italianism was influential on other singers, such as **Henry Cooke**, his young contemporary in the Chapel Royal. **Samuel Pepys** records in his diary (4 September 1664) having sung Porter's two-voiced motets.

POWER, LEONEL (?–1445). Composer. Power is the most prolific of the composers in the **Old Hall Manuscript** and one of the major voices shaping the new sonorities that give rise to the Renaissance musical aesthetic. He appears in service to Thomas, Duke of Clarence, in 1418 and is with the duke in France from 1419 to 1421, a significant connection given the Franco-Flemish penchant for the *contenance angloise* in the early 15th century.

Power's works show a wide range of styles from isorhythm to chanson-like textures to the sonorous homophony of English discant. Additionally, his work in developing the musically unified mass ordinary is especially significant, with his composition of what is likely the first tenor cyclic mass, his *Missa alma redemptoris mater*. Power's later years are documented at Canterbury, where he joined the fraternity of the monastery in 1423 and was master of the choir singing in the Lady Chapel.

PRECES AND RESPONSES. In the morning and evening offices of the *Book of Common Prayer*, the various prayers offered between the Creed and the Collects, consisting of a Kyrie, the Lord's Prayer, and a set of versicles and responses. These latter prayers are variously on behalf of the queen, ministers, and the people of God, and for peace and cleanliness of heart. In cathedral practice, the dialogue of versicles and responses typically takes the form of alternating the officiant's formulaic, monophonic chant with the composed polyphony of the choir.

PRIVATE MUSICK. Body of musicians at court associated with the Privy Chamber, the private quarters of the monarch. Formalized under Charles I, the Private Musick, or the **"lutes, viols**, and voices," featured lutanists like **Robert Johnson** and **John Wilson**, and violists like **John Jenkins** and **Alfonso Ferrabosco.** In 1685 James II reformed the court musical structure, transforming the multiple court ensembles into a unified, single body, of which members of the former private musick were a part; this transformed ensemble—the new "private musick"—contained most prominently violins, but included winds, lute, voices, harpsichord, and composer, as well. *See also* ABELL, JOHN; AKEROYDE, SAMUEL; BABELL, WILLIAM; BALTZAR, THOMAS; BOWMAN, JOHN; HINGESTON, JOHN; KING, ROBERT; LAWES, HENRY; LAWES, WILLIAM; LOCKE, MATTHEW; PURCELL, HENRY; TURNER, WILLIAM.

PROFESSIONAL CONCERT. Subscription concert series started by Wilhelm Cramer and held in the **Hanover Square Rooms**, London, between 1785 and 1793. The series presented high-quality performances of symphonies and other works including those by **Franz Joseph Haydn**, usually presented 12 concerts in a season (from February to May), was for the profit of the orchestra, and limited the number of subscribers to 500. During the 1791 season, the Professional Concert invited Ignaz Pleyel, Haydn's pupil, to perform and conduct his compositions, as a rival to **Johann Peter Salomon**'s series featuring Haydn.

PROMS (ALSO HENRY WOOD PROMENADE CONCERTS; BBC PROMS). Concert series begun in 1895 by the impresario Robert Newman and conductor **Sir Henry Wood**. The Proms have always featured a mixture of old standards and new compositions, given in an informal setting, including standing-room listening. The Proms were given at the **Queen's Hall** until its destruction in 1941. Afterward, the series moved permanently to the **Royal Albert Hall**, except for a wartime hiatus at the Bedford Corn Exchange. Impresarios supporting the Proms include Edgar Speyer (1902–14), **Chappell & Co.** (1914–27), and the **British Broadcasting Corporation** (BBC; 1927–39 and 1942–present). Wood formed and conducted the **Queen's Hall**

Orchestra as its major ensemble. The BBC Symphony took over in 1930. Aside from Henry Wood, conductors of the Proms have included **Sir Adrian Boult**, **Sir Frederic Hymen Cowen**, Sir Colin Davis, **Constant Lambert**, Roger Norrington, **Sir Malcolm Sargent**, and others. A continued tradition at the last Proms concert of the season is to sing both **Sir Hubert Parry**'s **"Jerusalem"** and **Sir Edward Elgar**'s **"Land of Hope and Glory."** *See also* BRIAN, HAVERGAL; BRIDGE, FRANK; MACONCHY, DAME ELIZABETH; "RULE, BRITANNIA."

PROUT, EBENEZER (1835–1909). Music theorist, writer, teacher, and editor. Prout was one of the most important English music theorists of the second half of the 19th century. His many monographs, including *Instrumentation* (1876), *Harmony* (1889), and *Musical Form* (1893), went through numerous editions and were translated widely. Prout was largely self-taught (save for limited piano lessons) and began his career as a schoolmaster. Turning to music as a profession in 1859, he worked variously as a choral conductor, as organist at nonconformist chapels, and as a piano teacher, particularly at the **Crystal Palace** School of Art (1861–85). He also held positions at the National Training School for Music (the predecessor to the **Royal College of Music**), the **Royal Academy of Music** (2; from 1879), the **Guildhall School of Music** (from 1884) and was Professor of Music at Trinity College, Dublin, from 1894. Prout worked as a music critic for both the *Academy* and the *Atheaneum*, and edited the *Monthly Musical Record* between 1871 and 1875. Prout also edited editions of the music of **George Frideric Handel** and Wolfgang Amadeus Mozart.

PUBLIC CONCERTS. The development of the modern public concert can in significant part be traced to late 17th-century London, where factors such as the decentralizing of the musical establishment, the need of court musicians to seek supplemental income, the allure of foreign performers, and the broadening of musical venues gave rise to various concert series in a number of **concert rooms**. The first essays in London public concerts were informal in nature and setting, as witnessed by **John Bannister**'s concerts (begun 1672) at a Whitefriars tavern, eventually moving to **Lincoln's Inn Fields** and the Essex Buildings in the Strand. Other early ventures would include the fashionable concerts at the York Buildings in Villiers Street and **Thomas Britton**'s long-running concert series (ca. 1678–1714) above his small-coal shop in Clerkenwell.

The 18th century saw the increasing formality of the public concert and its programs, with **oratorios** and benefit concerts performed in the theater and concerts in venues such as **Hickford's Room** in James St. The subscription concert series led by **Johann Christian Bach** and **Carl Friedrich Abel** chiefly at the **Hanover Square Rooms** document the strong inroads of foreign musicians in London at the time and the home that public concerts gave to their endeavors. In the 18th century, public concerts were also offered at various **pleasure gardens**, including **Sadler's Wells** and **Vauxhall Gardens**. The first purpose-built concert halls came by mid-century, including the Holywell Music Room, Oxford (1748); the **Hanover Square Rooms** (1775) and hall beside King's Theatre, **Haymarket** (1796), in London; and the Music Hall (Bold Street) in Liverpool (1786). More frequent, however, was the borrowing of another space—theaters like **Drury Lane**, assembly halls like the **Pantheon**, taverns, and even churches and chapels—for a concert. At this point, concerts were still a fashionable, privileged affair: annual concert organizations like the **Concerts of Ancient Music** (1776) and even onetime celebrations like the **Handel Commemorations** (1784) counted on elite lists of subscribers. Foreign musicians were still courted for concerts, but progressively more indigenous English musicians were highlighted as soloists.

As subscription concerts increased in frequency throughout the 19th century, impresarios built more specialized halls, and strictures on attendance loosened, except in cases such as **John Ella**'s **Musical Union**, where, though all classes might buy tickets, the seating was segregated. Other institutions became more democratic: **Exeter Hall** (1831) welcomed members of all classes to attend and perform through regular concerts by such organizations as the **Sacred Harmonic Society** and the **Tonic Sol-fa Association**. As choirs and orchestras were founded in greater numbers, and touring of musicians, foreign and domestic, increased, the type and number of concerts available in England came to closely resemble the public concerts of today.

PURCELL, DANIEL (ca. 1664–1717). Organist and composer. Like his older brother **Henry Purcell**, Daniel was trained as a chorister in the **Chapel Royal**. In his early twenties he was appointed organist at Magdalen College, Oxford, and remained there until 1695, when he relocated to London. Much of his work is for the theater and includes contributions to Peter Motteux's *The Island Princess*; in 1701 he participated in *The Judgment of Paris* competition and won third prize, following **John Weldon** and **John Eccles**.

PURCELL, HENRY (1659–95). The predominant composer of the Restoration era. Purcell's training as a chorister in the **Chapel Royal** presaged his nearly lifelong association with the royal musical establishment: a gentleman of the Chapel Royal from 1682, keeper of the wind and keyboard instruments from 1683 (and for the decade preceding, he was **John Hingeston**'s assistant in this capacity), composer for the violins from 1677 with a hiatus during the reign of James II, resumed as composer in the **Private Musick** from 1689, harpsichord in the Private Musick from 1685, and **organ** tuner from 1688. He was also appointed organist of Westminster Abbey in 1679. And while his compositions in these royal and ecclesiastical capacities are plentiful and masterful—court **odes, anthems, ceremonial music,** etc.—it is his extensive work for the theater, emerging primarily in the last years of his life—that has most secured the perception of his greatness.

Purcell easily became, and has remained, an icon of musical Englishness, quickly seen, for instance, in the title of his two-volume posthumous song anthology, *Orpheus Britannicus* (1698, 1702), a title that seems well to encapsulate his rank among English composers of his day. And as his career blossomed at a time in which various continental styles had strong claims in England, his relationship with those styles and his forging of musical "Englishness" is particularly significant. Charles II's ties to the French court brought a strong French influence into play at the English court. Purcell's fluency in that idiom is clear, for instance, in works like his famous court **masque *Dido and Aeneas*,** where much of the music is devoted to French dances and much of the internal structure proceeds according to a Lullian pattern of solo air, choral repetition, instrumental (dance) repetition.

Italianism found its way into England in part through the activities of traveling virtuosos, and it finds an echo in Purcell's *Sonatas of III Parts* (1683) and the **cantata**-like construction of multisectional songs. In his preface to the 1683 *Sonatas,* he esteems the Italian "seriousness and gravity," especially in contrast with the "levity and balladry" of the French, and commends the elegancy of Italian music to English artists. Elsewhere, however, in his edition of **John Playford**'s *An Introduction to the Skill of Musick,* he writes of a technical point that "'tis the constant Practise of the *Italians* in all their Musick, either Vocal or Instrumental, which I presume ought to be a Guide to us." His "I presume" might seem to undermine the view.

With respect to national style and influence, his prefatory note to *Dioclesian,* a note perhaps by **John Dryden,** is also significant: "Musick is yet but in its Nonage, a forward Child, which gives hope of what it may be hereafter in *England,* when the Masters of it shall find more encouragement. 'Tis now learning *Italian,* which is the best Master, and studying a little of the *French* Air, to give it somewhat more of Gayety and Fashion. . . . [W]e [the English] must be content to shake off our Barbarity by degrees." Dryden himself was aware of national issues certainly and likely aroused the resentment of English composers when he collaborated with the Frenchman **Louis Grabu** in the royal music drama *Albion and Albanius* (1685), a collaboration which he defended: "When any of our countrymen excel him, I shall be glad, for the sake of old England, to be shewn my errour; in the meantime, let virtue be commended, though in the person of a stranger." However, Purcell, his collaborator in the 1690s, clearly had "shewn" him the errors of his ways, and English theater music was securely in native hands.

Wherein does the musical Englishness lie? Many have remarked on the fluency of Purcell's setting of English words and the naturalness of their musical declamation. Assuredly there is also an intensity of affective musical language that emerges especially in heightened moments of anguish, as in the final lament from *Dido and Aeneas* or the tortured, fearful moments of "The Blessed Virgin's Expostulation." And there is a clear lingering of earlier English styles that surfaces in the contrapuntal richness of his Fantasias (1680), the last of the English **viol** consorts, although by this point they may have been but "compositional exercise" (Holman, *NG*, 2001), and some of the anthems, like the dramatic fragment "Hear My Prayer" or the large-scale "Blow Up the Trumpet in Sion."

Purcell's works are wide ranging. The anthems are written in full, verse, and symphony styles, including one of the most expansive of the Restoration symphony anthems, "My Heart Is Inditing" for the coronation of James II (1685), and anthems that cavort in their textual pictorialism, such as "They That Go Down to the Sea in Ships." He wrote a large number of bawdy **catches**, and yet also elegant court odes like "Sound the Trumpet" (1687) and "Come ye Sons of Art" (1694). His work in the theater began in 1680 with music for Nathaniel Lee's *Theodosius*, and he continued to supply incidental music and songs for plays until the final year of his life. Though the conventions of the spoken theater may have constrained the integrality of Purcell's music, many of his musical contributions are substantial, dramatic, and richly memorable, such as "Music for a While" from *Oedipus* or "Let the Dreadful Engines Roar" from *Don Quixote*.

The "**opera**" *Dido and Aeneas* remains unique in Purcell's output and rare in the Restoration theater, with its sister, **John Blow**'s *Venus and Adonis*, one of few works to essay the fully sung dramatic style. Typically "operatic" in England was the hybrid **semi-opera** or **dramatick opera**, in which a spoken play is infused with often-extensive musical entertainments. Purcell composed the music for four semi-operas, *Dioclesian* (1690); *King Arthur* (1691), with its famous shivering frost scene indebted to Lully's *Isis*; *The Fairy Queen* (1692); and *The Indian Queen* (1695), completed by his brother Daniel. *The Indian Queen* powerfully breaks down the wall between the musical "entertainment" and the drama with an integral and "operatic" conjuration scene. The music for Ismeron, the conjuror, is a necessary agent for the action itself and in its musical content—key and chromatic descent—revelatory of Queen Zempoalla's dire fate.

With Purcell's untimely death in 1695, the growth of the English musical theater was dealt a tragic blow. And while others, notably **John Eccles**, were still available to carry the semi-operatic tradition forward, the encroachment of Italian opera was ascendant and the musical theater in the first part of the 18th century would belong to **George Frideric Handel** and foreigners. *See also* BALLAD; BOWEN, JEMMY; BOWMAN, JOHN; BRITTEN, BENJAMIN; CROSS, LETITIA; DORSET GARDEN THEATRE; DRURY LANE THEATRE; DURFEY, THOMAS; ENGLISH SLIDE TRUMPET; GIBBONS, CHRISTOPHER; GOSTLING, JOHN; HERBERT, GEORGE; HOLST, IMOGEN; HUMFREY, PELHAM; LEHMANN, LIZA; LEVERIDGE, RICHARD; MAD SONGS; MUSICAL ANTIQUARIAN SOCIETY; NOVELLO, VINCENT; ORGAN; PATE, JOHN; PURCELL CLUB; PURCELL SOCIETY; REGGIO, PIETRO; ROOTHAM, CYRIL; ST. CECILIA'S DAY OBSERVANCE; SHORE; TALBOT, JAMES.

PURCELL CLUB. Organization founded to promote the music of **Henry Purcell**. Members met twice a year to sing a morning service of Purcell's music at Westminster Abbey and an evening concert of secular music. The group formed in 1836 and disbanded in 1863, and celebrated Purcell's bicentenary early in January of 1858.

PURCELL ROOM. *See* ROYAL FESTIVAL HALL.

PURCELL SOCIETY. Organization founded in 1876 to study, publish, and promote the music of **Henry Purcell**. The society completed publishing all the known music of Purcell in 1965 and has since concentrated on releasing revised versions of the scores. The society has released both scholarly editions and performing editions of Purcell's music.

PURITANS. The Puritans were a religious sect in 16th- and 17th-century England that sought a purification of the established Anglican Church. Drawn to a Calvinistic Presbyterianism, the Puritans represented an influential force not only in the dynamics of the church but in the state as well, as manifest in the English Civil War. The Puritans were famously known for a zealous sobriety of life and piety, and this would have a strong affect on music. During the Puritan Commonwealth, the closing of theaters put an end to a major activity for English musicians, as did the removal of **organs** from churches and the disbanding of choirs. Complex church music, especially that which might use instruments or smack of the secular, was renounced, though the **metrical psalm** was nurtured.

Against this background a historical cliché arose that depicts the Puritans as opposed to music: the Purtian as a music hater. **Percy Scholes** (1934) offered a strong corrective, noting such things as the blossoming of **John**

Playford's music publishing during the Commonwealth and the Lord Protector Cromwell's embrace of music, which extended to the employ of **John Hingston**, the ownership of an organ, and the hiring of a large ensemble for his daughter's wedding. In Scholes's view, it is clear that religious discipline and propriety always trumped music's allure, but this did not make the latter problematic in nature, only in degree.

PURKIS, JOHN (1781–1849). Organist and teacher. Purkis was blind from birth (though he achieved limited sight after a series of operations in 1811), was considered to be a child prodigy, and studied with Thomas Grenville, organist of the **Foundling Hospital**. His posts included St. Olave Southwark (1793) and St. Clement Danes (1802). The firm of Flight and Robinson consulted with him on the construction of the **Apollonicon**, and he performed Saturday-afternoon recitals on that instrument regularly for nearly 21 years. The fantasias on **opera** themes he performed at these recitals were published for the middle-class piano market by William Hodsoll; these were extremely popular at the end of the 1820s. Among his students was the music historian and organist William Smith Rockstro.

QUEEN ELIZABETH HALL. *See* ROYAL FESTIVAL HALL.

QUEEN'S CONCERT ROOMS. *See* HANNOVER SQUARE ROOMS.

QUEEN'S HALL. London concert hall in Langham Place, completed in 1893 and destroyed by an incendiary bomb in 1941. The hall included two concert venues: a smaller one, seating about 500, and a larger one, seating up to 3,000. Queen's Hall was home to many of London's most famous concert series and ensembles, including the **Queen's Hall Orchestra**, the **Proms** (1895–1940), the **Royal Philharmonic Society**, and the **British Broadcasting Corporation** Symphony Orchestra (1930–41).

QUEEN'S HALL ORCHESTRA. London orchestra founded by **Sir Henry Wood** in 1895; renamed the New Queen's Hall Orchestra in 1915. The Queen's Hall Orchestra was the main orchestra for the **Proms** between 1895 and 1924. It was also one of the first major professional ensembles to hire women as regular members. Since the destruction of the **Queen's Hall** in 1941, the Orchestra has performed in a variety of locations in and around London. Prominent conductors of the orchestra have included **Sir Malcolm Sargent**, among others. *See also* CLARKE, REBECCA; COATES, ERIC; GOOSSENS, SIR EUGENE; LONDON SYMPHONY ORCHESTRA.

QUILTER, ROGER (1877–1953). English composer. Quilter composed songs (for which he is best known), arrangements of folk tunes, choral works, and numerous instrumental works. He was educated at Eton and then at the Hoch Konservatorium in Frankfurt (1897–1901), where he also studied privately with Iwan Knorr; he is considered one of the **Frankfurt Group**. His songs became extremely popular in the first few decades of the 20th century and were featured in the performances of Gervase Elwes and other prominent vocalists of the time. He was a founder of the Musicians' Benevolent Fund (1921).

R

RAINIER, PRIAULX (ALSO IVY PRIAULX; 1903–86). Composer, teacher, and violinist of South African origin. Rainier studied violin at the South African College of Music, Capetown (1913), won a scholarship to the **Royal Academy of Music (2 [RAM]; 1920–25)**, and settled in England permanently. After leaving the RAM, she taught violin privately and at the Badminton School, Bristol, and played in a string quartet and in cinema orchestras. She studied privately with Nadia Boulanger in 1937 and began further essays in composing, mixing approachable elements of contemporary styles. She was a professor of composition at the RAM from 1943–61. After her retirement, she was given a Civil List pension. Performances of her works increased from the 1960s until her death, as did her compositional output.

RAMSEY, ROBERT (?–1644). Composer. Ramsey was both a graduate of Cambridge and the organist and master of the children at Trinity College there. His works include Latin and English liturgical works, the style of the former showing the progressive influence of Italy. Ramsey is also the composer of a number of **dialogues** on biblical and mythological subject in GB Obo Don. c. 57. The biblical dialogues, though logically essays that might prepare the way for English **oratorio**, do not historically lead in that direction. However, Ramsey's "In Guilty Night," a setting of the story of Saul and the Witch of Endor, points to **Henry Purcell**'s well-known setting, and both find an echo in **George Frideric Handel**'s *Saul.*

RANDALL, JOHN (1717–99). Organist and composer. Randall was trained at the **Chapel Royal** and at King's College, Cambridge (MusB, 1744; MusD, 1756). He was organist at various colleges of Cambridge, including King's, St. John's, Pembroke, and Trinity, and was named Professor of Music in 1755. His compositions include **anthems**, psalm-tune settings, **hymn** tunes, and an **ode** performed at the installation of the Duke of Grafton as chancellor to Cambridge University (1769; now lost).

RANDEGGER, ALBERTO (1832–1911). Conductor, singer, teacher, and composer of Italian birth. Randegger was trained in Italy (where he sang with

Giuseppe Verdi) and settled in London in 1854. He took numerous positions, including organist at St. Paul's, Regent Park (1854–70), and conductor of Italian **operas** at **St. James's Theatre, Covent Garden**, and **Drury Lane** and of various choirs and **musical festivals**, including Norwich (1881–1905), but he was known primarily in his own time as a teacher of singing. He taught at the **Royal Academy of Music (2)** from 1868 to 1911 and concurrently at the **Royal College of Music** from 1896 to 1911. His book *Singing* (1893) was in use for decades. Randegger's compositions are mostly forgotten, but he was known for his conducting of Wolfgang Amadeus Mozart and his interpretations of Richard Wagner and Giuseppe Verdi.

RANELAGH GARDENS. *See* PLEASURE GARDENS.

RAVENSCROFT, THOMAS (ca. 1592–ca. 1635). Editor, composer, and theorist. Ravenscroft was a chorister at St. Paul's Cathedral, London, and a student at Gresham College, Cambridge. For a period (1618–22) he was the music master at Christ's Hospital. He oversaw the publication of a number of collections, including the psalter *Whole Booke of Psalmes* (1621) and three anthologies of rounds, **catches**, and theatrical play songs: *Pammelia* (1609), *Deuteromelia* (1609), and *Melismata* (1611). The contents of these anthologies are strikingly diverse with drinking songs like "He That Will an Alehouse Keep" sharing the pages with street cries like "New Oysters" and devotional texts like "O Lord Turne Not away Thy Face." In the end, however, the anthologies point to the conviviality of informal music-making and are, in that light, rich documents of early 17th-century musical life.

In 1614 Ravenscroft published *A Brief Discourse of the true (but neglected) use of Charact'ring the Degrees*, a musical treatise focused on questions of mensuration and proportion. Some (Ian Spink in *Blwl*, 1992) have suggested the *Discourse* may have figured in Ravenscroft's teaching.

The modern assessment of Ravenscroft's compositions—**madrigals, anthems**, and fantasias—is not enthusiastic. Mateer and Payne (*NG*, 2001) note that his "extant compositions show him to have been a man of great versatility, though of slender talents."

RAWSTHORNE, ALAN (1905–71). Composer and pianist. Known to the public primarily for his film scores (including *Burma Victory* [1946]), Rawsthorne was a lauded and successful composer of orchestral and chamber music. He was trained at the **Royal Manchester College of Music** (1925–29) and studied piano with Egon Petri in Zakopane, Poland, and Berlin until 1932. He taught at Dartington Hall (1932–34) before moving to London to devote his time to composition. Aside from war service between 1939 and 1945, he composed in London (until 1953) and then in Essex for the remainder of his life. His compositions first gained public notice at the International Society for Contemporary Music festivals of 1938 and 1939, and he remained a well-known, if not popular, figure for the rest of his life. Rawsthorne was named a CBE in 1961.

REDFORD, JOHN (?–1547). Composer and organist. Redford was a **vicar-choral** at St. Paul's Cathedral, London, as early as 1534, later appointed as master of the choristers and almoner, and surely also functioning as organist. Redford's compositional work was tightly focused on liturgical **organ** pieces, surviving today in sources like the **Mulliner Book,** and he is unusual in the narrowness of his output as well as its high quality. In addition to his numerous organ settings, there are only a few Latin motets; the popular attribution to him of the famous vernacular **anthem** "Rejoice in the Lord Always" no longer stands.

REGGIO, PIETRO (1632–85). Composer and singer. Following service to Queen Christina of Sweden and travels in Spain, Germany, and France, the Italian Reggio immigrated to London by 1664, where he became an important channel for the transmission of the Italian style. His influence on **Henry Purcell** is often noted, a connection reinforced in the younger composer's setting of Cowley's "She Loves and She Confesses Too," which adopts the same ground bass as Reggio uses in his setting of the same text.

Reggio is mentioned by the diarists **Samuel Pepys** and **John Evelyn.** Evelyn, whose daughter Mary was a pupil of Reggio's, records that "Came to my house some German strangers, and Signor Pietro a famous Musitian, who had ben long in Sweden in Queene Christinas Court: he sung admirably to a Guitarr and has a perfect good tenor and base etc: and had set to Italian composure, many of Abraham Cowleys Pieces which shew'd extremely well" (23 October 1680). Pepys mentions him as "slovenly," but "one who sings Italian songs to the **theorbo** most neatly." The settings of Cowley's verse were published in 1680. Of the collection Spink (1974) observes: "it has to be confessed that, on the whole, they are rather unexciting settings of rather unexciting poems," leading him to conclude, "While he may not be an incompetent composer, he is, sad to say, a quite unmemorable one."

Reggio authored a treatise on vocal ornamentation, *The Art of Singing,* which was published in 1678, resurfacing only recently in 1997.

RICHTER, HANS (1843–1916). Austro-German conductor active in England between 1877 and 1911. Richter was trained in Vienna and played for or conducted Richard Wagner's music in the 1860s and 1870s. His first visit to London came in 1877, when he conducted in the place of Wagner at the Wagner Festival mounted there. Until his retirement in 1911, Richter split his time conducting in Vienna and England. He conducted a series called the "Richter Concerts" from 1879 to 1900, the Birmingham **Musical Festival** from 1885 to 1909 (including the premiere of **Sir Edward Elgar**'s *Dream of Gerontius*), the **Hallé Orchestra** from 1899 to 1911, and the **London Symphony Orchestra** from 1904 to 1911. He was named a CVO in 1907.

RIMBAULT, EDWARD FRANCIS (1816–76). Musicologist, editor, organist, and composer. Rimbault was one of the most important and influential musical antiquarians of the 19th century. He edited and helped publish many editions of early English music for societies such as the **Handel Society**, the **Motett Society**, the **Musical Antiquarian Society**, and the **Percy Society**, and he collected an immense musical library that sold for £2,000 in the year after his death. His early studies were with **Samuel Wesley** and **William Crotch**, and he was named organist at Swiss Church, Soho, when he was 16. He was the founder and coeditor of the journal the *Choir and Musical Record*. He published monographs on the harmonium (1857), the piano (1860), and the **Chapel Royal** (1872).

RITSON MANUSCRIPT. The Ritson Manuscript (GB Lbl Add. 5665) is one of the principal sources of early Tudor song. The collection, likely a provincial one from the vicinity of Devon, shows a number of scribal hands, probably reflecting a long period of compilation from the last decades of the 15th century through the first decades of the 16th. Much of the manuscript is devoted to **carols**, the principal composer of which is Richard Smert. Other works include secular songs in a continental cantilena style, masses, and motets.

ROBERTSBRIDGE CODEX. The Robertsbridge Codex (GB Lbl Add. 28550) represents the earliest surviving keyboard music. The manuscript, a fragment of only two leaves, likely dates from around 1325. Notationally distinctive, combining staff notation with letters, the manuscript presents three dances (*estampies*) and arrangements of three motets, two of which are from the French *Roman de Fauvel*.

ROGERS, BENJAMIN (1614–98). Organist, singer, and composer. Apart from a time as organist at Christ Church, Dublin, Rogers's training and early career center on Windsor and environs, as he was a chorister at St. George's Chapel, later a lay clerk there, and for a time a member of the chapel choir and later organist at Eton. His time at Eton brought him into contact with Nathaniel Ingelo, a fellow of the college who acted as Rogers's patron in several instances. In 1665 he began work in Oxford as master of the choristers at Magdalen, in which post he remained until 1686, when he was dismissed.

The composer of **services**, **anthems**, instrumental suites, and keyboard music, he was held in high esteem by his contemporaries. **Anthony Wood** (quoted by **Charles Burney**) relates: "His compositions for instruments . . . have been highly valued. . . . and Dr. **[John] Wilson**, the professor, *the greatest and most curious judge of Music that ever was*, usually wept when he heard them well performed, as being wrapt up in ecstasy; or, if you will, melted down: while others smiled, or had their hands and eyes lifted up, at the excellence of them."

ROOTHAM, CYRIL (1875–1938). Teacher, organist, conductor, and composer. Rootham was a force in the musical life of Cambridge University for much of his life as an organist at St. John's (1901–38) and lecturer and conductor of the Cambridge University Musical Society (1912–36). As a conductor, he was known mostly for his revivals of **Henry Purcell**, **George Frideric Handel**'s **oratorios**, and Wolfgang Amadeus Mozart's **operas**. He composed a great deal of vocal music, including **partsongs**, sacred works, and a few dramatic works. He was trained at St. John's College, Cambridge (BA in classics, 1897; BMus, 1900; MA, 1901; and DMus, 1910) and at the **Royal College of Music**, studying under **Sir Charles Villiers Stanford** and **Sir Walter Parratt**. Before returning to Cambridge, he held organist posts at Christ Church, Hampstead (1898–1901), and St. Asaph's Cathedral (1901).

ROSEINGRAVE, THOMAS (1690/91–1766). Organist and composer. Roseingrave was a member of a musical family; his organist father, Daniel, held various cathedral posts, including Gloucester, Winchester, Salisbury, and Christ Church, Dublin; his brother, Ralph, also an organist, succeeded Daniel in Dublin. As a young man, Roseingrave was sent to Italy (1709) to study and while there entered the circle of Domenico Scarlatti, whose works he would strongly champion in England, especially with an edition of 42 Scarlatti sonatas published in 1739 (*XLII Suites de Pièces Pour le Clavecin*). Roseingrave's Italianism was also clear in the publication of Italian-texted **cantatas** of his own composing.

He was appointed organist of St. George's, Hanover Square, in 1725, a parish prominent through both the size of its **organ** and also its association with **George Frideric Handel**. His career there and in general subsequently collapsed, however, in the wake of a frustrated love affair and its ensuing emotional difficulties.

ROSSETER, PHILIP (1567/68–1623). Lutanist and composer. Rosseter received court appointment as a lutanist in 1603. In 1601 he and **Thomas Campion** brought out a *Book of Ayres*, famous for its preface that scorns complex counterpoint and undue madrigalism, and thus charts a simpler course for the **ayre**. In 1609 he published a collection of **English consort** lessons. Also at that time he entered into a period of theater management in which he was active until 1617.

ROUNDELAY. English cognate for medieval French *rondelet* (*rondeau*) as a dance song in *forme fixe* whose name points to a circular choreography. **Thomas Ravenscroft**'s *Pammelia* (1609) is described on its title page as a "mixed varietie of pleasant roundelays and delightful **catches**." As none of the songs are specifically designated as "roundelay," he appears to be using it synonymously with "round."

ROYAL ACADEMY OF MUSIC (1). The Royal Academy of Music was a London **opera** company that was active in two incarnations; one from 1719 to 1728 and the second from 1729 to 1737. Both were musically led by **George Frideric Handel**, with **John Jacob Heidegger** in a managerial role. The first academy, performing at the **Haymarket** Theatre, featured operas by **Giovanni Bononcini** and Attilio Ariosti as well as Handel; the principal singers included **Senesino**, Francesca Cuzzoni, and Faustina Bordoni (Hasse). Financial difficulties, bad relationships among the singers, and a shift in audience taste led to the closing of the Academy in 1728. Its re-formation in 1729 was also financially challenging, and the founding of a rival company, the **"Opera of the Nobility"** in 1733, stretched patronal support to the point of mutual collapse in 1737.

ROYAL ACADEMY OF MUSIC (2; RAM). Oldest degree-granting musical school in England, founded in London in 1822. It was given a royal charter in 1830. It moved from its original premises on Tenterden Street to Marylebone Street in 1912 and was made a constituent college of the University of London in 1999. The facilities include a 450-seat concert hall, an **opera** house, a museum, and a library. Some of the principal professors there were **Thomas Attwood, Sir William Sterndale Bennett, Sir Lennox Berkeley, Alan Bush, Frederick Corder, William Crotch, John Ella, Sir Edward German, Thomas Greatorex, Robert Lindley, Kate Loder, Hamish MacCunn, Sir George Alexander Macfarren, Sir Alexander Campbell Mackenzie, Ignaz Moscheles, Ebenezer Prout, Alberto Randegger, Sir Arthur Sullivan, Samuel Sebastian Wesley,** and **Sir Henry Joseph Wood.** Prominent students who attended the RAM include **Sir**

Granville Bantock, Sir John Barbirolli, Sir Joseph Barnby, John Francis
Barnett, Sir Arnold Bax, Sterndale Bennett, Bush, Rebecca Clarke, Eric
Coates, Corder, John Spencer Curwen, Ella, German, Joseph Holbrooke,
Loder, Macfarren, Mackenzie, William Gray McNaught, Priaulx Rainier,
Sullivan, Arthur Goring Thomas, Maude Valérie White, and Wood. *See
also* CRAMER, JOHN BAPTIST.

ROYAL ALBERT HALL. London concert hall opened in 1871. The hall
uses a combination of standing room and seating; it has been the site of the
Proms concerts since 1941. The hall housed the Royal Albert Hall Choral
Society (1871; renamed the **Royal Choral Society** in 1888) and the Royal
Albert Hall Orchestra (1905). The Hall has been used for numerous popular-
music concerts as well.

**ROYAL CHORAL SOCIETY (ALSO ROYAL ALBERT HALL CHO-
RAL SOCIETY).** Large London choir (approximately 850 voices) founded
for the opening of the **Royal Albert Hall** in 1871. Its conductors have included Charles Gounod (to 1872), **Sir Joseph Barnby** (to 1896), **Sir Frederick Bridge** (to 1922), H. L. Balfour (to 1929), and **Sir Malcolm Sargent**
(to 1967).

ROYAL COLLEGE OF MUSIC (RCM). London conservatory founded
in 1882 as the successor to the National Training School for Music (NTSM).
The NTSM was founded in 1876 to help spur the reform of the **Royal Academy of Music (2)** and allow for training in **opera**, sacred music, and military
music; **Sir Arthur Sullivan** was its first principal. When he resigned in 1881,
Sir George Grove took the position and helped reorganize the institution into
the RCM. The RCM confers degrees in all aspects of music performance and
the academic study of music as well as the honorary FRCM (Fellow of the
Royal College of Music). Its current facilities, built in 1894 and expanded
in 1965 and 1968, include a 468-seat concert hall, a 400-seat theater, a 150-
seat recital hall, and an extensive library. Besides Grove, its principals and
directors have included **Sir Hubert Parry** (1894–1918), **Sir Hugh Percy
Allen** (1918–37), and **Sir George Dyson** (1938–52). Prominent members of
the RCM's faculty include **Havergal Brain, Sir Frederick Bridge, Edward
Dannreuther, Sir (Henry) Walford Davies, Cecil Armstrong Gibbs,
Herbert Howells, John Ireland, Jenny Lind, Charles Harford Lloyd, Sir
Walter Parratt, Alberto Randegger, Sir Malcolm Sargent, Humphrey
Searle**, and **Ralph Vaughan Williams**. Prominent students of the RCM in-
clude **Sir Malcolm Arnold, Sir Arthur Bliss, Sir Herbert Brewer, Frank
Bridge, Benjamin Britten, George Butterworth, Rebecca Clarke, Samuel**

Coleridge-Taylor, Davies, **Arnold Dolmetsch**, Dyson, **Peter Racine Fricker**, Gibbs, **Sir Eugene Goossens**, Ivor Gurney, Gustav Holst, Imogen Holst, Howells, Ireland, **Constant Lambert, Iris Lemare, Elisabeth Lutyens, Hamish MacCunn, Dame Elizabeth Maconchy, Robin Milford, E. J. Moeran, Cyril Rootham, Edmund Rubbra**, Searle, **Sir Michael Tippett**, Vaughan Williams, and **Charles Wood**. *See also* ENGLISH MUSICAL RENAISSANCE; *THE SCENES FROM THE SONG OF HIAWATHA.*

ROYAL COLLEGE OF ORGANISTS (ALSO RCO; COLLEGE OF ORGANISTS). Organization founded for the examination and encouragement of organists and sacred music in 1864. The RCO received its royal charter in 1893. Aside from examinations, the college also sponsors lectures and **organ** recitals. It awards diplomas on a hierarchical basis, starting with the ARCO (Associate), the FRCO (Fellowship), the Choir Training Diploma (CHM) and the Archbishop of Centerbury's Diploma in Choral Music (ACDM; awarded jointly with the **Royal School of Church Music**).

ROYAL FESTIVAL HALL. A 2,900-seat concert hall on the South Bank of the Thames in London. The hall was originally built for the **Festival of Britain** and opened in 1951. It was expanded in 1967 into the Southbank Arts Centre with the addition of connections with the Queen Elizabeth Hall (a 900-seat venue for popular music), the Purcell Room (a 370-seat chamber music hall), and the Hayward (an art gallery).

ROYAL ITALIAN OPERA. *See* COVENT GARDEN.

ROYAL MANCHESTER COLLEGE OF MUSIC. *See* ROYAL NORTHERN COLLEGE OF MUSIC.

ROYAL MUSICAL ASSOCIATION (RMA). Society founded in 1874 as the Musical Association for the study of music as an art and science and the promotion of that study. The association received the authority to be called "royal" in 1944. Early presidents included **Sir Frederic Gore Ouseley, Sir Hubert Parry, Sir Frederick Bridge, Charles Wood**, and **Edward J. Dent**. Papers given at meetings on acoustics, theory, history, and criticism, as well as the membership's comments on those papers, were published annually in the journal *Proceedings of the Musical Association* (1874–1944) and then the *Proceedings of the Royal Musical Association* (1944–87). This publication was succeeded by the biannual peer-reviewed *Journal of the Royal Musical Association* (1987–present). The RMA has also published the *Royal Musical Association Research Chronicle* since 1968.

ROYAL NORTHERN COLLEGE OF MUSIC (ALSO MATTHAY SCHOOL OF MUSIC; RNCM; ROYAL MANCHESTER COLLEGE OF MUSIC; RMCM). Conservatory founded by **Sir Charles Hallé** in Manchester in 1893 as the Manchester College of Music. Hallé was the first principal, followed by Arthur Brodsky (1895–1929). It merged with the Northern School of Music (founded as the Matthay School of Music in 1920) and moved into new premises in 1972. Performance spaces at the college include a 616-seat theater, a 466-seat concert hall, and a 150-seat chamber music venue, the Lord Rhodes Room. The college has a substantial library and archives and a historical instrument collection. It received its royal charter in 1923.

ROYAL OPERA HOUSE. *See* COVENT GARDEN.

ROYAL PHILHARMONIC SOCIETY (ALSO PHILHARMONIC SOCIETY). Organization founded in 1813 to give concerts of instrumental music in London. The society was founded by musicians, and unlike other contemporary societies (such as the **Professional Concerts**), membership often was awarded on the basis of artistic talent and promise, rather than social status. The society was granted the authority to use the sobriquet "royal" in 1911. The society gathered a freelance orchestra for six to eight concerts per season. In its history, it commissioned works by Beethoven (Symphony no. 9 in D minor, op. 125), Luigi Cherubini, **Felix Mendelssohn** (the *Italian* Symphony), and Louis Spohr. Conductors of the society have included **Johann Peter Salomon** (1813), **Muzio Clementi** (conducting at the keyboard, 1813–25), **Sir George Smart** (1813–49), **Ignaz Moscheles** (1832–41), **Sir Michael Costa** (1846–54), Richard Wagner (1855), **Sir William Sterndale Bennett** (1856–66), **Sir Arthur Sullivan** (1885–57), **Sir Frederic Hymen Cowen** (1888–92 and 1900–1907), and **Sir Alexander Campbell Makenzie** (1893–99), among others. *See also* ATTWOOD, THOMAS; AYRTON, WILLIAM; CHAPPELL & CO.; CRAMER, JOHN BAPTIST; CROTCH, WILLIAM; NOVELLO, VINCENT; QUEEN'S HALL; ST. JAMES'S HALL.

ROYAL SCHOOL OF CHURCH MUSIC (ALSO SCHOOL OF ENGLISH CHURCH MUSIC; RSCM). Organization founded by Sydney Nicholson in 1927 for the study and promotion of sacred music, particularly of the Anglican Church. The school was granted the authority to use the sobriquet "royal" in 1945. For a time (1929–74), it ran the College of St. Nicholas at various locations, where courses were offered in liturgy, sacred music, and choir training leading to the ACDM, which is now awarded by the **Royal**

College of Organists. It now serves largely as an examining body and affiliation center for sacred music.

ROYAL SOCIETY OF FEMALE MUSICIANS (ALSO SOCIETY OF FEMALE MUSICIANS; SOCIETY OF PROFESSIONAL FEMALE MUSICIANS). Philanthropic organization founded in 1839 to provide aid to older and indigent professional female musicians. It raised funds primarily through concerts and donations from its members. By 1861 it had £6,000 invested. It merged with the **Royal Society of Musicians** in 1866.

ROYAL SOCIETY OF MUSICIANS (ALSO SOCIETY OF MUSICIANS; FUND FOR DECAYED MUSICIANS). Philanthropic organization founded in 1738 for the care of older musicians as well as widows and orphans of musicians. It was granted its first royal charter in 1790 and its second in 1987. Fund-raising occurred initially through concerts and donations by members (**George Frideric Handel** gave the Society £1,000 on his death); later, membership fees also helped to raise funds. The society did not admit women until it merged with the **Royal Society of Female Musicians** in 1866.

RUBBRA, EDMUND (ALSO CHARLES EDMUND; 1901–86). Composer, critic, pianist, and teacher. Rubbra is best known for his symphonies (11) and his choral works, which include five masses and numerous other pieces for the Catholic Church. Rubbra was initially self-taught but took some private lessons with **Cyril Scott** at the age of 17. He won open scholarships to Reading University (1920–21) to study with **Gustav Holst** and then the **Royal College of Music** (1921–25), where he studied with Holst and **Ralph Vaughan Williams**. From 1925 to 1941 he worked as a private music teacher, accompanist, and performer. During World War II, he served as part of the Army Classical Music Group, a piano trio that successfully continued after the war until the 1950s as the Rubbra-Gruenberg-Pleeth Trio. Rubbra was a senior lecturer at Worcester College, Oxford (1947–68), and professor of music at the **Guildhall School of Music and Drama** (1961–74). He wrote music criticism in the 1930s for the *Monthly Musical Record* and the *Listener*, as well as a monograph on Holst (1947). Rubbra was named CBE in 1960.

"RULE, BRITANNIA." Patriotic song with choral refrain from the end of **Thomas Arne**'s **masque** *Alfred* (1740). Although in context of the masque, the triumphal exuberance of the song—"Rule, Britannia, Britannia, rule the waves / Britons never will be slaves"—celebrates Alfred's victory over the Danes, its sentiment made it easily and popularly appropriated, and one can imagine its first hearings took on timely meaning in the context of the "War of Jenkins's Ear" between England and Spain.

Its wide dissemination is a measure of its popularity. Arne published it out of context as an addition to his *Judgment of Paris* (1742), and a few years later it was sung with altered text by the supporters of the "Young Pretender," Charles Edward Stuart, in the final Jacobite uprising of 1745, the refrain becoming "Rule, Britannia, Britannia, rise and fight, / Restore your injured Monarch's right." **George Frideric Handel** quoted it in 1745 in his *Occasional Oratorio*, and Beethoven published his "Five Variations on Rule Britannia," WoO 79, in 1804. The song has achieved cult status, however, as a robust part of performances of **Sir Henry Wood**'s "Fantasia on British Sea Songs" (1905) at the "Last Night of the **Proms**."

RUSH, GEORGE (fl. 1760–80). Composer, harpsichordist, and guitarist. Little is known for certain about Rush's background and education. He published four keyboard concerti and assorted other pieces, and completed three **operas** for **Drury Lane**: *The Royal Shepherd* and *Capricious Lovers* (both 1764) and *The Statesman Foiled* (1768; its music is now lost). Some of his music was published in Holland as well as England.

S

SACCHINI, ANTONIO (1730–86). Italian composer active in London from 1772 to 1781. He was one of the leading 18th-century composers of *opera seria*. He trained at the Conservatorio S. Maria di Loreto, where he taught for a time, and composed and produced operas in Naples, Venice, and Rome. In London he produced operas at King's Theatre, **Haymarket**, that became extremely popular, including *Il Cid* (1773), *Tamerlano* (1773), and *Montezuma* (1775). Sacchini fled London ahead of his creditors in 1781 and settled in Paris for the remainder of his life.

SACKBUT. English term (variously "shagbutt," "shagbolt," "seykebuds," etc.) for the early trombone, derived from the French *saquir* (to pull, here in reference to the instrument's slide). The earliest English reference to the instrument is in the court records of Henry VII; under his son, Henry VIII, 12 players were employed (1530s); later in the century the numbers grew more modest, but increased in the early 17th century with as many as 14 players in 1635. Use of the trombone in England wanes in the 18th century—**George Frideric Handel**'s famous "Dead March" from *Saul* is a significant late example, however—and "it is virtually certain that there was not a single native-born trombonist in England during the entire 18th century" (Herbert, 1990).

In ensemble with **cornetts**, trombones played masking **ayres**—**John Adson**'s 1611 set is a good example—and likely arrangements of vocal music (cf. GB Cfm 24E). **John Hingeston** also uses the combination in a **fantasia-suite**. The use of the trombone and cornett ensemble to double the voices in church music was also adopted in England, perhaps especially so in the years following the Commonwealth when instrumental support would have been expedient. Herbert (1993) draws attention, however, to the possibility that this may not have been the practice of the English in the early 16th century, based on accounts of the musical proceedings at the Field of Cloth of Gold (1520).

SACRED HARMONIC SOCIETY. The Sacred Harmonic Society, active from 1832 to 1889, was one of the premier London choral associations of its day. At times, it was an organization of Dissenting choirs (particularly after the 1834 Handel Festival in Westminster Abbey excluded nonconformists).

Its membership included members of all social classes and musical abilities. Many members were trained only in sight-singing notations such as **Tonic Sol-fa** rather than staff notation. It was one of the first major choirs of the 19th century to forward a rational recreation agenda, combining a philanthropic morality with a social and educational organization. Its seasons included presenting whole works, usually **oratorios**, especially of **George Frideric Handel**, **Franz Joseph Haydn**, and **Felix Mendelssohn**, but many choral compositions received their London premieres from the body.

The society's most famous conductor was **Sir Michael Costa** (1848–82), who used it to create "monster concerts" with orchestras of about 700 and choruses of over 2,700. The society sang oratorios weekly during the Great Exhibition in 1851; it was also a great part of the choir for the Handel Festivals at the **Crystal Palace** as conducted by Costa. From 1836 until 1880, it held rehearsals and concerts in **Exeter Hall**; when the Young Men's Christian Association bought that building in 1880 and prohibited the performance of oratorios there, the choir moved to **St. James's Hall**. Besides Costa, other conductors of the Society included Joseph Sterman (1832–48) and **Sir Charles Hallé** (1883–85). *See also* LESLIE, HENRY DAVID; PUBLIC CONCERTS.

SADLER'S WELLS. Sadler's Wells started as a **pleasure garden** in 1684 in the London suburb of Clerkenwell. A music house was one of the major attractions there, and it was turned into a theater in 1784. A series of theaters on the site since that time have hosted drama, **opera** (frequently in English translation), and ballet. A major renovation to the fifth theater in 1931 culminated the organization of a company by Lilian Baylis to present drama at the Old Vic and opera and ballet at Sadler's Wells. One of the ballet companies founded for this organization became the Royal Ballet upon moving to **Covent Garden**; the opera company moved to the Coliseum in 1968 and was renamed the English National Opera in 1974. The sixth and current theater was opened in 1998. A notable premiere at Sadler's Wells was **Benjamin Britten**'s *Peter Grimes* (1945). The pleasure gardens at the site closed in 1879. *See also* FORCER, FRANCIS; LAMBERT, CONSTANT; PUBLIC CONCERTS; SEARLE, HUMPHREY.

ST. CECILIA'S DAY OBSERVANCE. In London, 22 November, the canonical feast day of St. Cecilia, patroness of music, was the occasion for celebrative "Musick Feasts," documented as an annual occurrence between 1683 and 1703 under the auspices of the Musical Society. The observance included a festival **service** at St. Bride's Church, including major service settings, such as **Henry Purcell**'s *Te Deum* and *Jubilate Deo* (1694), a new **anthem**, and a sermon on music. After the service, a concert presentation of a

Cecilian **ode** was given, followed by a banquet. The odes, including Nicholas Brady's "Hail, Bright Cecilia," set by Purcell in 1692, and **John Dryden**'s "Song for St. Cecilia's Day," set by **Giovanni Battista Draghi** in 1687 and memorably by **George Frideric Handel** in 1739, often focus on the affective powers of music and particular instruments, rather than on Cecilia herself, and are thus in the nature of **"hymns** to music" with reference to Cecilia, rather than hagiographic commemorations.

Inspired by **Sir Henry Wood,** a modern annual observance was revived in London in 1945 under the sponsorship of the Musicians' Benevolent Fund, with the service taking place at St. Sepulchre's, London, and drawing on the choirs of the **Chapel Royal**, Westminster Abbey, St. Paul's Cathedral, and St. George's Chapel, Windsor. The service has now relocated to an alternating venue of either St. Paul's, Westminster Abbey, or Westminster Cathedral, with the music provided by the choirs of those three institutions.

ST. JAMES'S HALL. London concert hall in use between 1858 and 1905. It seated about 2,000 people and included an **organ.** As the most central of London's mid-19th-century halls, it was used by numerous important groups for concerts, including **John Ella**'s **Musical Union** (1858–80), **Henry Leslie's Choir** (1858–87), the **Royal Philharmonic Society** (1869–94), **Novello's Oratorio Concerts** (starting in 1869), and concerts directed by **Hans Richter** (frequently called the "Richter Concerts"; starting in 1879). The hall, sponsored by the publishers Cramer, Beale & Chappell, also held its own series of Monday and Saturday Popular Concerts (given at various times between 1858 and 1904). Besides music concerts, the hall was also used for public meetings. *See also* SACRED HARMONIC SOCIETY; *VARIATIONS ON AN ORIGINAL THEME* ("ENIGMA"), OP. 36.

ST. MARTIN'S HALL. Concert hall (with 3,000 seats and an **organ**) and lecture room (with 500 seats) built for **John Hullah**, mainly for classes and concerts to promote his sight-singing notation. He began teaching singing classes to schoolteachers there in 1849; the concert hall was officially open in 1850 and hosted choral, instrumental, and organ concerts. St. Martin's Hall burned to the ground in a fire in 1860, was rebuilt solely as a concert hall in 1862, and then was rebuilt again as the 4,000-seat Queen's Theatre in 1867, which housed concerts, plays, and the occasional scientific demonstration until it closed in 1878.

ST. MICHAEL'S COLLEGE. School organized in 1854 at Tenbury Wells and dedicated in 1856 by **Sir Frederic Arthur Gore Ouseley** for the promotion of Anglican sacred music. St. Michael's included a chapel with a daily choral **service**, a school for 30 boys, and a library containing a collection of musical and theological tracts from all eras. The institution existed until 1985.

SALOMON, JOHANN PETER (1745–1815). German violinist, impresario, and composer of German birth active in London. Salomon is most famous for a series of subscription concerts begun in London in 1783 that brought **Franz Joseph Haydn** to the city twice (1790–91 and 1794–95) and spurred the composition of the *London* **Symphonies**, several string quartets, and *The Creation*. Salomon came from a musical family in Bonn, began working for the court there in 1758 as a violinist, and toured various courts in Germany. Once established in England in 1781, he made the country his home for the remainder of his life and became a major figure within various musical establishments. He was famous for his quartet playing and was one of the founders of the **Royal Philharmonic Society**, leading the ensemble at its first performance in 1813.

SALVATION ARMY. English evangelical philanthropic organization founded by William Booth in 1865 as the East London Christian Mission to minister to the urban poor and destitute and named the Salvation Army in 1878. Choral and brass band music quickly became integral to the organization, the former often being printed in the **Tonic Sol-fa** sight-singing notation. Bands and choirs freely adopted contemporary popular tunes for their Salvationist music and **hymns**, and Salvation Army musicians began composing some as well, which provided a revenue stream for the organization. Booth published several tune books, including *The Christian Mission Hymn Book* (1868), *Salvation Music* (1880), and *The Musical Salvationist* (1886); the last is still in print as *Sing to the Lord*.

SARGENT, SIR MALCOLM WATTS (ALSO HAROLD MALCOLM WATTS SARGENT; 1895–1967). Conductor. With **Sir Adrian Boult** and **Sir Thomas Beecham**, Sargent was one of the most important conductors of his era, known especially for his interpretations of English music. During his childhood at Stamford, he was encouraged by his father—whose avocation was church organist—to study **organ** and piano and sing in local choirs. He earned his associateship of the **Royal College of Organists** (ARCO) in 1911 and was articled to Haydn Keeton, organist at Peterborough Cathedral in that year. Sargent became parish organist at Melton Mobray in 1914. For the balance of the decade, he earned a BMus (1914) and a DMus (1919) from Durham University, while working as a conductor of amateur ensembles and a composer, frequently performing his own music.

Recognition came in 1921, when Sargent conducted **Sir Henry Wood**'s **Queen's Hall Orchestra**; shortly after this, he settled in London and focused almost solely on conducting. He taught conducting at the **Royal College of Music** from 1923 and conducted many of England's best-known ensembles, including the **Hallé Orchestra** (1939–42), the Liverpool Philharmonic Orchestra (1943–49), the **Proms** (1948–67), and the **British Broadcasting Corporation** Symphony Orchestra (1950–57), among others. Sargent was particularly known for his conducting of mass choral ensembles, and he directed the **Royal Choral Society** for 25 years, beginning in 1928. He conducted the premieres of **oratorios** and **operas** by **Gustav Holst, Ralph Vaughan Williams,** and **Sir William Walton** and was frequently in demand as a guest conductor throughout the world. Sargent was knighted in 1947. *See also THE SCENES FROM THE SONG OF HIAWATHA.*

SARUM USE. The liturgical practice, texts, and music for Salisbury Cathedral. The installation of the Norman aristocrat Osmund as bishop of Salisbury in 1078 ushered in a time of innovation at Salisbury that would eventually, if not proximally, extend to liturgy and chant, and in this create an adaptation of the Roman Rite reflecting Norman influence and constituting one of several local practices within the Church of Rome. Though beginning as a local practice, the Sarum Use became widespread in southern England and was legislated for the whole southern province in 1542.

SAVOY THEATRE. Theater built in 1881 by Richard D'Oyly Carte to house productions of operettas by **Sir William Schwenck Gilbert** and **Sir Arthur Sullivan**. The Savoy was host for many years of the **D'Oyly Carte Opera Company**. It seats about 1,300 and was the first theater in England to be lit entirely by electricity. It has undergone extensive renovations twice, in 1929 and 1993 (the latter after a fire).

THE SCENES FROM THE SONG OF HIAWATHA. **Cantata** trilogy by **Samuel Coleridge-Taylor**, based on the poems of Henry Wadsworth Longfellow. The first part, *Hiawatha's Wedding Feast*, was premiered at the **Royal College of Music** on 11 November 1898; the second, *The Death of Minnehaha*, was first heard on 26 October 1899 at the North Staffordshire **Musical Festival**; and the final cantata, *Hiawatha's Departure*, was first heard at the **Royal Albert Hall** on 22 March 1900, along with the first two parts of the trilogy. The whole work sets Longfellow's stories of the marriage of Hiawatha and Minnehaha, a famine, Minnehaha's death and funeral, the arrival of Europeans, and the departure of Hiawatha. Coleridge-Taylor uses reoccurring motives to link the three works together into a contiguous whole, and a performance of all three lasts about two hours. *Hiawatha's Wedding Feast* was particularly loved and was performed yearly at the **Royal Albert Hall**, with **Sir Malcom Sargent**

conducting, between 1924 and 1939. These performances included nearly a thousand costumed characters and were one of the last unabashed, naïve flowerings of exoticism in England before World War II.

SCHOLES, PERCY (1877–1958). Writer, critic, and teacher. Scholes was one of the most prolific writers on a wide range of English musical subjects of the first half of the 20th century. His major works include the first edition of the *Oxford Companion to Music* (1938), *The Mirror of Music: A Century of Musical Life in Britain as Reflected in the Pages of the* Musical Times, *1844–1944, The Concise Oxford Dictionary of Music* (1952), as well as monographs on **Charles Burney**, **Sir John Hawkins**, the **Puritans**, and many other subjects. He was largely self-taught, though he did later take an associate diploma from the **Royal College of Music** and a BMus from Oxford. He worked first as a teacher, and then as an editor (*Music Student*, 1908–21 [now *Music Teacher*], which he founded) and a music critic for the *Evening Standard* (1913–20), the *Observer* (1920–27), and the *Radio Times* (1923–29). He lived in Switzerland from 1928 to 1940, where he took a *doctorat ès letters* from Lausanne University in 1934 and began to work on several major dictionary and encyclopedia projects. He returned to England between 1940 and 1957, where he continued writing and was named to the Board of the Faculty of Music of Oxford University. He returned to Switzerland for the last two years of his life. Scholes was named to the OBE in 1957.

SCHOOL OF ENGLISH CHURCH MUSIC. *See* ROYAL SCHOOL OF CHURCH MUSIC.

SCHROETER, JOHANN SAMUEL (ALSO SCHRÖTER; ca. 1754–88). German keyboardist and composer active in England from 1767 until his death. Schroeter was raised in a musical family and had early training with Johann Adam Hiller in Leipzig. In London he was the organist of the German Chapel and became the music master to Queen Charlotte in 1782. He was also a musician to the Prince of Wales (later George IV). His wife, Rebecca, studied with **Franz Joseph Haydn** after Schroeter's death. Schroeter was known as a piano teacher and publisher of keyboard works.

SCOTT, CYRIL (1879–1970). Composer, writer, and poet. Scott was a member of the **Frankfurt Group** and as a composer inspired by the Decadent poets and artists (including Maurice Materlinck, Stephane George, and Aubrey Beardsley) as well as impressionism. He studied at the Frankfurt Hoch Konservatarium between 1892 and 1893 (with Engelbert Humperdinck) and from 1895 to 1898 (with Iwan Knorr) as a pianist and a composer. In the first three decades of the 20th century, his career flowered in both Great Britain and Europe, with frequent performances of large-scale works, including symphonies, a piano concerto, **cantatas** such as *Let Us Now Praise Famous Men* (Norwich **Musical Festival**, 1936) and *La Belle Dame sans Merci* (Leeds Musical Festival, 1937), and a one-act **opera**, but his popularity declined after World War II.

Scott continued composing after this point but also focused increasing energies on other pursuits, including poetry. For a time until a recording revival of his music in the first decade of the 21st century, much of his known output was songs and chamber music. Among Scott's literary output are several volumes of poems, unpublished plays, books on homeopathy, and two volumes of memoirs: *My Years of Indiscretion* (1924) and *Bone of Contention* (1969).

A SEA SYMPHONY. The first symphony of **Ralph Vaughan Williams**, premiered at the Leeds **Musical Festival** on 6 September 1910. The four-movement composition is a hybrid form, mixing elements of a dramatic **cantata** (a chorus and two soloists) and symphony, making it perfect for performance at the many early 20th-century English musical festivals. The texts are drawn from Walt Whitman's *Leaves of Grass* (the author being a particular favorite of Vaughan Williams's) and, unlike the typical cantata of the time, celebrate the technology of traveling the sea, combining it with a late-Romantic search for the infinite.

SEARLE, HUMPHREY (1915–82). Composer and writer on music. Searle studied at Winchester (1928–33) and Oxford (1933–37) before studying with Gordon Jacob and **John Ireland** for a year at the **Royal College of Music** (RCM) and then at the New Vienna Conservatory (1937–38), and privately with Anton Webern. He worked for the **British Broadcasting Corporation** (BBC) from 1938 to 1940 and again from 1946 yo 1948, at **Sadler's Wells** from 1951 to 1957, and as a professor of composition at the RCM from 1965 until his death. In his work at the BBC, his writing, and his own composition, he promoted serialism. Aside from books on 20th-century counterpoint, he wrote the seminal *Music of Franz Liszt* (1954; second edition 1966) and a translation of Hector Berlioz's letters. He was named CBE in 1968 and an FRCM in 1969.

SEIBER, MÁTYÁS (1905–60). Composer and teacher born in Hungary. Seiber was one of the first major figures in England to promote jazz and its analysis. He studied cello and composition at the Budapest Academy of Music (1919–24) before teaching at the Frankfurt Hoch Conservatory (1928–33) and working as the cellist of the Lenzewski Quartet. Seiber settled in England in 1935, composing music for film and writing and lecturing on jazz. He taught composition at Morley College from 1942 to 1957 and helped found the **Society for the Promotion of New Music** and the Dorian Singers. His musical works include a mixture of film scores, pop songs such as the semifamous "By the Fountains of Rome" (1965), folk song arrangements, and various orchestra, choral, and chamber pieces.

SEMI-OPERA. Sometimes referred to as **dramatick opera**, semi-opera is a uniquely English form of musical drama that combines a spoken play (often in adapted form) with **masque**-like musical entertainments that could be both lavish and extensive but were rarely integral to the drama itself. In fact, by convention, the principal characters of the drama never sang; rather the music fell to secondary characters and those for whom the singing might be rationalized, such as magicians, enchanters, etc. Semi-opera emerged in the 1670s in adaptations of **William Shakespeare**, such as the 1674 performance of *The Tempest* (a version by **Sir William Davenant** and **John Dryden**, likely adapted by Thomas Shadwell) including music by **Matthew Locke**, **Pelham Humfrey**, and **John Banister**, and in Shadwell's *Psyche* (1675), also with music by Locke. The genre came into its fullest blossom in the 1690s in the stage works of **Henry Purcell**, such as *Dioclesian* (1690), *King Arthur* (1691), and *The Fairy Queen* (1692). Other late 17th-century composers such as **John Eccles** made strong contributions to the genre as well, as in his setting of John Dennis's *Rinaldo and Armida* (1698).

Semi-opera may well have gratified a lingering taste for the Caroline masque, a taste that after the Commonwealth years presumably would prove safer in the public theater than at court. But in particular, its hybrid nature was held to be resonant with the national taste, a view emphasized by Peter Motteux in the *Gentleman's Journal* (1692): "[E]xperience hath taught us that our English genius will not relish that perpetual Singing [of fully sung opera]. . . . [O]ur *English* Gentlemen, when their Ear is satisfy'd, are desirous to have their mind pleas'd, and Music and Dancing industriously intermix'd with Comedy and Tragedy."

SENESINO (ALSO FRANCESCO BERNARDI; ?–d. by 1759). Castrato. The Italian castrato Senesino, so-called because of his birth in Siena, was brought to London in 1720 by **George Frideric Handel**, where he was a star figure on the stage in **operas** by Handel and **Giovanni Bononcini**, among others. A company member of the **Royal Academy of Music (1)** from 1720 to 1728 and in its second iteration from 1730 to 1733, Senesino's relationship with Handel was long-standing but also characteristically difficult. Unsurprisingly, Senesino was one of the key figures in the establishment of the so-called **"Opera of the Nobility,"** a rival company to Handel's. Abbé

Prévost, in *Le Pour et Contre* (October 1733) oberves, "You already know how there was an irreconcilable rupture between Senesino and Handel, and how the former produced a schism in the company and hired a separate theatre for himself and his partisans." Johann Joachim Quantz's description of his singing is often quoted:

> He had a powerful, clear, equal and sweet contralto voice, with a perfect intonation and an excellent shake. His manner of singing was masterly and his elocution unrivalled. Though he never loaded adagios with too many ornaments, yet he delivered the original and essential notes with the utmost refinement. He sang allegros with great fire, and marked rapid divisions, from the chest, in an articulate and pleasing manner.

His musical abilities were perhaps not matched by his acting skills, however, if the remarks of the aristocratic impresario Francesco Zambeccari are to be believed, for he likened him to a statue on stage, prone to make gestures opposite of the ones desired.

SERVICE. In the Anglican Church, choral settings of **canticles** and (often) **preces and responses** from Matins and **Evensong** or the Communion rite. Services might be elaborate—**William Byrd**'s *Great Service* is a notable example—or more modest in its demands, as seen, for instance, in **Thomas Tallis**'s *Short Service*. Oftentimes services are named by their key or modality—the Tallis *Short Service* is also the *Dorian Service*—but many make reference to places, such as **Herbert Howells**'s for King's College, Cambridge; St. John's College, Cambridge; Gloucester Cathedral; and Winchester Cathedral, among others. *See also* ALCOCK, JOHN; AMNER, JOHN; ANGLICAN CHANT; ANTHEM; BARNARD, JOHN; BARNBY, SIR JOSEPH; BATTEN, ADRIAN; BEVIN, ELWAY; BLOW, JOHN; BREWER, SIR HERBERT; COOKE, BENJAMIN; GREENE, MAURICE; JACKSON, WILLIAM (1); LUMLEY PARTBOOKS; MORLEY, THOMAS; *MUSICA BRITANNICA*; ORGAN; OUSELEY, SIR FREDERIC ARTHUR GORE; ROGERS, BENJAMIN; SMART, HENRY THOMAS; STAINER, SIR JOHN; *TE DEUM*; VOLUNTARY; WANLEY PARTBOOKS; WESLEY, SAMUEL SEBASTIAN.

SHAKESPEARE, WILLIAM (1564–1616). Shakespeare's dramas require music in varying degrees, some of which falls under the heading of "stage music," i.e., instrumental music to accompany various actions (processions, battle fanfares, etc.), while other instances draw on both popular **ballads** and "composed" song in ways that powerfully affect the drama itself. Rooted in the notion that music has the power to be a dynamic force, namely, to affect change, Shakespeare's use of music gives it an active agency in the lives of his characters. The magic songs of Ariel in *The Tempest* I/ii furnish a familiar example: Ferdinand is drawn by Ariel's "Come Unto These Yellow Sands," a song that both calms the sea and beckons him forth: "This music crept by me upon the waters, / Allaying both their fury and my passion / With its sweet air; thence I have follow'd it, / Or it hath drawn me rather." Elsewhere the agency of music is revivifying, as for instance, in the curing of the mad king in *King Lear* IV/vii. Lear's daughter Cordelia tellingly describes her father's condition as one of "untun'd and jarring senses," and the musical dissonance of her imagery is echoed in the Doctor's bidding "Louder the music there" as Cordelia seeks to "repair those violent harms" with a filial kiss.

Recent study (Duffin, 2004) has underscored the frequency with which the play texts allude to popular song, a rich and polyvalent intertextuality achieved through the quotation of lines and song titles and even the naming of characters. As Duffin notes, "Shakespeare's choice to insert, quote, or cite these songs in his plays reveals both the emotions and thoughts of his characters and something of his own state of mind as he wrote the plays."

Shakespeare's use of music in his texts, dramatic or otherwise, also shows an understanding of music's cosmological associations, as in the famous "How sweet the moonlight sleeps upon this bank" from *The Merchant of Venice* V/i. Here the Platonic "Harmony of the Spheres" is lyrically referenced in Lorenzo's instruction to Jessica:

> Look how the floor of heaven
> Is thick inlaid with patines of bright gold:
> There's not the smallest orb which thou behold'st
> But in his motion like an angel sings,
> Still quiring to the young-eyed cherubins;
> Such harmony is in immortal souls . . .

And the idea present here, that the cosmic harmony finds a microcosmic echo in the harmony of the soul, is what allows Cordelia to speak of her father's madness, referenced above, as "untun'd." To the early modern world, the notion of the soul as possessing harmony or dissonance was less metaphorical than an embrace of the broad, metaphysical understanding of music. Shakespeare, however, is no stranger to the metaphorical use of music; in Sonnet 8, musical concord is, for instance, likened to a familial consortial relationship. In the "true concord of well-tuned sounds,"

> Mark how one string, sweet husband to another,
> Strikes each in each by mutual ordering.
> Resembling sire and child and happy mother,
> Who all in one, one pleasing note do sing . . .

Musical reengagements of Shakespeare have been frequent, and began as early as the **semi-opera** productions of *The Tempest* (1674) and *Macbeth* (1694) in the late 17th century. The modern canon includes tone-poem evocations, such as **Sir Edward Elgar**'s *Falstaff* (1913) and Pytor Il'yich Tchaikovsky's *Romeo and Juliet* (1869); composed settings of Shakespearian texts, such as **Ralph Vaughan Williams**'s *Serenade to Music* (1938); a setting of "How sweet the moonlight sleeps upon this bank" from *The Merchant of Venice*; and a number of Shakespearian operas, of which Verdi's *Macbeth* (1847), *Otello* (1887) and *Falstaff* (1893) are particularly prominent. *See also* ARNE, THOMAS AUGUSTINE; BALLAD; CHOIRBOY PLAYS; FORESTER SONG; GERMAN, SIR EDWARD; "GREENSLEEVES"; JOHNSON, ROBERT.

SHARP, CECIL (1859–1924). Teacher, folklorist, and collector. Sharp remains one of the most influential and most divisive figures in the folk music revival of the first half of the 20th century. Sharp's work as a collector was colored by the prejudices of his time, but as a promoter of the importance and possibility of folk music and dance, he was tireless. His education at Uppingham School and Clare College, Cambridge (1879–82), included a great deal of amateur music-making and training in piano and voice. He took part of the BMus exam while at Cambridge but graduated with a BA in mathematics. Sharp spent a decade in Australia (1882–92), where he played the **organ** at Adelaide Cathedral and was a partner in a local music school. He also composed two light **operas** and various choral works for the cathedral while there.

Sharp returned to England in 1892 and worked first as a music master in the Ludgrove Preparatory School (1892–96) and then as the principal of the Hampstead Conservatory (1896–1905). From 1905 until his death, his income came almost exclusively from writing and lecturing about folk music and folk dance. To this end he worked at times with **Mary Neal**, though the two had disagreements about both the method and the reasons for folk music and dance collecting. Thereafter he collaborated with **Maud Karpeles**. His major publications of collections began in 1904 (*Folk Music from Somerset* [1904–9]) and continued with a systematic study of folk music (*English Folk Songs: Some Conclusions* [1907]) and books promoting the study of folk music and dance in elementary and secondary schools (1912 and 1917). He also helped to found the English Folk Dance Society (1911), which became the **English Folk Dance and Song Society**. His visits to the United States during World War I with Karpeles led to interest in collecting American folk music by local institutions. On Sharp's death in 1924, Karpeles became his literary executor.

SHAW, GEORGE BERNARD (1856–1900). Music critic, writer, and dramatist of Irish origin. While Shaw is more known for his plays and drama criticism, he is the most famous English-language music critic of the 19th century. His work is easily reread even today, as it is witty and erudite and always accessible, no matter what level of musical comprehension the reader has attained. Shaw began writing music criticism for the *Hornet* shortly after his arrival in London in 1876 as an anonymous "ghost" (deputizing for Vandeleur Lee). From 1888 to 1890 he wrote criticism under the pseudonym Cornetto di Bassetto for the *Star* before becoming the music critic of the *World* from 1890 to 1894. While he ended regular musical criticism at this point, he continued to write occasionally on musical topics, including *The Perfect Wagnerite* (1898; a political interpretation of the *Ring* cycle), as well as articles on **Sir George Grove** and **Sir Edward Elgar**, among others.

Shaw was a great friend to Elgar and convinced the **British Broadcasting Corporation** to commission the Third Symphony (left unfinished at the composer's death). Shaw's particular musical interests included the **operas** of Wolfgang Amadeus Mozart, Richard Wagner, and Giuseppe Verdi; he detested much of the work of Johannes Brahms, **Felix Mendelssohn**, and most **oratorios** by English composers. Collections of his music criticism are still in print.

SHEPPARD, JOHN (ca. 1515–58). Composer. One of the defining figures of the mid-16th-century liturgical style, Sheppard composed works that range from several mass settings and a significant body of music for the Latin Office to English **services** and **anthems**. Of the five masses, the "Cantate" mass, "a commanding monument to his genius" (Wulstan, 1985), is the most prominent. Based on an unidentified cantus firmus, some of its florid figuration is suggestive of ornamental improvisation (*Blwl*, vol. 2). His **"Western Wind"** mass is based on the same secular tune set in the masses of **Christopher Tye** and **John Taverner**. The richest of his works are his sonorous settings of responds, antiphons, and **hymns** for the Office.

The first documentation of Sheppard's musical activity places him as *informator choristarum* at Magdalen College, Oxford, from 1543 to 1548. He was appointed a gentleman of the **Chapel Royal** by 1552.

SHIELD, WILLIAM (1748/49–1829). Composer, writer, violist, and song collector. Shield was born in County Durham (there is no clear baptismal record of his birth). He had early lessons with his father, a music teacher, and studied with **Charles Avison** at Newcastle. He played violin in local concerts in Newcastle and worked as a bandleader in Scarborough and Durham before moving to London in 1772. In London he played violin and then viola at the King's Theatre, **Haymarket** (1772–91), and was house composer at **Covent Garden** from 1784 to 1797. From 1797 to 1817 he held no permanent position but was regarded as an important composer and violist. He composed music for more than 36 **operas**, afterpieces, and other dramatic works. With the famous antiquarian Joseph Ritson, Shield published collections of English songs (1793) and Scottish songs (1794); other folk songs were included in his 1800 *Introduction to Harmony* and *Rudiments of Thoroughbass*. Shield was a member of the **Society of Musicians** (1777), was a founding member of the **Royal Philharmonic Society** (1813), and was **Master of the King's Music** from 1817 until his death.

SHORE. Prominent musical family in Restoration London:

Matthias (d. 1700)—Trumpeter
William (d. 1700)—Trumpeter
John (ca. 1662–1752)—Trumpeter and lutanist
Catherine (1669–1734)—Singer-actress

The Shore family collectively led the court trumpet establishment for over six decades: Matthias became serjeant-trumpeter in 1687, followed by his son William in 1700, who was followed by his brother John in 1707, who held the post until his death. John was reputedly also the inventor of the tuning fork. **Sir John Hawkins** gives a significant description of John's playing, noting that he "had extended the power of that noble instrument [the trumpet] . . . beyond the reach of imagination, for he produced from it a tone as sweet as that of a hautboy," confirming that the trumpet was not only martial, but also an instrument of refinement. Hawkins also suggests that John suffered a disabling lip injury from playing.

One particularly famous reference to the family surfaces in the text to **Henry Purcell**'s "Come, Ye Sons of Art" (1694): the aria, "Sound the Trumpet"—significantly sung without trumpets—contains the line "You make the listening shores rebound," a compelling pun in that with no trumpet part here, the Shores in the orchestra for the **ode** (likely Matthias and William) would have had no other choice but to be "listening."

Matthias's daughter, Catherine, described by Hawkins as a student of Purcell, was a singer-actress on the London stage and the wife of the famous actor and theater manager Colley Cibber, whom she married in 1693.

SILAS, EDOUARD (1827–1909). Organist, pianist, teacher, and composer of Dutch origin. After training on piano and composition, including time spent at the Paris Conservatoire, Silas settled in England in 1850. He held various positions, including organist of a Roman Catholic chapel in Kingston and teacher of harmony at both the **Guildhall School of Music** and the

London Academy of Music. His compositions included symphonies, a mass, **cantatas**, and an **oratorio**, *Joash*, premiered at the Norwich **Musical Festival** in 1863. *See also* ORGAN.

SIMPSON, CHRISTOPHER (1602/6–69). Violist, composer, and writer. Simpson's compositions and his career as a violist exemplify the cultivation of virtuosic, florid division playing that rose to the fore during the interregnum. Enjoying the patronage of Sir Robert Bolles, Simpson wrote the *Division-Violist* (1659; revised as *Chelys/The Division Viol*, 1665) for the instruction of Sir Roberts's son, John. This highly regarded didactic work combined instruction in playing the **viol**, descant, and divisions upon a ground. In 1665 Simpson also published his theoretical treatise, *The Principles of Practical Musick* (later revised as *A Compendium of Practical Musick*, 1667), praised by the likes of **Henry Purcell** as "the most Ingenious Book I e're met with upon this Subject." Although by the late 18th century Simpson's style and, indeed, his instrument had passed out of fashion, **Charles Burney** still praised him as "a musician extremely celebrated for his skill in the practice of his art, and abilities on his particular instrument." His compositions, unsurprisingly, include a large number of division pieces, but also virtuosic **fantasia-suites**.

SMART, SIR GEORGE THOMAS (1776–1867). Conductor, impresario, organist, singing teacher, and composer brother of **Henry Smart** and uncle of **Henry Thomas Smart**. Smart was one of the major conductors of the first half of the 19th century and a well-regarded teacher of singing; his interpretations of **George Frideric Handel**'s arias were particularly sought after. His journals and annotated programs (held at the **British Library**) are a rich source of information about contemporary music, gleaned from both his own experience as a conductor and his travels to the Continent. He conducted—from the keyboard—many of the major **musical festivals** held in England between 1820 and 1840, including those at Bath, Cambridge, Derby, Hull, Liverpool, London (such as the 1834 Handel Festival at Westminster Abbey), Manchester, and Norwich. In addition, he was a founding member of the **Royal Philharmonic Society**, conducting 49 concerts between 1813 and 1849; one of the founders of the **Bach Society** (1854); the first chairman of the **Royal College of Organists** (1864); and conductor of the Lenten **Oratorios** at **Drury Lane** (1813–25) and the City Amateur Concerts (1818–22).

Smart was trained at the **Chapel Royal** (1783–93), where he was later appointed organist (1822) and composer (1838). Early in his career, he worked variously as a keyboardist, a teacher of singing, an **opera** singer, and an impresario, as well as a conductor. He was knighted in 1811 by the Lord Lieutenant of Ireland in appreciation for a series of concerts given in Dublin in that year.

SMART, HENRY (1778–1823). Violinist and violist; brother of **Sir George Thomas Smart** and father of **Henry Thomas Smart**. Smart studied violin with Wilhelm Cramer and joined the orchestras at **Covent Garden**, the **Academy of Ancient Music**, and the **Concerts of Ancient Music** in 1792. He led the orchestra at the **Lyceum Theatre** (1809–12) and at **Drury Lane** (1812–21), including performances of the Lenten **Oratorios** under the baton of his brother. He also played regularly for the **Royal Philharmonic Society**. In 1821 he founded a piano factory on Berners Street in London.

SMART, HENRY THOMAS (1813–79). Organist, **organ** designer, composer, and music critic; son of **Henry Smart** and nephew of **Sir George Thomas Smart**. Smart was known during his time as an opponent of plainsong, a great extemporizer, and an expert on all aspects of organ building. He was educated at Highgate School, and turned down careers in engineering, the military, and law before turning to music. He was mostly self-taught on the organ. He held organist positions at the Parish Church at Blackurn, Lancashire (1831–36); St. Philips, Regent Street (1836–44); St. Luke's, Old Street (1844–64); and St. Pancras New Church, Woburn Place (1864–79). This last church remained an evangelical "low church" without a choir until his death; he led a group of 40 boys to support the unison singing. He was a music critic for the *Atlas* from 1836. He was cofounder of the **Vocal Association** (1855) with **Sir Julius Benedict** and of the **Bach Society** (1854).

During his life Smart was a well-regarded composer of dramatic vocal works, **anthems**, **services**, and **partsongs**. His **opera** *Bertha* was performed at **Haymarket** in 1855, and **oratorio** *Jacob* at Glasgow in 1873. Smart's **cantata** *The Bride of Dunkerron* premiered at the Birmingham **Musical Festival** in 1864 and remained a popular staple of choral societies until World War I. Organs that he designed were placed in the Town Hall of Leeds and St. Adrian's Hall and the City Hall in Glasgow.

SMETHERGELL, WILLIAM (ca. 1751–ca. 1836). Organist, violist, teacher, and composer active principally in London. Smethergell was principal violist at the **Vauxhall pleasure gardens** and had symphonies performed there; he was organist at All Hallows, Barking-by-the-Tower (1770–1823), and St. Mary-at-Hill (1775–1826). Aside from symphonies, he composed numerous keyboard works and concertos.

SMITH, "FATHER" BERNARD (ca. 1630–1708). Organ builder. An émigré organ builder, Smith relocated to England in the early years of the Restoration, placing him (along with his competitor, **Renatus Harris**) as a central figure in rebuilding the English organ culture, dismantled by **Puritan**

rule. Smith is associated with instruments at the Sheldonian Theatre, Oxford; Christ Church, Oxford; Durham Cathedral; and St. Margaret's, Westminster (where he became the organist, as well), but he is most famously associated with the Temple Church. There, he and Harris entered into unusually overt competition—each built an instrument to be judged in situ—with Smith eventually getting the nod. He held a royal appointment as organ maker from 1671 until the year of his death.

SMITH, JOHN CHRISTOPHER (THE ELDER; 1683–1762/63), AND SMITH, JOHN CHRISTOPHER (THE YOUNGER; 1712–95). The former was **George Frideric Handel**'s amanuensis and treasurer and the latter his assistant, composer, and organist. Smith, the elder, was a German friend of Handel's from student years in Halle who came to London in 1716 under Handel's wing and became his chief copyist and treasurer. Smith, the younger, was a pupil of Handel, **Thomas Roseingrave**, and **Johann Christoph Pepusch** who composed both Italian **opera** and Handelian-styled **oratorio**, as well as functioning as an assistant to Handel, playing a significant role in bringing works to performance during the years of the composer's blindness. The younger Smith was also organist of the **Foundling Hospital** from 1754 to 1770, a venue importantly associated with benefit performances of *Messiah*.

SMITH, JOHN STAFFORD (1780–1836). Composer, organist, and early musicologist. Smith is best known today as an antiquarian and collector of 2,191 volumes of music, including such items as the **Old Hall Manuscript**. He published the first antiquary edition of English music, *A Collection of English Song* in 1779, and a series of English and continental transcriptions entitled *Musical Antiquaries* in 1812. He also put his considerable collection of manuscripts at the disposal of **Sir John Hawkins** when the latter worked on his history of music.

Smith was the son of a Gloucester Cathedral organist, sent to London to study with **William Boyce**. He became a chorister of the **Chapel Royal** in 1761, was made a gentleman there in 1784, and was its organist from 1802 until his death and master of the children from 1805 to 1817. He was also named a Lay Vicar of Westminster Abbey in 1785. During his life, Smith was known as a composer of **glees**, including "The Anacreontic Song," written for the London **Anacreontic Society** and now used as the tune of Francis Scott Key's "Star Spangled Banner."

SMITH, THEODORE (ALSO THEODOR SCHMIDT; ca. 1740–ca. 1810). Composer and keyboard player of German birth. Smith was likely born in Hanover and was performing in London by 1766. He played concerts at **Hickford's Room** and composed for the **pleasure gardens** and theaters of

London. Smith's output includes keyboard works, symphonies, and songs—especially for his wife, the singer Maria Harris. When Harris left Smith for a "Mr. Bishop," Smith was devastated and took employment at a school for poor girls in Chiswick. He was also the organist at Ebury Chapel, London, by ca. 1795.

SMYTH, DAME ETHEL (1858–1944). Composer, writer, and conductor. Smyth was one of the most important and powerful voices promoting the cause of women as composers and orchestral performers in the late 19th and early 20th centuries, and one of the original voices of the second generation of the **English Musical Renaissance**. Smyth was born into a middle-class family and began playing piano and singing early, as a matter of course. She attended the Leipzig Conservatory (1877–78) but left after a year, staying in the city to study privately with Heinrich von Herzogenberg. Smyth remained in Europe for over a decade and, through von Herzogenberg's circle, met Brahms, Clara Schumann, and other composers. Her compositions in the 1880s focused on chamber music and had many public and private performances.

By 1890 Smyth returned to London and began working on orchestral and large-scale vocal works, including the Mass in D (1893) and the **operas** *Fantasio* (Weimar, 1898), *Der Wald* (Berlin, 1902), *The Wreckers* (Leipzig, 1906), and *The Boatswain's Mate* (London, 1916). As the cities of premieres in the above list indicates, Smyth frequently found it easier to have her works performed on the Continent than in London; *The Wreckers*, perhaps her most important opera, was not heard in the city until 1909.

In the 1910s Smyth turned briefly to Suffrage work, writing **"The March of the Women"** (1911), one of the two main anthems of the movement (the other was Teresa del Reigo's **"The Awakening"** [1911]). During World War I, she worked as a radiologist in France and discovered her hearing was deteriorating. Following the war, she resumed composing both instrumental works and opera, including *Entente Cordiale* (London, 1925), and started conducting revivals of earlier works and broadcasting. She also began writing a series of memoirs of her life, including *Impressions That Remained* (1919), *Streaks of Life* (1921), *A Final Burning of Boats, Etc.* (1928), *Female Pipings in Eden* (1934), *As Time Went On . . .* (1936), and *What Happened Next* (1940). Smyth was named DBE in 1922 and received an honorary doctorate from Oxford University in 1926.

SNOW, VALENTINE (ca. 1700–1770). Trumpeter. Snow, the successor to **John Shore** as serjeant-trumpeter in 1753, is best known as the trumpeter for whom **George Frideric Handel** wrote a number of his most notable trumpet parts, including those in *Messiah*, *Atalanta*, and *Samson*, inter alia. **Charles Burney**'s reference to Snow's part in the overture to *Atalanta* is particularly interesting for its comment on the persistent tuning difficulties of certain harmonics on the natural trumpet: "the trumpet part, intended to display the tone and abilities of Snow . . . had fewer notes that are naturally and inevitably imperfect in the instrument, than common." Burney also offers strong praise for Snow's playing at **Vauxhall Gardens**: "Valentine Snow, afterwards serjeant trumpet, was justly a favourite here [at Vauxhall Gardens], where his silver sounds in the open air, by having room to expand, never arrived at the ears of the audience in a manner too powerful or piercing."

SOCIETY FOR THE PROMOTION OF NEW MUSIC (SPNM). Organization founded in 1943 to promote the music of younger British composers, now called Sound and Music after merging in 2008 with the British Music Information Centre, the Contemporary Music Network, and the Sonic Arts Network. Activities included promoting new music on the **British Broadcasting Corporation** as well as seminars to expose younger composers to acknowledged masters. Past presidents include **Benjamin Britten**, **Dame Elizabeth Maconchy**, and **Ralph Vaughan Williams**. *See also* SEIBER, MÁTYÁS.

SOCIETY OF BRITISH MUSICIANS. Organization extant between 1834 and 1865 devoted to promoting British music. Membership in the society was confined to indigenous British musicians, and the organization received little notice in the press. Its concert series presented premieres of more than 70 chamber works.

SOCIETY OF FEMALE MUSICIANS. *See* ROYAL SOCIETY OF FEMALE MUSICIANS.

SOCIETY OF MUSICIANS. *See* ROYAL SOCIETY OF MUSICIANS.

SOCIETY OF PROFESSIONAL FEMALE MUSICIANS. *See* ROYAL SOCIETY OF FEMALE MUSICIANS.

SOCIETY OF WOMEN MUSICIANS. Cooperative organization for women in music founded in 1911. The society created a library and founded a choir, a lecture series, and a concert series. Most of the important female musicians of the middle of the 20th century, including **Rebecca Clarke**, **Imogen Holst**, **Liza Lehmann**, **Dame Elizabeth Maconchy**, and **Dame Ethel Smyth** were members; it also allowed men to participate as associate members. The society disbanded in 1972.

SOMERVELL, SIR ARTHUR (1863–1937). Composer and music educator. Somervell held great influence during the first three decades of the 20th century as a teacher at the **Royal College of Music** (RCM; appointed 1894) and as an inspector of music for the Board of Education (appointed 1901; chief inspector, 1920; retired 1928). As a composer, he was well known for his choral works, including the **cantatas** *Helen of Kirkconnel* (Bristol, 1894) and the *Forsaken Merman* (Leeds, 1898), the **oratorio** the *Passion of Christ* (1914), as well as his song cycles, such as that on Tennyson's *Maud* (1898).

Somervell was educated at the Uppingham School and King's College, Cambridge (where he studied with **Sir Charles Villiers Stanford**); he completed his musical studies at the Berlin Hochschule für Musik (1883–85) and the RCM (1885–87, where he studied with **Sir Hubert Parry**). He was long associated with the competition **musical festivals**, especially the Kendall Festival. Somervell was knighted (KB) in 1929.

SPEM IN ALIUM. Motet in 40 parts by **Thomas Tallis**. Few works of Renaissance polyphony can rival Thomas Tallis's *Spem in alium* in either grandeur or scale. Scored for 40 independent voices configured in eight different choirs, the motet is a compositional tour de force that combines masterful architectural control with rare sumptuousness of sound. In the main, the motet proceeds through its vast landscape as an imitative chain linking the various choirs, one by one, and then back again. To this basic framework, Tallis also adds ten-voice antiphonal dialogue and a few instances of full tutti, sometimes with active counterpoint, but never more memorably than with homophonic acclamations on the word *respice* ("consider").

An early 17th-century anecdote in the Commonplace Book of Thomas Wateridge suggests that the motet was written at the behest of an English nobleman (presumably Thomas Howard, the Duke of Norfolk) in response to the performance of an Italian work in "30 parts." The anecdote further states that Tallis's work was sung in the "long gallery at Arundel House," the home of the Earl of Arundel, Norfolk's father-in-law. Significantly, the earl also owned Nonsuch Palace, whose library at one time held a now-lost copy of "A songe of fortie partes, made by Mr. Tallys," confirmed in a catalogue of 1596.

Davitt Moroney (2007) proposes that the Earl of Arundel was a likely person to have sponsored the unnamed Italian work, and proposes that the recently rediscovered *Missa sopra Ecco si beato giorno* by Alessandro Striggio, a mass in 40 and 60 parts, was a likely work to have instigated Tallis's response in the form of this extravagant motet. Earlier scholarship had cast Striggio's 40-voice motet, *Ecce beatam lucem*, in this role.

SQUARE. Mensural, monophonic melody derived from the bottom voice of preexistent polyphony for cantus-firmus use in liturgical composition and improvisation, especially in the context of the Lady Mass. Three masses "upon the square" by William Whytbroke and **William Mundy** appear in the **Gyffard Partbooks**. These masses are cantus-firmus works, and some of their scaffold melodies also appear in a separate monophonic source likely compiled to be an anthology of squares (Bent, *NG*, 2001). Additionally, **Nicholas Ludford**'s Lady Masses are *alternatim* works employing squares. Wulstan (1985) suggests that, as the monophonic *alternatim* sections—the squares—are not underlaid, they were to be used as cantus firmus for **organ** improvisation.

STAGGINS, NICHOLAS (?–1700). Violinist, wind player, and composer. Staggins began his career at court in the royal violin band in 1670, quickly also claiming an appointment as a wind player. In 1674 he become Master of His Majesty's Violins, to be followed shortly by appointment as **Master of the King's Music** in the same year, succeeding **Louis Grabu**, an appointment he held until his death in 1700 when he was succeeded by **John Eccles**.

Modern assessment of Staggins's compositions tends to be unenthusiastic, and Holman (1993) suggests this lack of enthusiasm may have extended to the contemporaneous view as well, noting the scant survival of his works. Staggins is best known as the composer for the court **masque** *Calisto* (1674/75), a work performed on a grand scale with as many as 51 instrumentalists taking part both in front of the stage and behind the scene. His theatrical interests were furthered, no doubt, in travels on the Continent in the mid-1670s following *Calisto*.

STAINER, SIR JOHN (1840–1901). Composer, musicologist, and organist. Stainer was one of the most important pedagogical figures of the **English Musical Renaissance**; the reforms he introduced in his various professional positions—as organist at St. Paul's Cathedral, regarding rehearsals, attendance, and salary (1872–88); as His Majesty's Inspector of Music in Elementary Schools, advocating movable doh and **Tonic Sol-fa** over fixed doh (1883–88); and as professor of music at Oxford University, publishing lecture schedules and assigning teaching duties based on specialization (1889–99)—all helped to reorganize and strengthen these institutions. His formal academic work, including editing a volume of Christmas **carols** (1871), a monograph on Guillaume Dufay (1898), and an edition entitled *Early Bodlean Music* (1901), as well as papers presented before the **Royal Musical Association**, was matched by his pedagogical primers on the **organ** (1877) and harmony (1878) and a dictionary of musical terms (1876).

Stainer's long association with St. Paul's Cathedral began when he was named a probationer (1848), then a chorister (1849); he began deputizing there as an organist by 1856. Early in his career he held posts of organist at St. Benet, Paul's Wharf (1854); **St. Michael's College**, Tenbury Wells (1857); Magdalen College, Oxford (1860); and organist to Oxford University (1861). While at Oxford, he took many degrees (BMus, 1859; BA, 1864; DMus, 1865; and MA 1866), founded numerous societies, including the Oxford Orpheus Society (1865) and the Oxford Philharmonic Society (1866), and directed others. While organist at St. Paul's and before returning to Oxford, Stainer also taught organ at the National Training School for Music (a forerunner of the **Royal College of Music**; 1876) and was its principal (1881–83), and was one of the instigators of the **Royal Musical Association** (president, 1889–1901).

Stainer's compositions include **musical festival** works, such as the **oratorios** *The Daughter of Jarius* (Three Choirs—Worcester, 1878) and *St. Mary Magdalen* (Three Choirs—Gloucester, 1883), **hymns**, **services**, and **anthems**; but his most famous work, frequently performed in his lifetime, the organ-accompanied oratorio *The Crucifixion*, was completed for St. Marylebone Parish Church (1887). Stainer was knighted in 1888.

STANFORD, SIR CHARLES VILLIERS (1852–1924). Composer, teacher, and conductor of Irish birth. Along with **Sir Hubert Parry** and **Sir Alexander Campbell Mackenzie**, Stanford was part of the first generation of great composers of the **English Musical Renaissance**. He was an important force, both compositionally and pedagogically. Stanford composed within most of the genres available to him at the time, succeeding in all save **opera**, and his students (including **Sir Arthur Bliss**, **Frank Bridge**, **Samuel Coleridge-Taylor**, **Sir George Dyson**, **Ivor Gurney**, **Gustav Holst**, **Herbert Howells**, **John Ireland**, and **Ralph Vaughan Williams**, among others) carried his legacy far into the 20th century.

Stanford was born and raised in Dublin by a professional family; he was grounded in the classics and amateur music-making (including study of violin, piano, and **organ**). Stanford's early training also included meetings with Joseph Joachim in 1862, as well as trips to London in 1862, 1864, and 1868, where he studied with **Ernst Pauer** and attended concerts at the **Crystal Palace**. Stanford was named a choral scholar at Queen's College, Cambridge, in 1870 and began classical studies there in 1871; he took a BA in 1874 and an MA in 1878. In these years he became the assistant conductor (1871) and then conductor (1873–93) of the Cambridge University Musical Society and the organist of Trinity College (1874–92).

Stanford was granted leave for the last six months of the years 1874, 1875, and 1876 to study on the Continent with Carl Reinecke in Leipzig and Frederich Kiel in Berlin. From 1877 to 1887, when he was named professor of music at Cambridge, his reputation as a composer and conductor steadily grew, and he was appointed professor of composition and conductor of the orchestra at the newly formed **Royal College of Music** (RCM) in 1883; he ceased conducting the orchestra there only in 1921. The positions at the

RCM and Cambridge led to further important appointments, including that as director of the **Bach Choir** (1886–1902), the Leeds Philharmonic Society (1897–1909), and the Leeds **Musical Festival** (1901–10), as well as three commissions from the Birmingham Musical Festival for large-scale choral works, namely the **oratorios** *Three Holy Children* (1885) and *Eden* (1891) as well as the *Requiem* (1897). His symphonies and choral works were performed internationally. In his later years, Stanford's music fell out of favor, and he criticized modern techniques and trends in various editorial-style writings, but much of his liturgical choral music maintains a place within the Anglican tradition. Stanford was knighted in 1902.

STANLEY, JOHN (1712–86). Organist, violinist, and composer. Stanley was blinded at the age of two, "falling on the marble hearth with a china bason in his hand" (**Charles Burney**). Studying under **Maurice Greene**, he achieved acclaim as organist of St. Andrew's, Holborn. His apparently prodigious memory enabled a diverse music career that included directing **George Frideric Handel**'s **oratorios** at **Covent Garden** and elsewhere and, notably, performances of *Messiah* at the **Foundling Hospital** in 1775–77.

As a composer Stanley wrote concerti grossi in the tradition of Arcangelo Corelli (1742), although later in his life his approach to the concerto moved to the ritornello style, as in op. 10 (1775). He was also a prolific composer of English **cantatas** and a few **oratorios**. However, he is best known for his **voluntaries, organ** works that helped to solidify a two-movement form in which the first movement for principal stop is slow, featuring some imitation and often suspensions; the second movement, a fast movement, features a solo stop (trumpet or cornet) and echoing phrases.

Toward the end of his life (1779), he received appointment as Master of the King's Band, reflecting his status as an "extraordinary musician" (Burney).

STORACE, STEPHEN (1762–96). Composer. Storace's career in England was short but included numerous innovations in **opera** borrowed from continental sources, such as action finales in *The Pirates* (1792) and *The Cherokee* (1794). Born in England to an Italian father, Storace studied harpsichord and violin before studying at the San Onofrio Conservatory in Naples. He performed in Florence with his sister, the singer Nancy Storace (the first Susanna in Wolfgang Amadeus Mozart's *Le Nozze di Figaro*, and Vienna's prima donna between 1783 and 1787) in 1774. Though nominally based in England in the early 1780s, he composed two Viennese comic operas, *Gli sposi malcontenti* (1785) and *Gli equivoci* (1786). When he and his sister settled permanently in London in 1787, he composed for King's Theatre, **Haymarket**, until 1789, when the theater burned down, and again during 1792–93 and 1793–94 with the singer Michael Kelly, and at **Drury Lane** for **Thomas Linley (the elder)**. His compositions remained popular for several decades after his death.

SULLIVAN, SIR ARTHUR SEYMOUR (1842–1900). Composer and conductor. Sullivan was the most famous composer in Great Britain during his own lifetime. While many of his non-operetta compositions were highly praised and successful, he was best known internationally because of his operetta collaborations with **Sir William Schwenk Gilbert**. Born into a musical family (his father was a bandmaster at Sandhurst and later a clarinet teacher at the Royal Military School of Music), Sullivan early learned elements of orchestration. He was admitted late as a singer to the **Chapel Royal** (1854–57) and won the **Mendelssohn Scholarship**, funding initially a year of study at the **Royal Academy of Music (2;** 1856, where he worked with **Sir William Sterndale Bennett** and John Goss), and then time in Leipzig (1859–61; studying with **Ignaz Moscheles** and Julius Rietz).

Sullivan returned to London and spent the 1860s establishing a reputation within most of the grand genres, presenting works for **musical festivals**, such as the **cantata** *Kennilworth* (Birmingham, 1864) and the **oratorio** *The Prodigal Son* (Three Choirs—Worcester, 1869), a symphony (1866), a cello concerto (1866), as well as incidental music for numerous plays. During this time, he also composed a great deal of chamber music and religious music, including **anthems** and **hymn** tunes (including "Onward, Christian Soldiers" [1871]). Other contemporary famous work includes the song "The Lost Chord" (1877), popular in parlor concerts in the last decades of the century and frequently sung to Sullivan's accompaniment by his longtime mistress, Mary Frances ("Fanny") Ronalds. Sullivan also took on a typical variety of professional engagements, such as organist (1861–72), first at St. Michael's, Chester Square, and then St. Peter's, Cranley Gardens, and conductor of the Civil Service Music Society and the Glasgow Choral Union (1875–77). For a time he was also the principal of the **National Training School for Music** (1876–81).

Sullivan began to work in operetta in 1866 with *The Sapphire Necklace*, to a libretto by **Henry Frothergill Chorley**. His first collaboration with Gilbert, *Thespis*, came in 1871 (most of the music for this composition is lost). An additional collaboration, *Trial by Jury* (1875), led to a formal partnership between the two, brokered by Richard D'Oyly Carte and the formation of the **D'Oyly Carte Opera Company**; in all, 13 operettas came from this partnership, many of which are still in repertoire today, including *H.M.S. Pinafore* (1878), *The Pirates of Penzance* (1880), and *The Mikado* (1885). The partnership did not always run smoothly; Sullivan often felt that his music was being held back by Gilbert's words, and he felt considerable pressure to abandon popular operetta in order to pursue more "serious" genres.

In the 1880s until his death, Sullivan therefore established himself in other parts of the musical world, conducting the Leeds Musical Festival (1880–99); for this organization he composed both the oratorio *The Martyr of Antioch* (1880) and the cantata *The Golden Legend* (1886), and both received hundreds of performances by choral societies during his lifetime. He also conducted the **Royal Philharmonic Society** (1885–87) and composed his only grand **opera**, *Ivanhoe* (1891; libretto by Julius Sturgis after the novel by Sir Walter Scott). While little known today, it ran for 160 performances, in a theater specially built for it by D'Oyly Carte. In the decade after his death, the critical press savaged his reputation as a composer, but Sullivan's music remains popular to this day, with performances by both professional and amateur companies; many "G & S" societies, started in the 19th and 20th centuries, continue to thrive. Sullivan was knighted in 1883 and named to the RVO in 1897.

"SUMER IS ICUMEN IN." Known as the "Reading Rota" or the "Summer Canon," "Sumer is icumen in" is preserved in GB lbl Harl. 978, written around 1250. The canon, in modern reception one of the Middle Age's best-known works, is a four-voice construction (the rota) over a two-voice *pes*, which gives an interlocked (via *Stimmtausch*) ground pattern. Significantly, the use of the repeating ground pattern may also link the composition to the tenor-based motet, evolving at the same time. The manuscript records some alterations to the melody as well as a later stemming of the note characters, pointing to a continuing engagement of the work. The manuscript also includes a Latin Easter text, *Perspice, christicola*, as a contrafactum to the secular summer text. Some (Obst, 1983) have proposed that the contrafactum was the original text.

T

TALBOT, JAMES (1664–1708). Writer on music. Talbot was Regius Professor of Hebrew at Cambridge from 1699 to 1704, although his interests and energies extended to an important consideration of musical instruments, recorded in a manuscript at Christ Church, Oxford (GB Och Music Ms. 1187), a manuscript once owned by the music collector **Henry Aldrich**. Talbot seems to have had a close friendship with **Henry Purcell** as well, noting in his copy of Purcell's *Dioclesian* that it was a gift from Purcell's own library and that in death Purcell was "mourned by many but by nobody more than by his friend and admirer James Talbot" (trans. Unwin, 1987). Talbot also wrote commemorative poetry on the death of Purcell.

TALLIS, THOMAS (ca. 1505–85). Composer and organist. Tallis is not only one of the most prominent of 16th-century English composers, but owing to his longevity in royal service, he is an icon of the religious turbulence of the day. A memorial at Greenwich, no longer extant, observed:

> He serv'd long Time in Chappell with grete prayse,
> Fower Soverenes Reynes (a Thing not often seen)
> I mean Kyng Henry and Prynce Edward's Dayes,
> Queene Mary, and Elizabeth our Queene.

Tallis's works span the richness of pre-Reformation counterpoint, the Cranmerian constraints of an emerging Anglican devotional style, the floridity of the return of Romanism under Mary Tudor and Cardinal Pole, and the stylistic breadth of Elizabeth's reign. And while there is surely a degree to which his range represents a technical adaptability that is impressive indeed, it is also much the case that the range represents the pragmatic demands of the day.

Tallis held brief appointments at Dover Priory and the Parish Church of St. Mary-at-Hill, London, prior to his work at Waltham Abbey (1538–40). The dissolution of the monasteries under Thomas Cromwell led to the closing of the abbey. Tallis briefly resurfaced at Canterbury and by 1543–44 was a gentleman of the **Chapel Royal**, an appointment he held until his death some 40 years later.

Like his Chapel Royal colleague **William Byrd**, Tallis may well have been Roman Catholic, a supposition supported by his relationship with the recusant Anthony Roper. And in this light, motets like the penitential "In jejunio" may take on added personal resonance (" . . . et ne des hereditatem tuam in perditionem" [and give not thine inheritance to perdition]) in the same manner as Byrd's motets on themes of the desolation of Jerusalem ("Ne irascaris," for example).

The **votive antiphon** best captures Tallis's florid, "Roman" style and its links to the sonorous world of the **Eton Choirbook**. The early "Salve intemerata" and the impressively large-scale "Gaude gloriosa" are important examples, the latter perhaps from the resurgence of Romanism under Mary Tudor. This resurgence would provide the impetus for one of Tallis's most splendid works, the seven-voice *Missa Puer natus*, perhaps sung in 1544 by the combined chapels of Mary and her Spanish husband, Philip II. Tallis here brings not only an expansive sense of sonority but at the same time also a rigorous rational control of the writing; vowels of the unsung text to the cantus firmus, for instance, systematically unfold a scheme for the mensural durations of the melody.

Some of Tallis's English music clearly reflects the emerging Protestant idioms of the day. The **anthems** "Hear the Voice and Prayer" and the well-known "If Ye Love Me," both from the **Wanley Partbooks**, are simple and largely syllabic, with ample chordal homophony to secure the integrity of the text, and yet with a degree of undeveloped imitation to lend grace. Tallis also treated the **metrical psalm** with nine harmonized settings for Archbishop Matthew Parker's Psalter (1567). Two of these psalms have gained particular modern familiarity; "The Third Tune" ("Why Fumeth in Fight") is the basis of **Ralph Vaughan Williams**'s *Fantasia on a Theme by Thomas Tallis*, and "The Eighth Tune" ("God graunt with grace") presents in a more extended form the **hymn** melody known as the "Tallis Canon."

The Elizabethan via media in piety would give the Latin motet a renewed life in England, drawing on such factors as the monarch's taste for ceremony and the existence of a Latin prayer book (*Liber precum publicarum*, translated by Walter Haddon) for use at the universities. Byrd and Tallis's collaborative anthology, *Cantiones Sacrae* (1575), is an important example; significantly, its dedication to Elizabeth implies the royal approval of the genre. The anthology, the first publishing venture of Byrd and Tallis under their monopoly for the printing of music, presents 17 motets from each composer, perhaps a numerical salute to the 17th year of the monarch's reign. The Latin motet *Spem in alium*, also with an English contrafactum, "Sing and Glorify," is

Tallis's tour de force composition in 40 parts, written perhaps in response to Alessandro Striggio's *Missa sopra Ecco si beato giorno*.

Although overshadowed by his vocal church music, Tallis wrote both liturgical and nonliturgical keyboard pieces, the former cantus-firmus based, as well as a few consort *In nomines* and secular **partsongs**.

"TALLIS" FANTASIA. *See FANTASIA ON A THEME BY THOMAS TALLIS.*

TAVERNER, JOHN (ca. 1490–1545). Composer. Taverner emerges as one of the most significant composers of the reign of Henry VIII. Caldwell (*OHEM*, vol. 1) compellingly underscores his melodic gift and "superlative command of contrapuntal resources," as well as his combination of the distinctive traits of his contemporaries: "**[William] Cornysh**'s clarity of texture, **[Robert] Fayrfax**'s sensitivity to the text, [and] **[Nicholas] Ludford**'s grandeur of design." His compositions include several large-scale cantus-firmus masses, of which the *Missa Gloria tibi Trinitas* furnishes the model for the popular consort *In nomine*. Other masses include a variation setting on the secular song "Western Wynde" (also known as **"Western Wind"**). Unsurprisingly, **votive antiphons** also figure prominently in his output, reflecting the statutory requirement for three antiphons to be sung after Compline at Cardinal College (later Christ Church), Oxford, where Taverner was *informator choristarum* from the college's opening in 1526 until 1530. With the political demise and death of Cardinal Thomas Wolsey, the college's patron, Taverner moved to Boston (Lincolnshire), where he was associated with St. Boltolph's and the Guild of St. Mary until 1537.

Older accounts of Taverner's life have built a picture of a reform-minded zealot, repentant of having "made songs to popish ditties" (*Foxe's Book of Martyrs*, 1563), involved in the suppression of the monasteries, and a figure who had stopped composing by 1530. Modern scholarship (see for instance Bowers, *NG*, 2001) has found little to support these claims, however. In 1528 Taverner was implicated in a purge of illegal books at Oxford, but his prosecution was dismissed. Additionally, he was involved ten years later in the removal of the rood in the Boston parish church, but these instances fall short of the traditional depiction of the composer as religious fanatic. Peter Maxwell Davies' **opera**, *Taverner* (1962–68) gives modern voice to the traditional view.

TE DEUM. The *Te Deum*, whose origins are traditionally held to have been joyfully extemporized by St. Augustine and St. Ambrose at Augustine's baptism, was liturgically prescribed as a **hymn** of praise at the end of Sunday Matins, but it also emerged as a standard song of state celebration. See for instance **William Shakespeare**'s *Henry V*, IV/viii, commanding after the victory at Agincourt:

> Do we all holy rites;
> Let there be sung "Non nobis" and "Te Deum;"
> The dead with charity enclosed in clay:
> And then to Calais; and to England then:
> Where ne'er from France arrived more happy men.

It reappears as the vernacular "We Praise Thee, O God" as one of the morning **canticles** in the ***Book of Common Prayer***. As such, many composers of the 19th century and beyond set it in polyphonic versions, either quoting its melody, as heard in **Henry Smart**'s **Service** in F, or within its own context, such as **Sir Charles Villiers Stanford**'s Morning **Service** in C major, op. 115. A number of composers also used the *Te Deum* as the basis for large-scale **musical festival** works, including **Sir Arthur Sullivan** (1872), Stanford (1898), **Sir Hubert Parry** (1911), **Ralph Vaughan Williams** (1928), and **Sir William Walton**, whose 1953 version was heard at the **Coronation** of Elizabeth II.

THEORBO. A form of **lute** with an extended neck, accommodating longer stopped courses than found on the conventional lute, and a second peg-box for unstopped diatonic courses in the bass range. The stopped courses employ reentrant tuning. Originating in Italy, where it was nominally interchangeable with the *chitarrone*, it was introduced into England in the early 17th century, possibly by Inigo Jones or the composer Angelo Notari (Spencer, 1976), where it had a long usage in the continuo accompaniment of vocal music for much of the century. Both **Thomas Mace** and **John Wilson** offer solo music for the theorbo, as well, though solo repertory was always a secondary concern. In *Musick's Monument* (1676), Mace gives a compelling description of the instrument, though he unusually puts it forth as an echo of "the old English lute":

> *The Theorboe*, is no other, than *That* which we call'd *the Old English Lute*; and is an *Instrument* of so much *Excellency*, and *Worth, and of so Great Good Use*, That in dispite of all *Fickleness*, and *Novelty*, It is still made use of, in the *Best Performances in Musick, (Namely, Vocal Musick.)*
>
> But because, I said It was the *Old English Lute*, It may be ask'd, Why is It not then *still so Call'd; but by the Name of the Theorboe?*
>
> I Answer, That although *It be the Old English Lute*, yet as to the *Use of It Generally, there is This Difference*, viz. *The Old Lute was Chiefly us'd, as we now use our French Lutes, (So call'd') that is, only to Play Lone-Lessons upon, &c. But the Theorboe-Lute is Principally us'd in Playing to the Voice, or in Consort; It being a Lute of the Largest Scize; and we make It much more Large*

in Sound, by contriving unto *It a Long Head, to Augment and Increase that Sound, and Fulness of the Basses, or Diapasons, which are a great Ornament to the Voice, or Consort.*

THOMAS, ARTHUR GORING (1850–92). Composer. Until his suicide, Thomas was considered one of the best dramatic composers of his time. His choral **ode** *The Sun-Worshippers* (Norwich, 1881) was a staple on the English **musical festival** circuit, and his **opera** *Esmeralda* (1883), written for the **Carl Rosa Opera Company**, was extremely popular in England and abroad. Thomas's family wished a career in the civil service for him. He turned from this path to study music in Paris with Émile Duran (1873–75). Thomas later studied with **Sir Arthur Sullivan** and **Ebenezer Prout** at the **Royal Academy of Music (2;** 1877–80) and began to make his way as a dramatic composer. Thomas's period of creativity lasted from about 1878 to the completion of his opera *Nadeshda* in 1885; after this, composition was fitful. His last works were finished by others, including *The Golden Web*, an operetta (S. P. Waddington), and *The Swan and Skylark*, a **cantata** (**Sir Charles Villiers Stanford**).

THREE CHOIRS MUSICAL FESTIVAL. *See* MUSICAL FESTIVALS.

TIPPETT, SIR MICHAEL KEMP (1905–98). Composer and conductor. Tippett was a major compositional force in the 20th century, one of the first British composers to use popular musics postmodernly as a method of instilling political commentary within the art music tradition. Tippett was raised in a political family; his mother was imprisoned briefly as a suffragette. He learned piano as a child while attending Stamford Grammar School in Lincolnshire, and taught himself rudiments of composition. He attended the **Royal College of Music** (RCM) between 1923 and 1928 (failing his degree examinations in his first attempt), studying composition with **Charles Wood** and C. H. Kitson and conducting with **Sir Adrian Boult** and **Sir Malcolm Sargent**. Dissatisfied with his technique after presenting a concert of his own music in 1930, he returned to the RCM to study with R. O. Morris (1930–32).

Tippett settled initially in Oxted, Surrey (1928–50), where he led numerous amateur musical ensembles. Throughout the 1930s, Tippett became increasingly involved in workers' politics but decided by the end of the decade to subsume political action into his compositions. This is first seen in *A Child of Our Time* (1941), which described the murder of a German diplomat by a displaced Jewish refugee in the form of a **Passion**, using African American spirituals in the place of Johann Sebastian Bach–style chorales.

From 1940 to 1951 (except for a three-month period in jail due to his conscientious objection to World War II), he was the music director of Morley

College, London. After leaving his position at Morley College, Tippett broadcast musical commentary for the **British Broadcasting Corporation**, taught at numerous summer **musical festivals**, including Aspen in the United States of America (1965), and directed, for a time, the Bath Festival (1969–74). His compositions continued to touch on issues of alienation, such as *A Midsummer Marriage* (1946–52), and finding a place within a chaotic world, like *New Year* (1986–88), which used jazz, rap, and reggae as part of its musical materials. Like many composers of the 20th century, Tippett's musical style changed frequently. Tippett was named CBE in 1966 and OM in 1983.

TOMKINS, THOMAS (1572–1656). Composer and organist. It is likely that Tomkins was trained as a chorister at St. David's Cathedral, Pembrokeshire, Wales, where his father was organist; he also claimed to be a student of **William Byrd**. In 1596 he was appointed *instructor choristarum* at the cathedral in Worcester, a post that he held until the cessation of choral **services** there in 1646 with the capture of the city by Thomas Rainsborough and Parliamentary forces. Tomkins also held appointments in the **Chapel Royal**, as gentleman from 1620 and organist from 1621. In this capacity he made substantial contributions to the **coronation** of Charles I (1626), rendering his later "Sad Pavan for These Distracted Times" on the king's death all the more poignant. The lamentative tone that characterizes the "Sad Pavan" also marks several of his most powerful works, including the two **anthems** "When David Heard" and "Then David Mourned."

Tomkins was prolific in a variety of genres. His keyboard music, most of which is collected in an autograph manuscript (F Pbn 1122) and some of which appears in the **Fitzwilliam Virginal Book**, includes contrapuntal works, cantus-firmus compositions, and dances. In 1622 he published a collection of **madrigals**, *Songs of 3.4.5. and 6. Parts*, the dedications of which bear testament to his network of friends. His substantial body of English church music was published posthumously in 1668 as *Musica Deo Sacra*.

TONIC SOL-FA. Movable-doh notation system to teach sight-singing based on solfège, invented by **Sarah Glover** and modified and propagated by **John Curwen** and **John Spencer Curwen**. In a century when many such sight-singing systems existed in Great Britain, including those promoted by **John Hullah** and **Joseph Mainzer**, Tonic Sol-fa was supreme. The system represented solfège syllables with individual letters (e.g., doh=d, ray=r, me=m, etc.) and rhythm via spacing and punctuation markings; it was based on moveable doh (the tonic would always be doh, instead of the syllable doh always representing the pitch C). The height of the system's popularity was in the last half of the 19th century; for a time (from 1883 forward), it was even the recommended method to teach English schoolchildren musical notation. Many philanthropic organizations of the century used the notation, including the children's education, temperance, and women's suffrage movements. British and North American missionaries used the notation within numerous mission fields, especially Africa, India, and East Asia, and the **Salvation Army** used it well into the 20th century. John Curwen founded a journal (later edited by John Spencer Curwen), the *Tonic Sol-fa Reporter*, which ran in various incarnations, including the *Musical Herald* and the *Musical News and Herald*, from 1851 to 1928; a school, the **Tonic Sol-fa College**; and an organization, the **Tonic Sol-fa Association**, to propagate the notation.

TONIC SOL-FA ASSOCIATION. Organization founded in 1853 by **John Curwen** for the propagation of **Tonic Sol-fa**. The association organized demonstrations, classes, and concerts to forward the sight-singing method in venues including the **Crystal Palace** and **Exeter Hall**, and occasionally published method books and scores in the notation. *See also* MCNAUGHT, WILLIAM GRAY; *MESSIAH*; PUBLIC CONCERTS.

TONIC SOL-FA COLLEGE. London school, founded in 1878 by **John Curwen** to train educators to teach the **Tonic Sol-fa** sight-singing system.

TREBLE. Designation for a boy soprano in Anglican choirs. St. Paul's dictum *mulieres in ecclesiis taceant* (1 Corinthians 14:34) has spawned a long tradition of all-male church choirs that has been particularly resilient in Anglican cathedrals and not uncommon in Anglican collegiate chapels and some parish churches as well. The restriction to an all-male choir does not in itself require the use of boys, although they are pervasively documented as oblates in monasteries and choristers in secular cathedrals. Additionally, some repertories, such as the music of the **Eton Choirbook**, present an extended high register that musically would require them.

Controversially, the use of girl sopranos in alternation with boy trebles was first instituted at Salisbury Cathedral in 1991, a practice that has gained acceptance in a number of Anglican cathedrals, while at St. David's Cathedral, Wales, the cathedral choir soprano section is constituted by girls alone.

TRINITY COLLEGE OF MUSIC. London conservatory of music founded in 1872 as the Church Choral Society. It was renamed the College of Church Music, London, in 1873 and became Trinity College in 1876. At this time it also went from a focus on sacred choral music to general music. The institution was located in central London until 2001, when it moved to Greenwich. It awards BMus and MMus degrees. Notable faculty of Trinty include **Sir**

Frederick Bridge and **Samuel Coleridge-Taylor**. Prominent students of Trinity include **Sir Granville Bantock** and **Sir John Barbirolli**.

THE TRIUMPHS OF ORIANA. A **madrigal** anthology edited by **Thomas Morley**, published in 1601. Morley's anthology of 24 madrigals by a range of composers, including himself, **John Wilbye**, and **Thomas Weelkes**, is modeled on the Italian collection *Il Trionfo di Dori* (1592). The diverse madrigals are linked by the common refrain "Then sang the shepherds and nymphs of Diana, long live fair Oriana." Oriana was familiarly the wife of Amadis of Gaul in the famous eponymous Spanish romance, and traditionally she has been seen in the anthology as the allegorical representation of Elizabeth, the queen. Recent work by Jeremy Smith (2005) suggests, however, that Oriana is Anne of Denmark, wife of James VI of Scotland, and thus originally a reference to the attempt by Essex to replace Elizabeth with James, an unsuccessful attempt that resulted in Essex's execution. In this interpretation, Diana represents Essex's sister, Penelope Rich.

The madrigals, typical of the Elizabethan adaptation of Italian models, are light in tone and rich in text painting.

TUCKET. A trumpet fanfare. Emerging in dramatic contexts in the late 16th century, *tucket* refers to a fanfare or flourish played by trumpets. Earlier scholarship sought to derive the term from the Italian toccata, with works like the toccata to Monteverdi's *L'Orfeo* (1607) an inviting corollary. However, more recent study (Tarr and Downey, *NG*, 2001) traces the term to the late Middle Ages in the use of "tuck" to refer to flourishes played by trumpets or drums.

TUDWAY, THOMAS (ca. 1650–1726). Composer and organist. Following his training as a chorister in the **Chapel Royal** during the early years of the Restoration, Tudway went on to a long appointment as organist at King's College, Cambridge, from 1670 until his death, a tenure interrupted by a brief suspension for remarks critical of the queen (1706) but resumed after public apology.

In 1714 Tudway began to compile a six-volume manuscript anthology of English church music (GB Lbl Harl 7337–42) for Edward, Lord Harley. Completed in 1720, it is a valuable predecessor to **William Boyce**'s better-known collection. In the anthology, Tudway also offers an important account of the development of the Restoration symphony **anthem** and its relation to the musical tastes of the newly restored Charles II.

TURNER, WILLIAM (1651–1740). Countertenor and composer. Turner was trained as a chorister both at Christ Church, Oxford, and in the **Chapel**

Royal, where he was one of the first generation of trebles at the Restoration. His youthful talent is acknowledged in being one of the collaborators with fellow choristers **John Blow** and **Pelham Humfrey** in the composition of the so-called **Club Anthem**.

He was appointed master of the choristers at Lincoln in 1667 and shortly after (1669) began an extremely long tenure as gentleman of the Chapel Royal, holding the post for a staggering seven decades. His London activities also included solo singing and membership in the choirs of both St. Paul's and Westminster Abbey. In 1672 he also received appointment as a member of the King's **Private Musick**.

TYE, CHRISTOPHER (ca. 1505–73). Composer. Tye received the BMus at Cambridge in 1536, the year before he became lay clerk at King's College. In the early 1540s he took up duties at Ely Cathedral as *magister choristarum* and was associated with the **Chapel Royal** in the 1550s. He does not appear on the surviving rosters of the Chapel Royal, but he is identified as "one of the Gentylmen of hys [Edward VI's] graces most honourable Chappell" in the publication of his *Actes of the Apostles* (1553), as well as in a livery warrant from that year. He was ordained in 1560 and left Ely to take up the clerical living at Doddington-cum-Marche.

Tye's mass *Euge bone* is perhaps his most impressive work; another mass, like that of **John Taverner** and **John Sheppard**, is on the popular tune **"Western Wind,"** which he fashions into a variation scheme. His *Actes of the Apostles* is a four-voice setting of a metricized version of the scriptural book of Acts, which **Charles Burney** thought must surely have been "the delight of the Court in which he lived," but also "doubtless an absurd undertaking." Tye is also the composer of a number of **anthems** and *In nomines*.

In the 17th century, the antiquary **Anthony Wood** described him as "a peevish and humoursome man." In the 18th century, Burney noted that he "contributed greatly to the perfection of our Cathedral Music" and was "as great a musician as Europe could then boast"; **Sir John Hawkins** was equally laudatory, describing Tye as "a man of some literature" and noting that "there are very few compositions for the church of equal merit with his anthems."

VALENTINE, JOHN (1730–91). Composer, violinist, and music teacher. Valentine owned a music shop in Leicester, and in his time he was one of the most important performers and teachers in Leicestershire and taught many instruments besides the violin. Most of his compositions were written with amateur and student performance in mind, including his op. 6, *Eight Easy Symphonies* (1782). The Valentine family remained important music-makers in Leicester until the middle of the 19th century.

VAN DIEREN, BERNARD (1887–1936). Composer, music critic, and writer on music of Dutch origin. Van Dieren was part of a group of composer-critics, active in the 1920s, who saw their mission to be the reevaluation of music history in general and recent British music in particular. His musical circle included **Cecil Gray**, **Philip Heseltine**, and **Constant Lambert**; his wide-ranging intellectual curiosity, however, put him into contact with many other great and creative minds of his generation.

Van Dieren was largely self-taught musically but encouraged by Arnold Schoenberg and Ferruccio Busoni (he met both while in Berlin in 1911 and 1912 as a music correspondent). He settled in London in 1909. His major critical work, *Down among the Dead Men* (1935), called for—among other things—the reappraisal of the reputations of Charles-Valentin Alkan, Gaetano Donizetti, and Giacomo Meyerbeer. His music was much more praised by his critic-friends than performed, though a string quartet was heard in Frankfurt in 1927, and the **British Broadcasting Corporation** broadcast some of his works in the early 1930s.

VARIATIONS ON AN ORIGINAL THEME* ("ENIGMA"), OP. 36 (ALSO "ENIGMA" VARIATIONS).** Theme and variations for orchestra by **Sir Edward Elgar**, premiered at **St. James's Hall** on 19 June 1899. The "Enigma" Variations, along with his great **oratorio *The Dream of Gerontius, made Elgar famous internationally. The piece is programmatic in nature, with Elgar composing each one of the 13 variations in the voice of one of his friends. Particularly evocative are the movements "Nimrod," commemorating a discussion Elgar had with his friend August Jaeger about

Ludwig van Beethoven, and "Dorabella," which portrays the antics of Dora Penny (later Dora Powell), a particular friend of Elgar and his wife. The sobriquet "Enigma" was applied to the work because Elgar later mentioned that a secondary theme—not stated by the orchestra—interlocks with the primary theme; a great amount of scholarly ink has spilled in the ensuing century since the work's premiere to discern this theme, with little success. The composition uses traditional key relationships to distinguish between masculine and feminine variations; "Nimrod," for instance, is in a heroic E-flat major.

VAUGHAN WILLIAMS, RALPH (1872–1958). English composer, teacher, conductor, and writer. Vaughan Williams, with **Gustav Holst**, was the most important musical voice of his generation and brought the use of Elizabethan and folk music models for composition into great prominence. He composed in every genre available to him, including symphonies (nine), **operas** (five), **masques**, ballets, and even film music (11 scores completed, starting in 1940), and was particularly known by his contemporaries as a public music figure who could compose for any skill level from unskilled children to the most virtuosic professional, and proud to do so, so long as it would improve the musical life of Great Britain.

Coming from a genteel family (he was related to both the Wedgewoods and the Darwins), his early musical training included lessons on piano and violin from an aunt and study of the viola while attending Charterhouse School (1887–90). Additional training occurred at the **Royal College of Music** (RCM; 1890–92), at Trinity College, Cambridge (1892–95; BMus, 1894; BA, 1895), and at the RCM again (1895–96). At these institutions, Vaughan Williams studied with **Sir Hubert Parry**, **Sir Charles Villiers Stanford**, and **Charles Wood** and met Holst, forming an important musical friendship that would last to the end of the latter's life. He married Adeline Fisher in 1897.

Until 1910 Vaughan Williams interspersed employment in typical musical fields (organist, editor of the *English Hymnal* [1906 edition], folk song collector [starting in 1903], conductor, etc.) with private studies abroad, first with Max Bruch (1897) and later with Maurice Ravel (1908). Vaughan Williams found fame in the first decade of the 20th century through the publication of folk song transcriptions and then a series of **musical festival** premieres, including "Toward the Unknown Region" (Leeds, 1907), *A Sea Symphony* (Leeds, 1910), and the *Fantasia on a Theme by Thomas Tallis* (Three Choirs—Gloucester, 1910). During this time he also began a long association with the competition festival at Leith Hill in Dorking (1905–53); like his work with the **English Folk Dance and Song Society**, the efforts he spent with Leith Hill were aimed at all times toward introducing the public to good works of music. For this reason, he instituted massed concerts there at the end of the competitions. His frequent conducting of Johann Sebastian Bach's *St. Matthew Passion* between the wars became nationally famous. Vaughan Williams spent World War I in a variety of jobs, including ambulance driver, officer in the Royal Garrison Artillery, and after the armistice, music director of the First Army of the British expeditionary force (he demobilized in 1919).

After the war, Vaughan Williams's international compositional impact strengthened; while his operas were performed primarily in Great Britain—*Hugh the Drover* (1920), *Sir John in Love* (1928), *The Poisoned Kiss* (1929), and *Riders to the Sea* (1932)—his symphonies became well known both on the Continent and throughout North America. He began teaching composition at the RCM in 1919 and conducted the **Handel Society** (1919–21) and the **Bach Choir** (1921–28), prestigious positions that showed the continued regard musicians held for him. After the deaths of **Sir Edward Elgar** and Holst in 1934, Vaughan Williams became in essence the most important living British composer. His music—whether in premieres or revivals—was heard frequently at the remaining music festivals and presented in recordings and broadcasts on the **British Broadcasting Corporation**, and he was frequently sought out as a conductor or speaker both nationally and internationally.

During World War II, Vaughan Williams undertook a variety of tasks, including working for what would eventually become the Arts Council of Great Britain. From the end of the war forward, he remained extremely productive, completing four of his nine symphonies, his last opera, *The Pilgrim's Progress* (1951), numerous choral works, and lecturing on folk music at Cornell University (1954). In 1951 Adeline died; he married Ursula Wood, a poet and family friend, in 1953. She became his staunch companion in the last few years of his life and brilliant champion of his works and legacy after his death.

Aside from his teaching work at the RCM and involvement with competition festivals such as that at Leith Hill, Vaughan Williams was also an important writer on music, always advocating a place for the British composer and the importance of educating the audience through treating it intelligently; many of his important writings can be seen in the collection *National Music and Other Essays*, gathered posthumously (1963). Vaughan Williams turned down a knighthood but was named OM in 1935.

VAUXHALL GARDENS. London **pleasure garden** located at Lambeth. One of several pleasure gardens flourishing in the 18th century, Vauxhall Gardens came to the fore under the entrepreneurship of Jonathan Tyers (1732). **Sir John Hawkins** notes that the original house on the land belonged to Sir Samuel Moreland and that the garden had "a great number of stately trees, and [was] laid out in shady walks." The garden became "a place of musical entertainment for every evening during the summer season." The covered bandstand, the "orchestra," was equipped with an **organ**, making the performance of popular organ concertos possible, and later another music room was erected as well.

A number of composers were featured at the gardens, notably **Thomas Arne**, **William Boyce**, and **George Frideric Handel**. Tyers held the latter in particularly high esteem and commissioned the well-known statue of Handel by Louis-François Roubiliac, which was installed in a "conspicuous part of the garden" (Hawkins). A public rehearsal of Handel's *Royal Fireworks Musick* drew a staggering 12,000 people to the gardens.

VENUS AND ADONIS. Short **opera** or **masque** by **John Blow**. Styled a "masque" in a surviving score, but an "opera" in the libretto, Blow's *Venus and Adonis* is a short, fully sung dramatic work performed at court in the presence of Charles II, with his mistress **Mary "Moll" Davis** taking the part of Venus and their daughter, Lady Mary Tudor, the role of Cupid.

The performance date at court would have been sometime after December 1680 when the daughter Mary received her title (Baldwin and Wilson, *DNB*) but prior to April 1684 when the work was performed at "Mr. Josias Priest's Boarding School at Chelsey" (Luckett, 1989). The connection to Priest's boarding school also strengthens the similarity to **Henry Purcell**'s *Dido and Aeneas*; Purcell's work was performed at Priest's school, alludes to the Venus and Adonis narrative in its hunting scene, and shares the unusual status of being a fully sung English dramatic work. Additionally, given the similarities in the works, the performance history of *Venus and Adonis*—performances at court and at Chelsea—has invited speculation that *Dido* may also have had a court performance in addition to its lone documentable performance at Priest's school (Schmalfeldt, 2001).

VERSE ANTHEM. *See* ANTHEM.

VICAR-CHORAL. (L. *vicarius choralis*.) The common designation for adult, professional singers in cathedral choirs, lay or ordained, though generally not in holy orders, hence often "lay vicar." Usage, of course, varies from cathedral to cathedral; thus, for instance the vicars-choral at York are the "songmen," and in university settings the equivalent term would be "choral scholar."

VIOL. Family of fretted and bowed strings, generally built in treble, tenor, and bass ranges, and played held downward between the legs or, with smaller sizes, on the player's lap. Viols appear in England under the patronage of Henry VIII, with his inventory in 1547 listing 19 instruments in a variety of sizes. Interest in the instrument would swell in the latter part of the century and was characteristically widespread in the first half of the 17th century. The "chest of viols"—the family of instruments in different sizes—found rich deployment in England, including the accompaniment of **anthems** and songs and in fantasias, dance pieces, and cantus-firmus compositions, such as the *In nomine* and the *Browning*. Apart from the full consort of viols, single viols were used to play the bass line in the instrumentally mixed **English consort** and also played florid solos and polyphonic pieces. These latter two repertories are associated with smaller forms of the bass instrument, the "division viol" for the ornamental playing and the yet smaller "lyra viol" for chordal polyphonic playing. The divison viol is closely associated with **Christopher Simpson**, who published *The Division Violist* in 1659; the lyra viol is closely associated with the music of **Tobias Hume**.

In the last part of the 17th century, the aristocratic contrapuntal viol consort waned in the face of the Italian violin school and its practitioners, foreign advances that were nurtured by the Continental ties of the late Stuarts. With the triumph of the violin secure in the 18th century, the persistence of the solo viol in the career of **Carl Friedrich Abel** well into the second half of the century is striking. His 1787 obituary in the *Morning Post* confirmed both the contemporary rarity of the viol and that it "would probably die with him."

The English viol tradition was nurtured in part by skilled viol makers, of whom the family of John Rose is particularly notable. *See also* COPRARIO, JOHN; FERRABOSCO, ALFONSO, (THE YOUNGER); FINGER, GODFREY; FORD, THOMAS; HINGESTON, JOHN; HUME, TOBIAS; JENKINS, JOHN; LAWES, WILLIAM; LUPO, THOMAS.

VIOTTI, GIOVANNI BATTISTA (1755–1824). Italian virtuosic violinist, composer, and impresario active in London primarily between 1792 and 1798. His early training in Italy included studies with Antonio Celoniati and Gaetano Pugnani. A tour undertaken with Pugnani led Viotti to Paris, where he established himself as a performer at the *Concerts Spirtuels*, a performer in the retinue of Marie Antoinette, and the manager of the Théâtre de Monsieur (1788; from 1791, the Théâtre Feydeau). Fleeing the French Revolution in 1792, Viotti settled in London, where be performed in **Johann Peter Salomon**'s concerts, for **Franz Joseph Haydn**, and as acting manager of Italian **opera** (1794–95) and director of the orchestra (1797–98) at the King's Theatre, **Haymarket**. After an exile in Germany, Viotti returned to England and eschewed music, taking up a wine business for several years. He was one of the founding members of the London **Royal Philharmonic Society** (1813) but seldom played in its concerts. The failure of his wine business led to a brief period in Paris (1819–21) as the director of the Académie Royale de Musique (the Paris Opéra), but Viotti returned to London in late 1823, where he died.

VIRGINAL. A term that in England during the 16th and 17th centuries referred generically to all forms of plucked strung keyboard instruments and particularly to a small form that featured a rectangular shape and a single set of keys running laterally parallel to the keyboard. A clear depiction may be seen on the title page of ***Parthenia*** (1613), "the first musicke that ever was printed for the virginalls." As this image shows a young woman playing the instrument, it is suggestive of the probable connection between the gender of performers and the term itself, although this is difficult to clarify. Marcuse (1975) suggests the name may be derived from a confusion between the biblical "timbrel," played by women, and "cymbel," which in turn etymologically parents "cembalo."

The *Memoirs* of Sir James Melville preserve an account of his having heard Queen Elizabeth I play the virginals:

> [T]hat same day after dinner my lord of Hunsdon drew me up to a quiet gallery, that I might hear some music . . . where I might hear the Queen play upon the virginals. After I had hearkened a while, I took by the tapestry that hung before the door of the chamber, and seeing her back was towards the door, I entered within the chamber, and stood a pretty space hearing her play excellently well. But she left off immediately so soon as she turned her about and saw me. She appeared to be surprised to see me, and came forward, seeming to strike me with her hand; alleging she used not to play before men, but when she was solitary, to shun melancholy.

The emphasis on private music-making and its therapeutic use significantly underscores important contexts in which music was engaged by the nobility. *See also* BYRD, WILLIAM; COSYN, BENJAMIN; FARNABY, GILES; FITZWILLIAM VIRGINAL BOOK; TOMKINS, THOMAS.

VOCAL ASSOCIATION. Large London choir founded in 1855 by **Sir Julius Benedict** and **Henry Thomas Smart**. Until its dissolution around 1865, the association created a library of about 18,000 items and had a membership of 300. It presented concerts in the **Crystal Palace** and had audiences ranging from 6,000 to 18,000. Just before its dissolution, it was renamed "Mr. J. Benedict's Choral Society"; Smart ceased contact with the association sometime around 1857.

VOLUNTARY. An **organ** piece for Anglican church use, either composed or improvised. The term itself may refer either to an improvisatory cast to the music or to the fact that the music was a nonprescribed, i.e., "voluntary," part of the **service**. Usage has varied, but historically voluntaries have been common at the offices of Matins and **Evensong** just prior to the first lesson or at communion during the offertory. In modern practice, the term applies to the prelude and postlude that frame the service.

A "double voluntary" is one making use of two manuals; a "trumpet voluntary," popular in the late 17th and 18th centuries, is an organ work that features the solo trumpet stop, usually in alternation with echo repetitions, as seen, for instance, in the music of **John Stanley**.

VOTIVE ANTIPHON. A devotional text appended to the conclusion of the evening office, generally Compline, that is offered typically in praise of the Blessed Virgin Mary. Familiar from the Roman Rite are the seasonal Marian antiphons "Regina coeli," "Alma redemptoris mater," "Ave regina coelorum," and "Salve regina" (*see* ANTHEM), though the rich flourishing of this repertory in the early 16th century shows a range of other texts as well. The music of the **Eton Choirbook** is a substantial trove of votive antiphons, generally set in sections that alternate lavish full textures with florid soloistic ones. The several votive antiphons set by **Thomas Tallis**, of which the six-voice "Gaude gloriosa" is especially notable, mark the end of the tradition, one that ultimately fell to religious reform after Mary Tudor. *See also* TAVERNER, JOHN.

WAITS. An instrumental ensemble of civic musicians, descended from watchmen who sounded alarms with horns, and, as Wulstan (1985) has pointed out, an ensemble that bridged the social gap between music at court and music of the street. Typically composed of four or five versatile players along with apprentices, waits could range in activity from street patrols to concerts, weddings, civic ceremonies, and liturgy.

In the early stages of its transformation from a watch group to a musical ensemble, outdoor instruments held sway, most traditionally shawms and slide trumpet or trombone, corresponding to the continental *alta capella*. (From this association, the shawm was also known as a "wait pipe.") However, with increasing diversity in venue and function, the instrumentation also grew. Violins, for instance, appeared in the London Waits from 1619; earlier than that at Cambridge and Colchester. The Norwich Waits played with an **English Consort** instrumentation, as presumably did the London Waits, to whom **Thomas Morley**'s *English Consort Lessons* were dedicated. **Cornetts** and trombones were also common, with players like the cornettist **John Adson** in the London Waits an important example of the association. *See also* AVISON, CHARLES; BALLS, ALPHONSO AND RICHARD; WILSON, JOHN.

WAKEFIELD, MARY (ALSO AUGUSTA MARY; 1853–1910). Music philanthropist and singer; with **John Spencer Curwen**, one of the founders of the **musical festival** competition movement. Wakefield came from a well-off family, and after attending a finishing school in Brighton, where she learned some piano, she was able to study in London with **Alberto Randegger** and George Henschel; she also studied in Rome with Giovanni Sgambati. Contemporary accounts refer to her as an "amateur" vocalist, though she was skilled enough to sing as a soloist in the Three Choirs Festival at Gloucester in 1880 and was invited to sing at festivals in Leeds and Norwich.

Between 1880 and 1885, she organized numerous London charity concerts, where she often performed. Seeing the social good achieved through the choral work of **Henry Leslie**, Wakefield founded the Kendal Festival in 1885 (now called the "Mary Wakefield Westmorland Music Festival"), using

Spencer Curwen's competition festival at Stratford as a model. She directed the festival until 1900 and remained active in the competitive festival movement until her death. A great friend and admirer of John Ruskin, she compiled and edited the volume *Ruskin on Music* (1894).

WALKER, ERNEST (1870–1949). Musicologist, conductor, teacher, organist, and composer. For many years, Walker was synonymous with music in Oxford, and his writings on music remain an important point of departure for any discussion of the **English Musical Renaissance**. Walker was born in India to a mercantile family. When his family returned to London, he studied piano with Ernst Pauer. Walker attended Balliol College, Oxford, beginning in 1887, taking a BA (1891), BMus (1893), and DMus (1898). By 1891 he was also assistant organist (to John Farmer) at Balliol and was organist from 1901 to 1913. From 1901 to 1925 he was director of music there and organized a series of important concerts on Sunday evenings that featured many prominent artists and included premieres of chamber music. He resigned his post in 1925 to concentrate on composition but remained in Oxford until his death.

As a scholar, Walker edited the *Musical Gazette* (1899–1902), contributed articles to J. A. Fuller-Maitland's second edition of the *Grove Dictionary of Music and Musicians* (1902) and to the *Times* and the *Manchester Guardian*, and wrote monographs on Ludwig van Beethoven (1905) and the magisterial *A History of Music in England* (1907; rev. ed. 1924). Some of his writings were anthologized in *Free Thought and the Musicians* (1946).

WALSH, JOHN (THE ELDER; 1665/66–1736), AND WALSH, JOHN (THE YOUNGER; 1709–66). Music publishers. The elder John Walsh was appointed Instrument Maker-in-Ordinary to William III in 1692, an appointment to which his son succeeded in 1731 under George II, but it is chiefly as music publishers that they are both known. The Walsh company began publishing in 1695, and a change to pewter plates and the use of punches in 1700 allowed the printing process to be quicker and with greater quantity more easily accomplished. Significantly, the extent of the Walsh catalogue corresponds to a rise in the domestic market for printed music, a market in which the Walshes proved savvy businessmen.

The Walsh catalogue included both English and continental composers (Arcangelo Corelli and Antonio Vivaldi, for example), but it is as **George Frideric Handel**'s publisher that the firm is best known. The relationship with Handel began around 1730, corresponding largely to the younger Walsh's assuming leadership for the firm. From 1739 the firm held a 14-year monopoly on the printing of Handel's works.

WALTON, SIR WILLIAM TURNER (1902–83). English composer. Walton was one of the most striking musical voices during the interwar period; his popularity only fell because of the subsequent rise of that of **Benjamin Britten** and **Sir Michael Tippett** after World War II. Walton's early musical education came from his experiences as a choirboy at St. John's church in Werneth, where his father was choirmaster. His education continued at Oxford, where he was a choirboy at Christ Church Cathedral (1912–18) under the patronage of Thomas Strong and an undergraduate (1918–20; he failed to take a degree).

Patronage became a theme in Walton's life: in the 1920s he was given an annuity by the Sitwell family and lived for a time in their house in Chelsea. His work *Façade* (1922–29) stemmed from a trip to Italy in 1920 sponsored by the Sitwells, and the poetry set was that of Edith Sitwell. *Façade* was well received. But *Belshazzar's Feast*, commissioned by the **British Broadcasting Corporation** as a work for chorus and small orchestra and eventually premiered at the Leeds **Musical Festival** in 1931 as a work for soloist, choir, and full orchestra, made his early reputation. Osbert Sitwell compiled the libretto. In the 1930s Walton received the patronage of Sigfried Sassoon, Mrs. Samuel Courtauld, and Lady Alice Windbourne. He also began composing film scores. The 1937 commission for the *Crown Imperial March* for the **coronation** of George VI showed the official regard in which the establishment held Walton.

During World War II, Walton composed numerous patriotic film scores, of which the best known is that for Laurence Olivier's *Henry V* (1944). After the war, Walton attempted to recoup some of his interwar popularity with the **opera** *Troilus and Cressida* (1954), but the work was not received well by the critics. Walton married Susanna Gil Passo in 1948 and with a bequest from Lady Wimbourne was able to build an expansive villa on the Mediterranean island of Ischia. He continued to conduct his own works in Great Britain and abroad and work on additional scores until his death. Walton was knighted in 1951 and named OM in 1967.

WANLEY PARTBOOKS. An incomplete set of Edwardian partbooks (GB Ob Mus. Sch.E. 420–22) presenting **anthems** and **service** music, textually drawing on vernacular Primers that antedate the *Book of Common Prayer*. Two alto partbooks and a bass partbook survive; the tenor partbook is missing. In the manuscript, all of the works are unattributed, but concordances confirm that **John Sheppard**, **John Taverner**, and **Thomas Tallis** are represented, the latter, for instance, with his well-known anthem, "If Ye Love Me."

WARD, JOHN (ca. 1589–1638). Composer. Trained as a chorister at Canterbury, in maturity Ward enjoyed the patronage of the family of Sir Henry

Fanshawe. He was prolific as a composer of consort fantasias and *In nomines*, and he was distinctive in the Italianate seriousness that he brought to the more generally light Elizabethan **madrigal**. His madrigals unusually draw on serious literary texts—poems by Sidney and Drayton, for instance—although admittedly sometimes with a seeming disregard to original context. His only madrigal collection, *The First Set of English Madrigals*, was published in London in 1613. Modern criticism has noted his distinctions but also his shortcomings: "What he lacks is imagination, and especially coming from the work of his model **John Wilbye** one finds his music sententious and always a little uninteresting" (Kerman, 1962).

WARLOCK, PETER. *See* HESELTINE, PHILIP.

WEBBE, SAMUEL (1740–1816). Composer, organist, and singer. Widely known in his own time as a **glee** composer, Webbe also composed a great deal of Catholic liturgical music for the Sardinian (1775–95) and Portuguese (1776–96) chapels in London. An autodidact, Webbe was mostly self-taught, save for some lessons from Charles Barbandt, organist at the Bavarian Embassy Chapel. Sometime after these lessons commenced, Webbe converted to Catholicism. Beginning in 1766, he composed regularly for the **Noblemen and Gentlemen's Catch Club**, was elected a privileged member (1771), and was secretary of it as well (1784–1812). He sang at **Drury Lane**; the King's Theatre, **Haymarket**; and **Covent Garden**, and at the **pleasure gardens** of Marylebone and **Vauxhall**.

Webbe was the father of Samuel Webbe, the younger (1768–1843), a composer and organist active in London (like his father, at the embassy chapels for Catholic countries) and in Liverpool; the younger Samuel Webbe was also a director of the **Royal Philharmonic Society** for the 1815–16 and 1817–18 seasons.

WEELKES, THOMAS (1576–1623). Composer and organist. Weelkes held appointment as organist of Winchester College (1598) and of Chichester Cathedral (1602–17) and was dismissed from the latter post for drunkenness, a dismissal that seems not to have led to a reform of his behavior. His compositions include a large number of **anthems**, both verse and full, and a significant number of **madrigals**, the genre in which he was most prolific. Four volumes of madrigals appeared in print (1597, 1598, 1600, and 1608), and he was a contributor to the well-known *The Triumphs of Oriana* as well. His madrigal in that collection, the popular "As Vesta Was from Latmos Hill Descending," is an impressive display of counterpoint, exuberance, and pictorial text setting.

Though recent scholarly literature is not blind to his shortcomings, it has been quick to praise Weelkes at his best. Kerman (1962), for instance, in reference to the 1600 anthology, observes, "the style is still rough sometimes, more from impatience than incompetence, but Weelkes writes with a flair and vigorous enjoyment that is not approached by any of his contemporaries."

WELDON, JOHN (1676–1736). Composer and organist. Weldon was a chorister at Eton, where he studied with the organist John Walters and also with **Henry Purcell**. He was variously employed as organist at New College, Oxford; gentleman of the **Chapel Royal** (from 1701); organist and composer in the Chapel Royal (from 1708); organist of St. Bride's, Fleet Street (from 1702); and organist of St. Martin-in-the-Fields (from 1713/14). He rose to prominence as winner of the "Musick Prize" in 1700, a contest centered on setting William Congreve's *The Judgment of Paris* to determine the best of the English composers, echoing the theme of the story. It is also speculated that the setting of music for *The Tempest* once attributed to Purcell is likely by Weldon (Laurie, 1963/64). In certain of his songs he shows an awareness of the popularity of musical Italianism, as seen in his "When Perfect Beauty," a song identified as "in Imitation of Mr. **Nicola's [Matteis]** Manner."

WESLEY. Family of musicians and theologians in the 18th and 19th centuries:

John Wesley (1703–91)
Charles Wesley (1; 1707–88)
Charles Wesley (2; 1757–1834)
Samuel Wesley (1766–1837)
Samuel Sebastian Wesley (1810–76)

WESLEY, CHARLES (1; 1707–88). Clergyman, **hymn** composer, and brother of **John Wesley** and father of **Charles Wesley** (2) and **Samuel Wesley**. Wesley supported his brother, particularly through his hymn writing and itinerant preaching as a Methodist, but was buried as an Anglican. He was a prolific hymn writer; he composed thousands of hymns, some of which—including "Christ Is Risen Today" and "Hark! The Herald Angels Sing"—are in common use in multiple denominations of Christianity today. In order to promote the great talent of his two musical sons, he held a private subscription concert series at his home in Maryleborne from 1779 to 1787.

WESLEY, CHARLES (2; 1757–1834). Composer and keyboardist; son of **Charles Wesley** (1), brother of **Samuel Wesley**, and nephew of **John Wesley**. Wesley showed a prodigious early talent and was offered a place in the

Chapel Royal, which his father refused on account of not wishing his sons to become professional musicians. Instead, the younger Charles received training from an organist in Bristol until the family moved to London in 1771 so that Charles (2) and his brother Samuel could receive advanced training. While in London, the Wesleys gave private subscription concerts at their house between 1779 and 1787. These concerts were usually attended by from 30 to 50 people and included music written by the Wesleys, as well as that of **George Frideric Handel**, **Francesco Geminiani**, and Arcangelo Corelli. Charles (2) had lessons with Joseph Kelway and **William Boyce** and became a good organist; he held positions at Anglican chapels at Surrey, South Street, Walbeck, **Lock Hospital** (1797–1801), Chelsea Hospital, and Marylebone Parish Church. He wrote a typical complement of concertos, sonatas, **glees**, and even a Handelian **cantata**, *Caractacus* (1791). He composed few works after 1785, living by giving lessons and by his organist positions.

WESLEY, JOHN (1703–91). Clergyman and founder of Methodism; brother of **Charles Wesley** (1) and uncle to **Charles Wesley** (2) and **Samuel Wesley**. Wesley, like many religious figures of his time, believed music to have great power, and consequently he published numerous collections of **hymns** and tunes that were influential not just with the new Methodist church but for many of the 18th-century Dissenting churches, including the *Collection of Psalms and Hymns* (1737; translations of German and Moravian hymns Wesley heard while a missionary in Georgia, North America), *Foundery Tune Book* (1742), *Select Hymns with Tunes Annext* (1761), and the *Collection of Hymns for the Use of the People Called Methodists* (1780).

WESLEY, SAMUEL (1766–1837). Composer and keyboardist; son of **Charles Wesley** (1); brother of **Charles Wesley** (2); nephew of **John Wesley**; and father of **Samuel Sebastian Wesley**. Samuel Wesley's widely recognized talent as a musical prodigy was offset by a stormy personal life, partially caused by depression and partially by his own choices; he lived out of wedlock for several years before marrying Charlotte Louisa Martin and left her several years later for Sarah Suter, their housekeeper, whom he never wed but stayed with for the remainder of his life. Living outside typical cultural mores, as well as his public conversion to Catholicism in 1784, meant that solid professional positions eluded Samuel Wesley for much of his career. He therefore made his way teaching privately, lecturing (including at the Royal Institution), and writing journalism and criticism.

Like his brother Charles (2), he received early training in Bristol before moving to London in 1771. Both brothers played in a concert at **Hickford's Room** in 1777 and then for a series of subscription concerts in their own home, from 1779 to 1787. Around this time, Samuel began attending the various Catholic chapels in London and writing music for the Catholic liturgy. The few professional positions he did hold, such as assistant to **Vincent Novello** at the Portuguese Chapel (1811–24), organist at **Covent Garden** (1813–17), director of the **Royal Philharmonic Society** (1815), and Camden Chapel organist (1824–30), were offset by severe bouts of depression, keeping him from work for months, even years at a time. In spite of this, Samuel was a prolific composer of Catholic liturgical music, **anthems**, **odes**, **oratorios**, **glees**, and **organ** music, and was one of the major figures in the early revival movement of the music of Johann Sebastian Bach.

WESLEY, SAMUEL SEBASTIAN (1810–76). Composer and organist; son of **Samuel Wesley**. Wesley was the most important composer of Anglican music during the first half of the 19th century. The relative poverty of Samuel Sebastian Wesley's youth, due to his father's inability to work because of frequent bouts of depression, was somewhat alleviated when he was appointed a chorister at the **Chapel Royal** (1817–26), where he was trained by William Hawes, among others. When he left the chapel, he took on a number of positions at London churches, never staying for too long; this would become a pattern of Wesley's career. He also directed the chorus at the English Opera House (1828–32) and was organist at the Lenten **Oratorios** (1830–32). In 1832 Wesley left London to work in a number of important country churches, including Hereford Cathedral (1832–35), Exeter Cathedral (1835–42), Leeds Parish Church (1842–49), Winchester Cathedral (1849–65), and Gloucester Cathedral (1865–76). His frequent changes in position were caused at least in part by his acerbic personality and inability to convince church administrative authorities of his musical vision.

Accordingly, Wesley made attempts to gain a number of academic positions, first by taking a BMus and DMus from Oxford (1839); these applications came to nothing, aside from an appointment as professor of **organ** at the **Royal Academy of Music** (2; 1850). Throughout this time, Wesley was in much demand as a recitalist, and he conducted the Three Choirs **musical festivals** at Hereford (1834) and Gloucester (1865, 1868, 1871, and 1874) as part of his duties as organist. He also performed and conducted at the Birmingham Musical Festival (1843, 1849, and 1852). Wesley's output features a great deal of Anglican liturgical music, including the Morning and Evening **Service** in E (1845), **anthems** (some of the best of which were published as a set of 12 in 1853), and other works; he also composed many **glees**. Wesley was offered a knighthood in 1873 but decided instead to take a Civil List pension of £100 per annum.

"WESTERN WIND" (ALSO "WESTERN WYNDE"). A secular melody, likely popular, that forms the basis of three Tudor masses by **John Sheppard**, **Christopher Tye**, and **John Taverner**. The source melody is preserved in GB Lbl Royal App. 58 with the words:

> Western wind, when will thou blow?
> The small rain down can rain.
> Christ, if my love were in my arms
> And I in my bed again.

WHITE, MAUDE VALÉRIE (1855–1937). Composer particularly known for her song settings in numerous languages. She studied with **Sir George Alexander Macfarren** and Frank Davenport at the **Royal Academy of Music (2)** and won the **Mendelssohn Scholarship** in 1879. White also studied briefly with Robert Fuchs in Vienna (1883). She began a career in the early 1880s teaching piano and performing her own works. Her compositions quickly became popular and well regarded and were championed by some of the most important singers of her day, including Clara Butt, Nellie Melba, and Charles Santley. White began to split her time between London and Italy in 1901. Following World War I, her music was increasingly out of fashion, and she turned to translation and memoir writing (*Friends and Memories*, 1914; *My Indian Summer*, 1932).

WHYTE, ROBERT (ALSO ROBERT WHITE; ca. 1538–74). Composer. Trained as a chorister at Trinity College, Cambridge, Whyte held the post of master of the choristers at Ely (appointed 1562, succeeding his father-in-law, **Christopher Tye**), Chester (appointed 1567), and Westminster Abbey (appointed 1570). His output includes Latin motets, some English **anthems**, and consort pieces (*In nomines* and fantasias). That Latin works figure so prominently here underscores the persistence of that genre under Elizabeth I. *See also* GYFFARD PARTBOOKS.

WHYTHORNE, THOMAS (1528–96). Lutanist and composer. Whythorne held positions in service to a number of individuals, including John Heywood, the Duchess of Northumberland, and her son; in the 1570s he was also chapel master to the archbishop of Canterbury, Matthew Parker. His compositions include a collection of **partsongs** (1571) and a collection of duets (1590). However, his chief historical distinction lies in his authorship of his autobiography, a work that supplies interesting detail of Elizabethan life. *See also* LUTE.

WILBYE, JOHN (1574–1638). **Madrigal** composer. Wilbye enjoyed an unusually long patronal relationship with the Kytson family at Hengrave Hall near St. Edmundsbury, working under their sponsorship from the late 1590s until 1628. Wilbye's compositions focus on the madrigal, and he is among the most sensitive and accomplished of the English composers to engage that genre. The texts that he set reveal an appreciation for a more literary style than was common and also often for textual Italianism. However, it is in the strength of his expressive vocabulary that he proves most singular, as seen in madrigals like the poignantly sensitive "Draw On Sweet Night," a musical essay in melancholia. Wilbye's madrigals are found chiefly in two collections (1598 and 1609), the latter of which is seen as "the finest English madrigal collection" (Brown, *NG*, 2001); he also contributed the madrigal "The Lady Oriana" to the famous *The Triumphs of Oriana*.

WILSON, JOHN (1595–1674). Composer and lutanist. Known chiefly for his body of songs, Wilson wrote for the King's Men company during the reigns of both James I and Charles I. Following his appointment to the London City **Waits** in 1622, he received a court appointment (1635), in which capacity he accompanied Charles I to Oxford during the Civil War, taking the DMus there in 1644. His association with Oxford would become even more substantial following his being named professor there in 1656, a post that allowed him, as **Sir John Hawkins** notes, to have a stimulating effect on the musical scene. Shortly after the Restoration, Wilson returned to court and the King's Musicke (1661) and was named a gentleman of the **Chapel Royal** in 1662.

His skills as a lutanist were praised in superlative tones by **Anthony Wood**, echoed by Hawkins. Modern assessment of his compositions, however, is mixed. Spink (1974) suggests that "[H]is **ballads** show that he had a pleasing melodic gift, popular in character and undeniably attractive. But with few exceptions his declamatory **ayres** are dull and spoiled by awkward passages that now seem inept." *See also* LUTE.

WINCHESTER TROPER. Two manuscript collections of liturgical music ("tropers") from Winchester, each from around the beginning of the 11th century, are historically significant. The manuscript GB Ccc473 contains two-part polyphonic settings of mass movements of the Ordinary, tracts, Alleluias, and other responds. Although its neumatic notation resists accurate transcription, one can discern in its counterpoint the use of contrary motion, a significant development in moving polyphony beyond parallel and heterophonic voice derivation. This earliest surviving polyphonic source (apart from theoretical examples) may have belonged to Wulfstan, the cantor at Winchester (Caldwell, *OHEM*, vol. 1). The other manuscript, GB Ob 775, is a monophonic source, copied around 1050, containing the earliest dramatic version of the Easter sepulchre play based on "Quem quaeritis in sepulchro."

WISE, MICHAEL (ca. 1647–87). Organist, cornettist, singer, and composer. Wise was trained as a chorister in the **Chapel Royal** under Captain **Henry Cooke,** and there, in the first years of the Restoration, he would find himself in the company of fellow choristers **John Blow** and **Pelham Humfrey.** With the breaking of his voice he took up singing posts at St. George's, Windsor, and at Eton, and after a few years (1668) was appointed organist and instructor of the choristers at Salisbury. Court appointments followed— gentleman of the Chapel Royal (1676) and cornettist (1684)—although he simultaneously retained his position at Salisbury. Just prior to his death, he was appointed to be master of the choristers at St. Paul's, London. His death proceeded from an altercation with the Night Watch at Salisbury, an event that underscores the patterns of troubled and troubling behavior that followed him throughout his career. Nevertheless, **Sir John Hawkins** styles him a "most sweet and elegant composer." *See also* CORNETT; ORGAN.

WOOD, ANTHONY (1632–95). Oxford antiquary. Wood, self-styled "à Wood," was closely tied to Oxford throughout his life, and he devoted much of his energies to being a historian of both the university and its distinguished people, as seen in his *Athenae Oxonienses* and *Historia et Antiquitates Oxon.* He was also, especially during the Commonwealth, much given to music. In his autobiographical *The Life and Times of Anthony à Wood,* he describes that in 1651 he

> began to exercise his natural and insatiable genie he had to musick. He exercised his hand on the violin; and having a good eare to take any tune at first hearing, he could quickly draw it out from the violin, but not with the same tuning of strings that others used.

Later he would study with Charles Griffiths, an Oxford musician, who taught him to play with conventional tunings. He took part in weekly Oxford music meetings and recorded opinions of the participants ("Dr. **John Wilson,** the public professor, the best **lute** in all England," for example).

Wood's temperament was apparently notably sour. Llewelyn Powys observes, "Just as naturally as a cuttle fish ejects poisonous ink, so did Mr. Wood eject spite" ([Wood], 1961).

WOOD, CHARLES (1866–1926). Composer and teacher of Irish birth. Wood's early training as a chorister at Armagh Cathedral, Ireland, led him easily into study as a scholarship student at the **Royal College of Music** (1883–89) with **Sir Hubert Parry** and **Sir Charles Villiers Stanford.** He won an **organ** scholarship to Selwyn College, Cambridge, in 1888 and was an organ scholar at both Gonville and Caius colleges; at the latter, he was made lecturer in harmony and counterpoint (1889). He took the BA and BMus degrees in 1890, was appointed organist of Caius in 1891, took the degrees of MA and DMus in 1894, and was named a fellow at Caius. He spent most of his career at Cambridge, being named University Lecturer in Harmony and Counterpoint in 1897, and eventually professor of music there (1924–26). Wood's compositions included dramatic music works, but he is most famous for his Anglican liturgical music, especially settings of the Magnificat and Nunc Dimittis, still in use today.

WOOD, SIR HENRY JOSEPH (1869–1944). Conductor. Henry Joseph Wood was for nearly five decades synonymous with the **Proms** concerts at **Queen's Hall**, conducting them from 1895 to his death in 1944; he survived changes in sponsorship of the series from Robert Newman to the **British Broadcasting Corporation**. Under his baton, the Proms ensemble premiered hundreds of works, and Wood was instrumental in reforming 19th-century orchestra practices, such as his abolishment of the "deputy system" in 1904, where a performer could send a substitute if a more lucrative opportunity presented itself, and his allowing women to join a professional orchestra in 1913.

Wood received early training on **organ** and was taught by **Ebenezer Prout**, among others, at the **Royal Academy of Music (2; RAM; 1886–88)**. For a few years, Wood concentrated on **opera**, conducting at the Olympic Theatre and the **Carl Rosa Opera Company** before beginning his work with the **Queen's Hall Orchestra** in 1895. Aside from the Proms, Wood conducted at many **musical festivals**, such as those at Birmingham and Sheffield, as well as the student orchestra at the RAM (1923–42) and the amateur Hull Philharmonic Orchestra (1923–39). He was a frequent guest conductor for many ensembles in Great Britain, including the **London Symphony Orchestra** and the **Hallé Orchestra**, as well as in North America, such as the New York Philharmonic Orchestra, Boston Symphony Orchestra, and the orchestra at the Hollywood Bowl. He was the author of *The Gentle Art of Singing* (1927–28) and *My Life of Music* (1938). Wood was knighted in 1911 and named CH in 1944.

WORGAN, JOHN (1724–90). Organist, composer, and publisher. Worgan came from a family of organists and singers and worked in London throughout his life. He had early lessons from **Thomas Roseingrave** and **Francesco Geminiani**, and he took both a MusB (1748) and a MusD (1775) from Cambridge. His professional appointments included organist at various churches, such as St. Mary Axe with St. Andrew, Undercroft; St. Botolph, Aldgate; and St. John's Chapel, Bedford Row; he was also organist at the **Vauxhall pleasure gardens** from 1751 to 1761 and again from 1770 to

1773. He composed songs for Vauxhall as well as two **oratorios**: *Hannah* (1764) and *Manasseh* (1766).

WYLKYNSON, ROBERT (ca. 1475/80–1515 or LATER). Composer. Wylkynson is documented at Eton from 1496 and was *informator choristarum* from ca. 1500 to 1515. His contributions to the **Eton Choirbook**, the sole source for his music, include two richly scored settings, the nine-voice "Salve regina," in which each voice is associated with one of the angelic orders, and the 13-voice Credo, which also contains a 13-voice canon on "Jesus autem." These works well represent the interest in sonority that characterizes English music in the late 15th century.

YOUNG, NICHOLAS (?–1619). Editor and singer. Young can be documented as a singer at St. Paul's, London, between 1594 and 1618. His historical significance resides, however, in his editing of two collections of Italian **madrigals** with "Englished" texts, both of them appearing under the title *Musica Transalpina* (1588 and 1597).

YOUNG, POLLY (1749–99). Soprano, composer, and keyboardist. Young came from a musical family; her sisters were singers in various London theaters, and her father and uncles played for churches in the area. She was taken by a sister to Dublin when six years of age and began performing there; she returned to London in 1762 and sang at **Covent Garden** and then the King's Theatre, **Haymarket**, where she met and married the violinist and composer **François-Hyppolyte Barthélemon** in 1766. Together they performed in London at the **opera** theaters and **pleasure gardens** and on a successful continental tour (1776–77). She composed harpsichord sonatas, songs (in English and Italian), and **hymns**

Select Bibliography

INTRODUCTION

The field of English musical studies is currently robust, and the entries within this Select Bibliography reflect this. Significantly, the past 30 years have seen the emergence of a rich literature in support of this endeavor: several full-scale histories have been completed or are in progress, most notably John Caldwell's *The Oxford History of English Music* and *The Blackwell History of Music in Britain*, Ian Spink, general editor; *Festschriften* celebrating scholars of English music have offered new infusions of research and criticism, as in *Music in Eighteenth-Century England: Essays in Memory of Charles Cudworth*, *Essays on the History of English Music in Honor of John Caldwell: Sources, Style, Performance, Historiography*, and *Music and British Culture, 1785–1914: Essays in Honour of Cyril Ehrlich*; major anniversaries of English composers, such as Henry Purcell, George Frideric Handel, and Sir Edward Elgar, have occasioned impressive commemorative volumes; and archival resources, such as Andrew Ashbee and David Lasocki's remarkable *A Biographical Dictionary of English Court Musicians, 1485–1714* or Ashbee's *Records of English Court Music*, have powerfully enabled new levels of detailed study, as have archivally rich monographs like Peter Holman's *Four and Twenty Fiddlers: The Violin at the English Court, 1540–1690*. Two publishers' series—Ashgate Press's Music in 19th-Century Britain (Bennet Zon, general editor) and Boydell and Brewer's Music in Britain, 1600–1900 (Rachel Cowgill and Peter Holman, series editors)—have ensured a continuing number of excellent monographs on English music.

Here it is also necessary to acknowledge the pioneering work of Nicholas Temperley, longtime advocate of British music in general, whose articles and monographs, as well as his work with the journal *Victorian Studies*, brought a great deal of post-Purcellian music into the realm of acceptable musicological discussion and allowed such book series to be founded in the first place. Through Prof. Temperley's work, the study of English music has indeed undergone a renaissance in the last 30 years and is no longer simply a national enterprise: in the following Select Bibliography, scholarship is cited from authors working in Great Britain, North America, and throughout the rest of the world.

As is the case within any specialist field, the literature presented below contains both wholly approachable general histories as well as highly specialized scholarly studies. The study of English music, though, has a distinct advantage over many other fields of music history: frequently, the best contemporary descriptions of this rich musical and cultural tapestry were written by some of the best contemporary writers. A simple way to begin research in this history would be to read the works of Anthony Wood, Samuel Pepys, Charles Burney, John Hawkins, and George Bernard Shaw, listed below; all of these writers are both informative and enjoyably entertaining. General secondary sources that are approachable include the volumes listed in the first paragraph of this introduction to the Select Bibliography: these histories and essays provide orientations to English music that may be genre-based, such as the *Oxford History of English Music* and the *Blackwell* series, or based within social history, such as James Day's *"Englishness" In Music: From Elizabethan Times to Elgar, Tippett and Britten*. Extremely readable and informative social histories also include Simon McVeigh's *Concert Life in London from Mozart to Haydn* and Dave Russell's *Popular Music in England*. Further details can be gleaned on most composers from either the *New Grove Dictionary of Music and Musicians*, second edition (either in print or in its electronic format at *Oxford Music Online*), or the *Oxford Dictionary of National Biography*.

The studies of individual composers and genres are listed within this bibliography because they are generally the best available; of particular note is Howard Smither's four-volume *History of the Oratorio*, which lavishes a great deal of attention on the genre's English manifestations. Studies of the periods from the Middle Ages to the 17th century are extremely diverse and include such wide-ranging sources as Harrison's *Music in Medieval Britain*, Stevens's *Tudor Church Music*, and Wulstan's *Tudor Music*; the last is particularly engaging as it is from the point of view of a scholar-performer. More focused (but still eminently readable) studies include Bent's essay "The Old Hall Manuscript," which provides a model overview of a major manuscript source of English music; Kerman's *The Elizabethan Madrigal*, which investigates both literary and musical elements of the genre; and Winkler's *"O Let Us Howle Some Heavy Note": Music for Witches, the Melancholic, and the Mad on the Seventeenth-Century English Stage*, which is recent and rich in its interdisciplinary apparatus.

While there are not as many "classic" sources for the periods from the 18th to the 20th centuries, there are a number of foundational ones, such as Percy Scholes's *The Mirror of Music, 1844–1944: A Century of Life in Britain as Reflected in the Pages of the* Musical Times. Written by subject in a chronicle format, the work provides contemporary voices at times as witty as Shaw's, without some of the latter's prejudices. These centuries are particularly rich in well-written contextual histories, such as Weber's *The Rise of Musical Classics in Eighteenth-Century England*, Gatens's *Victorian Cathedral Music in Theory in Practice*, Hyde's *New-Found Voices: Women in Nineteenth-Century English Music*, and Riley's *British Music and Modernism*. It needs to be emphasized, though, that all of the sources in the Select Bibliography below are important works within the field of English musical studies, and that most of them are of an excellent quality.

In addition to having many brilliant writers on English music, there are many outstanding libraries and archives throughout Great Britain that include resources for the further study of British music. First and foremost among these is the British Library, London, which includes much of the primary and secondary source material on British music for the period from the 18th century to the present and has an extensive electronic presence as well. The British Library is followed closely by the Bodleian Library, Oxford, and the Cambridge University Library, which have extensive manuscript and secondary source holdings. However, most cities and towns in the United Kingdom have libraries and archives with some relevant information, be it within a cathedral library like that at Lincoln, a centralized city library such as the Manchester Central Library, or an excellent local history section, as at Birmingham Archives and Heritage Center. Students will also be quickly able to find many colleagues studying English music, either through the many conferences for the study of British music founded in the last few decades, including the biennial Music in Nineteenth-Century Britain conference (MNCB) and the conference of the North American British Music Studies Association (NABMSA). Academic programs for the specific study of English music now exist: the Leeds University Centre for English Music (LUCEM) and the Centre for the History of Music in Britain, the Empire, and the Commonwealth (CHOMBEC) at Bristol University. Both offer graduate degrees in the study of English music through their affiliated universities.

REFERENCE WORKS

Ashbee, Andrew. *Records of English Court Music*. Multivolume set. Aldershot, UK: Ashgate, 1986–96.

Ashbee, Andrew, and David Lasocki. *A Biographical Dictionary of English Court Musicians, 1485–1714*. Aldershot, UK: Ashgate, 1998.

Fuller, Sophie. *The Pandora Guide to Women Composers: Britain and the United States, 1629–Present*. London: Pandora, 1994.

Hefling, Charles, ed. *The Oxford Guide to the Book of Common Prayer*. Oxford: Oxford University Press, 2006.

The New Grove Dictionary of Music and Musicians. Edited by Stanley Sadie. New York: Grove, 2001.

The Oxford Book of Oxford. Edited by Jan Morris. Oxford: Oxford University Press, 1978.

Oxford Dictionary of National Biography. Edited by Lawrence Goldman. http://www.oxforddnb.com.

Strunk, Oliver. *Source Readings in Music History*. New York: W. W. Norton, 1950.

Strunk's Source Readings in Music History: The Renaissance. Edited by Gary Tomlinson. New York: W. W. Norton, 1998.

Swain, Joseph P. *Historical Dictionary of Sacred Music*. Lanham, MD: Scarecrow Press, 2006.

Unger, Melvin P. *Historical Dictionary of Choral Music*. Lanham, MD: Scarecrow Press, 2010.

GENERAL WORKS

Allen, Warren Dwight. *Philosophies of Music History: A Study of General Histories of Music, 1600–1960*. New York: Dover, 1962.

Apel, Willi. *The History of Keyboard Music to 1700*. Bloomington: Indiana University Press, 1972.

The Blackwell History of Music in Britain. Edited by Ian Spink. 6 vols. Oxford: Blackwell, 1988–96.

Bumpus, John S. *A History of English Cathedral Music, 1549–1889*. London: T. Werner Laurie [1908].

Burney, Charles. *A General History of Music*. 1776–89. Reprint, New York: Dover, 1957.

Caldwell, John. *English Keyboard Music Before the Nineteenth Century*. Oxford: Blackwell, 1973.

———. *The Oxford History of English Music*. 2 vols. Oxford: Clarendon Press, 1991, 1999.

Cowgill, Rachel, and Julian Rushton, eds. *Europe, Empire, and Spectacle in Nineteenth-Century British Music*. Aldershot, UK: Ashgate, 2006.

Cowgill, Rachel, and Peter Holman, eds. *Music in the British Provinces, 1690–1914*. Aldershot, UK: Ashgate, 2007.

Day, James. *"Englishness" in Music: From Elizabethan Times to Elgar, Tippett and Britten*. London: Thames, 1999.

Ehrlich, Cyril. *The Music Profession in Britain Since the Eighteenth Century*. Oxford: Clarendon Press, 1985.

Harrison, Frank Ll., Mantle Hood, and Claude Palisca. *Musicology*. Englewood Cliffs, NJ: Prentice-Hall, 1963.

Hawkins, John. *A General History of the Science and Practice of Music*. 1776. Reprint, New York: Dover, 1963.

Hollander, John. *The Untuning of the Sky: Ideas of Music in English Poetry, 1500–1700*. Princeton, NJ: Princeton University Press, 1961.

Hughes, Anselm. "Music of the Coronation over a Thousand Years." *Proceedings of the Royal Musical Association* 79 (1952–53): 81–100.

Hyde, Norman. *Four Faces of British Music*. Worthing: Churchman, 1985.

Krummel, David. *English Music Printing, 1553–1700*. Oxford: Oxford University Press, 1975.

Langley, Leanne. "The English Musical Journal in the Early Nineteenth Century." PhD diss., University of North Carolina at Chapel Hill, 1983.

Lebrecht, Norman. *Music in London*. London: Aurum Press, 1992.

Mackerness, E. D. *Somewhere Further North: A History of Music in Sheffield*. Sheffield: J. W. Northend Limited, 1974.

McVeigh, Simon. *Concert Life in London from Mozart to Haydn*. Cambridge: Cambridge University Press, 1993.

Russell, Dave. *Popular Music in England: A Social History*. Kingston and Montreal: McGill-Queen's University Press, 1987.

Tanner, Lawrence S. *The History of the Coronation*. London: Pitkin, 1952.

Walker, Ernest. *A History of Music in England*. Oxford: Oxford University Press, 1907.

Young, Percy. *A History of British Music*. London: Benn, 1967.

GENRES

Dramatic Music: Opera and Oratorio

Baldwin, Olive, and Thelma Wilson. "An English Calisto." *Musical Times* 112 (1971): 651–53.

Dent, Edward J. *Foundations of English Opera*. 1928. Reprint, New York: Da Capo, 1967.

Hall-Witt, Jennifer. *Fashionable Acts: Opera and Elite Culture in London, 1780–1880*. Durham: New Hampshire University Press, 2007.

Lew, Nathaniel. "A New and Glorious Age: Constructions of National Opera in Britain, 1945–1951." PhD diss., University of California, Berkeley, 2001.

Luckett, Richard. "A New Source for 'Venus & Adonis.'" *Musical Times* 130 (1989): 76–79.

Pinnock, Andrew, and Bruce Wood. "A Mangled Chime: The Accidental Death of the Opera Libretto in Civil War England." *Early Music* 36 (2008): 265–84.

Smither, Howard. *A History of the Oratorio*. 4 vols. Chapel Hill: University of North Carolina Press, 1977–2000.

White, Eric Walter. *A History of English Opera*. London: Society for Theatre Research, 1983.

Sacred Music

Bowers, Roger. *English Church Polyphony*. Aldershot, UK: Ashgate, 1999.

———. *Singers and Sources: English Polyphony, 14th–17th Centuries*. Aldershot, UK: Ashgate, 1998.

———. "To Chorus from Quartet: The Performing Resource for English Church Polyphony c. 1390–1559." In *English Choral Practice, 1400–1650*, edited by John Morehen, 1–47. Cambridge: Cambridge University Press, 1995.

———. "The Vocal Scoring, Choral Balance and Performing Pitch of Latin Church Music in England, c.1500–58." *Journal of the Royal Musical Association* 112 (1987): 38–76.

Johnstone, Andrew. "'As it was in the beginning': Organ and Choir Pitch in Early Anglican Church Music." *Early Music* 31 (2003): 507–25.

Johnstone, H. Diack. "The Genesis of Boyce's Cathedral Music." *Music & Letters* 56 (1975): 26–46.

Le Huray, Peter. *Music and the Reformation in England*. Cambridge: Cambridge University Press, 1978.

Long, Kenneth R. *The Music of the English Church*. New York: St. Martin's Press, 1971.

Mould, Alan. *The English Chorister: A History*. London: Hambledon Continuum, 2007.

Phillips, Peter. *English Sacred Music, 1549–1649*. Oxford: Gimmell, 1991.

Plank, Steven. *The Way to Heavens Doore: An Introduction to Liturgical Process and Musical Style*. Lanham, MD: Scarecrow Press, 1994.

———. "*Wrapped all in Woe*: Passion Music in Late-Medieval England." In *The Broken Body: Passion Devotion in Late-Medieval Culture*, edited by A. A. MacDonald, H. N. B. Ridderbos, and R. M. Schlusemann, 93–108. Groningen: Egbert Forsten, 1998.

Rankin, Susan, and David Hiley, eds. *Music in the Medieval English Liturgy: Plainsong & Mediaeval Music Society Centennial Essays*. Oxford: Clarendon Press, 1993.

Spink, Ian. *Restoration Cathedral Music, 1660–1714*. Oxford: Oxford University Press, 1995.

Stevens, Denis. *Tudor Church Music.* New York: W. W. Norton, 1966.

Temperley, Nicholas. *Music of the English Parish Church.* Cambridge: Cambridge University Press, 1979.

Watson, J. R. *The English Hymn: A Critical and Historical Study.* Oxford: Clarendon Press, 1999.

Wilson, Ruth. *Anglican Chant and Chanting in England, Scotland, and America, 1660–1820.* Oxford: Clarendon Press, 1996.

Song

Johnson, David. "The 18th-Century Glee." *Musical Times* 120 (1979): 200–202.

Lichtenwagner, William. "The Music of the 'Star-Spangled Banner': Whence and Whither?" *College Music Symposium* 18 (1978): 34–81.

Plank, Steven. "'A Song in Imitation of Mr Nicola's Manner': A Melismatic 'Mouthfull.'" *BACH* 27 (1986): 16–23.

Spink, Ian. *English Song: Dowland to Purcell.* New York: Scribner's Sons, 1974.

HISTORICAL PERIODS

Medieval

Bent, Margaret. "New and Little-Known Fragments of English Medieval Polyphony." *Journal of the American Musicological Society* 21 (1968): 137–56.

Duffin, Ross W. "The *Sumer* Canon: A New Revision." *Speculum* 63 (1988): 1–22.

Harrison, Frank Ll. *Music in Medieval Britain.* London: Routledge and Kegan Paul, 1963.

Obst, Wolfgang. "'Svmer is icumen in'—A Contrafactum?" *Music & Letters* 64 (1983): 151–61.

Renaissance

Austern, Linda Phyllis. *Music in English Children's Drama of the Later Renaissance.* Philadelphia: Gordon and Breach, 1992.

———. "Nature, Culture, Myth, and the Musician in Early Modern England." *Journal of the American Musicological Society* 51 (1998): 1–47.

Bent, Margaret. "The Earliest Fifteenth-century Transmission of English Music to the Continent." In *Essays on the History of English Music in Honour of John Caldwell,* edited by Emma Hornby and David Maw, 83–96. Woodbridge: Boydell and Brewer, 2010.

———. "Initial Letters in the Old Hall Manuscript." *Music & Letters* 47 (1966): 225–38.

———. "The Old Hall Manuscript." *Early Music* 2 (1974): 2–14.

———. "The Progeny of Old Hall: More Leaves from a Royal English Choirbook." In *Gordon Athol Anderson (1929–1981) in Memoriam,* edited by L. A. Dittmer, 1:1–54. Henryville and Ottawa: Institute of Mediaeval Music, 1984.

Bent, Margaret, and Andrew Hughes. "The Old Hall Manuscript: An Inventory." *Musica Disciplina* 21 (1967): 130–47.

Boyd, Morrison Comegys. *Elizabethan Music and Musical Criticism*. Philadelphia: University of Pennsylvania Press, 1962.

Fallows, David. "The Contenance Angloise: English Influence on Continental Composers of the Fifteenth Century." *Renaissance Studies* 1 (1987): 189–208.

Kerman, Joseph. "Elizabethan Anthologies of Elizabethan Madrigals." *Journal of the American Musicological Society* 4 (1951): 122–138.

———. *The Elizabethan Madrigal: A Comparative Study*. N.p.: American Musicological Society, 1962.

Nordstrom, Lyle. "The English Lute Duet and Consort Lesson." *Lute Society Journal* 43 (1976): 5–22.

Price, David C. *Patrons and Musicians of the English Renaissance*. Cambridge: Cambridge University Press, 1981.

Ravens, Simon. "'A Sweet Shrill Voice': The Countertenor and Vocal Scoring in Tudor England." *Early Music* 26 (1998): 122–34.

Skinner, David. "Discovering the Provenance and History of the Caius and Lambeth Choirbooks." *Early Music* 25 (1997): 245–66.

Smith, David. "Print Culture." Review of *Thomas East and Music Publishing in Renaissance England* by Jeremy Smith. *Musical Times* 144 (2003): 63–64.

Smith, Jeremy. "Music in late Elizabethan Politics: The Identities of Oriana and Diana." *Journal of the American Musicological Society* 58 (2005): 507–58.

———. *Thomas East and Music Publishing in Renaissance England*. Oxford: Oxford University Press, 2003.

Stevens, John. *Music and Poetry in the Early Tudor Court*. Cambridge: Cambridge University Press, 1979.

Williamson, Magnus. "*Pictura et scriptura*: The Eton Choirbook in Its Iconographical Context." *Early Music* 28 (2000): 359–82.

Woodfield, Ian. *English Musicians in the Age of Exploration*. Stuyvesant, NY: Pendragon, 1995.

Wulstan, David. *Tudor Music*. London: Dent, 1985.

Seventeenth Century

Clark, J. Bunker. *Transposition in Seventeenth-Century English Organ Accompaniments and the Transposing Organ*. Detroit: Information Coordinators, 1974.

Corp, E. T. "The Exiled Court of James II and James III: A Centre of Italian Music in France 1689–1712." *Journal of the Royal Musical Association* 120 (1995): 216–31.

Duffin, Ross W. "To Entertain a King: Music for James and Henry at the Merchant Taylors Feast of 1607." *Music & Letters* 83 (2002): 525–41.

Harwood, Ian. "Instrumental Pitch in England c1600." *Early Music* 11 (1983): 76–78.

Haynes, Bruce. "Pitch Standards in the Baroque and Classical Periods." PhD diss., University of Montreal, 1995.

Mabbett, Margaret. "Italian Musicians in Restoration England (1660–1690)." *Music & Letters* 67 (1986): 237–47.

Monson, Craig. *Voices and Viols in England, 1600–1650: The Sources and the Music.* Ann Arbor, MI: UMI Research, 1982.

Scholes, Percy. *The Puritans and Music in England and New England.* London: Oxford University Press, 1934.

Tilmouth, Michael. "A Calendar of References to Music in Newspapers Published in London and the Provinces (1660–1719)." *Royal Musical Association Research Chronicle*, no. 1 (1961).

Wainwright, Jonathan. *Musical Patronage in Seventeenth-Century England: Christopher, First Baron Hatton (1605–1670).* Aldershot, UK: Ashgate, 1997.

Westrup, J. A. "Foreign Musicians in Stuart England." *Musical Quarterly* 27 (1941): 70–89.

Eighteenth Century

Baldwin, Olive, and Thelma Wilson. S.v. "Tom Trollope's Mother-in-Law." http://www.florin.ms/garrows.html (accessed June 3, 2009).

Beechey, Gwilym. "Songs and Cantatas in Eighteenth-Century England." *Consort* 49 (1993): 30–40.

Castle, Terry. "Eros and Liberty at the English Masquerade, 1710–90." *Eighteenth-Century Studies* 17 (1984–85): 156–76.

Fiske, Roger. *English Theatre Music in the Eighteenth Century.* Oxford: Oxford University Press, 1986.

Hunter, David. "Bridging the Gap: The Patrons-in-Common of Purcell and Handel." *Early Music* 37 (2009): 621–32.

Jones, David Wyn, ed. *Music in Eighteenth-Century Britain.* Aldershot, UK: Ashgate, 2000.

Lovell, Percy. "'Ancient' Music in Eighteenth-Century England." *Music & Letters* 60 (1979): 401–15.

Weber, William. *The Rise of Musical Classics in Eighteenth-Century England: A Study in Canon, Ritual, and Ideology.* Oxford: Clarendon Press, 1992.

Wollenberg, Susan, and Simon McVeigh, eds. *Concert Life in Eighteenth-Century Britain.* Aldershot, UK: Ashgate, 2004.

Long Nineteenth Century/(Second) English Musical Renaissance

Bashford, Christina. "Historiography and Invisible Musics: Domestic Chamber Muisc in Nineteenth-Century Britain." *Journal of the American Musicological Society* 63 (2010): 291–359.

Bashford, Christina, and Leanne Langley, eds. *Music and British Culture, 1785–1914: Essays in Honour of Cyril Ehrlich.* Oxford: Oxford University Press, 2000.

Beedell, A. V. *The Decline of the English Musician, 1788–1888: A Family of English Musicians in Ireland, England, Mauritius, and Australia.* Oxford: Clarendon Press, 1992.

Fuller, Sophie. "Women Composers during the British Musical Renaissance, 1880–1918." PhD diss., University of London, 1998.

Gatens, William J. *Victorian Cathedral Music in Theory and Practice.* Cambridge: Cambridge University Press, 1986.

Gillett, Paula. *Musical Women in England, 1870–1914: "Encroaching on All Man's Privileges."* New York: St. Martin's, 2000.

Howes, Frank. *The English Musical Renaissance.* New York: Stein and Day, 1966.

Hueffer, Francis. *Half a Century of Music in England, 1837–1887: Essays Towards a History.* Philadelphia: Gebbie and Company; London: Chapman and Hall, 1889.

Hughes, Meirion, and Robert Stradling. *The English Musical Renaissance, 1840–1940: Constructing a National Music.* 2nd ed. Manchester: Manchester University Press, 2001.

Hyde, Derek. *New-Found Voices: Women in Nineteenth-Century English Music.* 3rd ed. Aldershot, UK: Ashgate, 1998.

McGuire, Charles Edward. *Music and Victorian Philanthropy: The Tonic Sol-fa Movement.* Cambridge: Cambridge University Press, 2009.

Pearsall, Ronald. *Victorian Popular Music.* Newton Abbot: David and Charles, 1973.

Schaarwächter, Jürgen. "Chasing a Myth and a Legend: 'The British Musical Renaissance' in 'A Land without Music.'" *Musical Times* 149 (2008): 53–59.

Scholes, Percy. *The Mirror of Music, 1844–1944: A Century of Musical Life in Britain as Reflected in the Pages of the* Musical Times. London: Novello & Company; Oxford: Oxford University Press, 1947.

Temperley, Nicholas, ed. *The Lost Chord: Essays on Victorian Music.* Bloomington: Indiana University Press, 1989.

Trend, Michael. *The Music Makers: The English Musical Renaissance from Elgar to Britten.* New York: Schirmer Books, 1985.

Twentieth Century

Pearsall, Ronald. *Edwardian Popular Music.* Newton Abbot: David and Charles, 1975.

Pirie, Peter J. *The English Musical Renaissance: Twentieth Century British Composers and Their Works.* New York: St. Martin's, 1979.

Riley, Matthew, ed. *British Music and Modernism.* Aldershot, UK: Ashgate, 2010.

MUSIC AND THEATER

Arundell, Dennis Drew. *The Story of Sadler's Wells.* Newton Abbott: David and Charles, 1978.

Chan, Mary. *Music in the Theatre of Ben Jonson.* Oxford: Clarendon Press, 1980.

Duffin, Ross W. *Shakespeare's Songbook.* New York: W. W. Norton, 2004.

Fuller, David. "The Jonsonian Masque and Its Music." *Music & Letters* 54 (1973): 440–52.

Gooch, Bryan, and David Thatcher. *A Shakespeare Music Catalogue.* Oxford: Clarendon Press, 1991.

Lindley, David. *Shakespeare and Music.* London: Arden Shakespeare, 2006.

Lowerre, Kathryn. "Music in the Productions at London's Lincoln's Inn Fields Theater, 1695–1705." PhD diss., Duke University, 1997.

Mellers, Wilfred. *Harmonious Meeting: A Study of the Relationship between English Music, Poetry and Theatre, c. 1600–1900*. London: Dennis Dobson, 1965.

Milhous, Judith, and Robert D. Hume. "The Haymarket Opera in 1711." *Early Music* 17 (1989): 523–38.

———. "Heidegger and the Management of the Haymarket Opera, 1713–17." *Early Music* 27 (1999): 65–84.

Plank, Steven. "'And Now About the Cauldron Sing': Music and the Supernatural on the Restoration Stage." *Early Music* 18 (1990): 393–407.

Price, Curtis. *Music in the Restoration Theatre*. Ann Arbor, MI: UMI Research, 1979.

Walls, Peter. *Music in the English Courtly Masque*. Oxford: Oxford University Press, 1996.

Winkler, Amanda Eubanks. *"O Let Us Howle Some Heavy Note": Music for Witches, the Melancholic, and the Mad on the Seventeenth-Century English Stage*. Bloomington: Indiana University Press, 2006.

MUSIC AND DANCE

Playford, John. *The English Dancing Master*. London, 1651. Reprint, Brooklyn, NY: Dance Horizons, n.d.

Sachs, Curt. *World History of the Dance*. New York: W. W. Norton, 1965.

Thorp, Jennifer. "'So Great a Master as Mr Isaac': an Exemplary Dancing Master of Late Stuart London." *Early Music* 35 (2007): 435–46.

Ward, John. "The Morris Tune." *Journal of the American Musicological Society* 39 (1986): 294–331.

MUSICAL INSTITUTIONS

Baldwin, David. *The Chapel Royal: Ancient & Modern*. London: Gerald Duckworth, 1990.

Bashford, Christina. "John Ella and the Making of the Musical Union." In *Music and British Culture, 1785–1914: Essays in Honour of Cyril Ehrlich*, edited by Christina Bashford and Leanne Langley, 193–214. Oxford: Oxford University Press, 2000.

Cowgill, Rachel. "Disputing Choruses in 1760s Halifax: Joah Bates, William Herschel, and the Messiah Club." In *Music in the British Provinces, 1690–1914*, edited by Rachel Cowgill and Peter Holman, 87–113. Aldershot, UK: Ashgate, 2007.

———. "The London Apollonicon Recitals, 1817–1832: A Case-Study in Bach, Mozart, and Haydn Reception." *Journal of the Royal Musical Association* 123 (1998): 190–228.

Craufurd, J. G. "The Madrigal Society." *Proceedings of the Royal Musical Association*, 82 (1955–56): 34–46.

Doctor, Jenny. *The BBC and Ultra-Modern Music: Shaping a Nation's Tastes.* Cambridge: Cambridge University Press, 1999.

Doctor, Jenny, and David Wright, eds. *The Proms: A New History.* London: Thames and Hudson, 2007.

Fuller-Maitland, J. A. "The People's Concert Society: Valedictory." *Musical Times* 77 (1936): 317–18.

Gladsone, Viscount, Guy Boas, and Harald Christopherson. *Noblemen and Gentlemen's Catch Club: Three Essays toward Its History.* London: Noblemen and Gentlemen's Catch Club at the Cypher Press, 1996.

Harrison, Bertha. "A Forgotten Concert Room." *Musical Times* 47 (1906): 602–5 and 669–72.

Keen, Basil. *The Bach Choir: The First Hundred Years.* Aldershot, UK: Ashgate, 2008.

McVeigh, Simon. "Music and the Lock Hospital in the 18th Century." *Musical Times* 129 (1988): 235–40.

———. "The Professional Concert and Rival Subscription Series in London, 1783–1793." *Royal Musical Association Research Chronicle* 22 (1989): 1–135.

Musgrave, Michael. *The Musical Life of the Crystal Palace.* Cambridge: Cambridge University Press, 1995.

Russell, Dave. "Abiding Memories: The Community Singing Movement and English Social Life in the 1920s." *Popular Music* 27 (2008): 117–33.

Simon, Herbert. *Song and Words: A History of the Curwen Press.* London: George Allen and Unwin, 1973.

Temperley, Nicholas. "The Lock Hospital Chapel and Its Music." *Journal of the Royal Musical Association* 118 (1993): 44–72.

Timms, Colin. "Steffani and the Academy of Ancient Music." *Musical Times* 119 (1978): 127–30.

COMPOSERS

Thomas Arne

Adas, Jane. "Arne's Progress: An English Composer in Eighteenth-Century London." PhD diss., Rutgers University, 1993.

Herbage, Julian. "Arne: His Character and Environment." *Proceedings of the Royal Musical Association* 87 (1960–61): 15–29.

Langley, Robin. "Arne's Keyboard Concertos." *Musical Times* 119 (1978): 233–36.

Malcolm Arnold

Jackson, Paul R. W. *The Life and Music of Sir Malcolm Arnold: The Brilliant and the Dark.* Aldershot, UK: Ashgate, 2003.

Thöne, Raphael D. *Malcolm Arnold—A Composer of Real Music: Symphonic Writing, Style and Aesthetics.* Moers: Edition Wissenschaft, 2007.

Arnold Bax

Bax, Arnold. *Farewell, My Youth and Other Writings by Arnold Bax*. Edited by Lewis Foreman. Aldershot, UK: Scolar, 1992.
Foreman, Lewis. *Bax: A Composer and His Times*. 3rd ed. Woodbridge, UK: Boydell, 2007.

Lennox Berkeley

Dickinson, Peter. *The Music of Lennox Berkeley*. Woodbridge, UK: Boydell, 2003.
Williamson, Malcolm. "Sir Lennox Berkeley (1903–1989)." *Musical Times* 131 (1990): 197–99.

Benjamin Britten

Brett, Philip. *Music and Sexuality in Britten: Selected Essays*. Edited by George E. Haggerty. With an introduction by Susan McClary and an afterword by Jenny Doctor. Berkeley: University of California Press, 2006.
Oliver, Michael. *Benjamin Britten*. London: Phaidon, 1996.

Alan Bush

Bush, Nancy. *Alan Bush: Music, Politics, and Life*. With essays on music by Lewis Foreman. London: Thames, 2000.
Craggs, Stewart R. *Alan Bush: A Source Book*. Aldershot, UK: Ashgate, 2007.

William Byrd

Bessler, Samantha. "London's Madrigal Society and the Reception of William Byrd's Music." Paper presented to the Fourth Biennial Conference of the North American British Music Studies Association, Des Moines, IA, July 2010.
Brett, Philip. *William Byrd and His Contemporaries*. Berkeley: University of California Press, 2007.
Brown, Alan, and Richard Turbet, eds. *Byrd Studies*. Cambridge: Cambridge University Press, 1991.
Byrd, William. Preface to *Cantiones Sacrae 1575*. In *The Byrd Edition*, edited by Craig Monson. London: Stainer and Bell, 1977.
Harley, John. *William Byrd: Gentleman of the Chapel Royal*. Aldershot, UK: Scolar, 1997.
Kerman, Joseph. *The Masses and Motets of William Byrd*. London: Faber and Faber, 1981.
McCarthy, Kerry. *Liturgy and Contemplation in Byrd's Gradualia*. New York: Routledge, 2007.
Monson, Craig. "Authenticity and Chronology in Byrd's Church Anthems." *Journal of the American Musicological Society* 35 (1982): 280–305.

Neighbour, Oliver. *The Consort and Keyboard Music of William Byrd*. London: Faber and Faber, 1978.

Thomas Campion

Campion, Thomas. *The Works of Thomas Campion; Complete Songs, Masques, and Treatises. . . .* Edited by Walter R. Davis. Garden City, NY: Doubleday, 1967.
Lindgren, Lowell. *Thomas Campion*. Leiden: E. J. Brill, 1986.
Ratcliffe, Stephen. *Campion on Song*. Boston: Routledge and Kegan Paul, 1981.
Wilson, Christopher. *Words and Notes Coupled Lovingly Together: Thomas Campion: A Critical Study*. New York: Garland, 1989.

Samuel Coleridge-Taylor

Carr, Catherine. "The Music of Samuel Coleridge-Taylor (1875–1912): A Critical and Analytical Study." PhD diss., University of Durham, 2005.
Self, Geoffrey. *The Hiawatha Man: The Life and Work of Samuel Coleridge-Taylor*. Aldershot, UK: Ashgate, 1995.

John Dowland

Holman, Peter. *Dowland—Lachrimae (1604)*. Cambridge: Cambridge University Press, 1999.
Poulton, Diane. *John Dowland*. Berkeley: University of California Press, 1982.
Rooley, Anthony. "New Light on Dowland's Songs of Darkness." *Early Music* 11 (1983): 6–22.
Wells, Robin Headlam. "John Dowland and Elizabethan Melancholy." *Early Music* 13 (1985): 5114–28.

John Dunstaple

Bent, Margaret. *Dunstaple*. London: Oxford University Press, 1981.
Stell, Judith, and Andrew Wathey. "New Light on the Biography of John Dunstable." *Music & Letters* 62 (1981): 60–63.
Wathey, Andrew. "Dunstable in France." *Music & Letters* 67 (1986): 1–36.

Edward Elgar

Adams, Byron. "The 'Dark Saying' of the Enigma: Homoeroticism and the Elgarian Paradox." *19th-Century Music* 23 (2000): 218–35.
———, ed. *Edward Elgar and His World*. Princeton, NJ: Princeton University Press, 2007.
Grimley, Daniel, and Julian Rushton. *The Cambridge Companion to Elgar*. Cambridge: Cambridge University Press, 2004.

Harper-Scott, J. P. E., and Julian Rushton, eds. *Elgar Studies*. Cambridge: Cambridge University Press, 2007.

Hodgkins, Geoffrey. *Somewhere Further North: Elgar and the Morecambe Festival*. Rickmansworth: Poneke Pres, 2004.

Kennedy, Michael. *Portrait of Elgar*. 3rd ed. Oxford: Clarendon Press, 1987.

McGuire, Charles Edward. *Elgar's Oratorios: The Creation of an Epic Narrative*. Aldershot, UK: Ashgate, 2002.

Moore, Jerrold Northrop. *Edward Elgar: A Creative Life*. Oxford: Oxford University Press, 1984.

Rushton, Julian. *Elgar: "Enigma" Variations*. Cambridge: Cambridge University Press, 1999.

Thomson, Aidan. "Re-Reading Elgar: Hermenutics, Criticism, and Reception in England and Germany, 1900–1914." DPhil diss., Oxford University, 2002.

Orlando Gibbons

Harley, John. *Orlando Gibbons and the Gibbons Family of Musicians*. Aldershot, UK: Ashgate, 1999.

Neighbour, Oliver. "Orlando Gibbons (1583–1625): The Consort Music." *Early Music* 11 (1983): 351–57.

Gilbert and Sullivan

Ainger, Michael. *Gilbert & Sullivan: A Dual Biography*. Oxford: Oxford University Press, 2002.

Dillard, Philip H. *Sir Arthur Sullivan: A Resource Book*. Lanham, MD: Scarecrow Press, 1996.

Young, Percy. *Sir Arthur Sullivan*. New York: W. W. Norton, 1972.

George Frideric Handel

Burrows, Donald, ed. *The Cambridge Companion to Handel*. Cambridge: Cambridge University Press, 1998.

——. "Handel and the Foundling Hospital." *Music & Letters* 58, no. 3 (July 1977): 269–84.

——. *Handel: Messiah*. Cambridge: Cambridge University Press, 1991.

——. "Handel's London Theatre Orchestra." *Early Music* 13 (1985): 349–58.

Burrows, Donald, and Robert Hume. "George I, the Haymarket Opera Company and Handel's *Water Music*." *Early Music* 19 (1991): 323–43.

Dean, Winton. *Handel and the Opera Seria*. Berkeley: University of California Press, 1969.

Dean, Winton, and John Merrill Knapp. *Handel's Operas, 1704–1726*. Oxford: Clarendon Press, 1987.

Hogwood, Christopher. *Handel*. London: Thames and Hudson, 1984.

Hurley, David Ross. *Handel's Muse: Patterns of Creation in his Oratorios and Musical Dramas, 1743–1751*. Oxford: Oxford University Press, 2001.

Lang, Paul Henry. *George Frideric Handel*. New York: W. W. Norton, 1966.

Larsen, Jens Peter. *Handel's Messiah*. New York: W. W. Norton, 1972.

Roberts, John. "False Messiah." *Journal of the American Musicological Society* 63 (2010): 45–97.

Shapiro, Alexander H. "'Drama of an Infinitely Superior Nature': Handel's Early English Oratorios and the Religious Sublime." *Music & Letters* 74 (1993): 215–45.

Smith, Ruth. *Handel's Oratorios and Eighteenth-Century Thought*. Cambridge: Cambridge University Press, 1995.

Strohm, Reinhard. *Essays on Handel and Italian Opera*. Cambridge: Cambridge University Press, 1985.

Gustav Holst

Holst, Imogen. *Gustav Holst: A Biography (with a Note by Ralph Vaughan Williams)*. London: Oxford University Press, 1958.

Mitchell, Jon C. *A Comprehensive Biography of Composer Gustav Holst, with Correspondence and Diary Excerpts, Including His American Years*. Lewiston, NY: Methuen, 2001.

Scheer, Christopher. "Fin-de-Siècle Britain: Imperialism and Wagner in the Music of Gustav Holst." PhD diss., University of Michigan, 2007.

Short, Michael. *Gustav Holst: The Man and His Music*. Oxford: Oxford University Press, 1990.

Hamish MacCunn

Oates, Jennifer. "Hamish MacCunn: A Scottish National Composer?" In *Europe, Empire, and Spectacle in Nineteenth-Century British Music*, edited by Rachel Cowgill and Julian Rushton, 145–157. Aldershot, UK: Ashgate, 2006.

——. "The Making of Scottish National Opera: Hamish MacCunn's *Jeanie Deans*." *Opera Journal* 35, no. 2/3 (June–September 2002): 3–28.

Hubert Parry

Beloliel, Bernard. *Parry before Jerusalem: Studies of His Life and Works with Excerpts from His Writings*. Aldershot, UK: Ashgate, 1997.

Dibble, Jeremy. *C. Hubert H. Parry: His Life and Music*. Oxford: Clarendon Press, 1992.

Henry Purcell

Baldwin, Olive, and Thelma Wilson. "Purcell's Sopranos." *Musical Times* 123 (1982): 602–9.

Burden, Michael, ed. *The Purcell Companion*. London: Faber and Faber, 1995.

———. "Where Did Purcell Keep His Theatre Band?" *Early Music* 37 (2009): 429–43.

Buttrey, John. "Dating Purcell's Dido and Aeneas." *Proceedings of the Royal Musical Association* 94 (1967/68): 51–62.

Charlton, David. "'King Arthur': Dramatick Opera." *Music & Letters* 64 (1983): 183–92.

Harris, Ellen. *Henry Purcell's Dido and Aeneas.* Oxford: Oxford University Press, 1987.

Holman, Peter. *Henry Purcell.* Oxford: Oxford University Press, 1994.

King, Robert. *Henry Purcell.* London: Thames and Hudson, 1994.

Laurie, Margaret. "Did Purcell Set the Tempest?" *Proceedings of the Royal Musical Association* 90 (1963/64): 43–57.

Plank, Steven. "Purcell, the Anthem, and the Culture of Preaching." *Musical Times* 150 (2009): 17–30.

Price, Curtis A. "*Dido and Aeneas*: Questions of Style and Evidence." *Early Music* 22 (1994): 115–25.

———. *Henry Purcell and the London Stage.* Cambridge: Cambridge University Press, 1984.

———. ed. *Purcell Studies.* Cambridge: Cambridge University Press, 1995.

Radice, Mark. "Sites for Music in Purcell's Dorset Garden Theatre." *Musical Quarterly* 81 (1997): 430–48.

Schmalfeldt, Janet. "In Search of Dido." *Journal of Musicology* 18 (2001): 584–615.

Walkling, Andrew. "The Dating of Purcell's *Dido and Aeneas*?" *Early Music* 22 (1994): 469–81.

———. "The Masque of Actaeon and the Antimasque of Mercury: Dance, Dramatic Structure, and Tragic Exposition in *Dido and Aeneas*." *Journal of the American Musicological Society* 63 (2010): 191–242.

———. "Political Allegory in Purcell's 'Dido and Aeneas.'" *Music & Letters* 76 (1995): 540–71.

Westrup, J. A. *Purcell.* London: J. M. Dent and Sons, 1937.

White, Bryan. "Letter from Aleppo: Dating the Chelsea School Performance of *Dido and Aeneas*." *Early Music* 37 (2009): 417–28.

Wood, Bruce. *Purcell: An Extraordinary Life.* London: ABRSM, 2009.

———. "Purcell's Odes: A Reappraisal." In *The Purcell Companion*, edited by Michael Burden, 200–253. London: Faber and Faber, 1994.

Wood, Bruce, and Andrew Pinnock. "'Unscarr'd by Turning Times'?: The Dating of Purcell's *Dido and Aeneas*." *Early Music* 20 (1992): 372–90.

Zimmerman, Franklin B. *Henry Purcell, 1659–1695: His Life and Times.* Philadelphia: University of Pennsylvania Press, 1983.

Charles Villiers Stanford

Dibble, Jeremy. *Charles Villiers Stanford: Man and Musician.* Oxford: Oxford University Press, 2002.

Rodmell, Paul. *Charles Villiers Stanford.* Aldershot, UK: Ashgate, 2002.

Thomas Tallis

Doe, Paul. *Tallis*. London: Oxford University Press, 1968.
Stevens, Denis. "A Song of Fortie Partes, Made by Mr Tallys." *Early Music* 10 (1982): 171–81.

John Taverner

Benham, Hugh. *John Taverner: His Life and Music*. Aldershot, UK: Ashgate, 2003.
Hand, Colin. *John Taverner: His Life and Work*. London: Eulenburg Books, 1978.

Michael Tippett

Bowen, Meirion. *Michael Tippett*. 2nd ed. London: Robson Books, 1997.
Kemp, Ian. *Tippett: The Composer and His Music*. London: Eulenberg; New York: Da Capo, 1984.

William Walton

Kennedy, Michael. *Portrait of Walton*. Oxford and New York: Oxford University Press, 1989.
Lloyd, Stephen. *William Walton: Muse of Fire*. Woodbridge, UK: Boydell, 2001.

Thomas Weelkes

Browne, David. *Thomas Weelkes*. London: Faber and Faber, 1969.
Shepherd, John. "Thomas Weelkes: A Biographical Caution." *Musical Quarterly* 64 (1980): 505–21.

The Wesley Family

Horton, Peter. *Samuel Sebastian Wesley: A Life*. Oxford: Oxford University Press, 2004.
Olleson, Philip. *Samuel Wesley: The Man and His Music*. Woodbridge, UK: Boydell, 2003.
Pratt, Andrew. *Indistinguishable Blaze: Meditations on Charles Wesley's Hymns*. Peterborough, UK: Inspire, 2007.
Tyson, John R. *Assist Me to Proclaim: The Life and Hymns of Charles Wesley*. Grand Rapids, MI: William B. Eerdmans, 2007.
Young, Carlton R. *Music of the Heart: John & Charles Wesley on Music and Musicians*. Carol Stream, IL: Hope, 1995.

Ralph Vaughan Williams

Adams, Byron, and Robin Wells, eds. *Vaughan Williams Essays*. Aldershot, UK: Ashgate, 2003.

Day, James. *Vaughan Williams*. 3rd ed. The Master Musicians, edited by Stanley Sadie. Oxford: Oxford University Press, 1998.

Foreman, Lewis, ed. *Ralph Vaughan Williams in Perspective*. Somerset, UK: Albion, 1998.

Frogley, Alain. *Vaughan Williams Studies*. Cambridge: Cambridge University Press, 1996.

Kennedy, Michael. *A Catalog of the Works of Ralph Vaughan Williams*. Oxford: Oxford University Press, 1996.

Onderdonk, Julian. "Ralph Vaughan Williams's Folksong Collecting: English Nationalism and the Rise of the Professional Society." PhD diss., New York University, 1998.

Saylor, Eric. "The Significance of Nation in the Music of Ralph Vaughan Williams." PhD diss., University of Michigan, 2003.

Thomson, Aidan, and Alain Frogley, eds. *The Cambridge Companion to Vaughan Williams*. Cambridge: Cambridge University Press, forthcoming.

Vaughan Williams, Ralph. *National Music and Other Essays*. 2nd ed. Oxford: Clarendon Press, 1986.

Other Composers

Anonymous. "Sir Julius Benedict." *Musical Times* 25 (1884): 384–85.

Ashbee, Andrew, ed. *William Lawes: Essays on His Life, Times, and Work*. Aldershot, UK: Ashgate, 1998.

Ashbee, Andrew, and Peter Holman, eds. *John Jenkins and His Time: Studies in English Consort Music*. Oxford: Clarendon Press, 1996.

Barlow, Michael. *Whom the Gods Love: The Life and Music of George Butterworth*. London: Toccata, 1997.

Boden, Anthony. *Thomas Tomkins: The Last Elizabethan*. Aldershot, UK: Ashgate, 2005.

Cunningham, Walker. *The Keyboard Music of John Bull*. Ann Arbor, MI: UMI Research, 1984.

Curtis, Liane. *A Rebecca Clarke Reader*. Bloomington: University of Indiana Press, 2004.

Dennison, Peter. *Pelham Humfrey*. Oxford: Oxford University Press, 1986.

Dibble, Jeremy. *John Stainer: A Life in Music*. Woodbridge, UK: Boydell, 2007.

Dickinson, Peter. *Lord Berners: Composer, Writer, and Painter*. Woodbridge, UK: Boydell, 2008.

Eatock, Colin Timothy. *Mendelssohn and Victorian England*. Farnham, UK: Ashgate, 2009.

Grogan, Christopher, ed. *Imogen Holst: A Life in Music*. Woodbridge, UK: Boydell, 2007.

Hurd, Michael. *Rutland Boughton and the Glastonbury Festivals*. Oxford: Clarendon Press, 1993.

Jackson, Francis. *Blessed City: The Life and Works of Edward C. Bairstow*. York: William Sessions, 1997.

Kroeger, Karl. "John Valentine: Eighteenth-Century Music Master in the English Midlands." *Notes* 44 (1988): 444–55.

Lindgren, Lowell. "Ariosti's London Years, 1716–29." *Music & Letters* 622 (1981): 331–51.

Lister, Warwick. *Amico: The Life of Giovanni Battista Viotti*. Oxford: Oxford University Press, 2009.

Little, Karen R. *Frank Bridge: A Bio-Bibliography*. New York: Greenwood, 1991.

Lloyd, Stephen. *H. Balfour Gardiner*. Cambridge: Cambridge University Press, 1984.

MacDonald, Malcolm. *John Foulds and His Music: An Introduction*. New York: Pro/Am Music Resources, 1989.

Marr, Peter. "John Alcock and Fanny Brown." *Musical Times* 118 (1977): 118–20.

Matthews, Betty. "Joah Bates: A Remarkable Amateur." *Musical Times* 126 (1985): 749–53.

———. "The Rise and Fall of Jonathan Battishill." *Musical Times* 133 (1992): 477–79.

McVeagh, Diana. *Gerald Finzi: His Life and Music*. Woodbridge, UK: Boydell, 2005.

Milligan, Thomas B. *John Baptist Cramer (1771–1858): A Thematic Catalogue of His Works*. Stuyvesant, NY: Pendragon, 1994.

Moroney, Davitt. "Alessandro Striggio's Mass in Forty and Sixty Parts." *Journal of the American Musicological Society* 60 (2007): 1–69.

Nettel, Reginald. *Havergal Brian and His Music*. Catalogue of works by Lewis Foreman. London: Dobson, 1976.

Palmer, Fiona M. *Domenico Dragonetti in England (1794–1846): The Career of a Double Bass Virtuoso*. Oxford: Oxford University Press, 1997.

———. *Vincent Novello (1781–1861): Music for the Masses*. Aldershot, UK: Ashgate, 2006.

Parrott, Isabel. "William Sterndale Bennett and the Bach Revival in Nineteenth-Century England." In *Europe, Empire, and Spectacle in Nineteenth-Century British Music*, edited by Rachel Cowgill and Julian Rushton, 29–44. Aldershot, UK: Ashgate, 2006.

Payne, Ian. "The Sacred Music of Thomas Ravenscroft." *Early Music* 10 (1982): 309–15.

Plantinga, Leon. *Clementi: His Life and Music*. Oxford: Oxford University Press, 1977.

Platt, Richard. "New Light on Richard Mudge." *Early Music* 28 (2000): 531–45.

Rees, Brian. *A Musical Peacemaker: The Life and Work of Sir Edward German*. Bourne End, Buckinghamshire, UK: Kensal, 1986.

Richards, Fiona. *The Music of John Ireland*. Aldershot, UK: Ashgate, 2000.

Rosen, Carole. *The Goossens: A Musical Century*. Boston: Northeastern University Press, 1993.

Shay, Robert. "Naturalizing Palestrina and Carissimi in Late Seventeenth-Century Oxford: Henry Aldrich and His Recompositions." *Music & Letters* 77 (1996): 368–400.

Skinner, David. "William Cornysh: Clerk or Courtier?" *Musical Times* 138 (1997): 5–12.

Smith, Barry. *Peter Warlock: The Life of Philip Heseltine*. Oxford: Oxford University Press, 1994.

Walsh, Basil. *Michael W. Balfe: A Unique Victorian Composer.* Foreword by Richard Bonynge. Dublin: Irish Academic Press, 2007.

Wells, Robin Headlam. "Ars amatoria: Philip Rosseter and the Tudor Court Lyric." *Music & Letters* 70 (1989): 58–71.

Wilcox, Helen. "My Mournful Style: Poetry and Music in the Madrigals of John Ward." *Music & Letters* 61 (1980): 60–70.

Wilson, Michael. *Nicholas Lanier: Master of the King's Musick.* Aldershot, UK: Scolar, 1994.

Wright, David. "Sir Frederick Bridge and the Musical Furtherance of the 1902 Imperial Project." In *Europe, Empire, and Spectacle in Nineteenth-Century British Music,* edited by Rachel Cowgill and Julian Rushton, 115–29. Aldershot, UK: Ashgate, 2006.

CONDUCTORS

Aldous, Richard. *Tunes of Glory: The Life of Malcolm Sargent.* London: Hutchinson, 2001.

Atkins, Harold, and Peter Coates. *The Barbirollis: A Musical Marriage.* London: Robson, 1983.

Blackwood, Alan. *Sir Thomas Beecham: The Man and the Music.* London: Ebury, 1994.

Fifield, Christopher. *True Artist and True Friend: A Biography of Hans Richter.* Oxford: Clarendon Press, 1993.

Jacobs, Arthur. *Henry J. Wood: Maker of the Proms.* London: Methuen, 1994.

Kennedy, Michael. *Adrian Boult.* London: Hamish Hamilton, 1987.

Lucas, John. *Thomas Beecham: An Obsession with Music.* Woodbridge, UK: Boydell, 2008.

Rothwell, Evelyn. *Life with Glorious John.* London: Robson, 2002.

CRITICS, JOURNALISTS, AND ASSORTED WRITERS ON MUSIC

Bledsoe, Robert Terell. *Henry Frothergill Chorley: Victorian Journalist.* Aldershot, UK: Ashgate, 1998.

Brett, Philip. "Musicology and Sexuality: The Example of Edward J. Dent." In *Queering the Pitch: Episodes in Music and Modern Identity,* edited by Sophie Fuller and Lloyd Whitesell, 177–88. Urbana and Chicago: University of Illinois Press, 2002.

Denke, Margaret. *Ernest Walker.* Oxford: Oxford University Press, 1951.

Dibble, Jeremy. "Edward Dannreuther and the Orme Square Phenomenon." In *Music and British Culture, 1785–1914: Essays in Honour of Cyril Ehrlich,* edited by Christina Bashford and Leanne Langley, 275–98. Oxford: Oxford University Press, 2000.

Dowland, John. *Andreas Ornithoparcus His* Micrologus. . . . London, 1609. Reprint, New York: Dover, 1973.

Evelyn, John. *The Diary of John Evelyn.* Edited by John Bowle. Oxford: Oxford University Press, 1983.

Grant, Kerry S. *Dr. Burney as Critic and Historian of Music.* Ann Arbor, MI: UMI Research, 1983.

Mace, Thomas. *Musick's Monument.* 1676. Reprint, Paris: Éditions du Centre National de la Recherche Scientifique, 1966.

Morley, Thomas. *A Plain and Easy Introduction to Practical Music.* 1597. Reprint, New York: W. W. Norton, 1973.

North, Roger. *Roger North on Music; being a selection from his essays written during the years c. 1695–1728.* Edited by John Wilson. London: Novello, 1959.

Pepys, Samuel. *The Diary of Samuel Pepys: A New and Complete Transcription.* Edited by Robert Latham and William Matthews. 11 vols. Berkeley: University of California Press, 1970–83.

Plank, Steven. "An English Miscellany: Musical Notes in Seventeenth-Century Diaries and Letters." *Consort* 41 (1985): 6–73.

Playford, John. *An Introduction to the Skill of Musick.* Edited by Henry Purcell. 1694. Reprint, New York: Da Capo, 1972.

Rainbow, Bernarr. "Bathe and his Introductions to Musicke." *Musical Times* 123 (1982): 243–47.

Shaw, George Bernard. *Music in London, 1890–1894.* New York: Vienna House, 1973.

White, Arthur. "Fabian Stedman: The First Group Theorist." *American Mathematical Monthly* 103 (1996): 771–78.

[Wood, Anthony]. *The Life and Times of Anthony à Wood.* Edited by Andrew Clark. Abridged by Llewelyn Powys. London: Oxford University Press, 1961.

Young, Percy. *George Grove, 1820–1900: A Biography.* Washington, DC: Grove's Dictionaries of Music, 1980.

MUSICAL INSTRUMENTS

Baines, Anthony. *European and American Musical Instruments.* New York: Viking Press, 1966.

Bicknell, Stephen. *The History of the English Organ.* Cambridge: Cambridge University Press, 1996.

Dickey, Bruce, and Michael Collver. *Catalog of Music for the Cornett.* Bloomington: Indiana University Press, 1996.

Herbert, Trevor. "The Sackbut and Pre-Reformation English Church Music." *Historic Brass Society Journal* 5 (1993): 146–58.

———. "The Sackbut in England in the 17th and 18th Centuries." *Early Music* 18 (1990): 609–16.

———. *The Trombone.* New Haven, CT: Yale University Press, 2006.

Holman, Peter. *Four and Twenty Fiddlers: The Violin at the English Court, 1540–1690.* Oxford: Clarendon Press, 1993.

Lasocki, David. "Professional Recorder Playing in England 1500–1740." *Early Music* 10 (1982): 23–29, 183–91.

Marcuse, Sibyl. *Musical Instruments: A Comprehensive Dictionary.* New York: W. W. Norton, 1975.

Praetorius, Michael. *Syntagma musicum II: De organographia.* Translated and edited by David Z. Crookes. Oxford: Clarendon Press, 1986.

Smithers, Don. *The Music and History of the Baroque Trumpet before 1721.* Carbondale: Southern Illinois University Press, 1988.

Spencer, Robert. "Chitarrone, Theorbo and Archlute." *Early Music* 4 (1976): 407–22.

Spring, Matthew. *The Lute in Britain.* Oxford: Oxford University Press, 2001.

Steele-Perkins, Crispian. *Trumpet.* London: Kahn and Averill, 2001.

Tarr, Edward. *The Trumpet.* Translated by S. E. Plank and Edward Tarr. Chandler, AZ: Hickman Music Editions, 2008.

Unwin, Robert. "An English Writer on Music: James Talbot 1664–1708." *Galpin Society Journal* 40 (1987): 53–72.

MISCELLANEOUS

Baldwin, Olive, and Thelma Wilson. "Alfred Deller, John Freeman and Mr. Pate." *Music & Letters* 50 (1969): 103–10.

Herissone, Rebecca. "Playford, Purcell, and the Functions of Music Publishing in Restoration England." *Journal of the American Musicological Society* 63 (2010): 243–89.

Jones, Simon. "The Legacy of the 'Stupendious' Nicola Matteis." *Early Music* 29 (2001): 553–69.

Ongaro, Giulio. "New Documents on the Bassano Family." *Early Music* 20 (1992): 409–16.

Pinto, David. "The Music of the Hattons." *Royal Musical Association Research Chronicle* 23 (1990): 79–108.

About the Authors

Charles Edward McGuire studies British music of the 19th and 20th centuries. His areas of interest include the music of Edward Elgar, Ralph Vaughan Williams, the British music festival, sight-singing techniques, and the intersection of choral singing and moral reform movements. His publications include the monographs *Elgar's Oratorios: The Creation of an Epic Narrative* (Ashgate, 2002) and *Music and Victorian Philanthropy: The Tonic Sol-fa Movement* (Cambridge, 2009) as well as essays in *Vaughan Williams Essays, The Cambridge Companion to Elgar, Elgar and His World, Elgar Studies, 19th-Century Music, Music & Letters, The Elgar Society Journal*, and the second edition of *The New Grove Dictionary of Music and Musicians*. Dr. McGuire holds bachelor's degrees from both Oberlin College and the Oberlin College Conservatory of Music and a PhD in music from Harvard University. He has taught in various capacities at Harvard University, Ball State University, the University of Maryland at College Park, and James Madison University. He is currently associate professor of musicology at the Oberlin College Conservatory of Music.

Steven E. Plank is professor and chair of the Department of Musicology at Oberlin College, where he has taught since 1980. His professional interests have focused on the music of Restoration England, the intertwining of liturgy and the history of musical style, the oratorio, performance practice, and brass organology. He is the author of two books, *The Way to Heavens Doore: An Introduction to Liturgical Process and Musical Style* (Scarecrow, 1994) and *Choral Performance: A Guide to Historical Practice* (Scarecrow, 2004), and a contributor to a number of journals, including *Musical Times, Music & Letters, Early Music*, and *Goldberg*, as well as to the encyclopedia *Musik in Geschichte und Gegenwart*. He is also the director of the Collegium Musicum of Oberlin College and received the Thomas Binkley Award from Early Music America in 2009 for his work as a university collegium director.

Breinigsville, PA USA
29 March 2011
258664BV00003B/1/P